藤崎 竜

(The stuffed
Supu in the
Jump giveaway
looks creepy.)

This volume contains "The Sheer
Precipice, Where is it Now?" "Hack
Writing," the results of the character
popularity poll, and two special pages.
I haven't done much for the special
pages, but I do try to think about
various stuff that will make the readers
happy. I really do!

Ryu Fujisaki

Ryu Fujisaki's *Worlds* came in second place for the
prestigious 40th Tezuka Award. His *Psycho +*, *Wāqwāq* and
Hoshin Engi have all run in *Weekly Shonen Jump* magazine,
and *Hoshin Engi* anime is available on DVD in Japan and
North America. A lover of science fiction, literature and
history, Fujisaki has made *Hoshin Engi* a mix of genres that
truly showcases his amazing art and imagination.

HOSHIN ENGI VOL. 5
The SHONEN JUMP Manga Edition

STORY AND ART BY RYU FUJISAKI

Based on the novel *Hoshin Engi*, translated by Tsutomu Ano,
published by Kodansha Bunko

Translation & Adaptation/Tomo Kimura
Touch-up Art & Lettering/Rina Mapa
Design/Sean Lee & Matt Hinrichs
Editor/Jonathan Tarbox

Editor in Chief, Books/Alvin Lu
Editor in Chief, Magazines/Marc Weidenbaum
VP of Publishing Licensing/Rika Inouye
VP of Sales/Gonzalo Ferreyra
Sr. VP of Marketing/Liza Coppola
Publisher/Hyoe Narita

Printed in the U.S.A.

Published by VIZ Media, LLC
P.O. Box 77010
San Francisco, CA 94107

SHONEN JUMP Manga Edition
10 9 8 7 6 5 4 3 2 1
First printing, February 2008

HOSHIN ENGI

封神演義

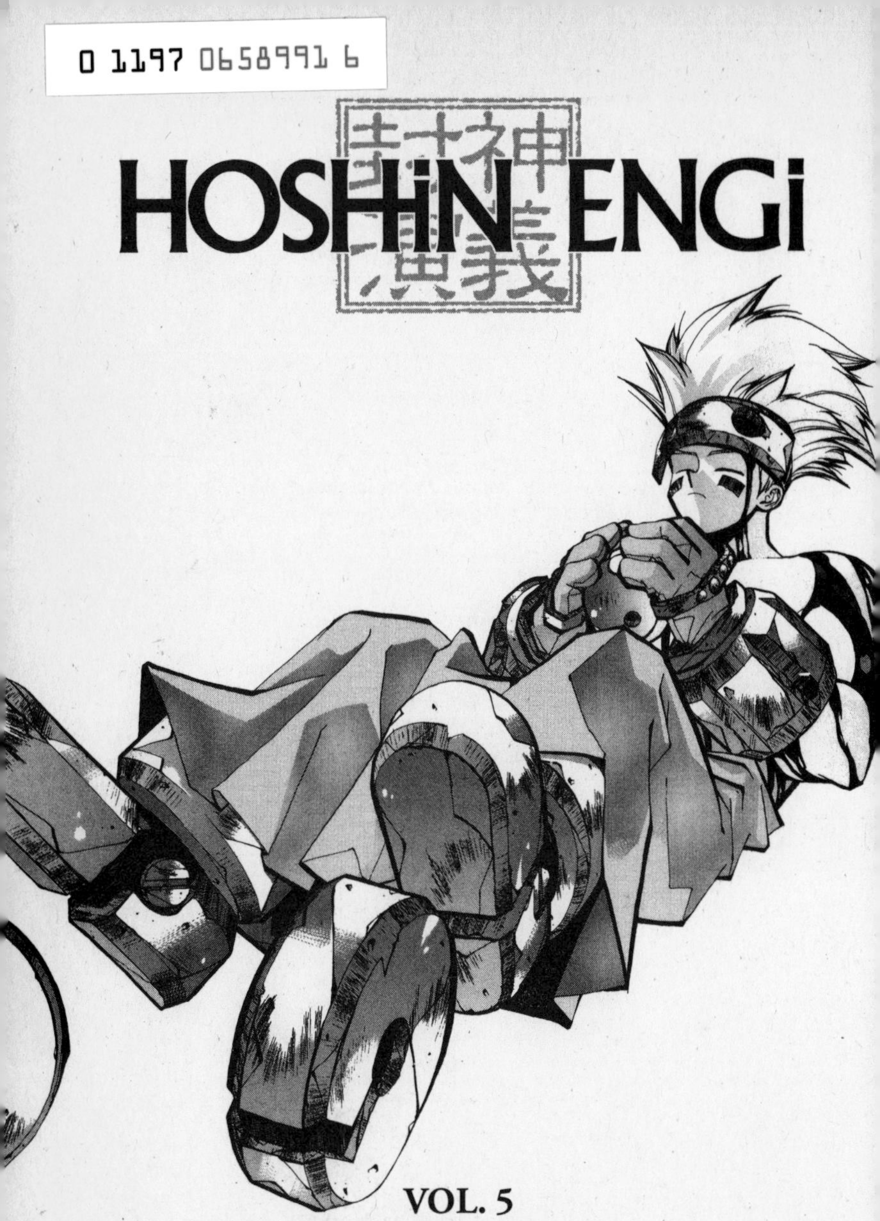

VOL. 5
COMRADES

STORY AND ART BY
RYU FUJISAKI

THE CHARACTERS

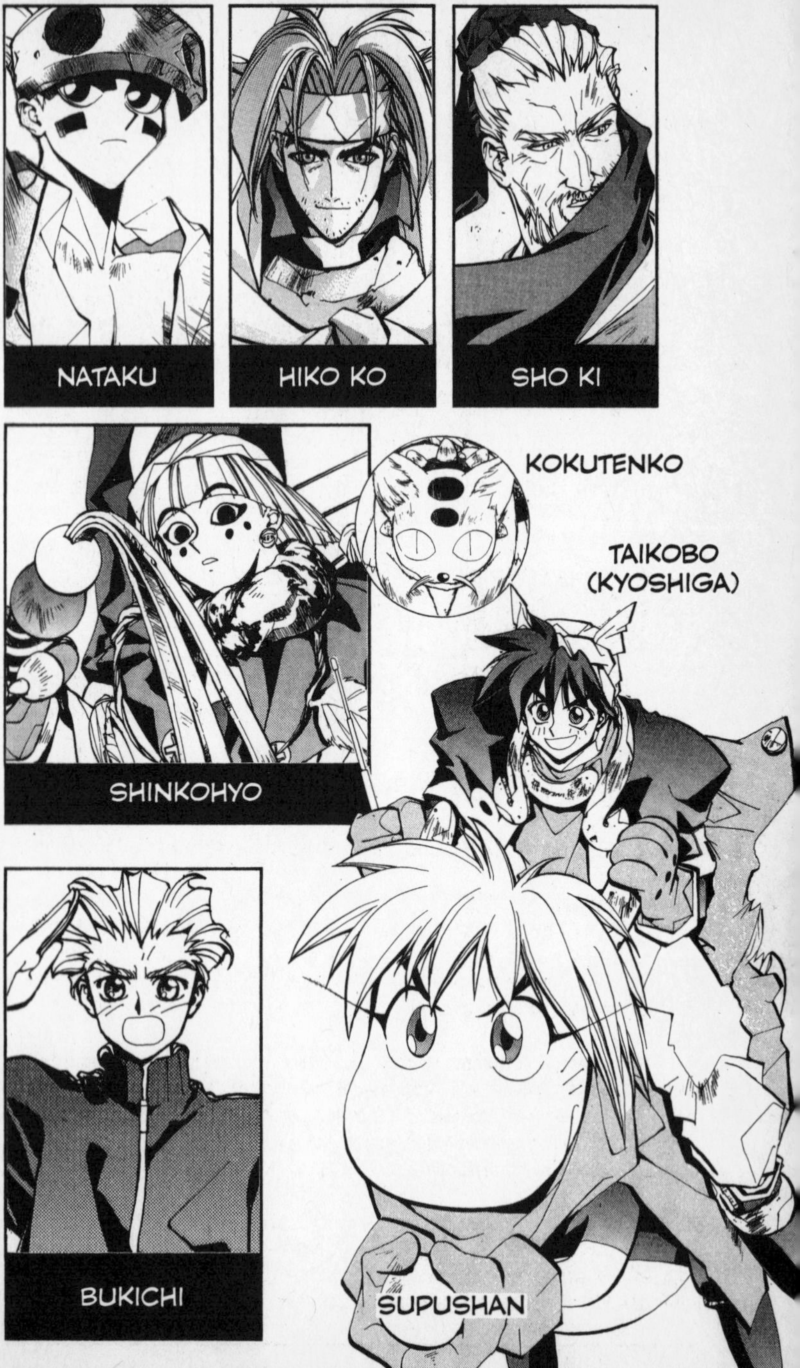
SHO KI
HIKO KO
NATAKU
KOKUTENKO
TAIKOBO (KYOSHIGA)
SHINKOHYO
SUPUSHAN
BUKICHI

KING CHU

BUNCHU

DAKKI

SHISEI

The Story Thus Far

Ancient China, over 3000 years ago. It is the era of the Yin Dynasty.

After King Chu, the emperor, married the beautiful Dakki, the good king was no longer himself, and became an unmanly and foolish ruler. Dakki, a Sennyo with a wicked heart, took control of Yin and the country fell into chaos.

To save the human world, the Hoshin Project was put into action. The project will seal evil Sennin and Doshi into the Shinkai and cause Seihakuko Sho Ki to set up a new dynasty to replace Choka. Taikobo, who was chosen to execute this project, visits Sho Ki in Seiki to encourage him to be the next king.

Right after Taikobo and Sho Ki meet, the Buseio, Hiko Ko, rebels and abandons King Chu. The Buseio is someone Taikobo greatly respects. Taikobo goes to protect Hiko Ko from the assassins that Dakki has sent, but the assassins get there first!

HOSHiN ENGi

VOL. 5
COMRADES

CONTENTS

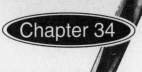

Chapter 34

THE BUSEIO REBELS, PART 6
THE PAOPE OF KINGO

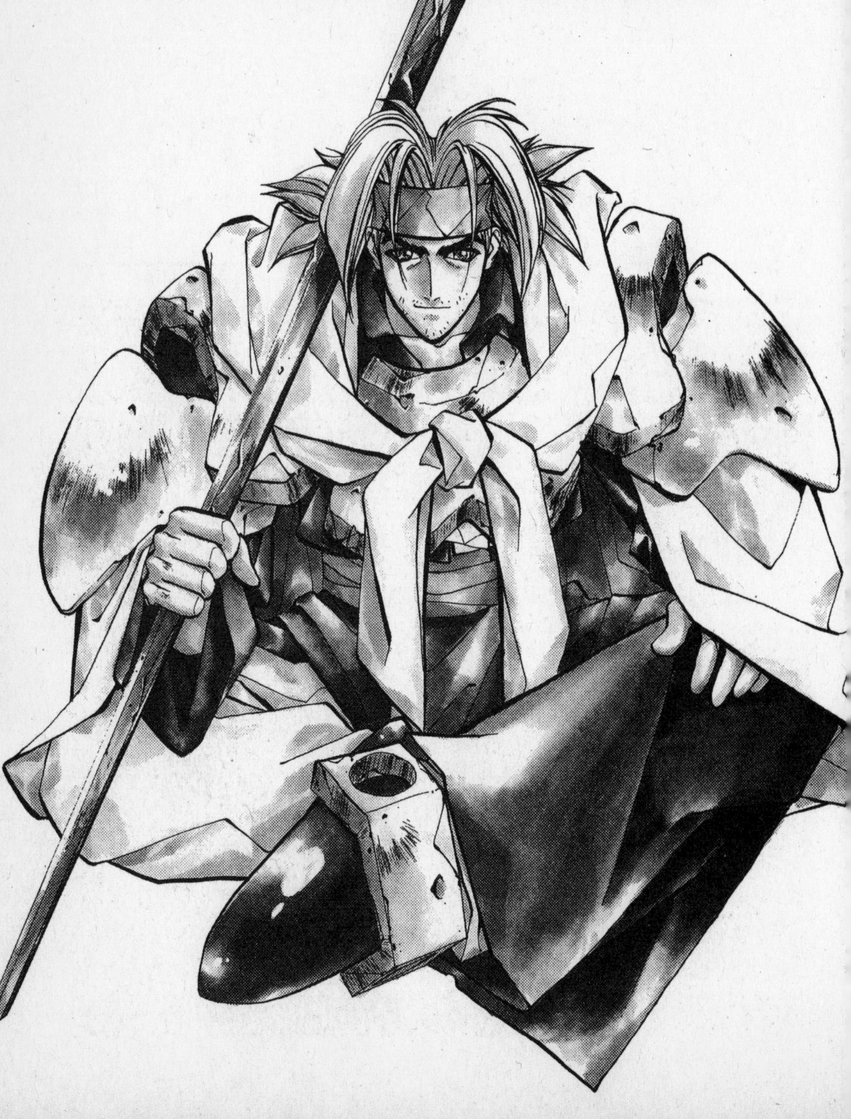

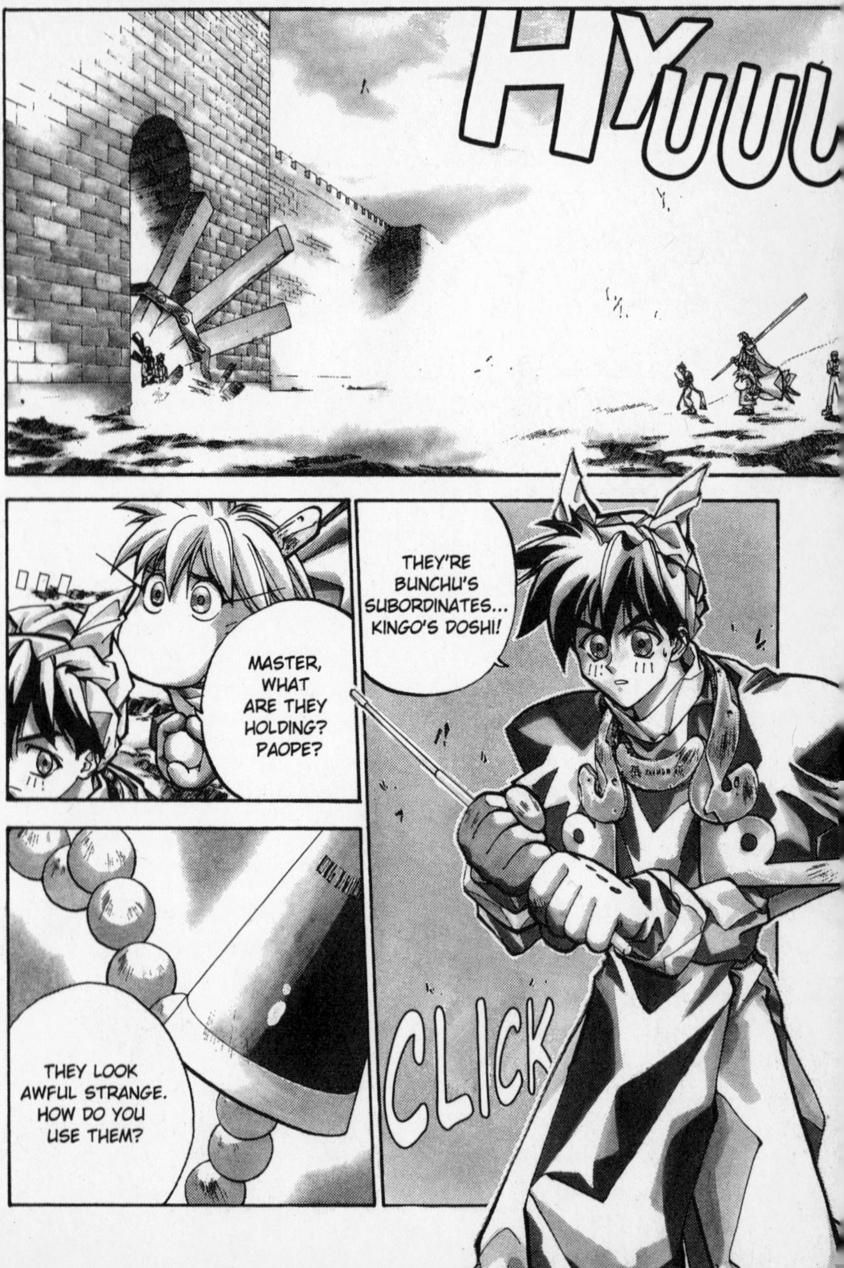
HYUUU
THEY'RE BUNCHU'S SUBORDINATES... KINGO'S DOSHI!
CLICK
MASTER, WHAT ARE THEY HOLDING? PAOPE?
THEY LOOK AWFUL STRANGE. HOW DO YOU USE THEM?

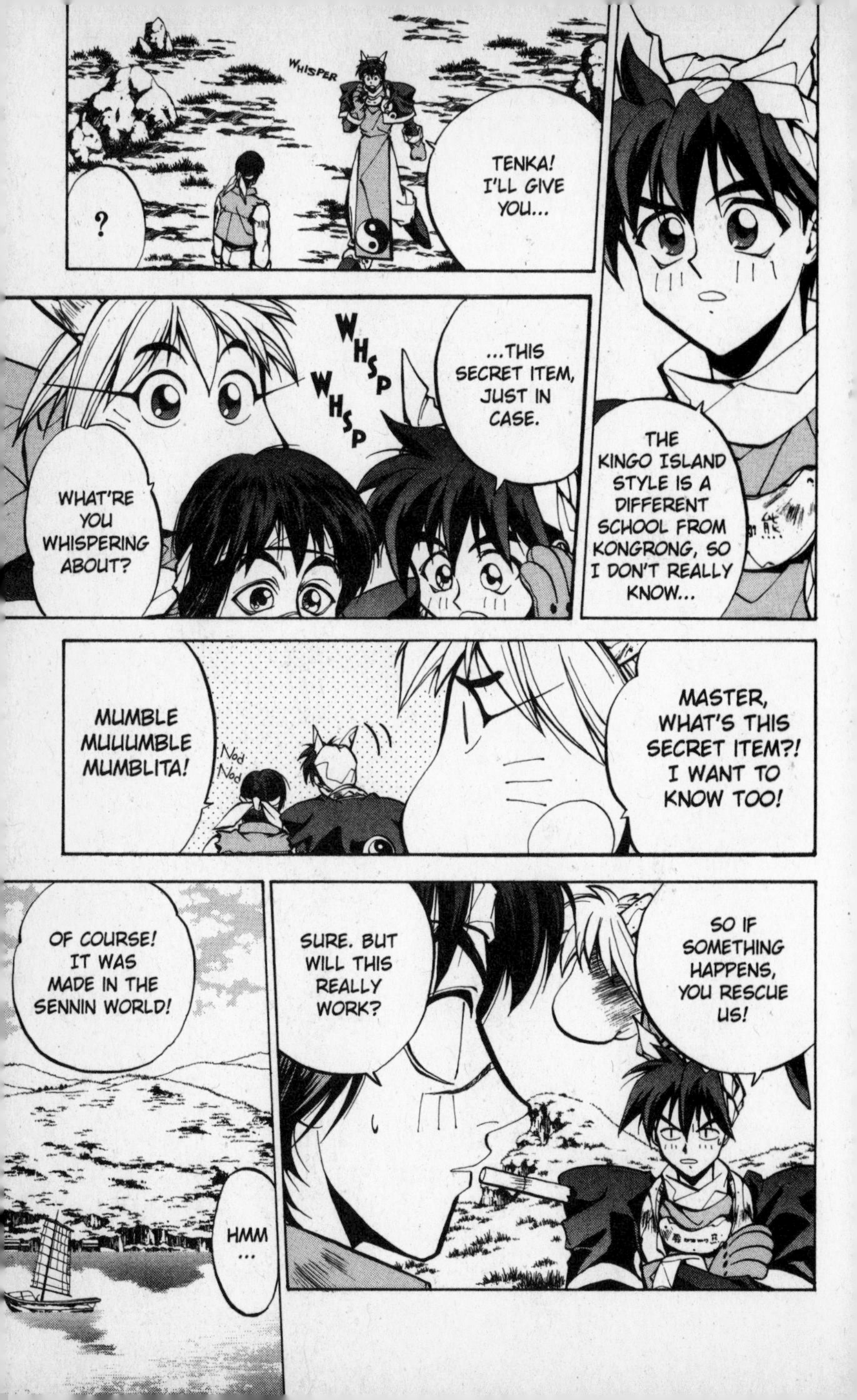
THE KINGO ISLAND STYLE IS A DIFFERENT SCHOOL FROM KONGRONG, SO I DON'T REALLY KNOW...
WHISPER
TENKA! I'LL GIVE YOU...
?
...THIS SECRET ITEM, JUST IN CASE.
WHSP WHSP
WHAT'RE YOU WHISPERING ABOUT?
MASTER, WHAT'S THIS SECRET ITEM?! I WANT TO KNOW TOO!
Nod Nod
MUMBLE MUUUMBLE MUMBLITA!
SO IF SOMETHING HAPPENS, YOU RESCUE US!
SURE. BUT WILL THIS REALLY WORK?
OF COURSE! IT WAS MADE IN THE SENNIN WORLD!
HMM ...

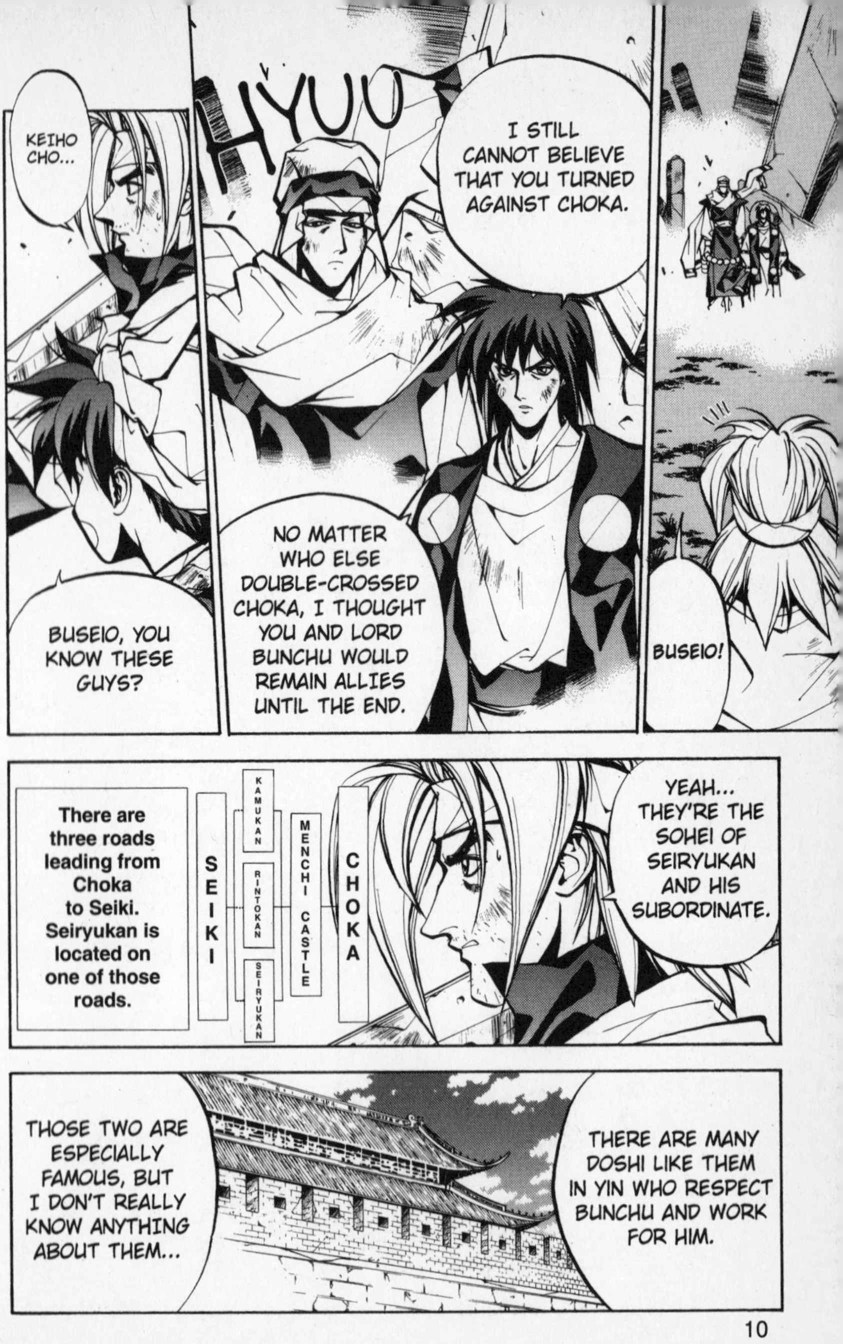
BUSEIO!
HYUU
I STILL CANNOT BELIEVE THAT YOU TURNED AGAINST CHOKA.
NO MATTER WHO ELSE DOUBLE-CROSSED CHOKA, I THOUGHT YOU AND LORD BUNCHU WOULD REMAIN ALLIES UNTIL THE END.
KEIHO CHO...
BUSEIO, YOU KNOW THESE GUYS?
YEAH... THEY'RE THE SOHEI OF SEIRYUKAN AND HIS SUBORDINATE.
CHOKA
MENCHI CASTLE
KAMUKAN
RINTOKAN
SEIRYUKAN
SEIKI
There are three roads leading from Choka to Seiki. Seiryukan is located on one of those roads.
THERE ARE MANY DOSHI LIKE THEM IN YIN WHO RESPECT BUNCHU AND WORK FOR HIM.
THOSE TWO ARE ESPECIALLY FAMOUS, BUT I DON'T REALLY KNOW ANYTHING ABOUT THEM...

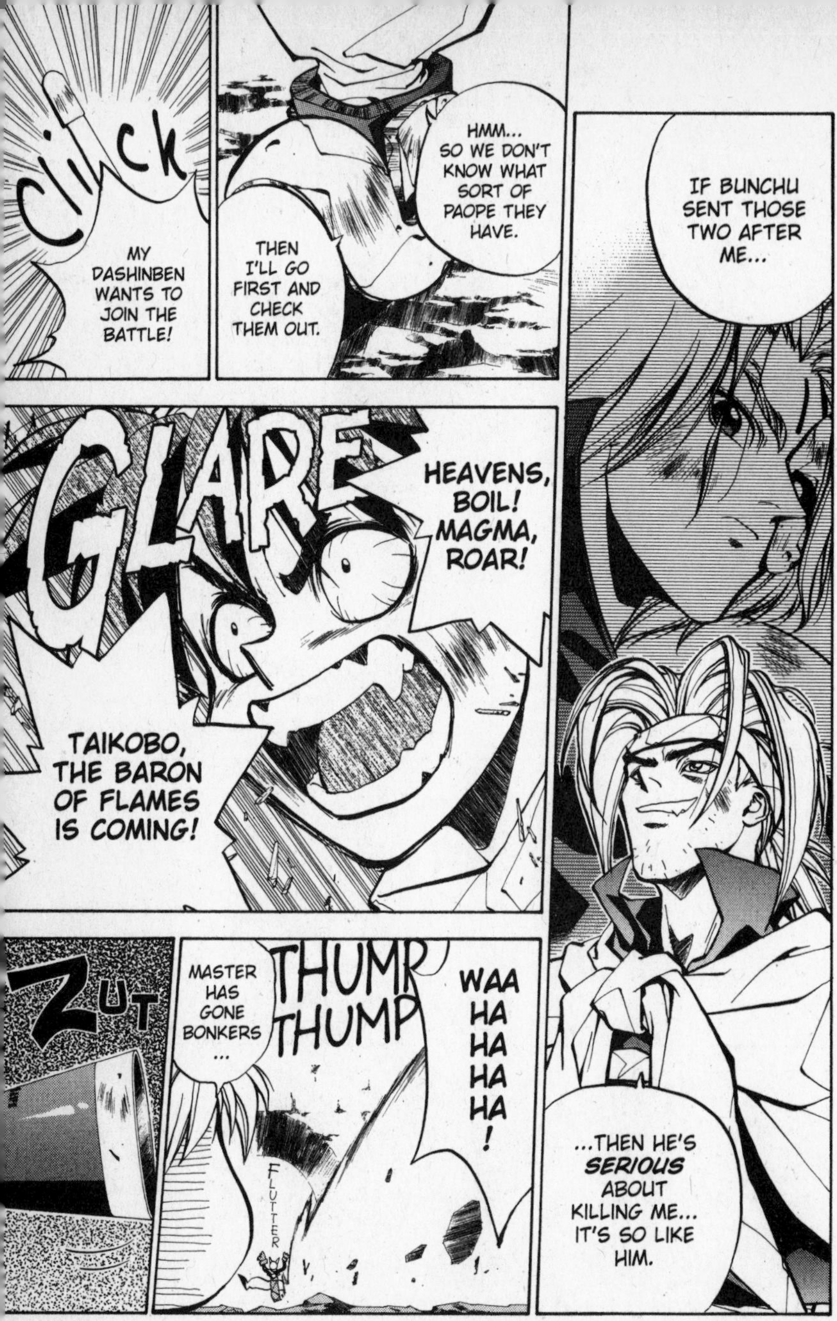
IF BUNCHU SENT THOSE TWO AFTER ME...
...THEN HE'S ***SERIOUS*** ABOUT KILLING ME... IT'S SO LIKE HIM.
HMM... SO WE DON'T KNOW WHAT SORT OF PAOPE THEY HAVE.
THEN I'LL GO FIRST AND CHECK THEM OUT.
CLIICK
MY DASHINBEN WANTS TO JOIN THE BATTLE!
HEAVENS, BOIL! MAGMA, ROAR!
GLARE
TAIKOBO, THE BARON OF FLAMES IS COMING!
WAA HA HA HA HA HA!
THUMP THUMP
MASTER HAS GONE BONKERS ...
FLUTTER
ZUT

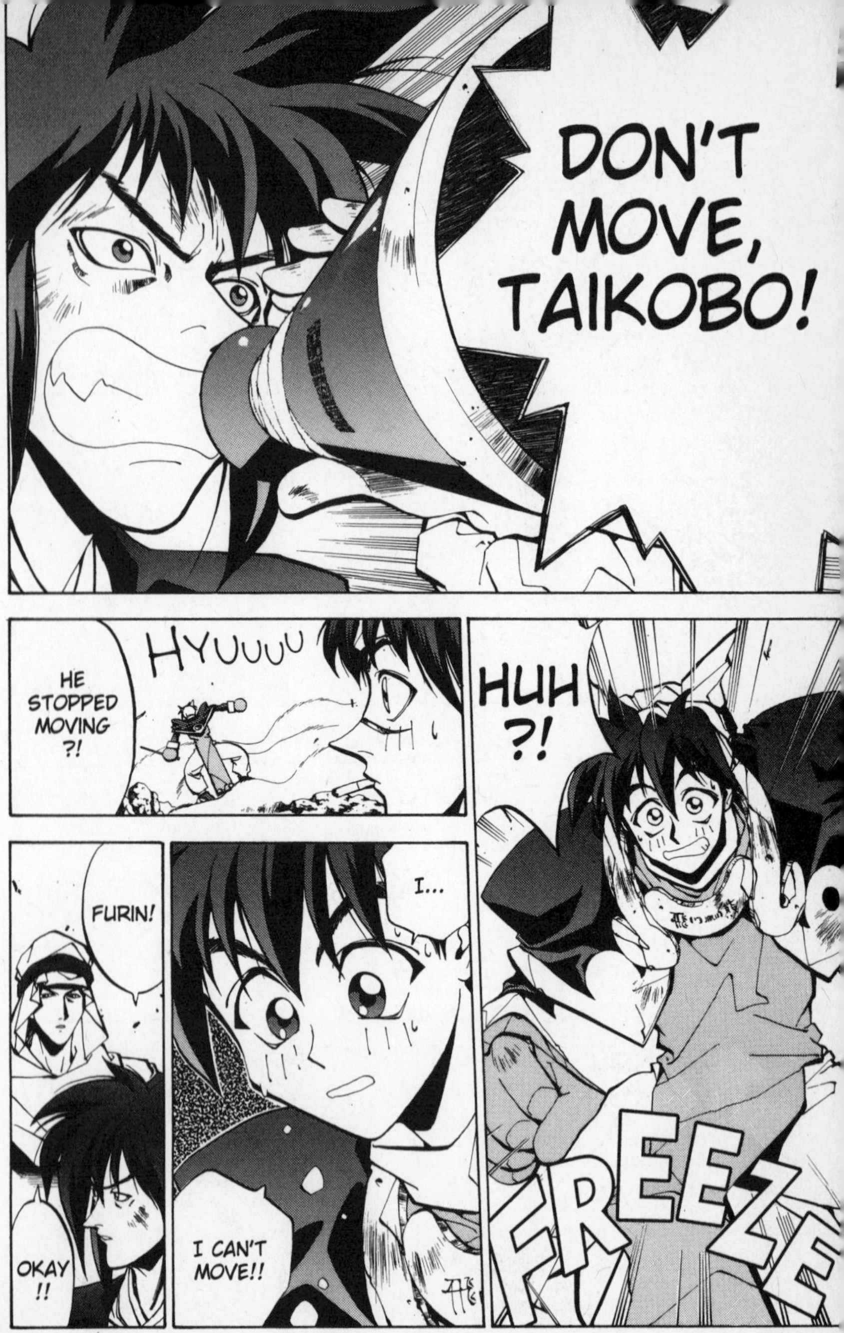
DON'T MOVE, TAIKOBO!
HUH ?!
FREEZE
HYUUUU
HE STOPPED MOVING ?!
I...
I CAN'T MOVE!!
FURIN!
OKAY !!

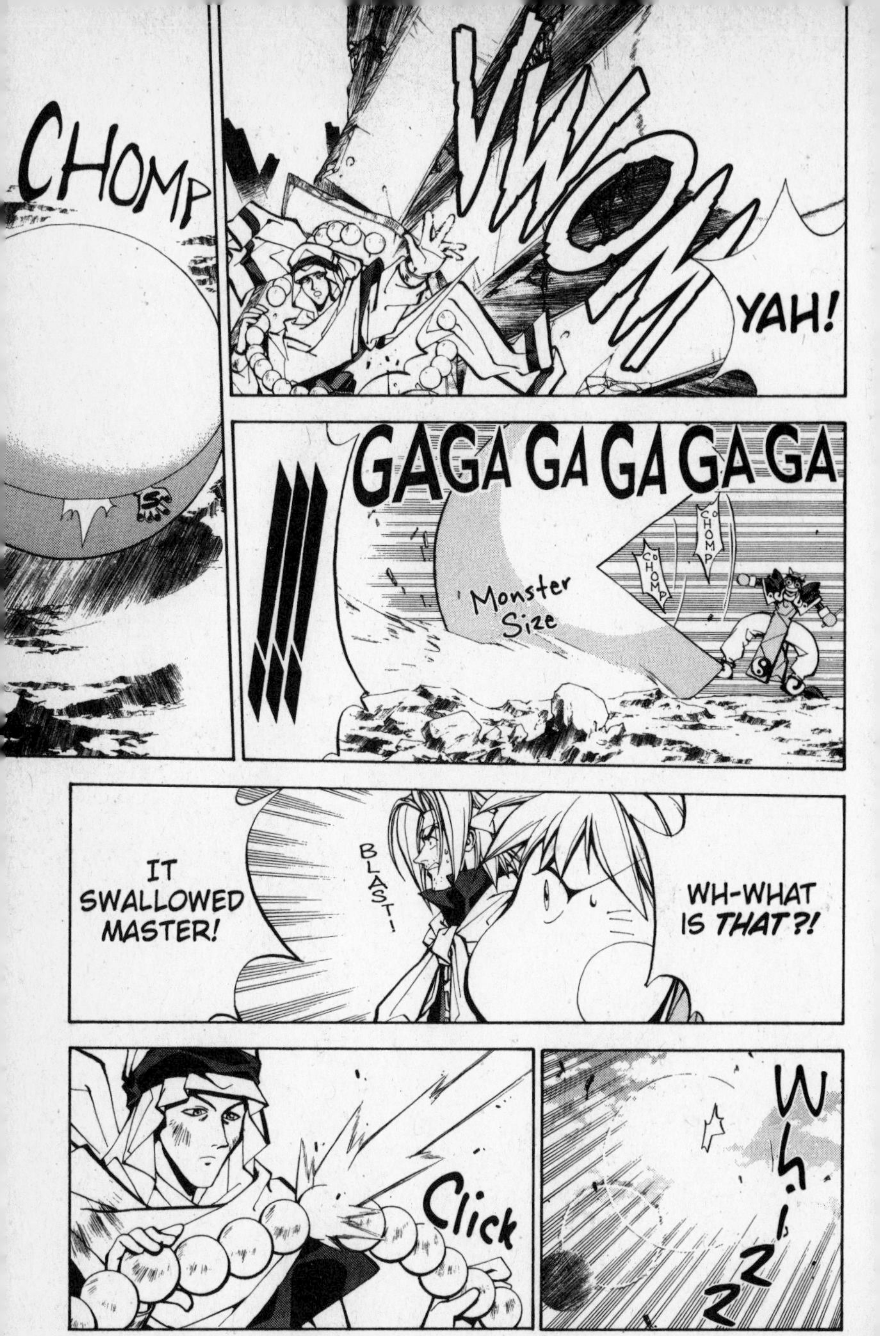
VWOM
YAH!
GAGA GA GA GA GA
CHOMP
CHOMP
Monster Size
CHOMP
WH-WHAT IS THAT?!
BLAST!
IT SWALLOWED MASTER!
Whizzz
Click

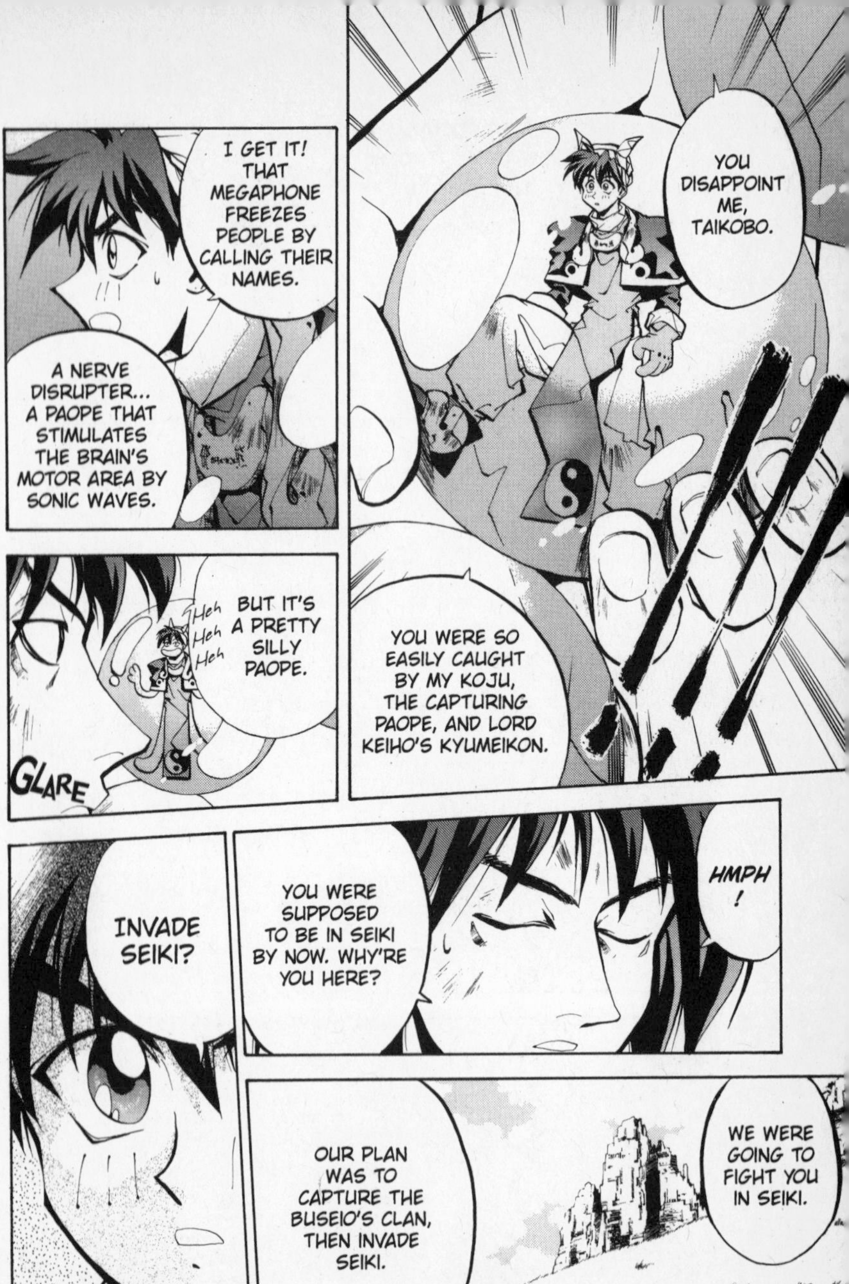
YOU DISAPPOINT ME, TAIKOBO.
YOU WERE SO EASILY CAUGHT BY MY KOJU, THE CAPTURING PAOPE, AND LORD KEIHO'S KYUMEIKON.
I GET IT! THAT MEGAPHONE FREEZES PEOPLE BY CALLING THEIR NAMES.
A NERVE DISRUPTER... A PAOPE THAT STIMULATES THE BRAIN'S MOTOR AREA BY SONIC WAVES.
Heh Heh Heh
BUT IT'S A PRETTY SILLY PAOPE.
GLARE
HMPH!
YOU WERE SUPPOSED TO BE IN SEIKI BY NOW. WHY'RE YOU HERE?
WE WERE GOING TO FIGHT YOU IN SEIKI.
OUR PLAN WAS TO CAPTURE THE BUSEIO'S CLAN, THEN INVADE SEIKI.
INVADE SEIKI?

READ THIS WAY

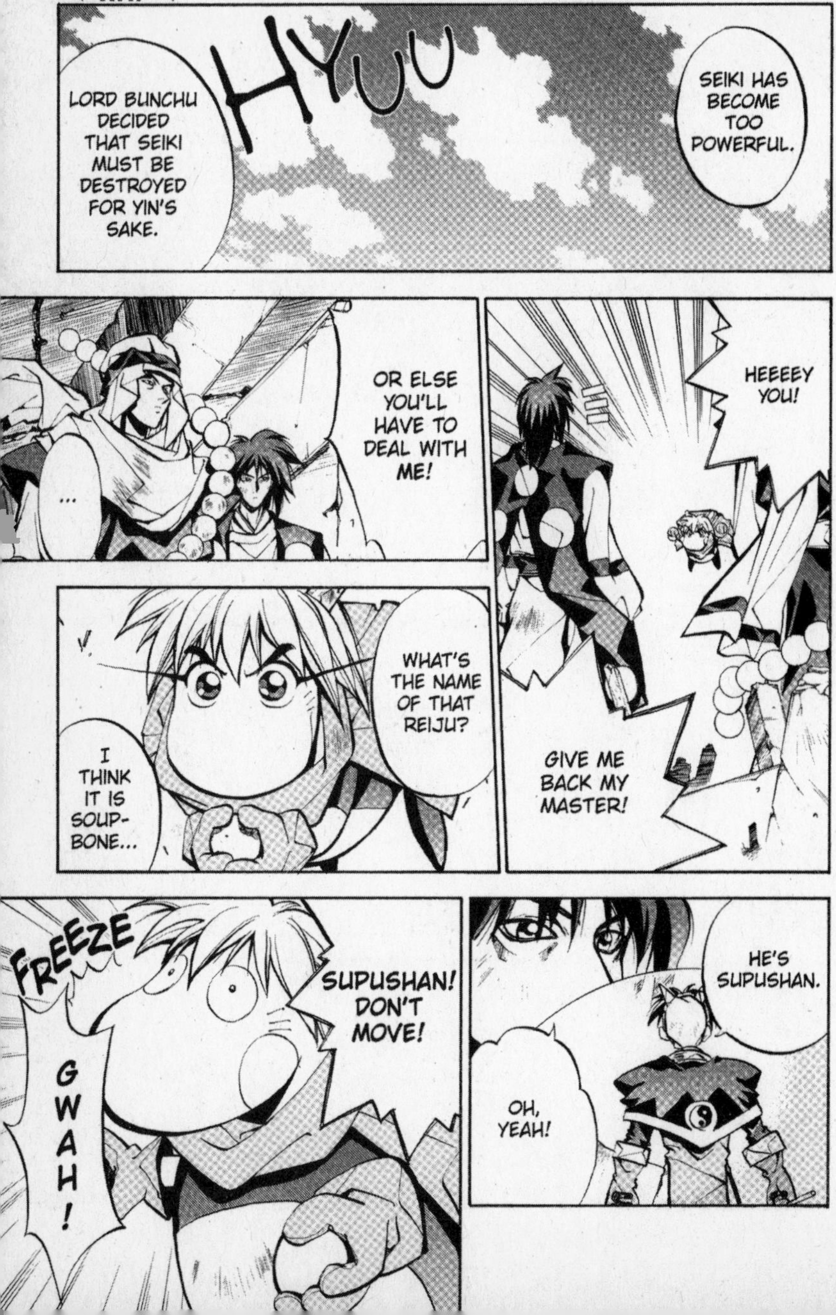
SEIKI HAS BECOME TOO POWERFUL.
HYUU
LORD BUNCHU DECIDED THAT SEIKI MUST BE DESTROYED FOR YIN'S SAKE.
HEEEEY YOU!
GIVE ME BACK MY MASTER!
OR ELSE YOU'LL HAVE TO DEAL WITH ME!
...
WHAT'S THE NAME OF THAT REIJU?
I THINK IT IS SOUP-BONE...
HE'S SUPUSHAN.
OH, YEAH!
SUPUSHAN! DON'T MOVE!
FREEZE
GWAH!

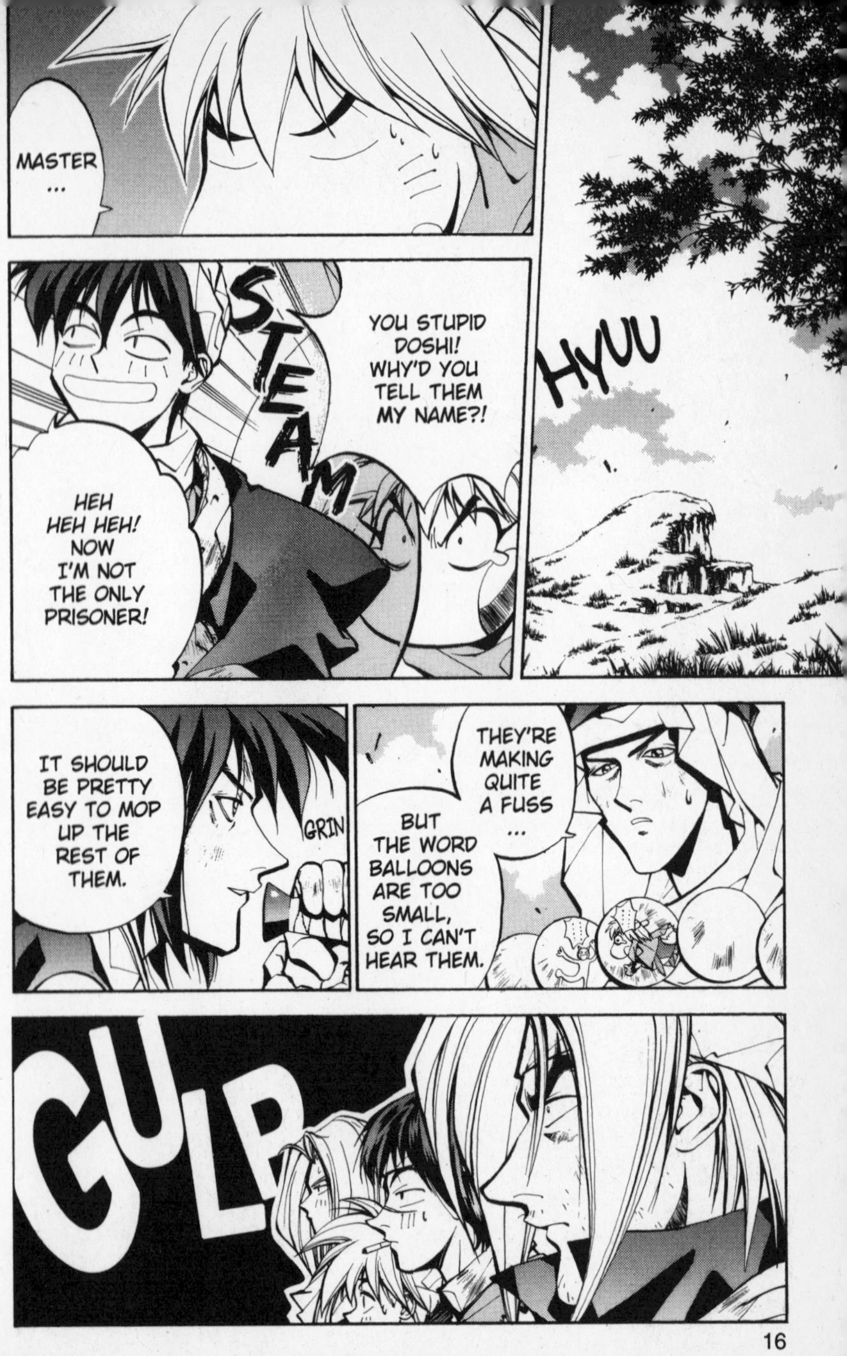
HYUU
MASTER ...
YOU STUPID DOSHI! WHY'D YOU TELL THEM MY NAME?!
STEAM
HEH HEH HEH! NOW I'M NOT THE ONLY PRISONER!
THEY'RE MAKING QUITE A FUSS ...
BUT THE WORD BALLOONS ARE TOO SMALL, SO I CAN'T HEAR THEM.
GRIN
IT SHOULD BE PRETTY EASY TO MOP UP THE REST OF THEM.
GULP

READ THIS WAY

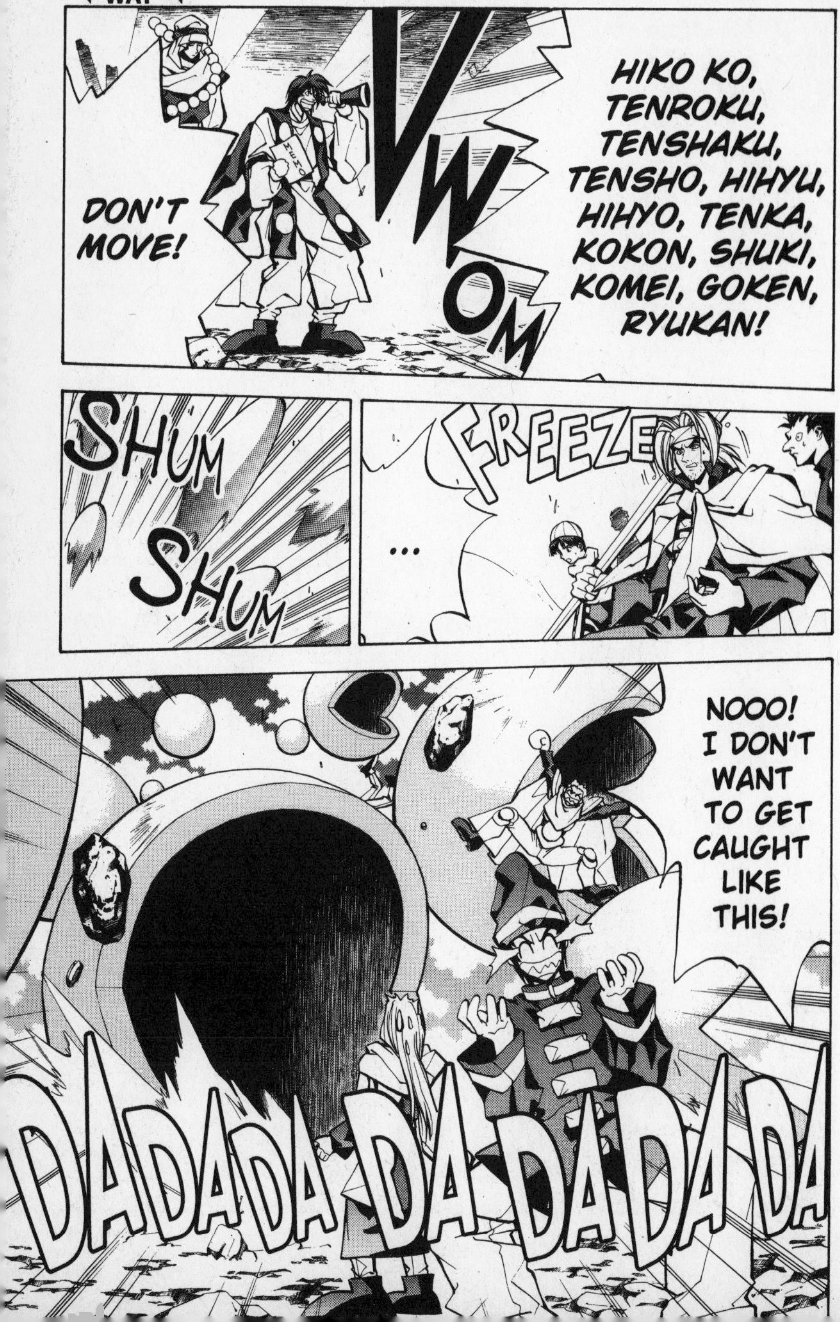
HIKO KO, TENROKU, TENSHAKU, TENSHO, HIHYU, HIHYO, TENKA, KOKON, SHUKI, KOMEI, GOKEN, RYUKAN!
VWOM
DON'T MOVE!
FREEZE
...
SHUM SHUM
NOOO! I DON'T WANT TO GET CAUGHT LIKE THIS!
DADADA DA DA DA DA DA DA

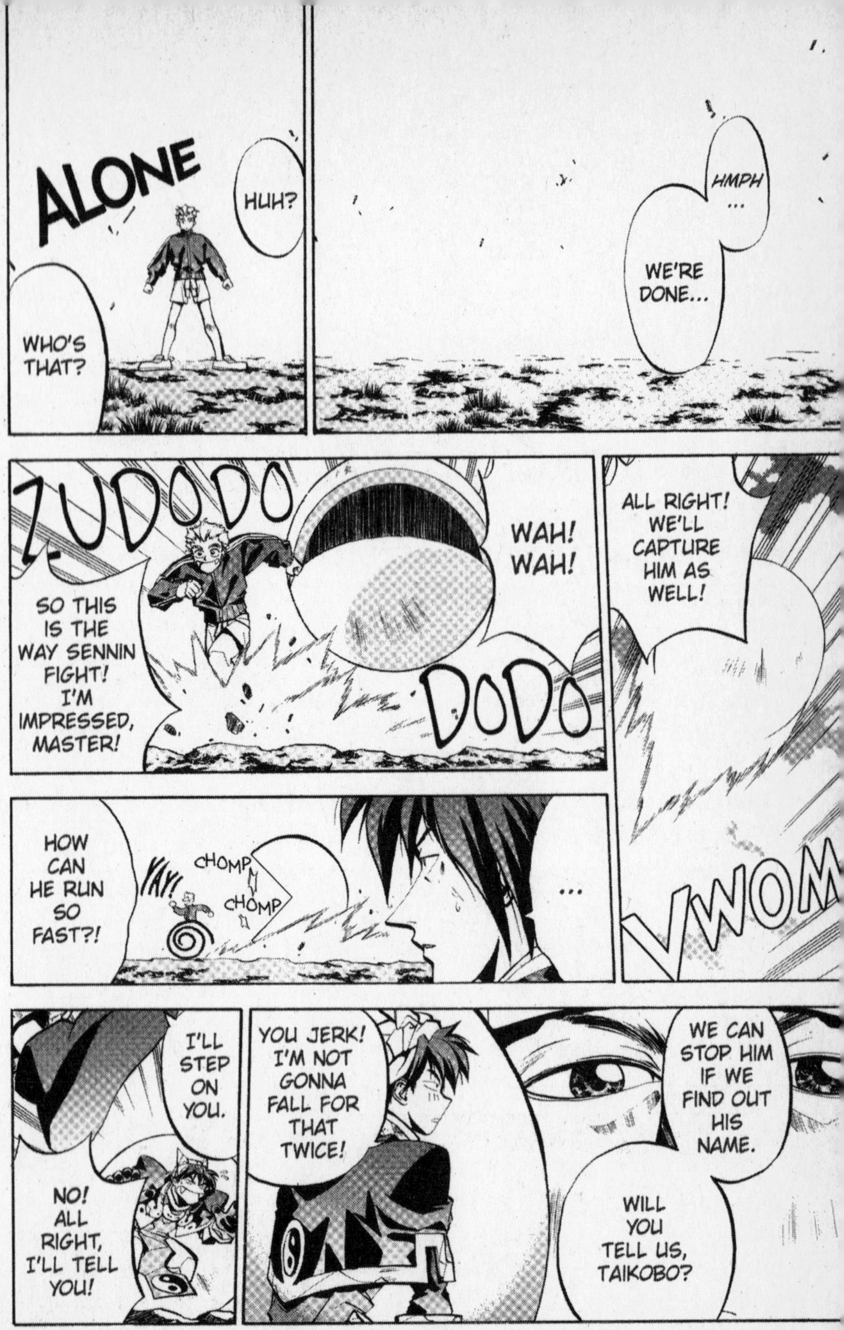
HMPH ...
WE'RE DONE...
HUH?
ALONE
WHO'S THAT?
ALL RIGHT! WE'LL CAPTURE HIM AS WELL!
VWOM
WAH! WAH!
ZUDODO
SO THIS IS THE WAY SENNIN FIGHT! I'M IMPRESSED, MASTER!
DODO
...
CHOMP CHOMP
YAY!
HOW CAN HE RUN SO FAST?!
WE CAN STOP HIM IF WE FIND OUT HIS NAME.
WILL YOU TELL US, TAIKOBO?
YOU JERK! I'M NOT GONNA FALL FOR THAT TWICE!
I'LL STEP ON YOU.
NO! ALL RIGHT, I'LL TELL YOU!

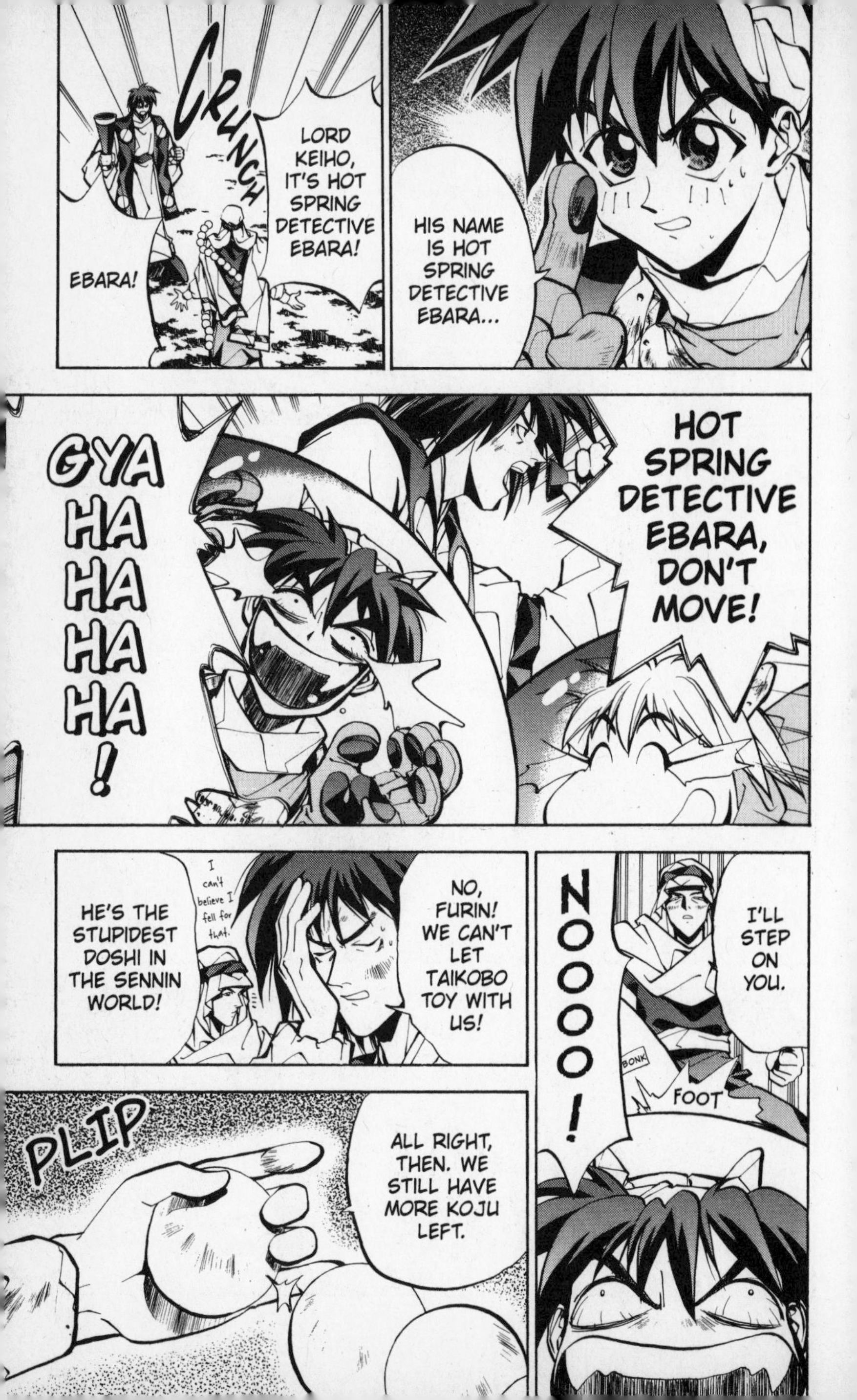
HIS NAME IS HOT SPRING DETECTIVE EBARA...
LORD KEIHO, IT'S HOT SPRING DETECTIVE EBARA!
CRUNCH
EBARA!
HOT SPRING DETECTIVE EBARA, DON'T MOVE!
GYA HA HA HA HA HA!
I'LL STEP ON YOU.
BONK
FOOT
NOOOO!
NO, FURIN! WE CAN'T LET TAIKOBO TOY WITH US!
I can't believe I fell for that.
HE'S THE STUPIDEST DOSHI IN THE SENNIN WORLD!
ALL RIGHT, THEN. WE STILL HAVE MORE KOJU LEFT.
PLIP

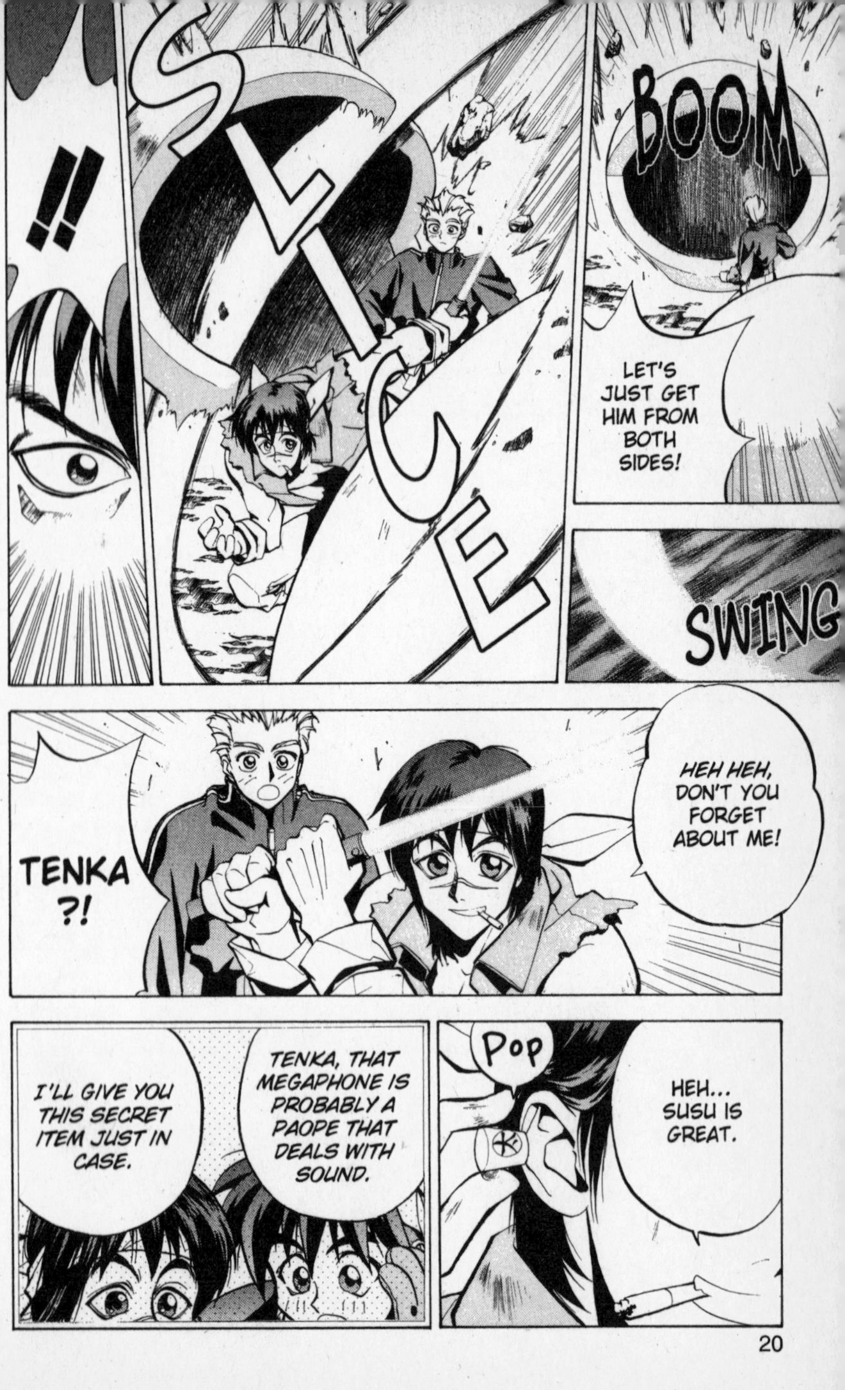
BOOM
LET'S JUST GET HIM FROM BOTH SIDES!
SWING
SLICE
!!
HEH HEH, DON'T YOU FORGET ABOUT ME!
TENKA ?!
Pop
HEH... SUSU IS GREAT.
TENKA, THAT MEGAPHONE IS PROBABLY A PAOPE THAT DEALS WITH SOUND.
I'LL GIVE YOU THIS SECRET ITEM JUST IN CASE.

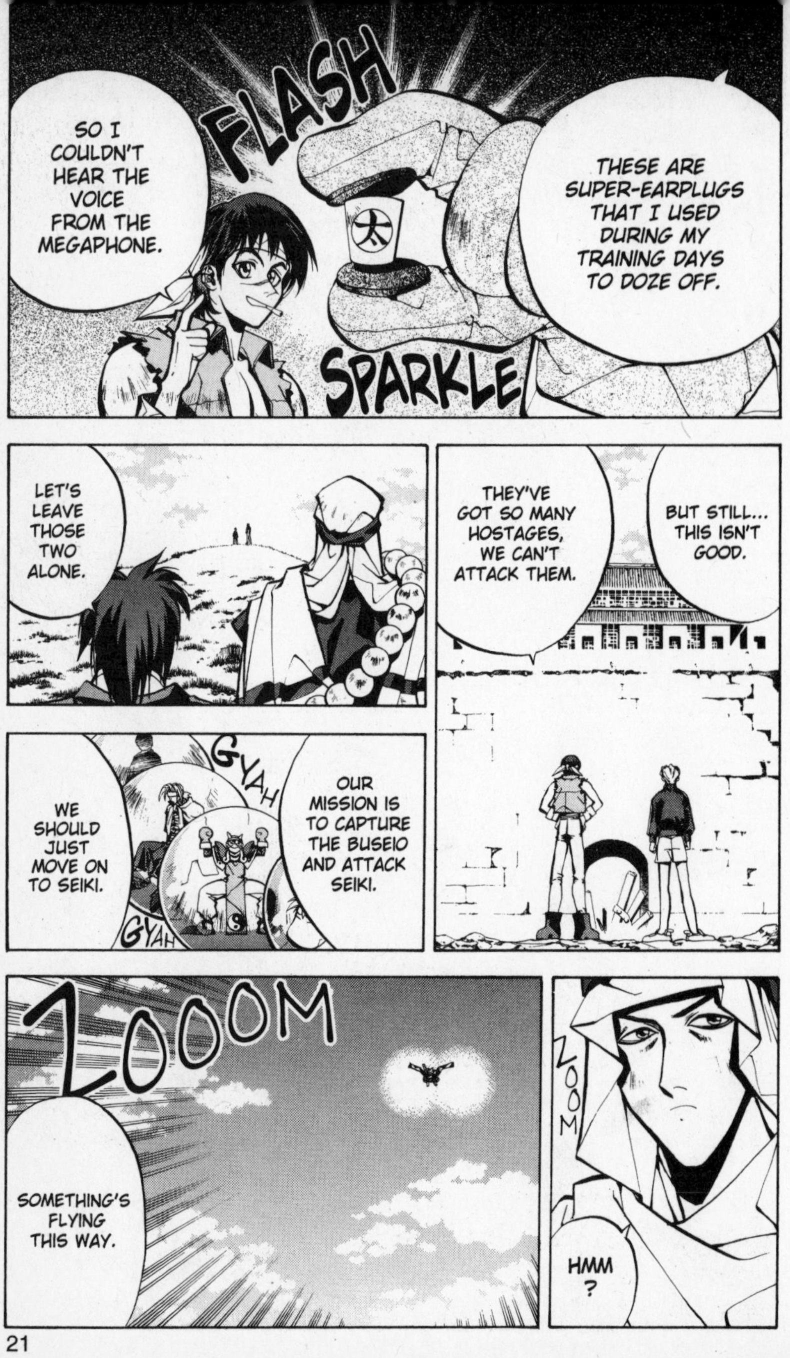
FLASH
THESE ARE SUPER-EARPLUGS THAT I USED DURING MY TRAINING DAYS TO DOZE OFF.
SO I COULDN'T HEAR THE VOICE FROM THE MEGAPHONE.
SPARKLE
BUT STILL... THIS ISN'T GOOD.
THEY'VE GOT SO MANY HOSTAGES, WE CAN'T ATTACK THEM.
LET'S LEAVE THOSE TWO ALONE.
GYAH
OUR MISSION IS TO CAPTURE THE BUSEIO AND ATTACK SEIKI.
WE SHOULD JUST MOVE ON TO SEIKI.
GYAH
ZOOM
HMM?
ZOOOM
SOMETHING'S FLYING THIS WAY.

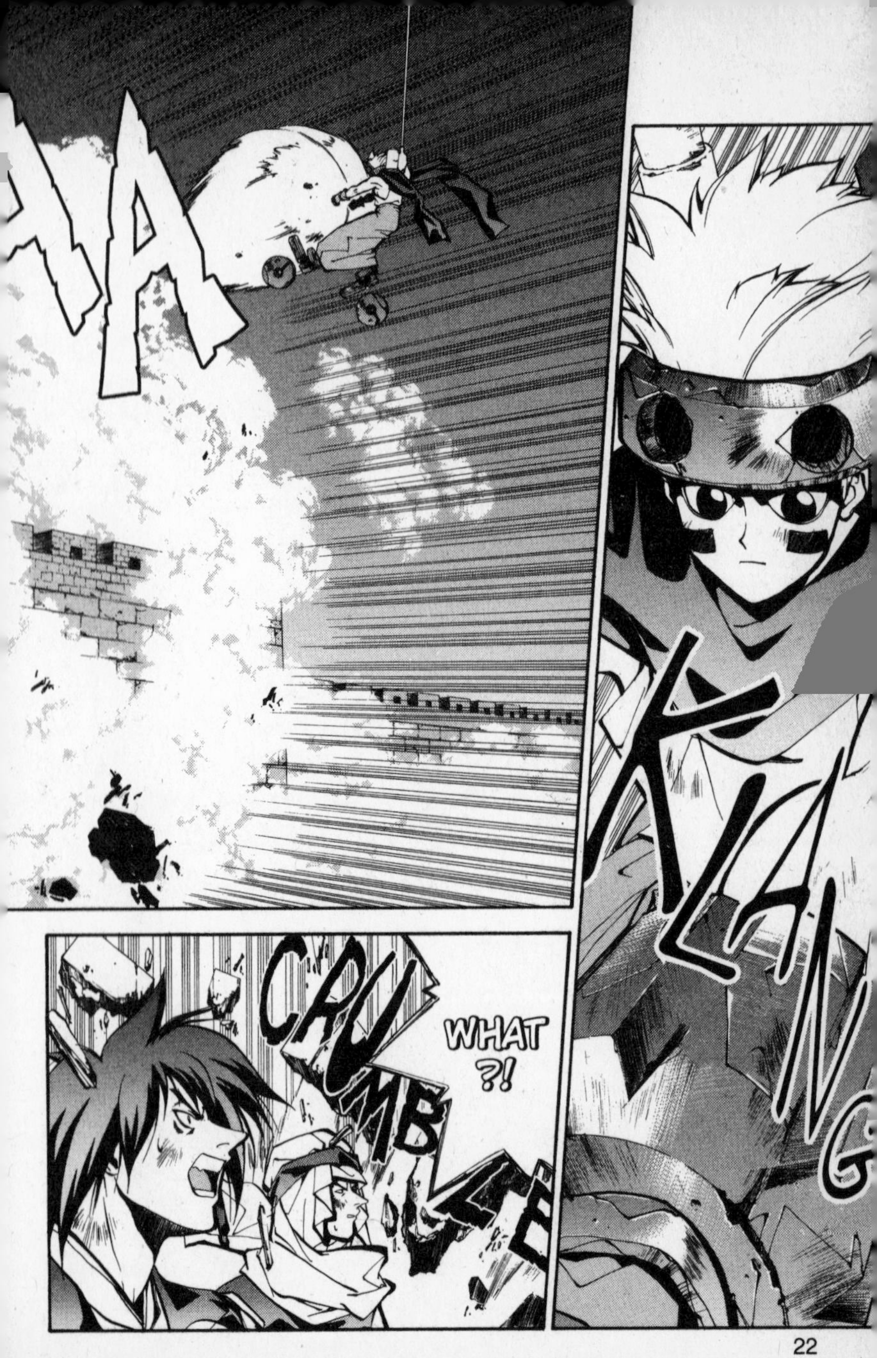
KLANG
AA
CRUMBLE
WHAT ?!

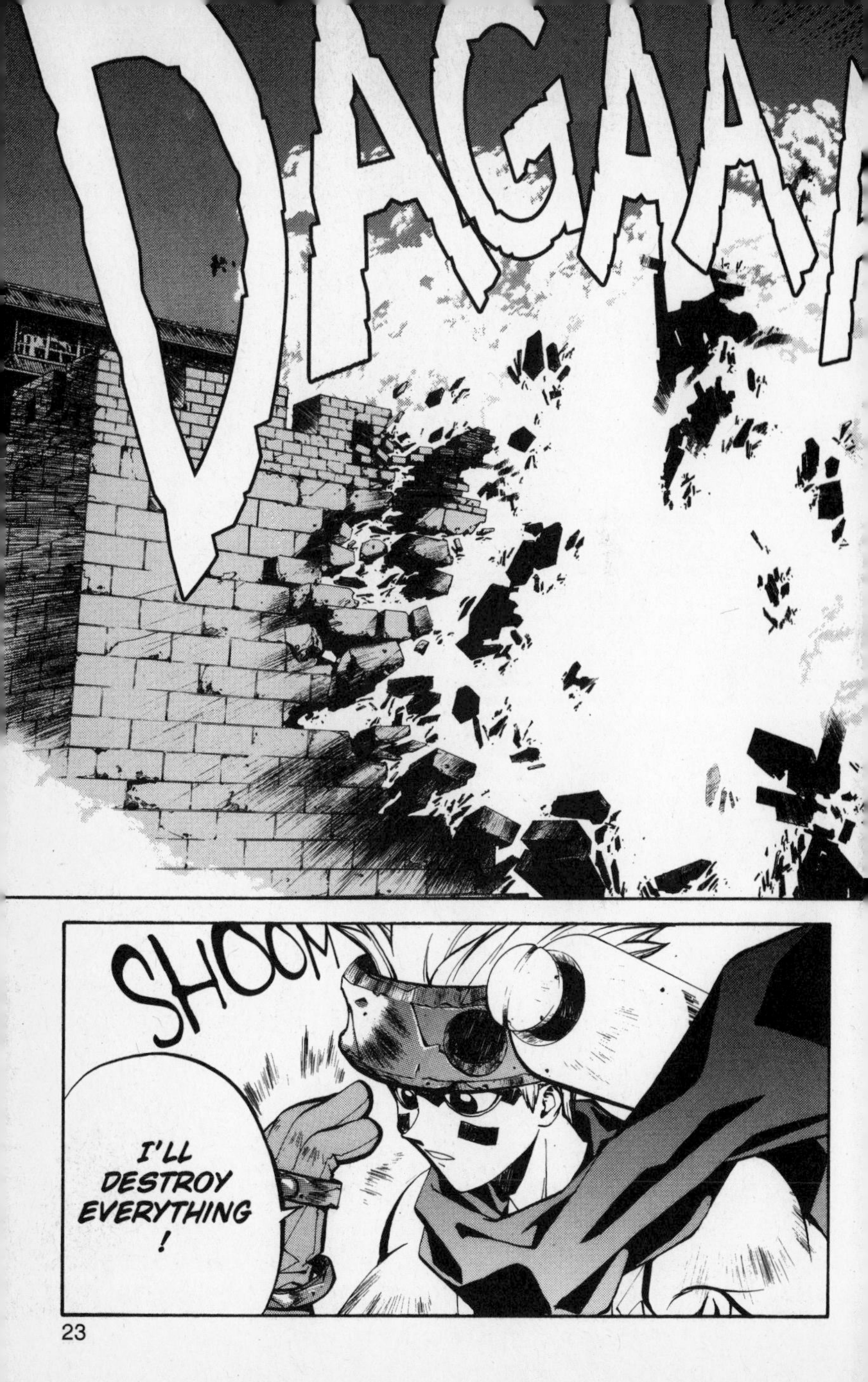
DAGAA
SHOOM
I'LL DESTROY EVERYTHING!

封神演義

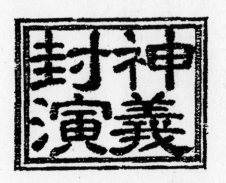

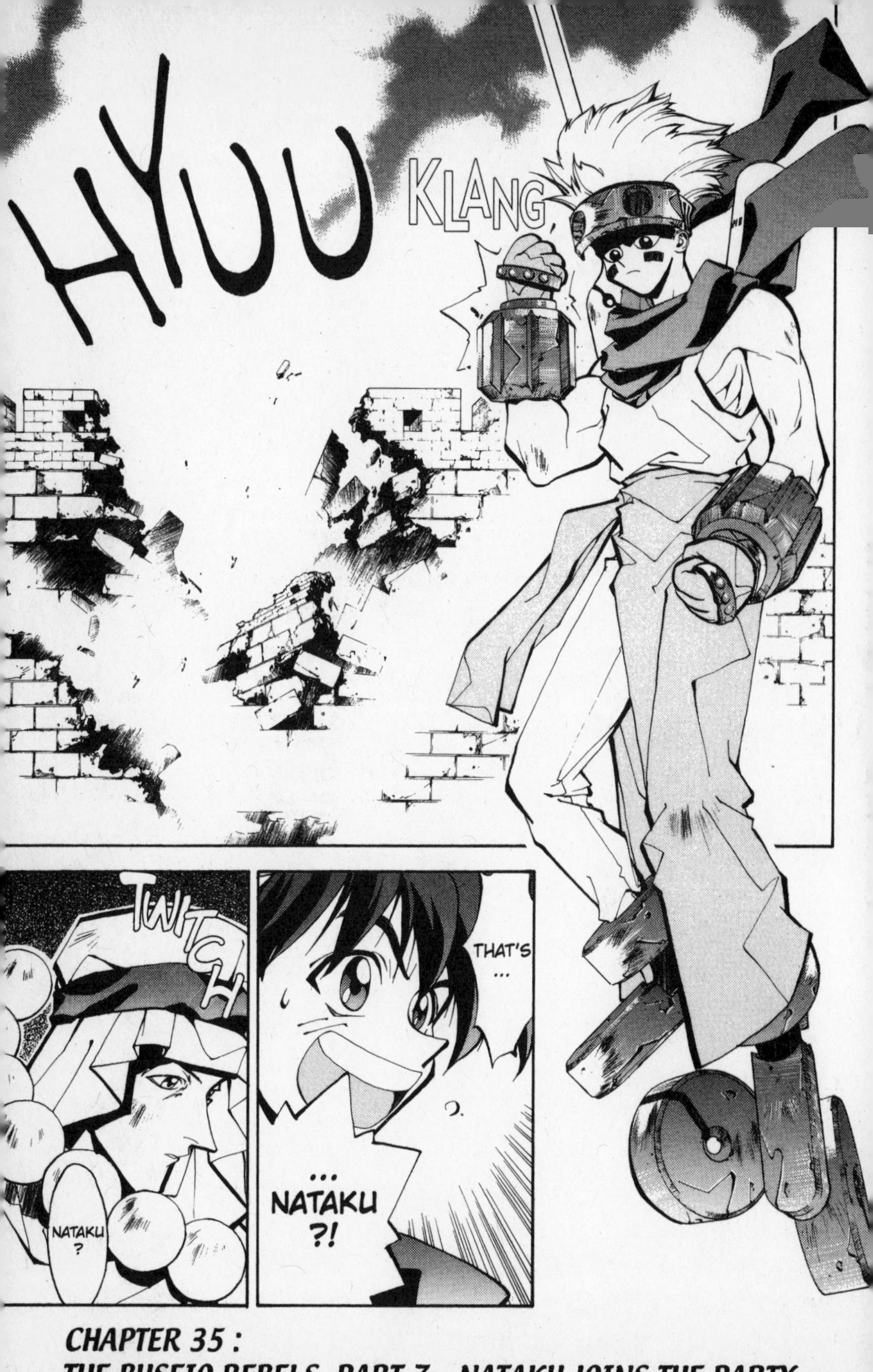
KLANG
HYUU
THAT'S ...
... NATAKU ?!
TWITCH
NATAKU ?

CHAPTER 35 :
THE BUSEIO REBELS, PART 7 - NATAKU JOINS THE PARTY

THE BUSEIO REBELS, PART 7
NATAKU JOINS THE PARTY

READ THIS WAY

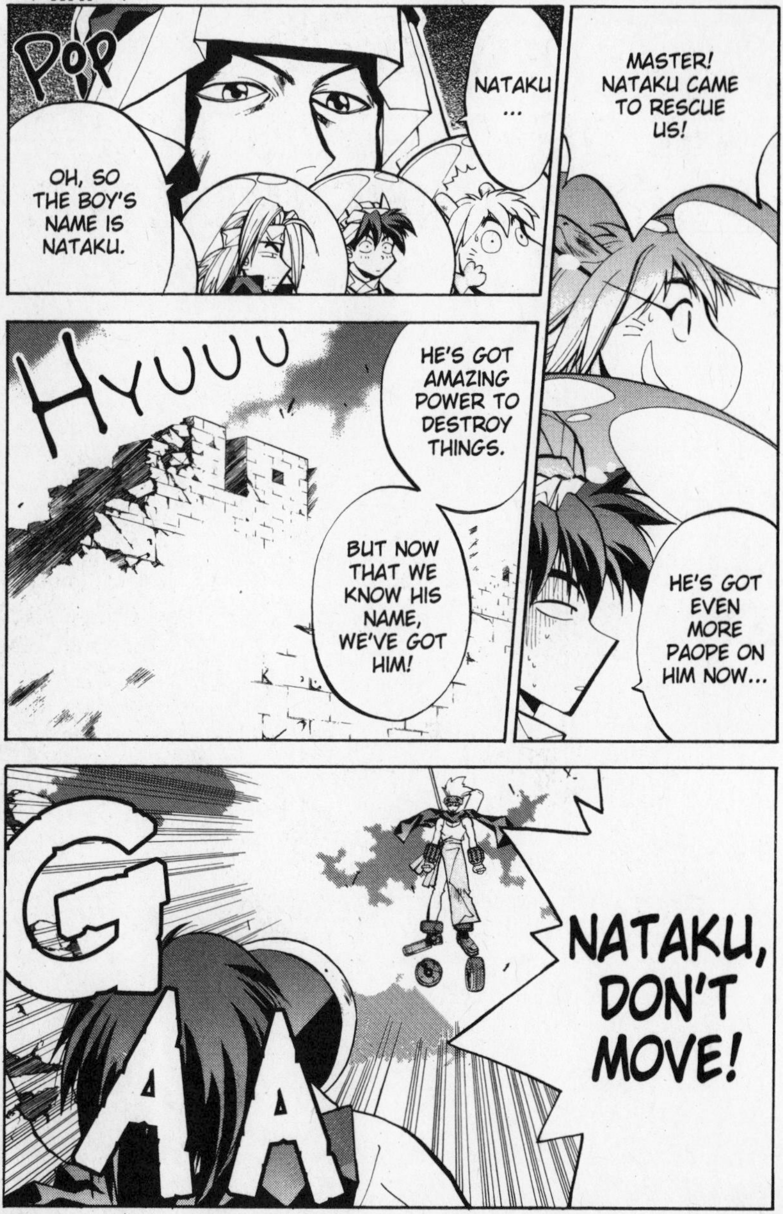
MASTER! NATAKU CAME TO RESCUE US!
HE'S GOT EVEN MORE PAOPE ON HIM NOW...
NATAKU ...
POP
OH, SO THE BOY'S NAME IS NATAKU.
HE'S GOT AMAZING POWER TO DESTROY THINGS.
BUT NOW THAT WE KNOW HIS NAME, WE'VE GOT HIM!
HYUUU
NATAKU, DON'T MOVE!
GAA

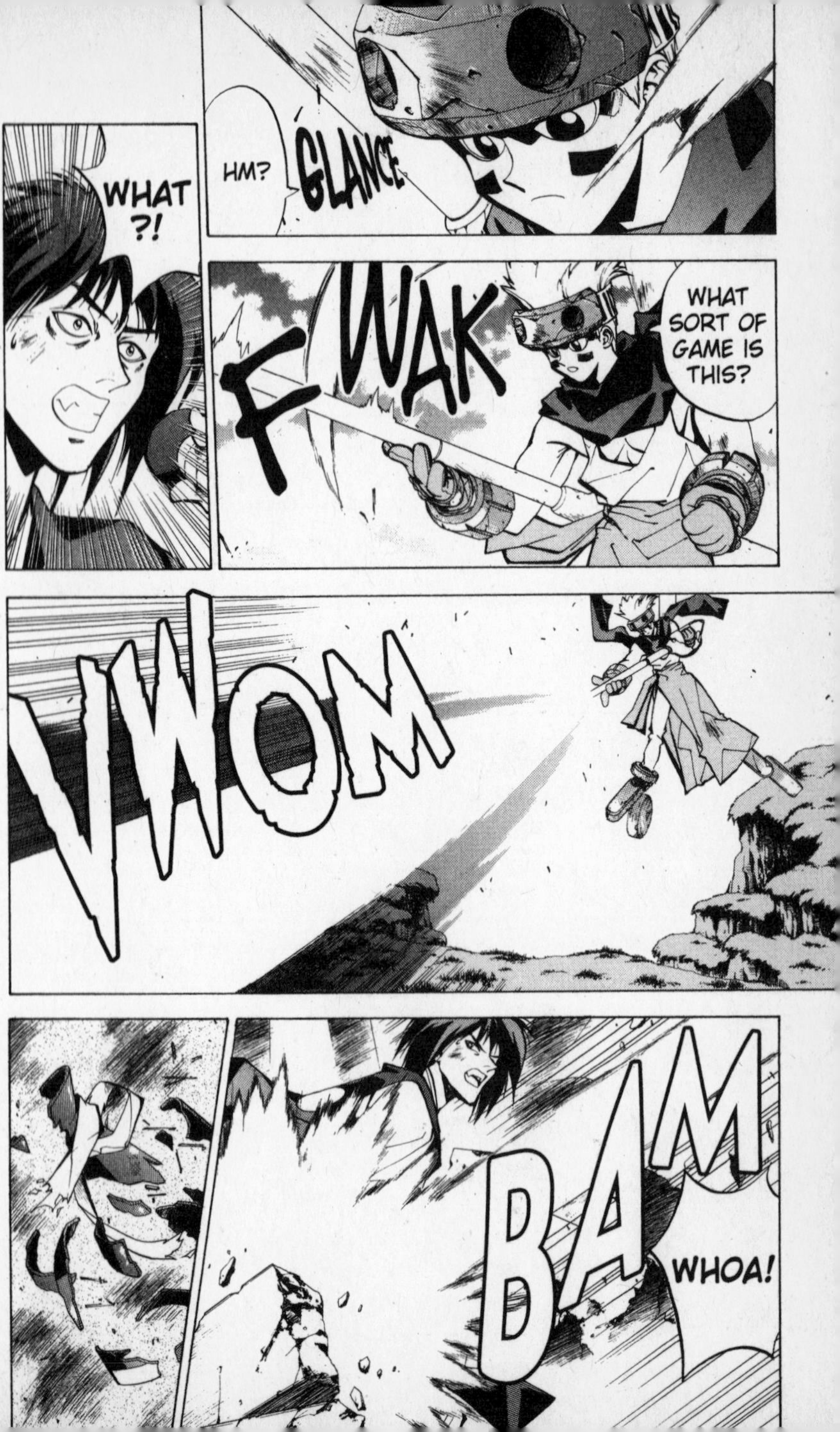
GLANCE
HM?
WHAT SORT OF GAME IS THIS?
FWAK
WHAT ?!
VWOM
BAM
WHOA!

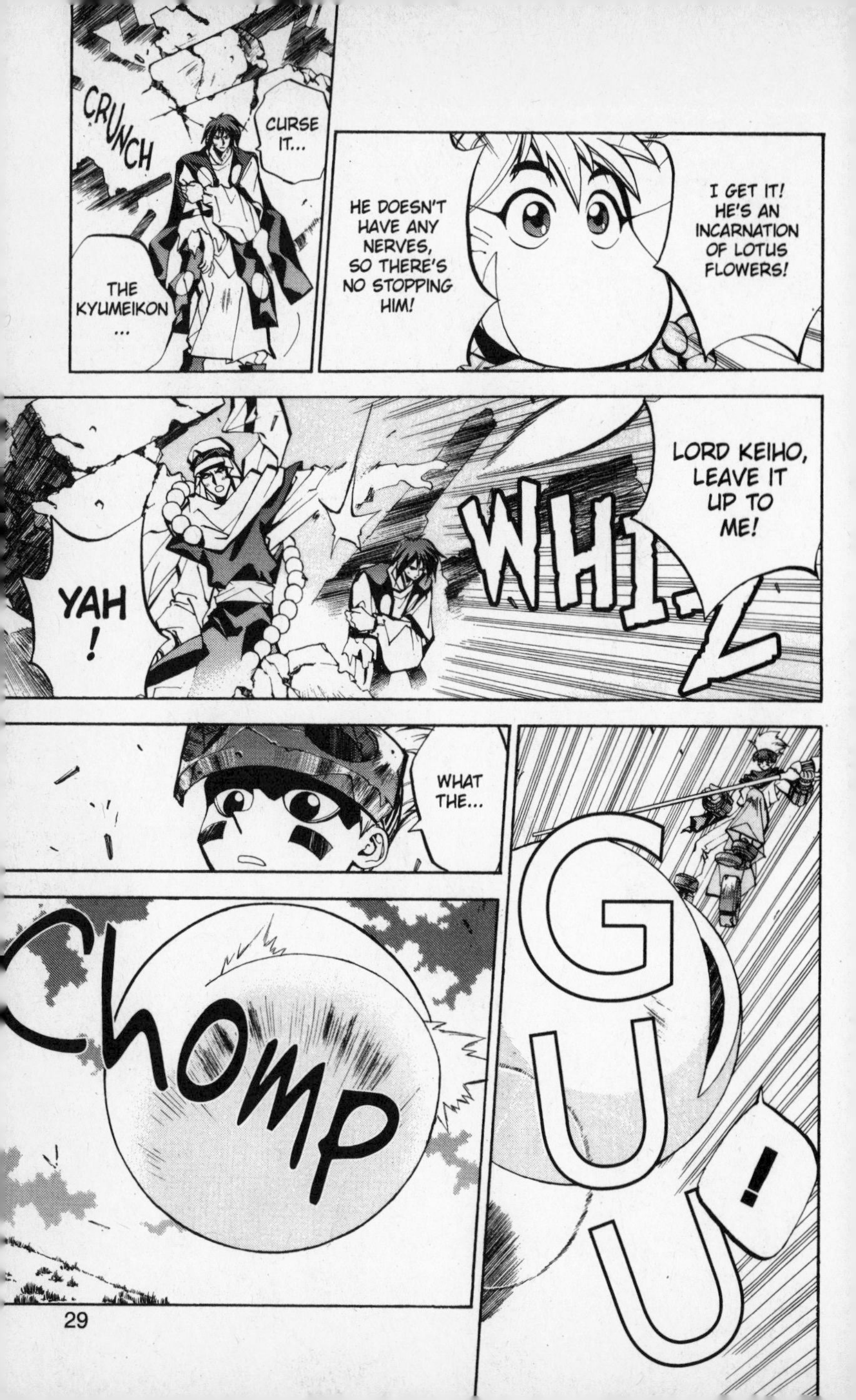
I GET IT! HE'S AN INCARNATION OF LOTUS FLOWERS!
HE DOESN'T HAVE ANY NERVES, SO THERE'S NO STOPPING HIM!
CRUNCH
CURSE IT...
THE KYUMEIKON ...
LORD KEIHO, LEAVE IT UP TO ME!
WHIZ
YAH !
GUUU !
WHAT THE...
Chomp

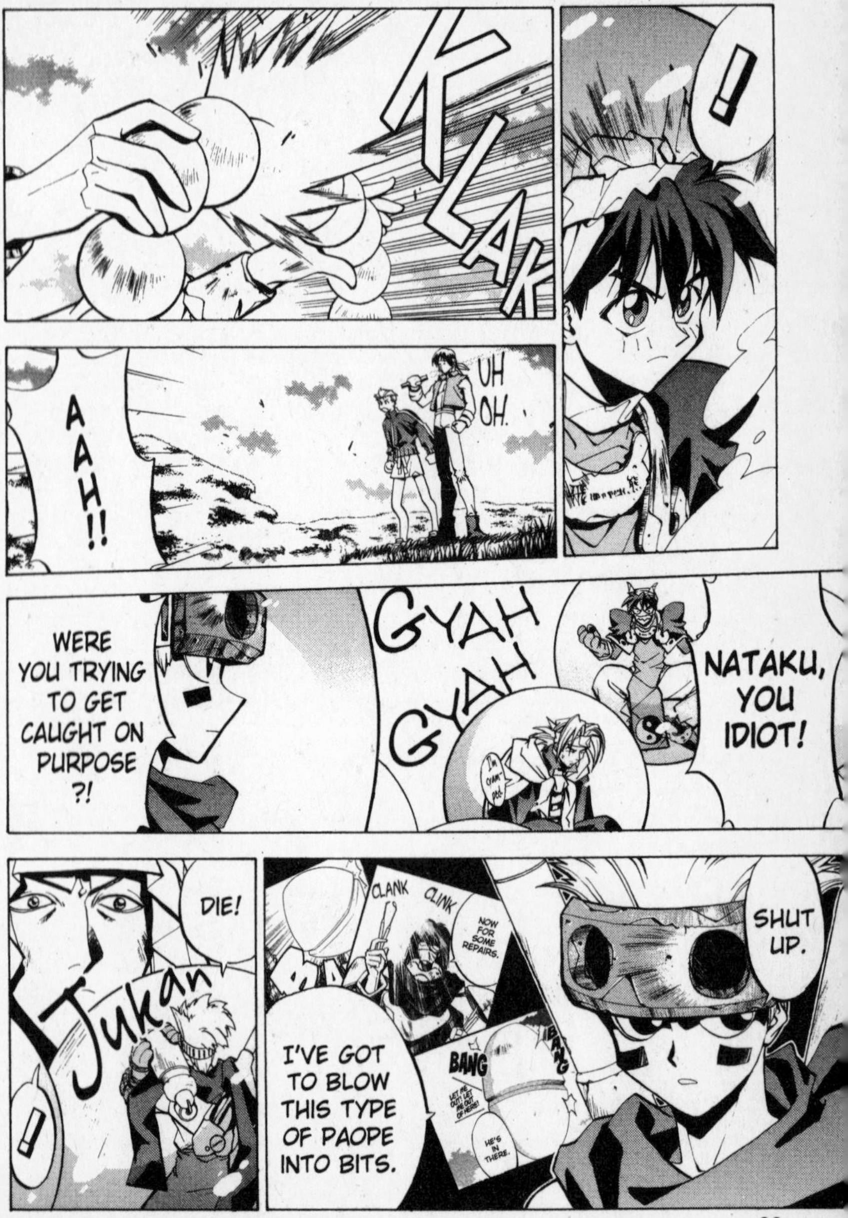
!
KLAK
UH OH.
AAH!!
NATAKU, YOU IDIOT!
GYAH GYAH
I'm cram-ped.
WERE YOU TRYING TO GET CAUGHT ON PURPOSE ?!
SHUT UP.
CLANK
CLINK
NOW FOR SOME REPAIRS.
BANG
BANG
LET ME OUT! LET ME OUT OF HERE!
HE'S IN THERE.
I'VE GOT TO BLOW THIS TYPE OF PAOPE INTO BITS.
DIE!
Jukan
!

READ THIS WAY

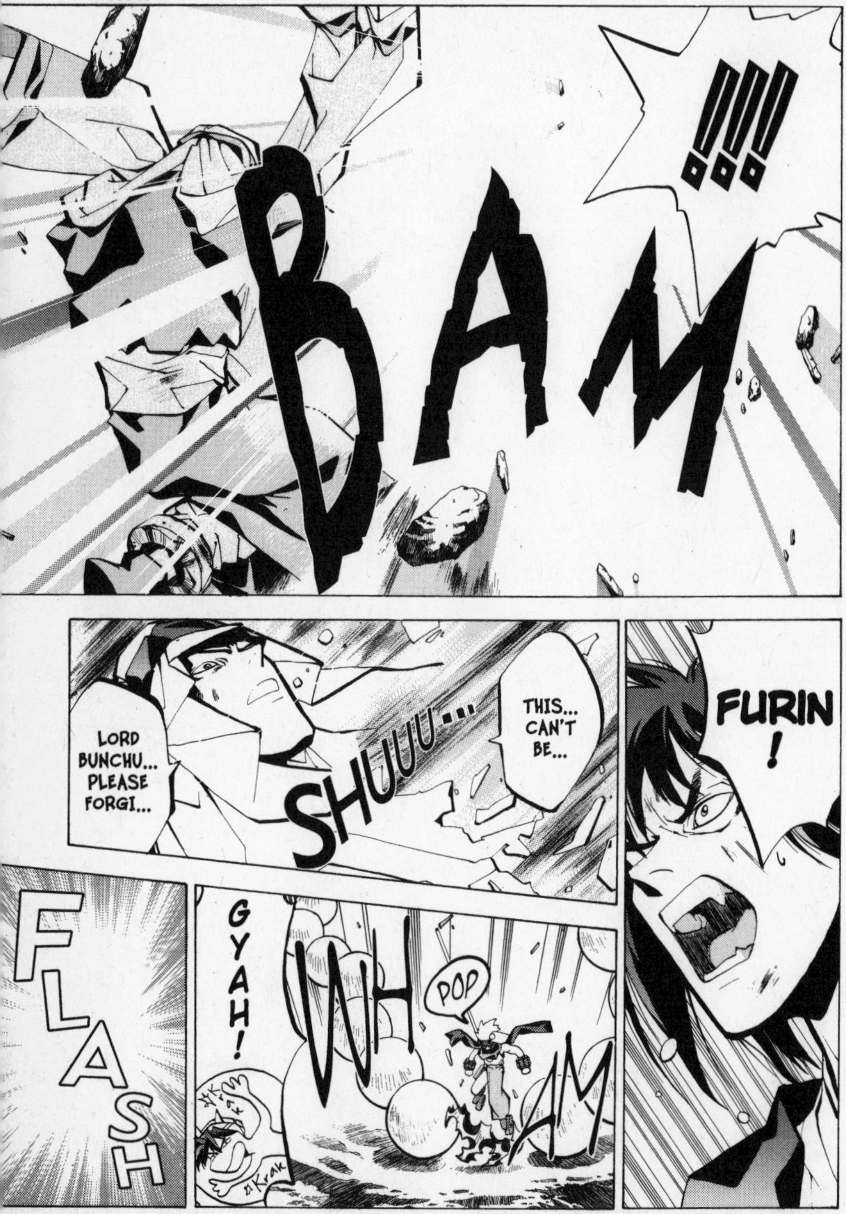
!!!!
BAM
FURIN!
THIS... CAN'T BE...
SHUUU...
LORD BUNCHU... PLEASE FORGI...
POP
WHAM
GYAH!
Krak
FLASH

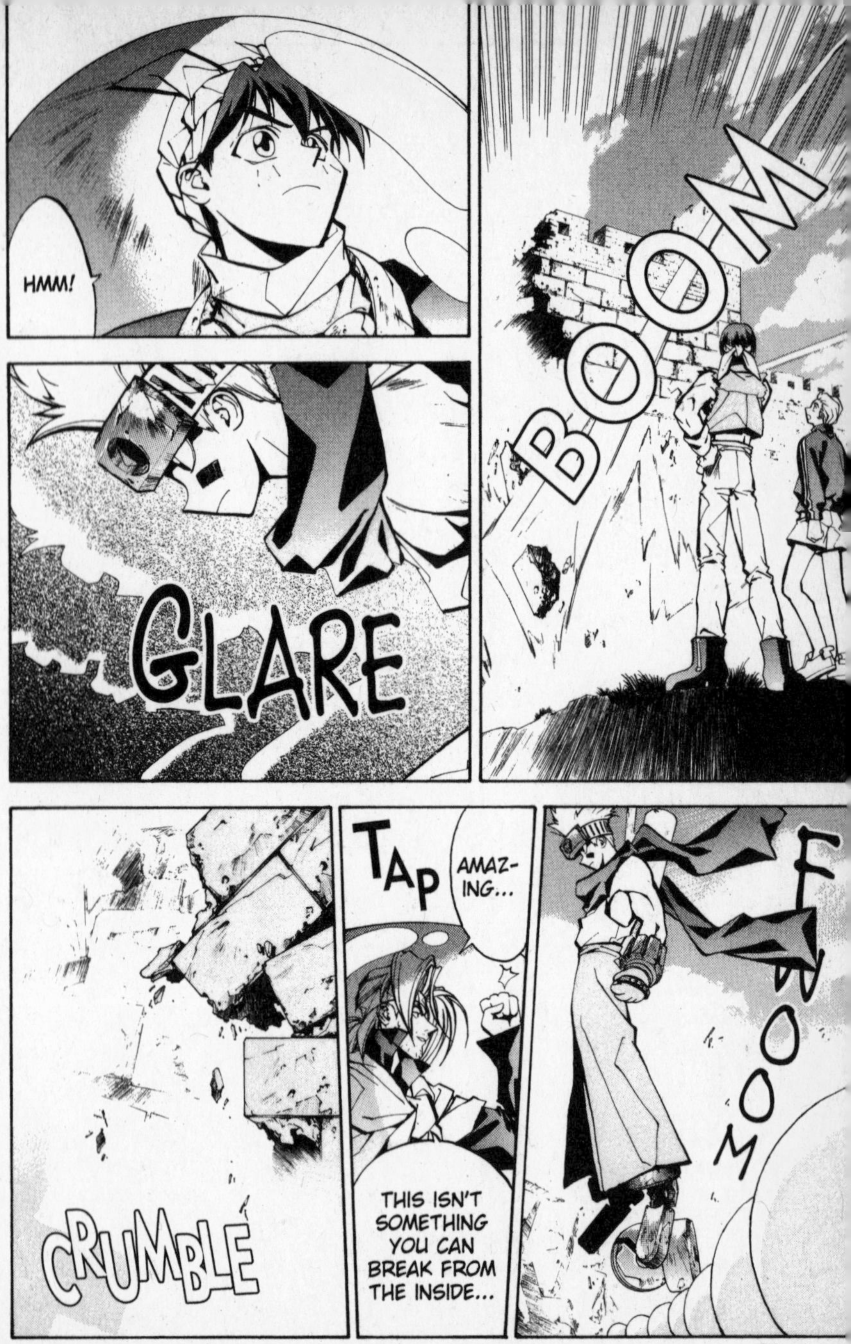
BOOOM
HMM!
GLARE
FWOOM
TAP
AMAZ-ING...
THIS ISN'T SOMETHING YOU CAN BREAK FROM THE INSIDE...
CRUMBLE

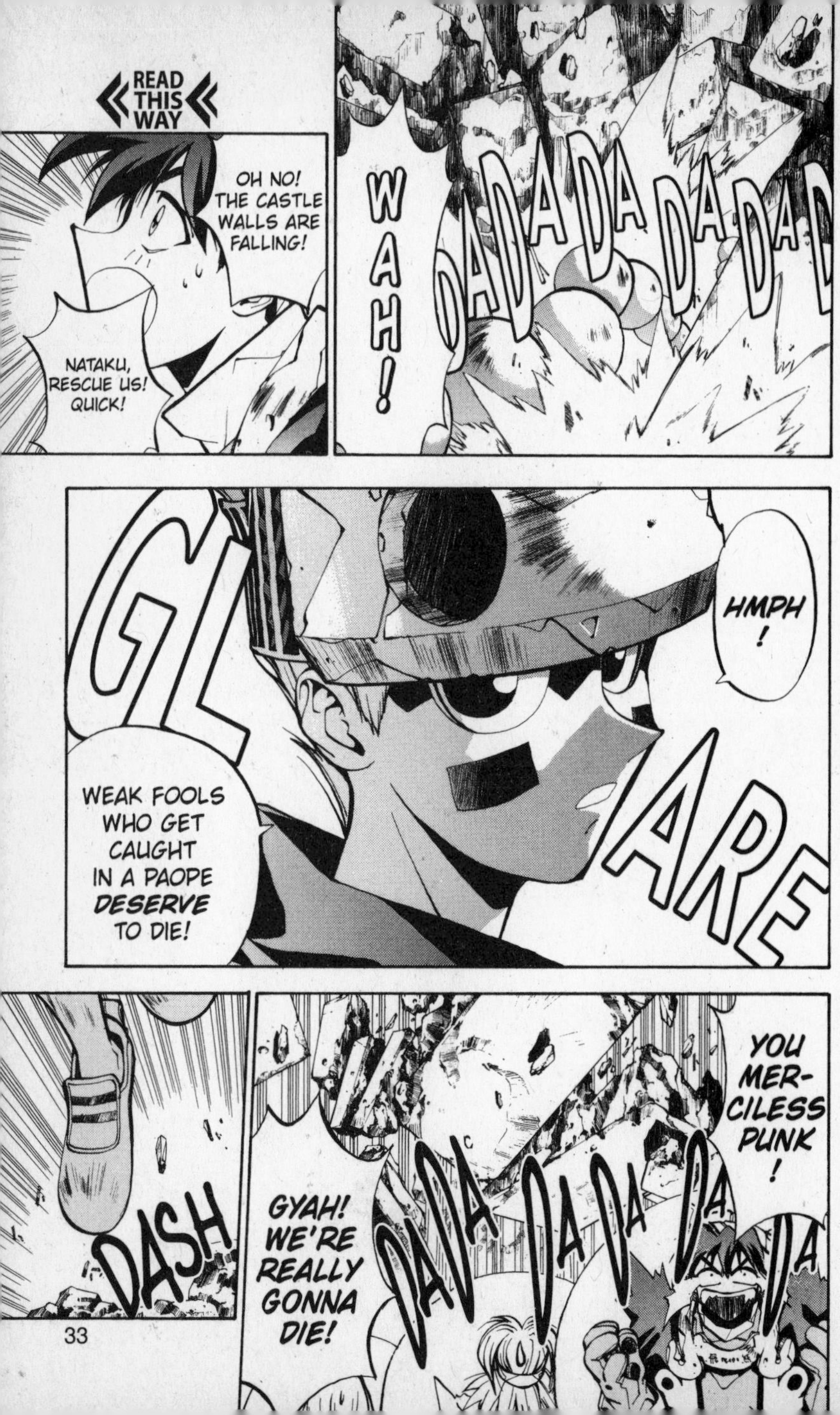

READ THIS WAY
DADADADADADADAD
WAH!
OH NO! THE CASTLE WALLS ARE FALLING!
NATAKU, RESCUE US! QUICK!
HMPH!
GLARE
WEAK FOOLS WHO GET CAUGHT IN A PAOPE DESERVE TO DIE!
YOU MERCILESS PUNK!
DADADADADADA
GYAH! WE'RE REALLY GONNA DIE!
DASH

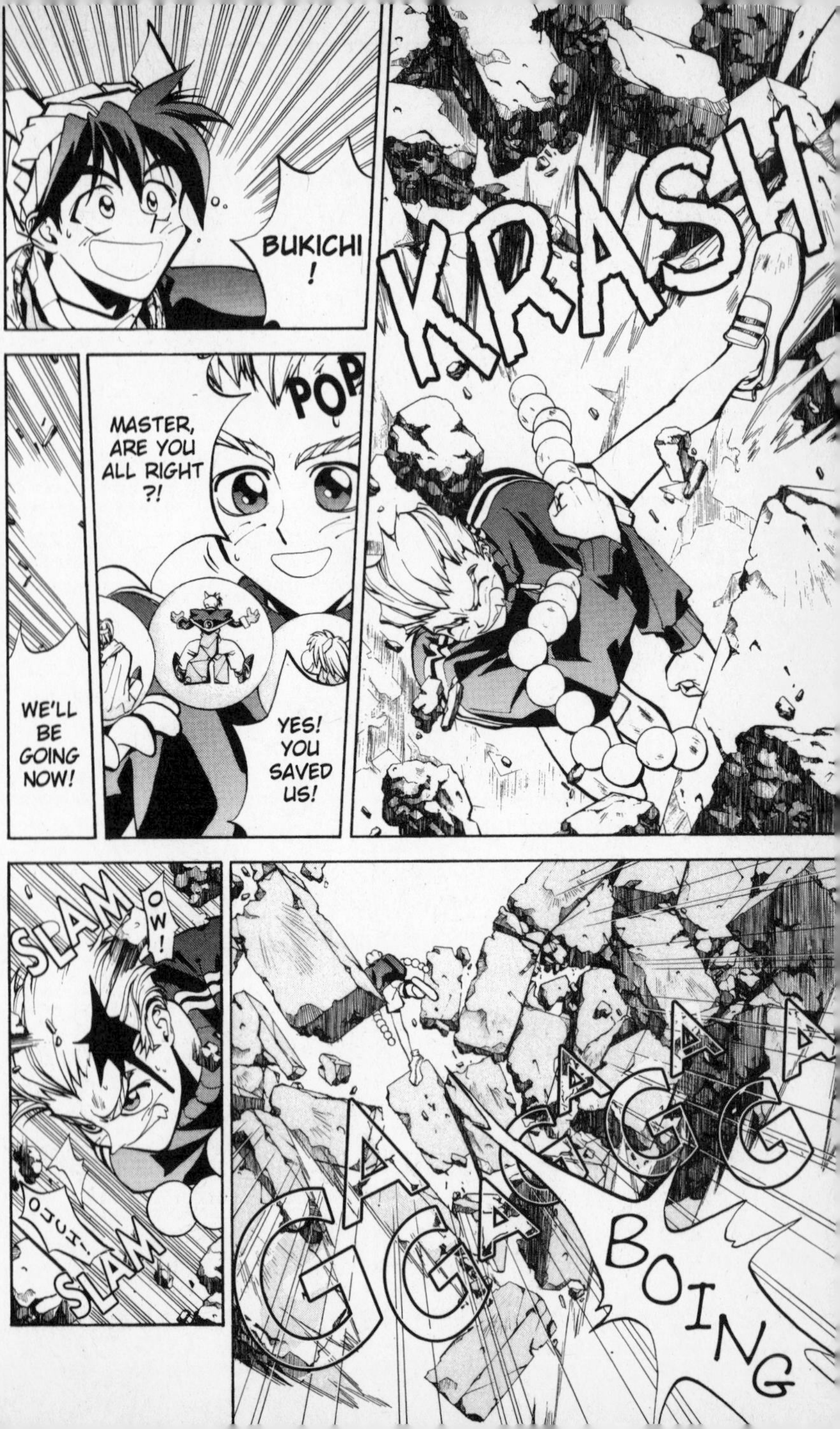
KRASH
BUKICHI !
POP
MASTER, ARE YOU ALL RIGHT ?!
YES! YOU SAVED US!
WE'LL BE GOING NOW!
GAGAGA
BOING
SLAM
OW!
OJUI-!
SLAM

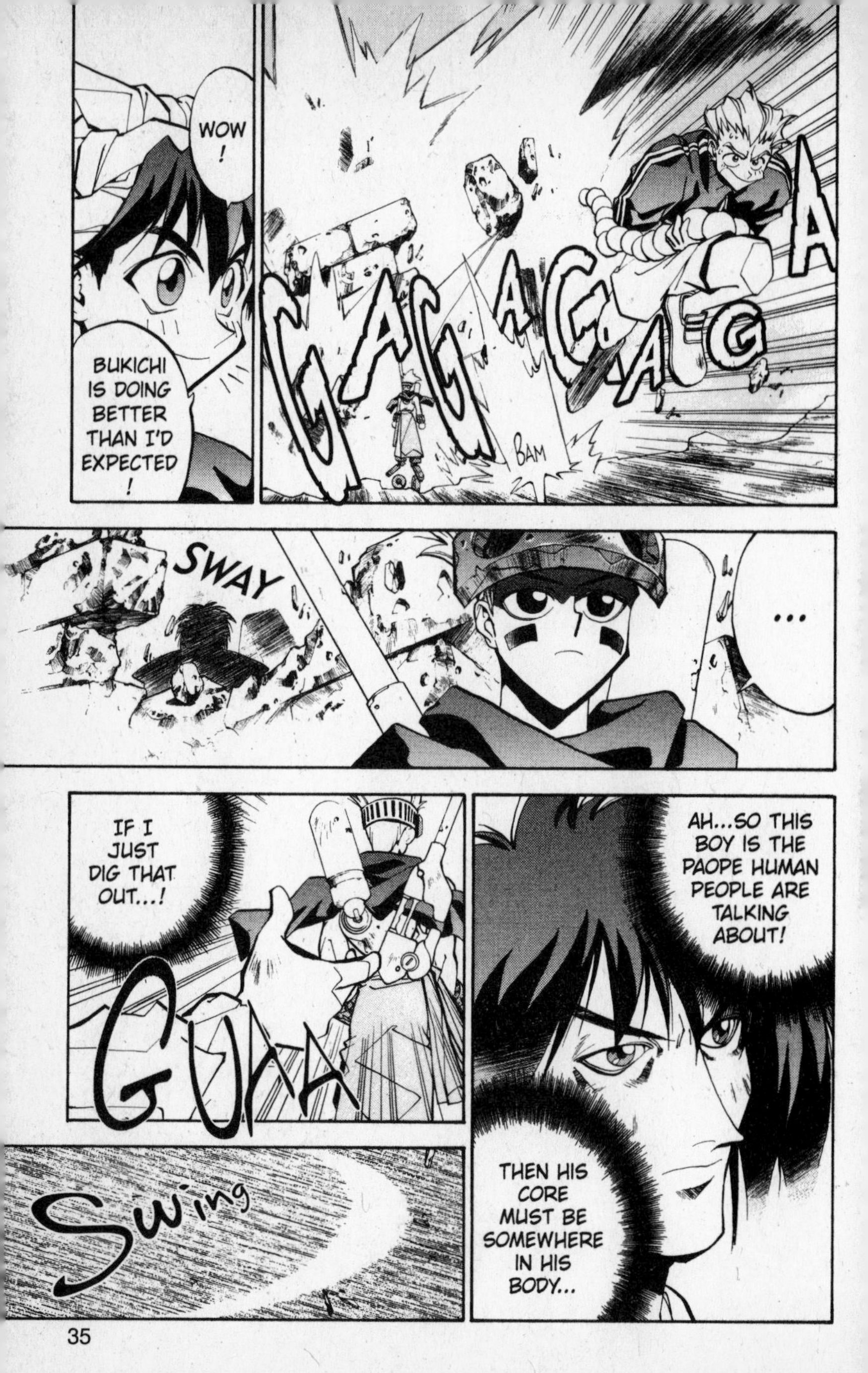
GAGAGAGA
BAM
WOW!
BUKICHI IS DOING BETTER THAN I'D EXPECTED!
...
SWAY
AH...SO THIS BOY IS THE PAOPE HUMAN PEOPLE ARE TALKING ABOUT!
THEN HIS CORE MUST BE SOMEWHERE IN HIS BODY...
IF I JUST DIG THAT OUT...!
GUA
Swing

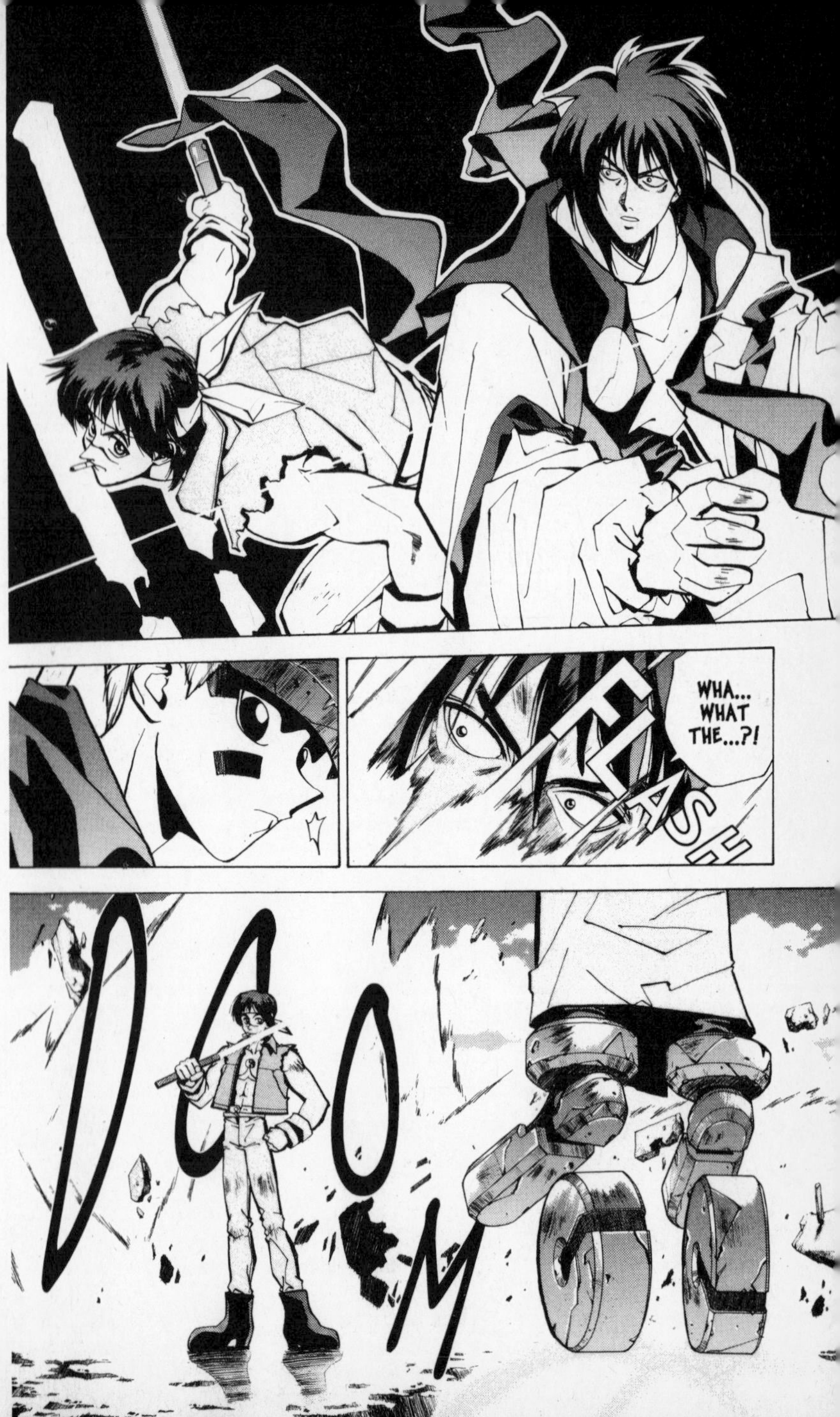
WHA... WHAT THE...?!
FLASH
DOOM

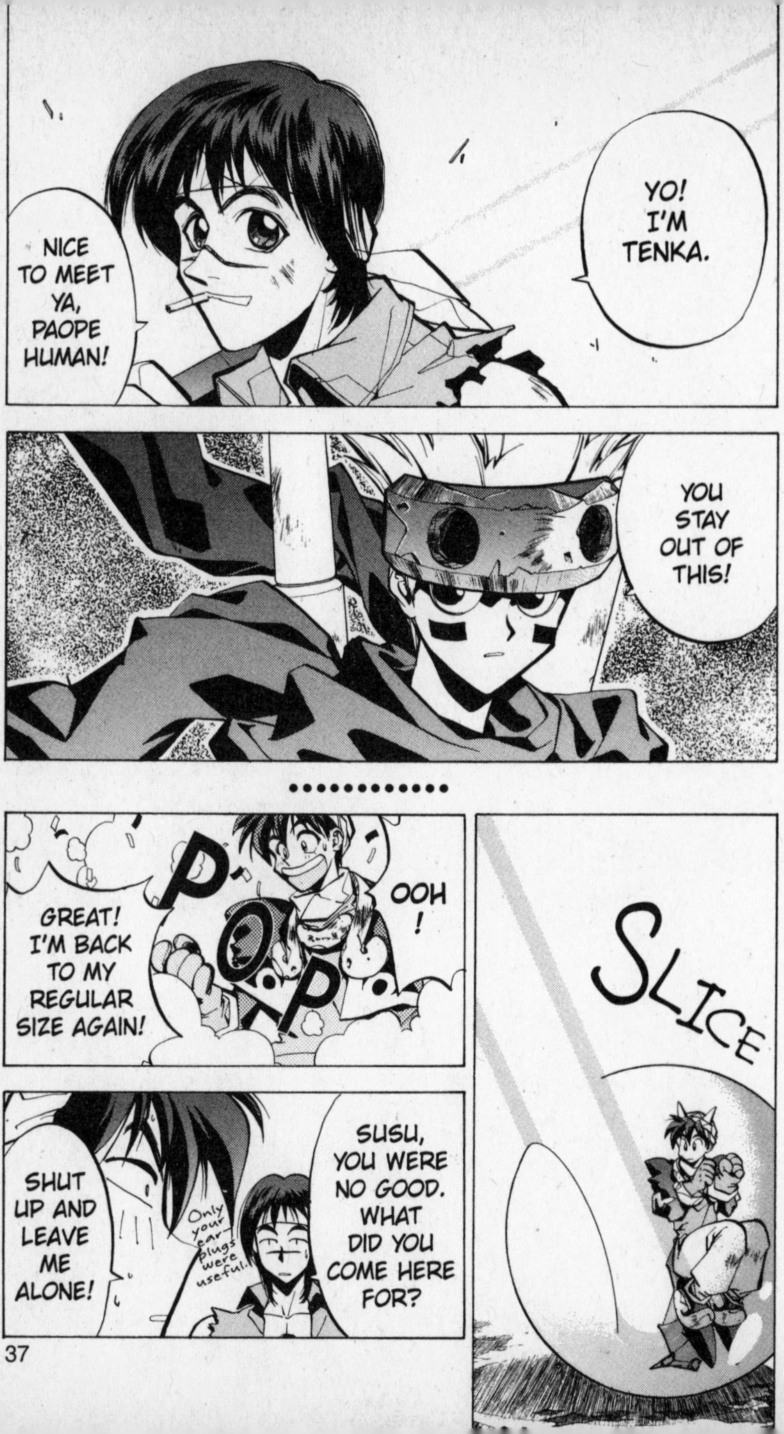
YO! I'M TENKA.
NICE TO MEET YA, PAOPE HUMAN!
YOU STAY OUT OF THIS!
....
SLICE
OOH!
POP
GREAT! I'M BACK TO MY REGULAR SIZE AGAIN!
SUSU, YOU WERE NO GOOD. WHAT DID YOU COME HERE FOR?
Only your ear-plugs were useful.
SHUT UP AND LEAVE ME ALONE!

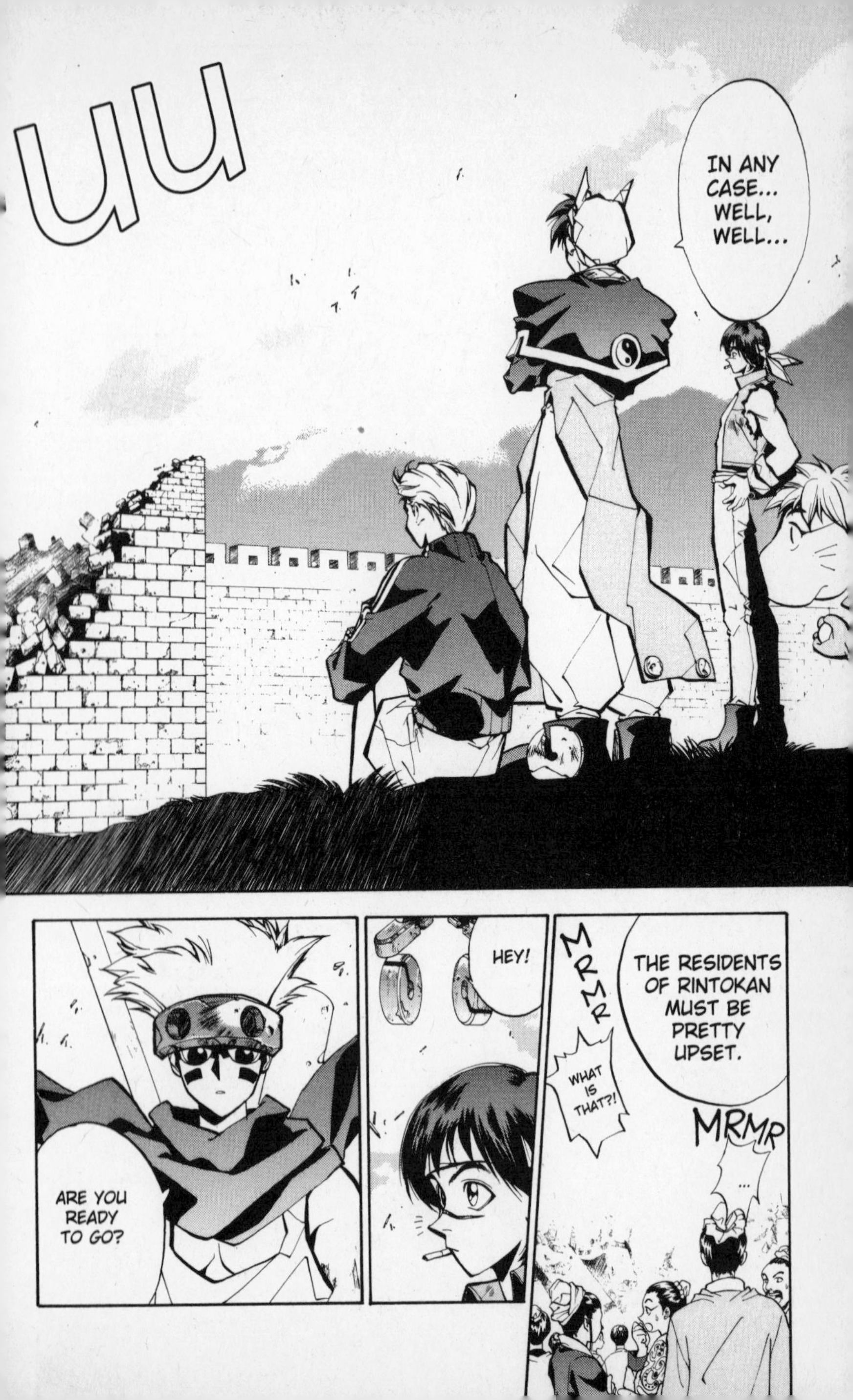
IN ANY CASE... WELL, WELL...
UU
THE RESIDENTS OF RINTOKAN MUST BE PRETTY UPSET.
MRMR
WHAT IS THAT?!
MRMR
...
HEY!
ARE YOU READY TO GO?

READ THIS WAY

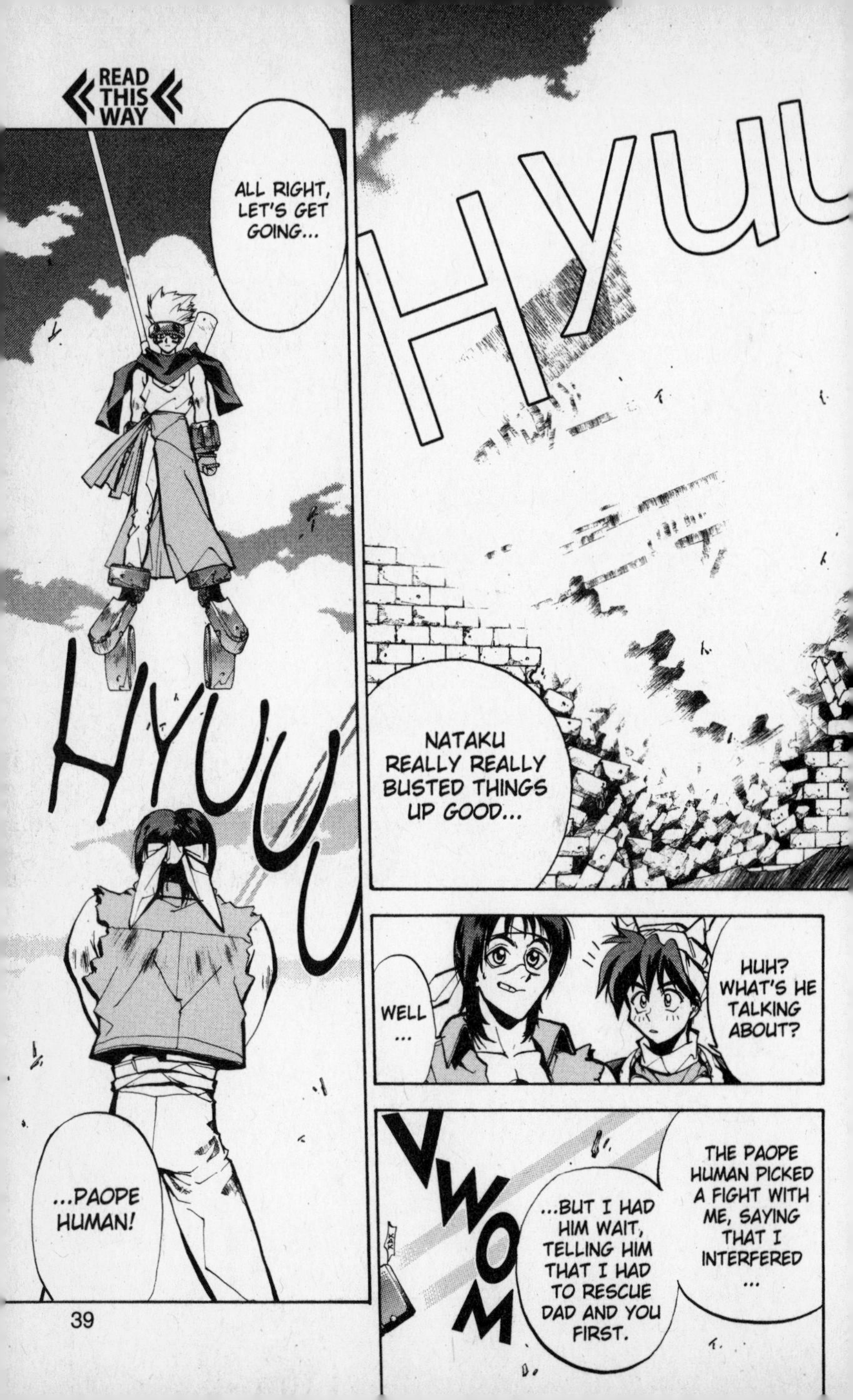
HYUU
NATAKU REALLY REALLY BUSTED THINGS UP GOOD...
HUH? WHAT'S HE TALKING ABOUT?
WELL ...
THE PAOPE HUMAN PICKED A FIGHT WITH ME, SAYING THAT I INTERFERED ...
...BUT I HAD HIM WAIT, TELLING HIM THAT I HAD TO RESCUE DAD AND YOU FIRST.
VWOM
ALL RIGHT, LET'S GET GOING...
HYUUU
...PAOPE HUMAN!

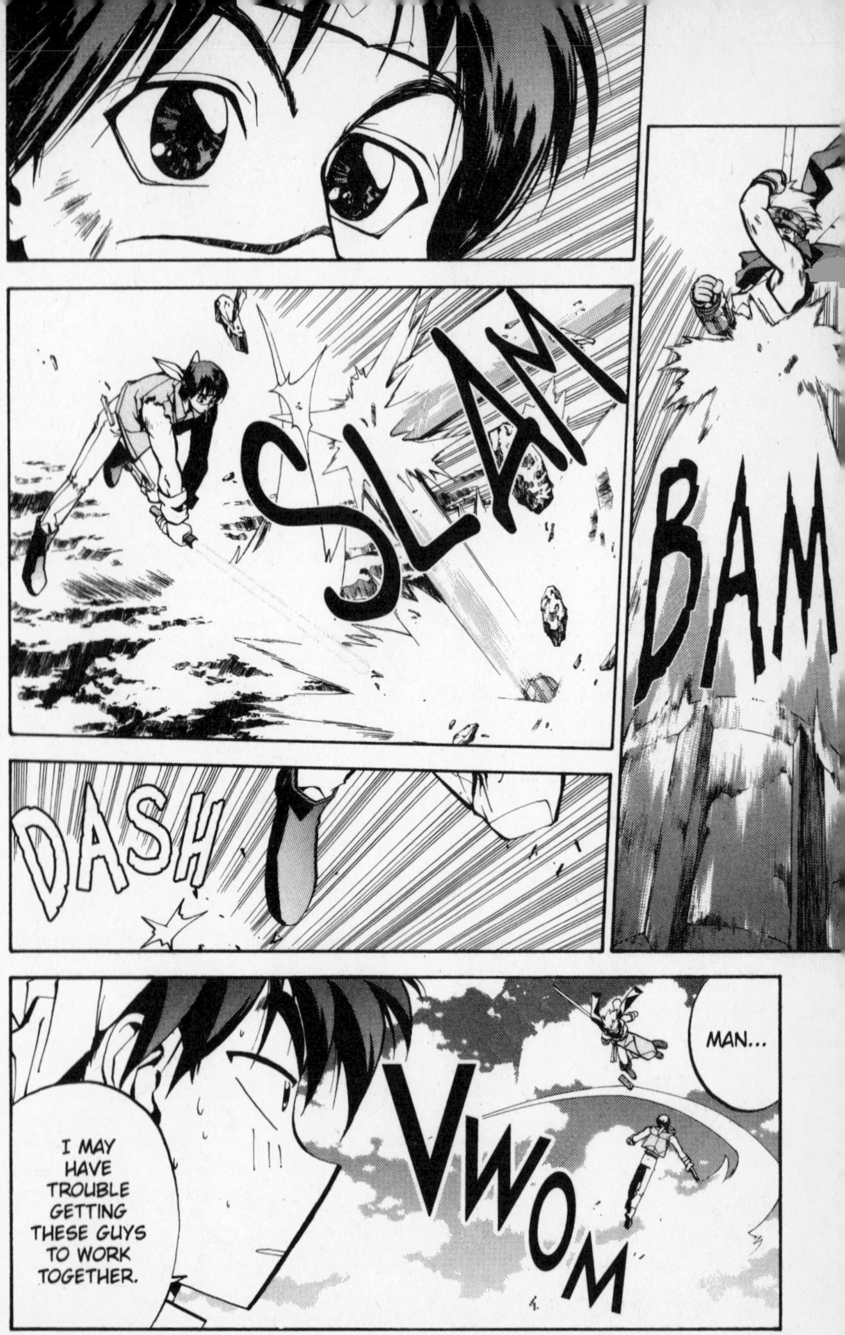
BAM
SLAM
DASH
MAN...
VWOM
I MAY HAVE TROUBLE GETTING THESE GUYS TO WORK TOGETHER.

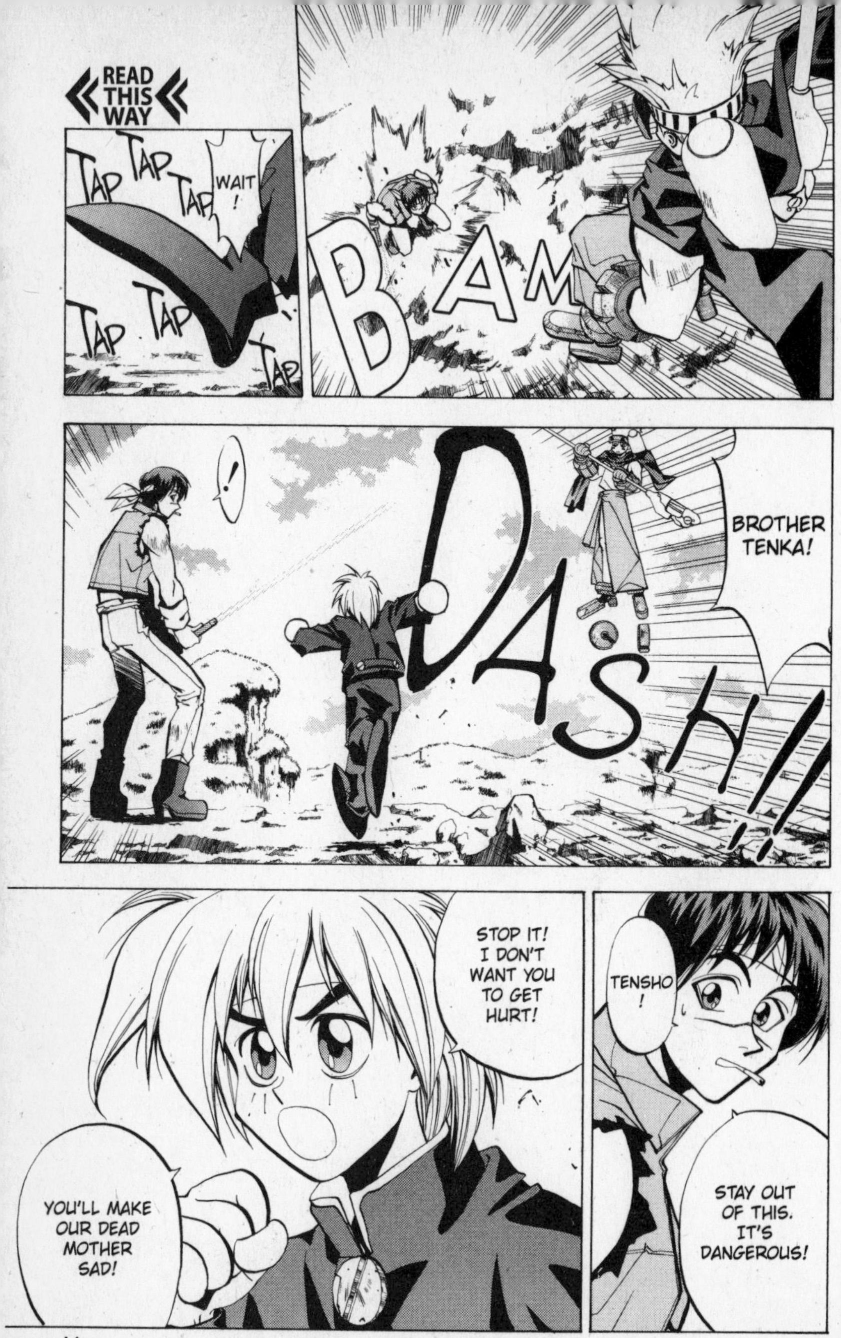
READ THIS WAY
BAM
TAP TAP TAP TAP
WAIT!
TAP TAP TAP
BROTHER TENKA!
!
DASH!!
TENSHO!
STAY OUT OF THIS. IT'S DANGEROUS!
STOP IT! I DON'T WANT YOU TO GET HURT!
YOU'LL MAKE OUR DEAD MOTHER SAD!

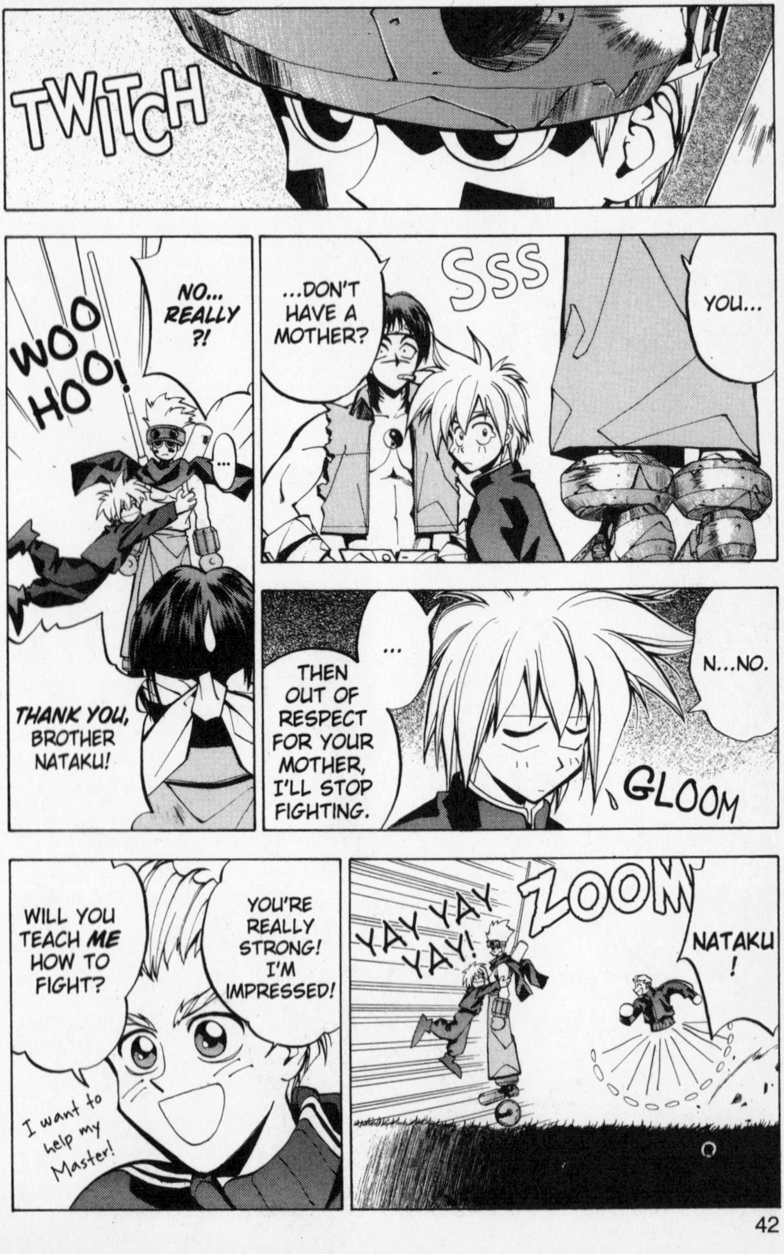
TWITCH
YOU...
SSS
...DON'T HAVE A MOTHER?
N...NO.
GLOOM
...
THEN OUT OF RESPECT FOR YOUR MOTHER, I'LL STOP FIGHTING.
NO... REALLY ?!
WOO HOO!
...
THANK YOU, BROTHER NATAKU!
NATAKU!
ZOOM
YAY YAY YAY YAY!
YOU'RE REALLY STRONG! I'M IMPRESSED!
WILL YOU TEACH *ME* HOW TO FIGHT?
I want to help my Master!

READ THIS WAY

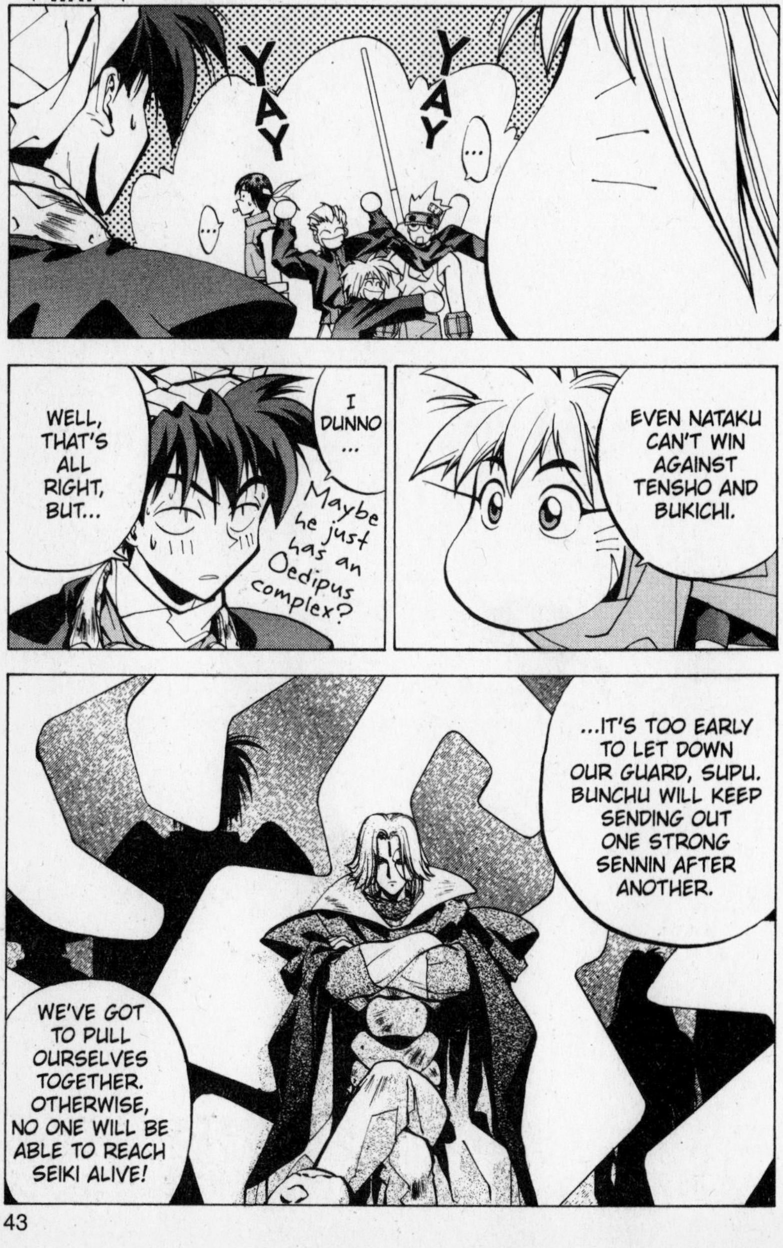
...
YAY
YAY
...
EVEN NATAKU CAN'T WIN AGAINST TENSHO AND BUKICHI.
I DUNNO ...
Maybe he just has an Oedipus complex?
WELL, THAT'S ALL RIGHT, BUT...
...IT'S TOO EARLY TO LET DOWN OUR GUARD, SUPU. BUNCHU WILL KEEP SENDING OUT ONE STRONG SENNIN AFTER ANOTHER.
WE'VE GOT TO PULL OURSELVES TOGETHER. OTHERWISE, NO ONE WILL BE ABLE TO REACH SEIKI ALIVE!

封神演義

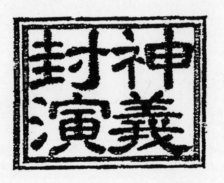

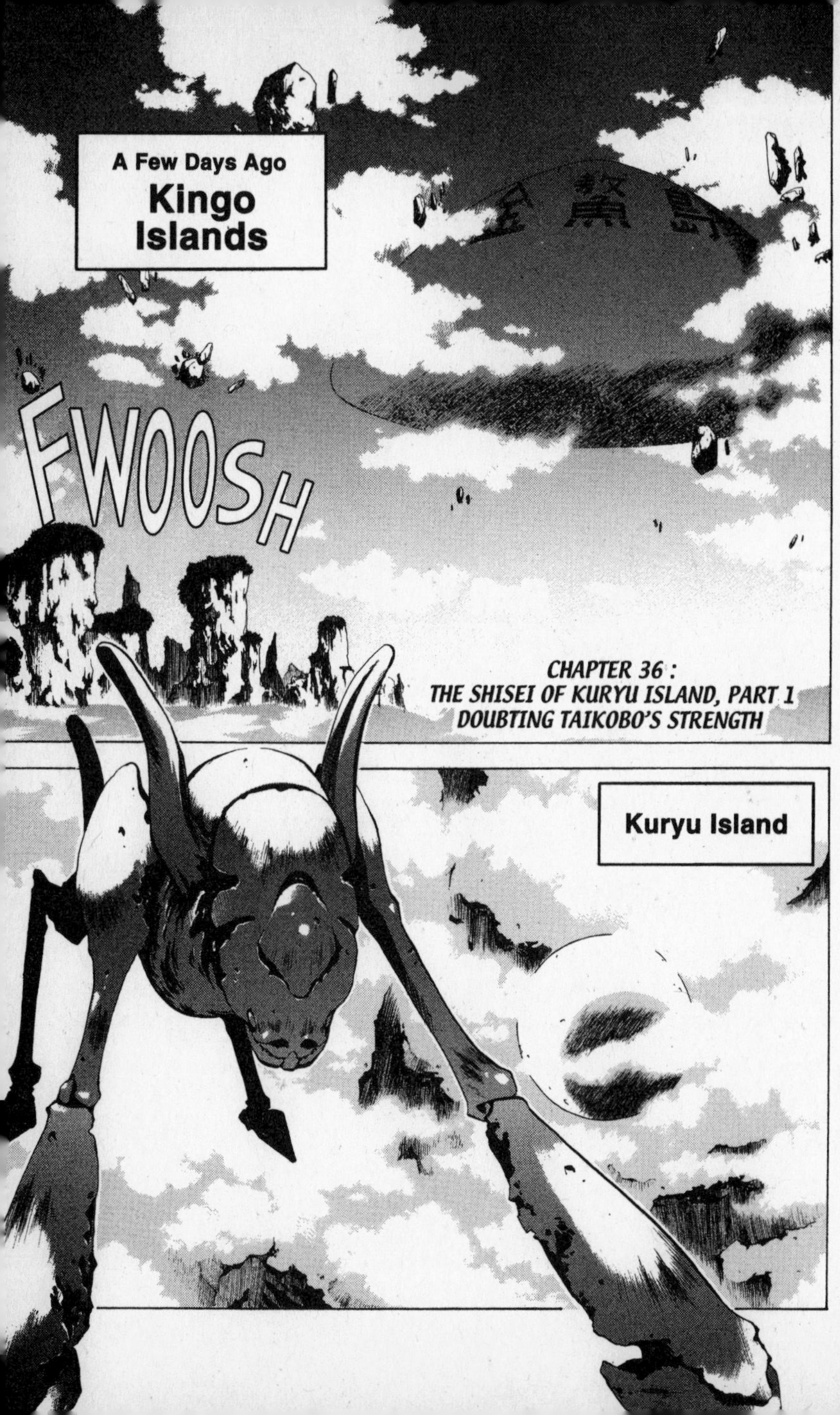
A Few Days Ago
Kingo Islands
FWOOSH
CHAPTER 36 :
THE SHISEI OF KURYU ISLAND, PART 1
DOUBTING TAIKOBO'S STRENGTH
Kuryu Island

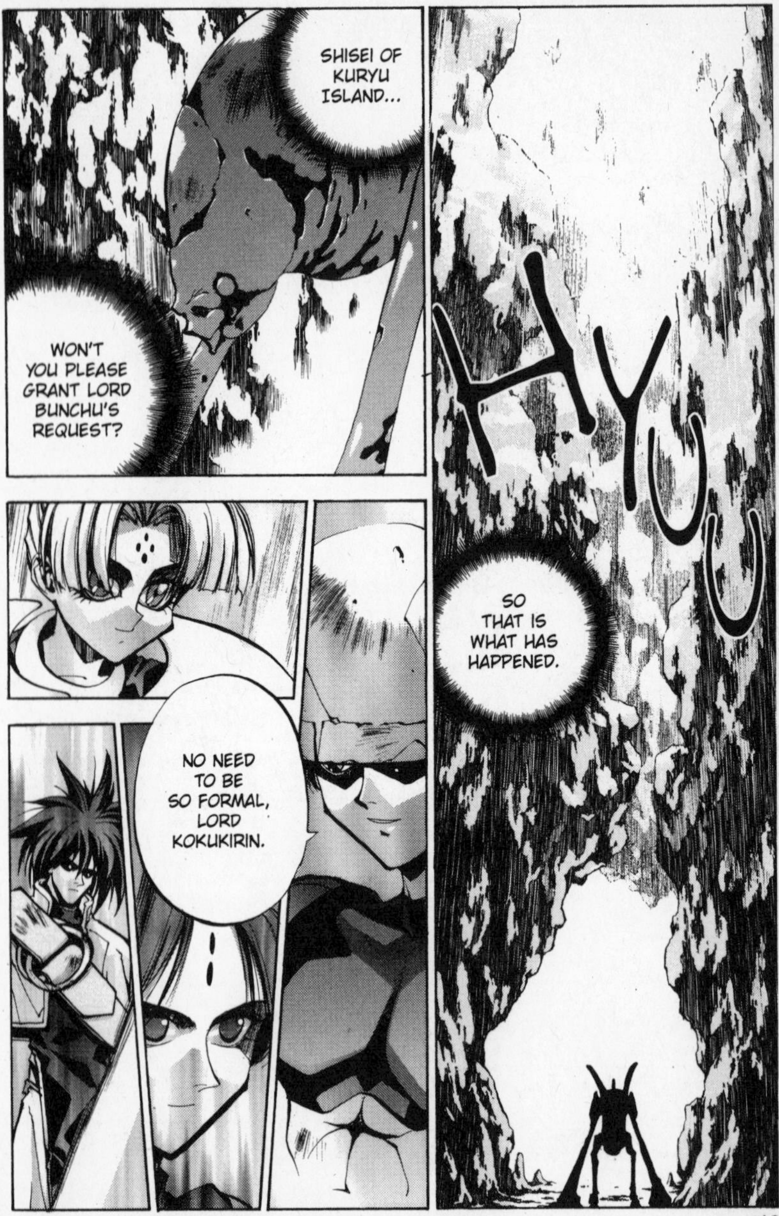
HYUU
SO THAT IS WHAT HAS HAPPENED.
SHISEI OF KURYU ISLAND...
WON'T YOU PLEASE GRANT LORD BUNCHU'S REQUEST?
NO NEED TO BE SO FORMAL, LORD KOKUKIRIN.
...

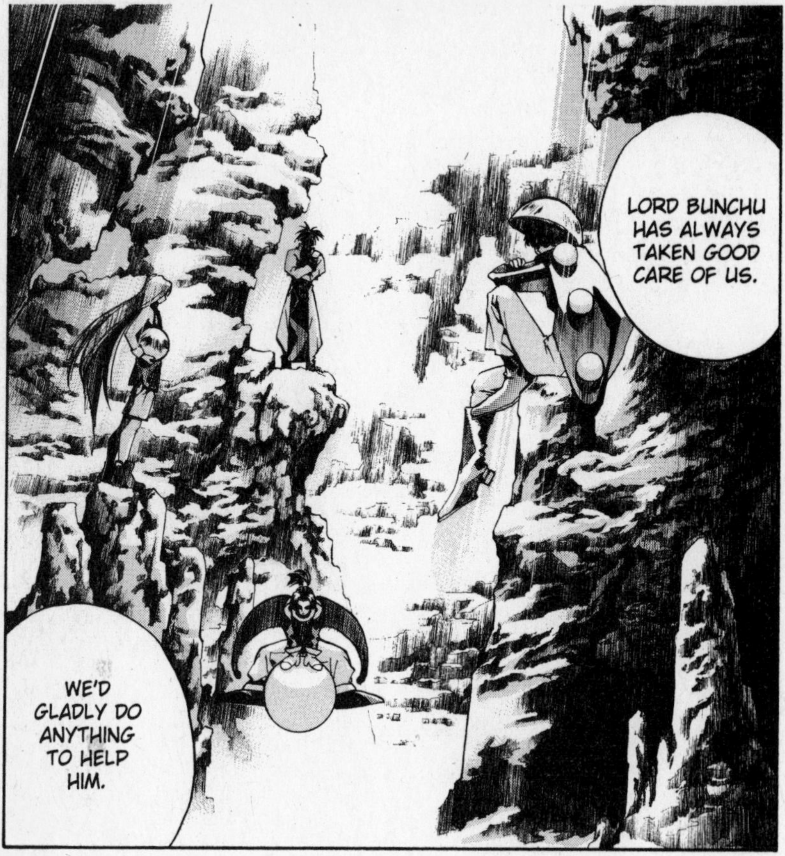
LORD BUNCHU HAS ALWAYS TAKEN GOOD CARE OF US.
WE'D GLADLY DO ANYTHING TO HELP HIM.

Chapter 36

THE SHISEI OF KURYU ISLAND, PART 1
DOUBTING TAIKOBO'S STRENGTH

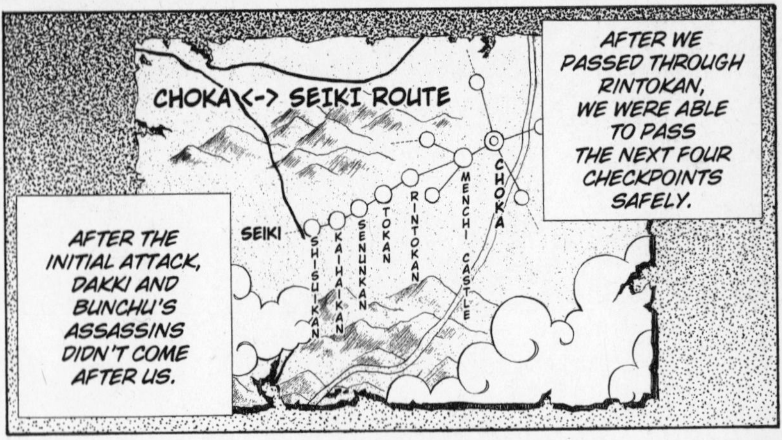
AFTER WE PASSED THROUGH RINTOKAN, WE WERE ABLE TO PASS THE NEXT FOUR CHECKPOINTS SAFELY.
CHOKA <-> SEIKI ROUTE
CHOKA
MENCHI CASTLE
RINTOKAN
TOKAN
SENUNKAN
KAIHAIKAN
SHISUIKAN
SEIKI
AFTER THE INITIAL ATTACK, DAKKI AND BUNCHU'S ASSASSINS DIDN'T COME AFTER US.

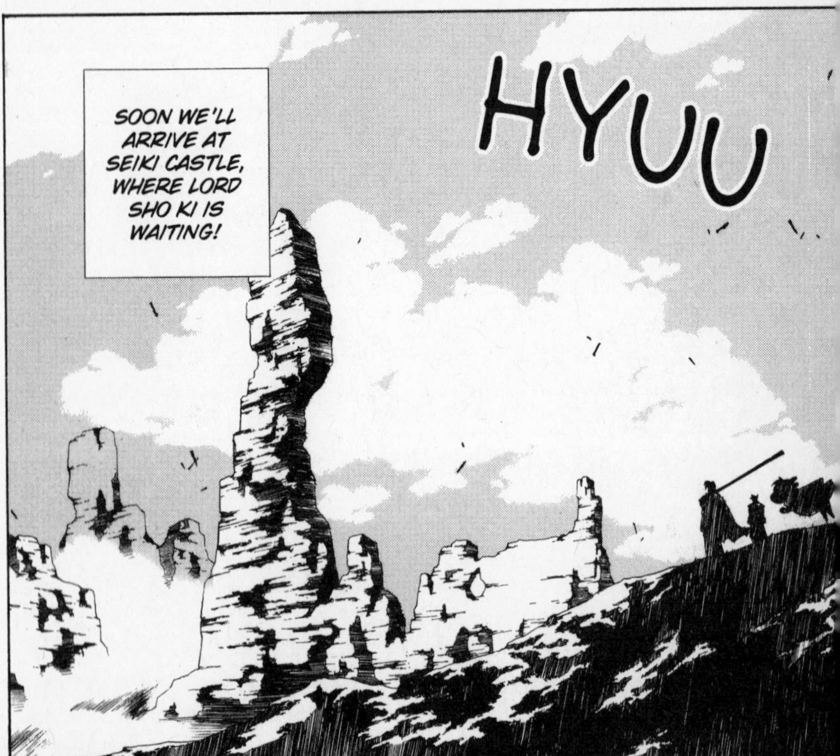
HYUU
SOON WE'LL ARRIVE AT SEIKI CASTLE, WHERE LORD SHO KI IS WAITING!

READ THIS WAY

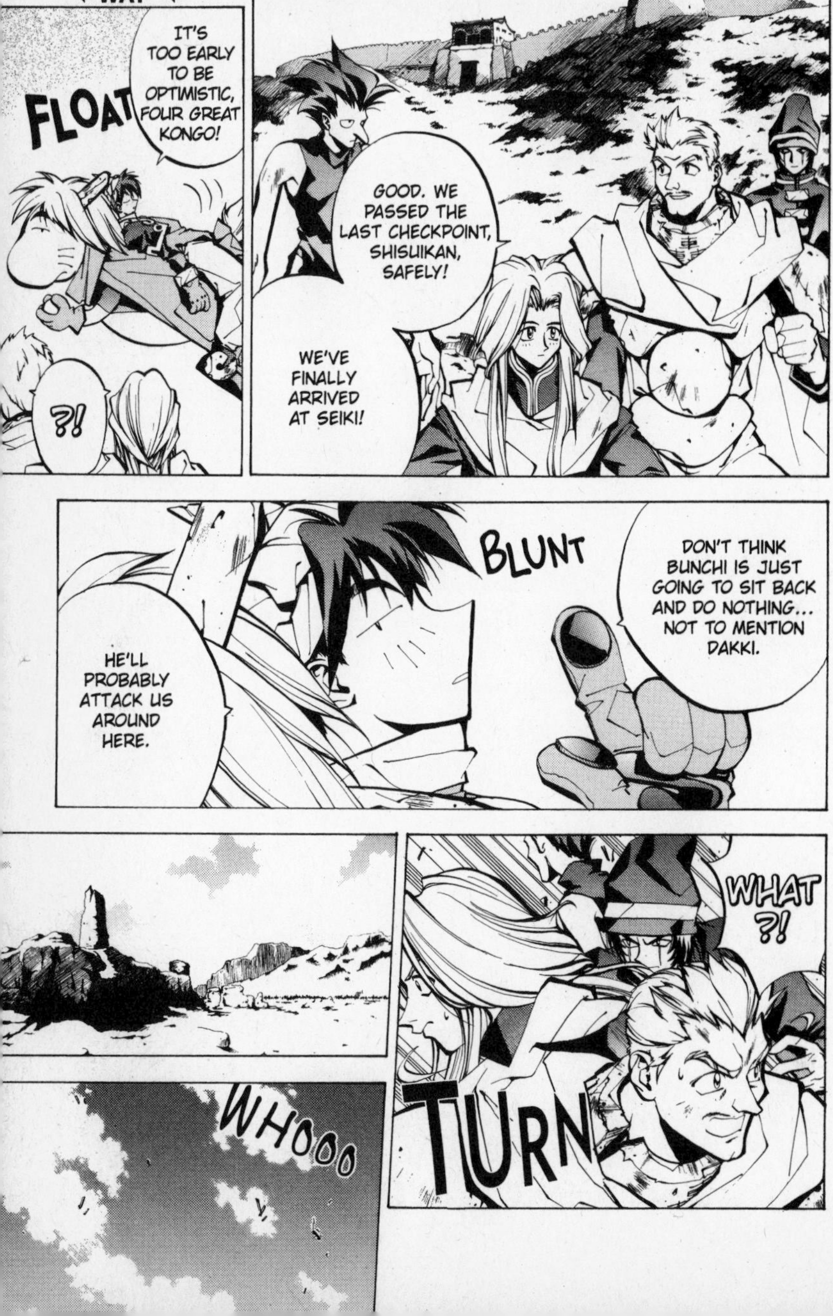
GOOD. WE PASSED THE LAST CHECKPOINT, SHISUIKAN, SAFELY!
WE'VE FINALLY ARRIVED AT SEIKI!
IT'S TOO EARLY TO BE OPTIMISTIC, FOUR GREAT KONGO!
FLOAT
?!
DON'T THINK BUNCHI IS JUST GOING TO SIT BACK AND DO NOTHING... NOT TO MENTION DAKKI.
BLUNT
HE'LL PROBABLY ATTACK US AROUND HERE.
WHAT ?!
TURN
WHOOO

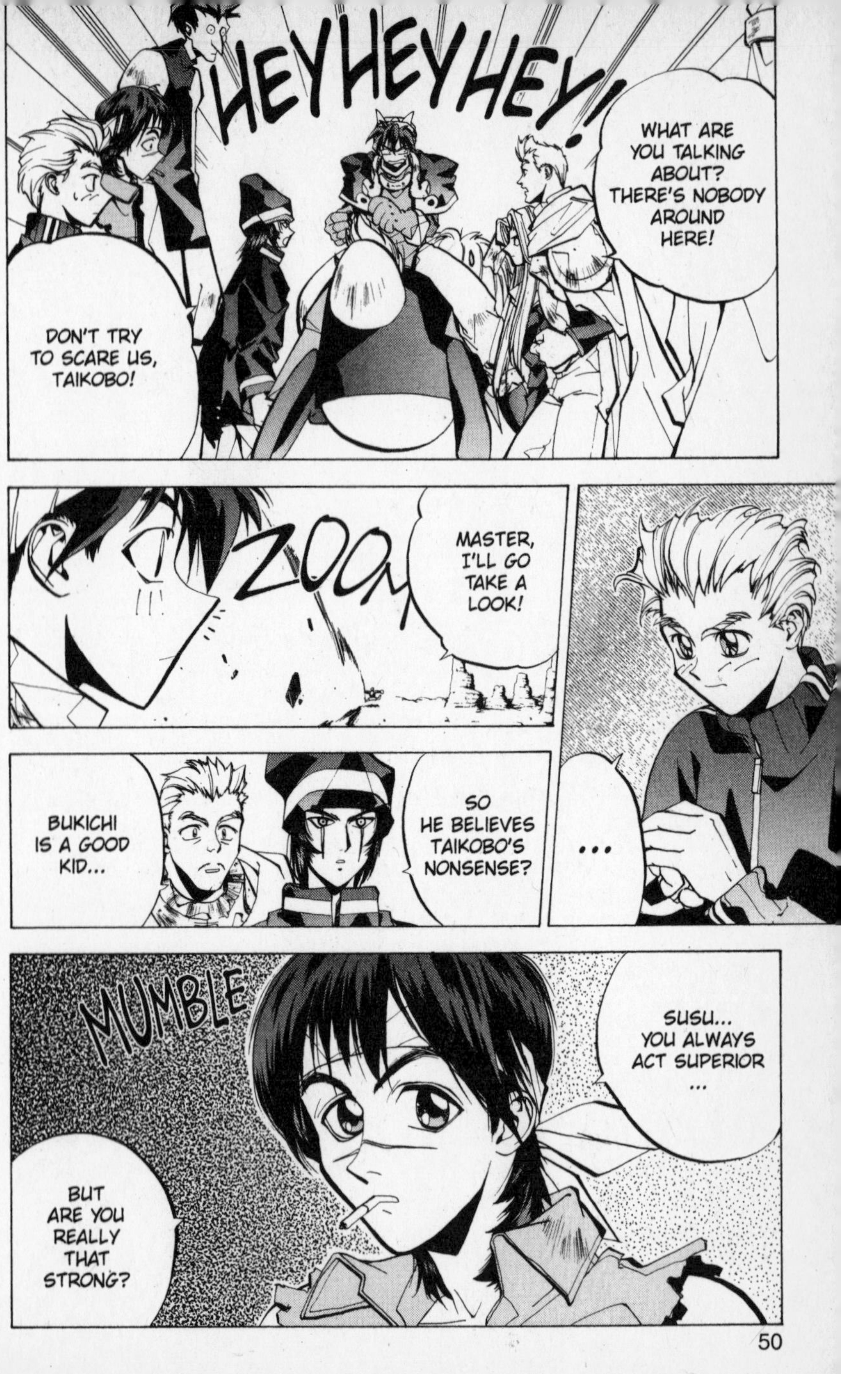
HEYHEYHEY!
WHAT ARE YOU TALKING ABOUT? THERE'S NOBODY AROUND HERE!
DON'T TRY TO SCARE US, TAIKOBO!
...
MASTER, I'LL GO TAKE A LOOK!
ZOOM
SO HE BELIEVES TAIKOBO'S NONSENSE?
BUKICHI IS A GOOD KID...
SUSU... YOU ALWAYS ACT SUPERIOR ...
MUMBLE
BUT ARE YOU REALLY THAT STRONG?

READ THIS WAY

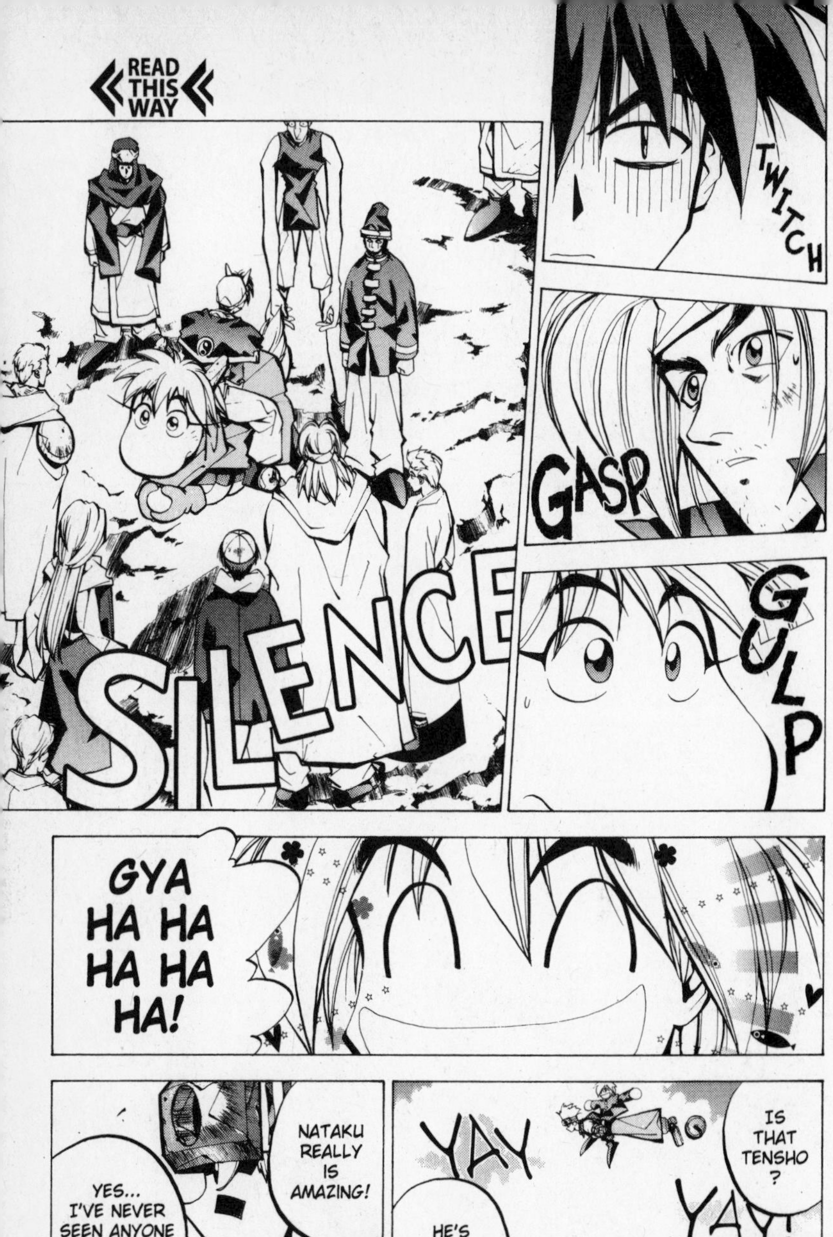

TWITCH
GASP
GULP
SILENCE
GYA HA HA HA HA HA!
IS THAT TENSHO?
YAY
YAY!
HE'S RIDING NATAKU.
NATAKU REALLY IS AMAZING!
YES... I'VE NEVER SEEN ANYONE THAT STRONG!

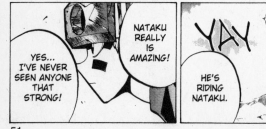

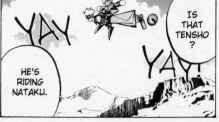

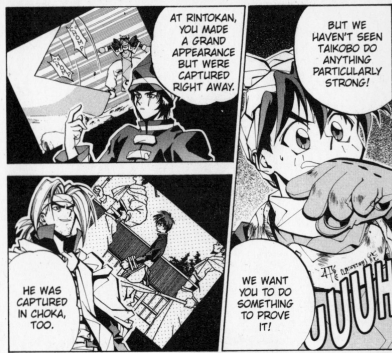

BUT WE HAVEN'T SEEN TAIKOBO DO ANYTHING PARTICULARLY STRONG!
UUUH
WE WANT YOU TO DO SOMETHING TO PROVE IT!
AT RINTOKAN, YOU MADE A GRAND APPEARANCE BUT WERE CAPTURED RIGHT AWAY.
CHOMP
CHOMP
HE WAS CAPTURED IN CHOKA, TOO.
Maybe you're good at getting captured?!
UHH...
EVERYBODY! MASTER MAY NOT BE THAT STRONG, BUT HE USUALLY WINS HIS BATTLES...
...USING CLEVER TACTICS!

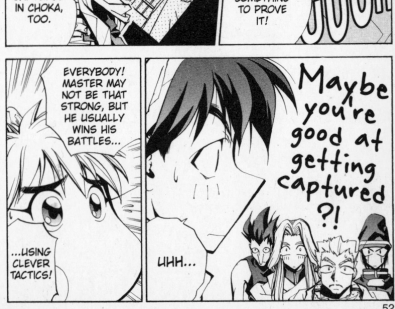

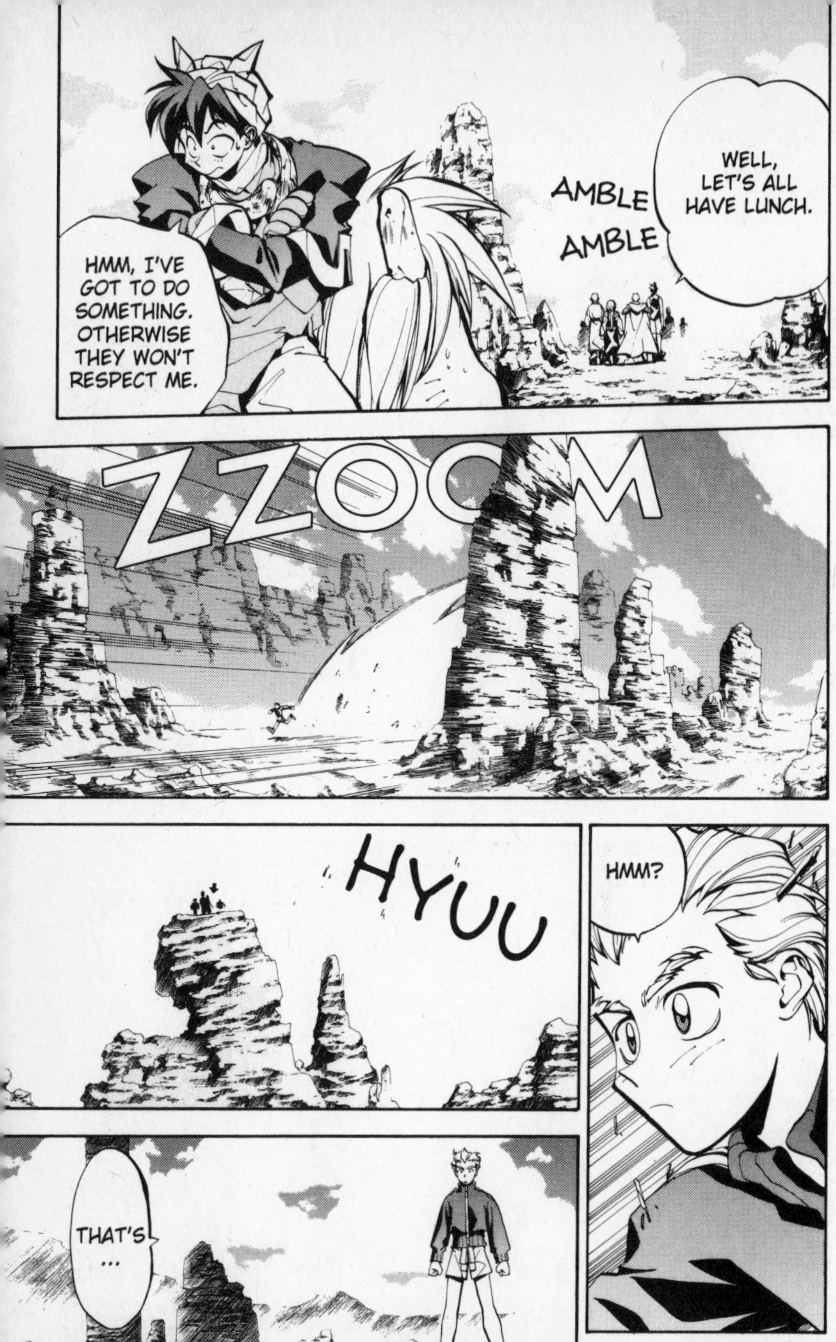
WELL, LET'S ALL HAVE LUNCH.
AMBLE
AMBLE
HMM, I'VE GOT TO DO SOMETHING. OTHERWISE THEY WON'T RESPECT ME.
ZZOOM
HMM?
HYUU
THAT'S ...

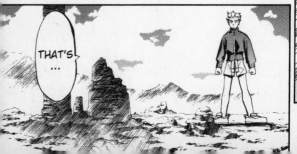

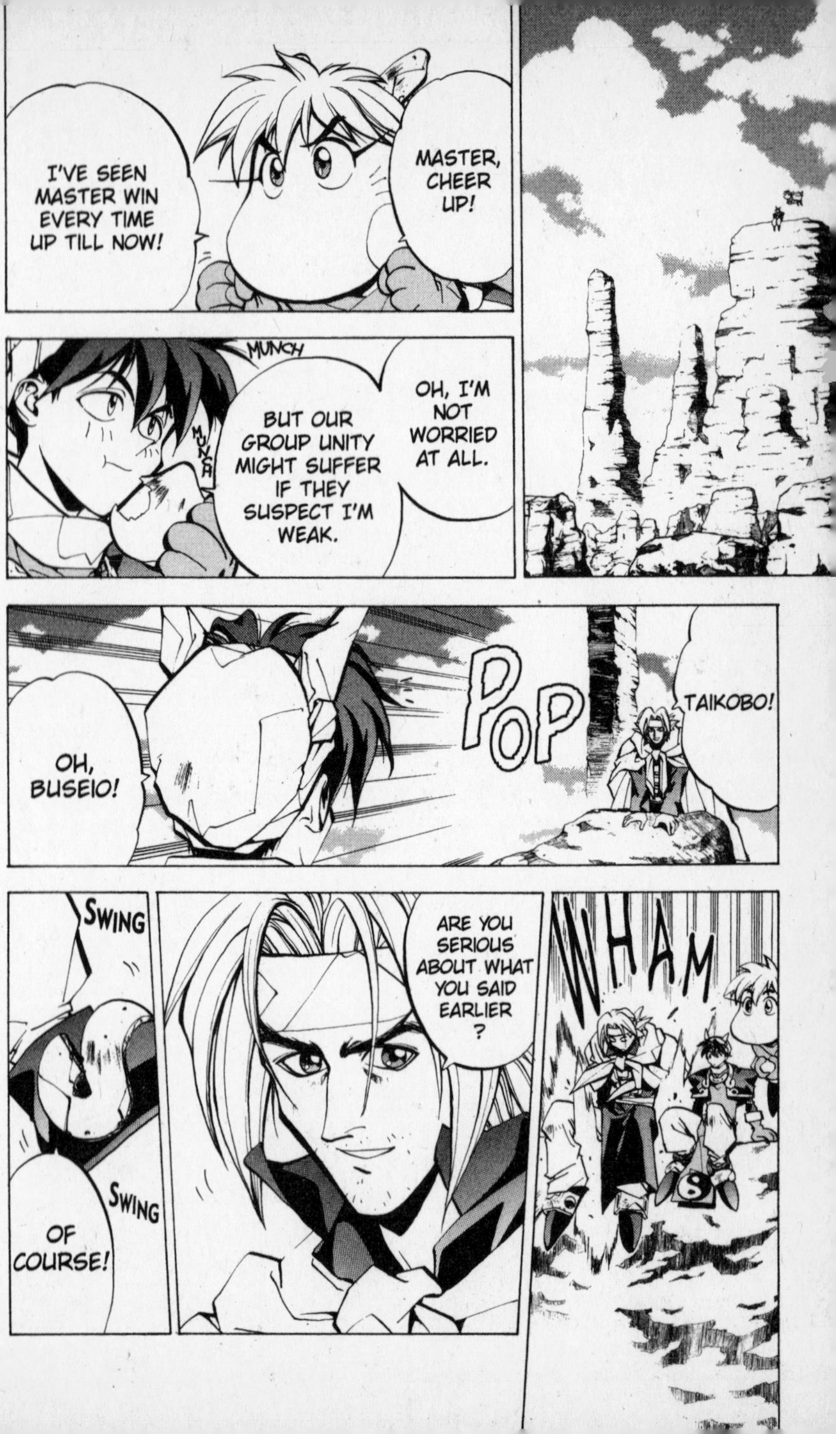
MASTER, CHEER UP!
I'VE SEEN MASTER WIN EVERY TIME UP TILL NOW!
MUNCH
OH, I'M NOT WORRIED AT ALL.
MUNCH
BUT OUR GROUP UNITY MIGHT SUFFER IF THEY SUSPECT I'M WEAK.
TAIKOBO!
POP
OH, BUSEIO!
WHAM
ARE YOU SERIOUS ABOUT WHAT YOU SAID EARLIER?
SWING
SWING
OF COURSE!

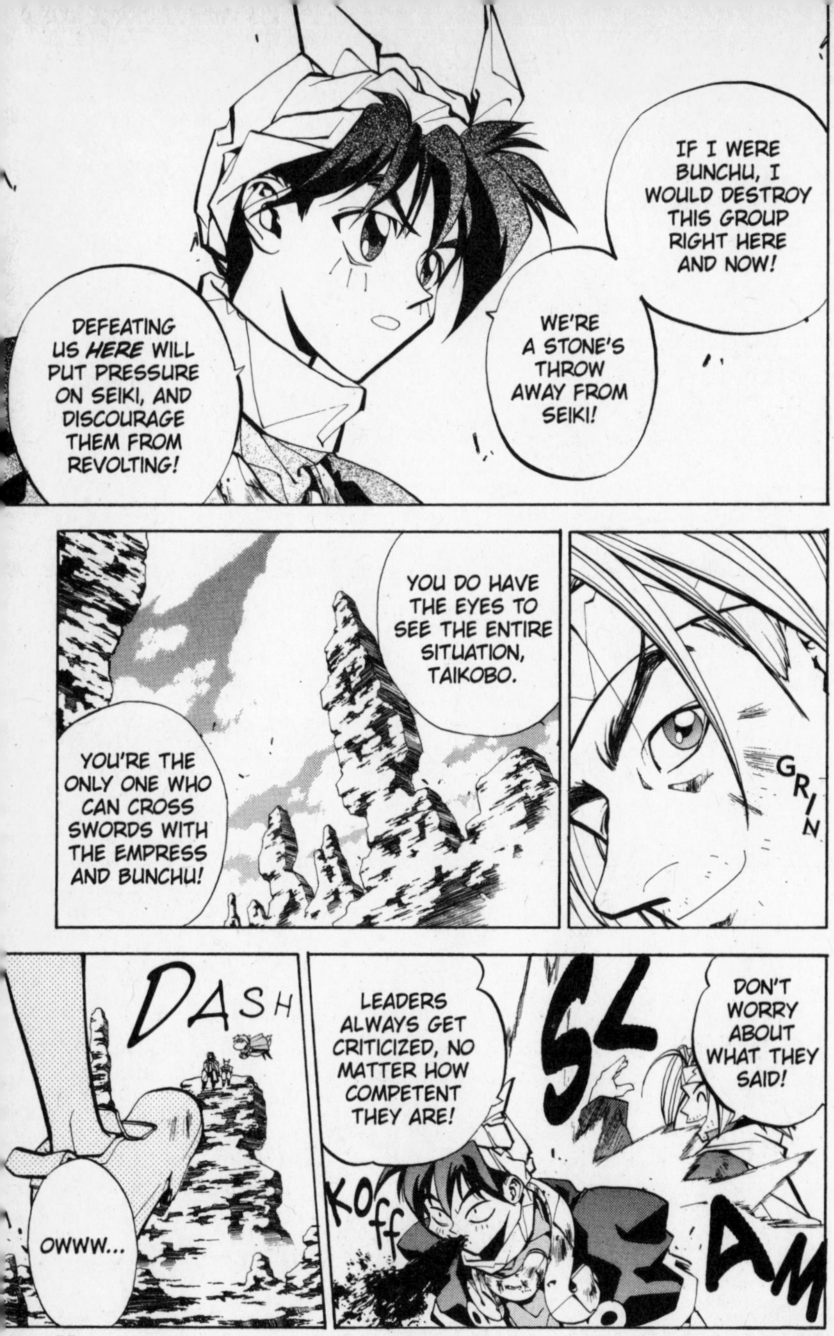
IF I WERE BUNCHU, I WOULD DESTROY THIS GROUP RIGHT HERE AND NOW!
WE'RE A STONE'S THROW AWAY FROM SEIKI!
DEFEATING US *HERE* WILL PUT PRESSURE ON SEIKI, AND DISCOURAGE THEM FROM REVOLTING!
GRIN
YOU DO HAVE THE EYES TO SEE THE ENTIRE SITUATION, TAIKOBO.
YOU'RE THE ONLY ONE WHO CAN CROSS SWORDS WITH THE EMPRESS AND BUNCHU!
DON'T WORRY ABOUT WHAT THEY SAID!
SLAM
LEADERS ALWAYS GET CRITICIZED, NO MATTER HOW COMPETENT THEY ARE!
KOff
DASH
OWWW...

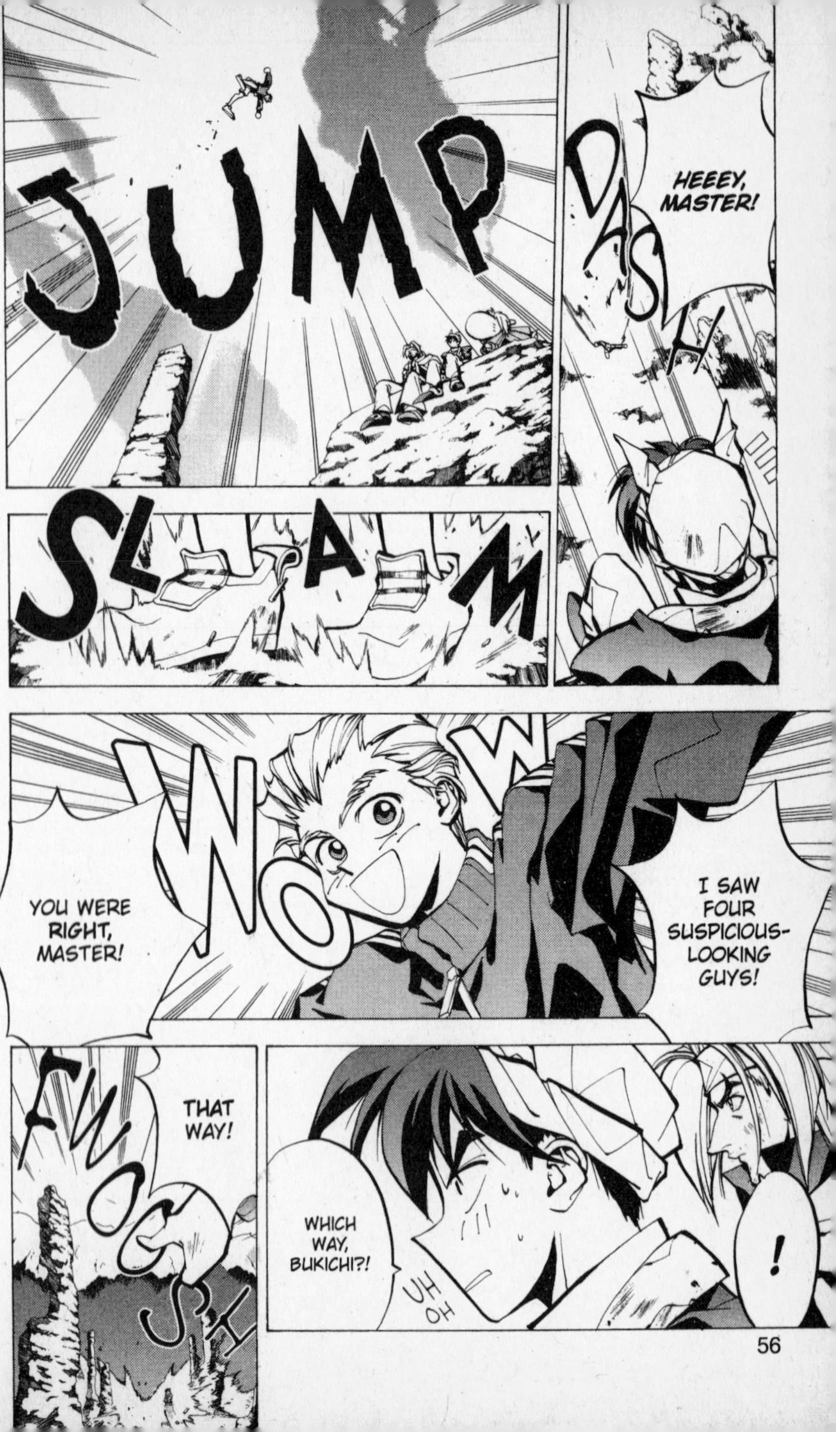
HEEEY, MASTER!
DASH
JUMP
SLAM
I SAW FOUR SUSPICIOUS-LOOKING GUYS!
WOW
YOU WERE RIGHT, MASTER!
!
WHICH WAY, BUKICHI?!
UH OH
THAT WAY!
FWOOSH

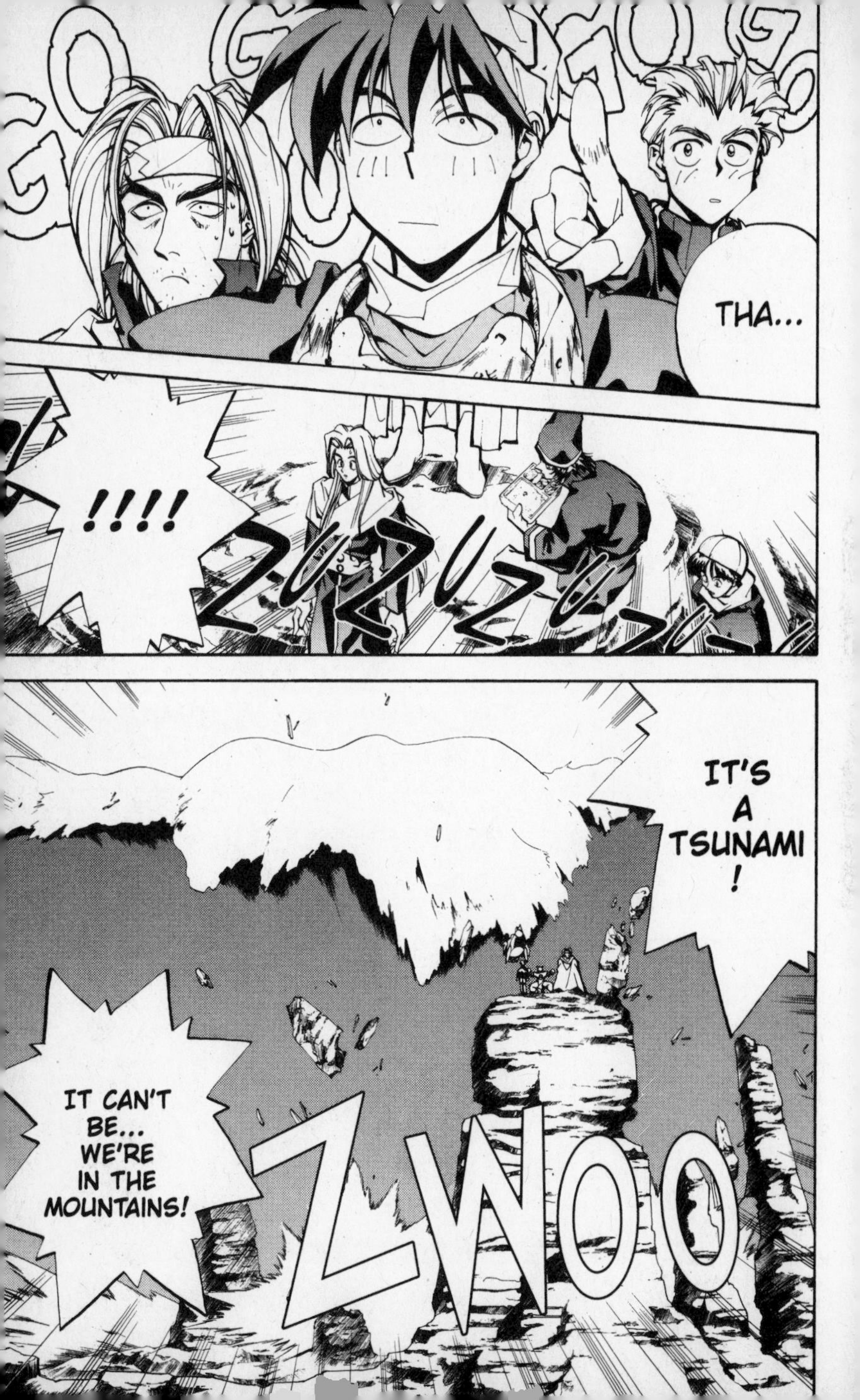
GO GO GO GO GO GO
THA...
!!!!
IT'S A TSUNAMI!
IT CAN'T BE... WE'RE IN THE MOUNTAINS!
ZWOO

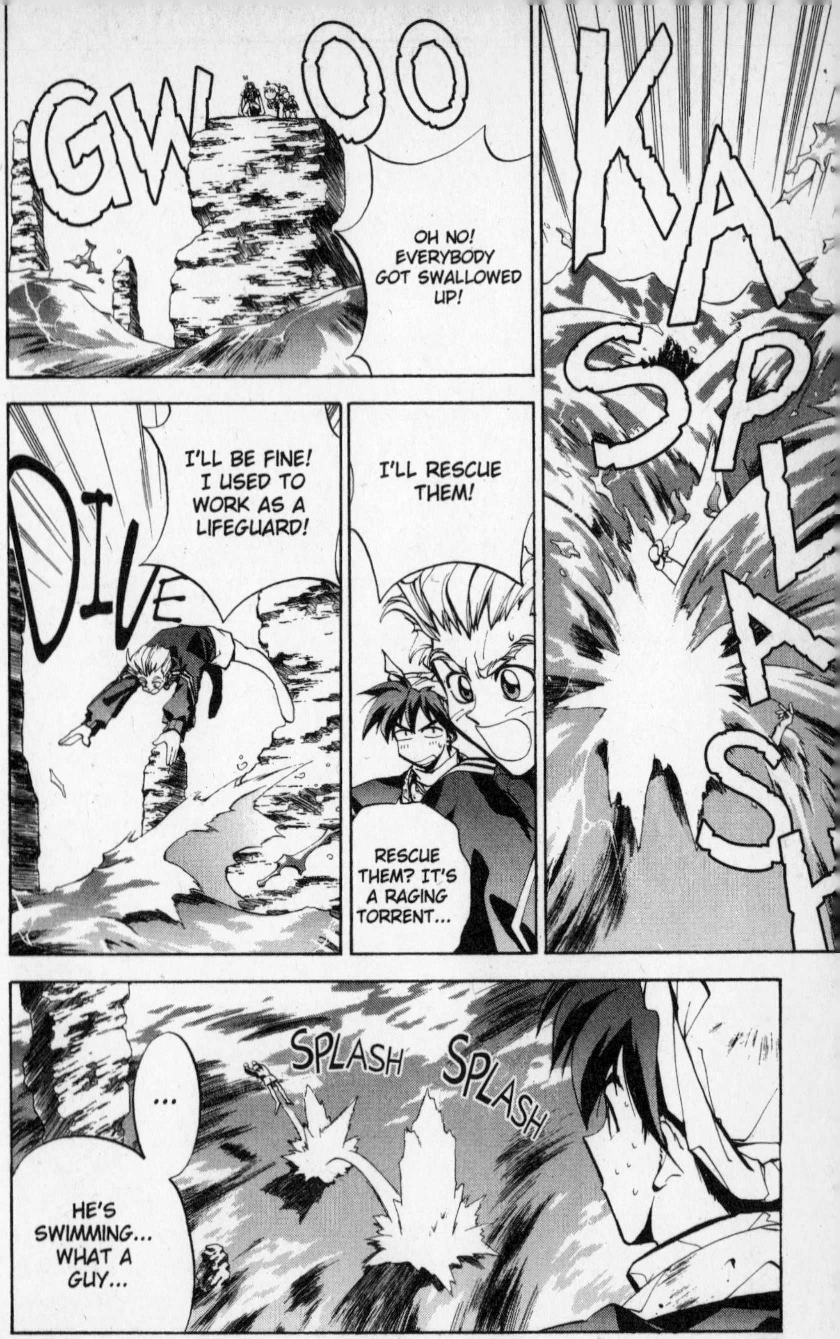
KA SPLASH
GWOOO
OH NO! EVERYBODY GOT SWALLOWED UP!
I'LL RESCUE THEM!
RESCUE THEM? IT'S A RAGING TORRENT...
I'LL BE FINE! I USED TO WORK AS A LIFEGUARD!
DIVE
SPLASH SPLASH
...
HE'S SWIMMING... WHAT A GUY...

READ THIS WAY

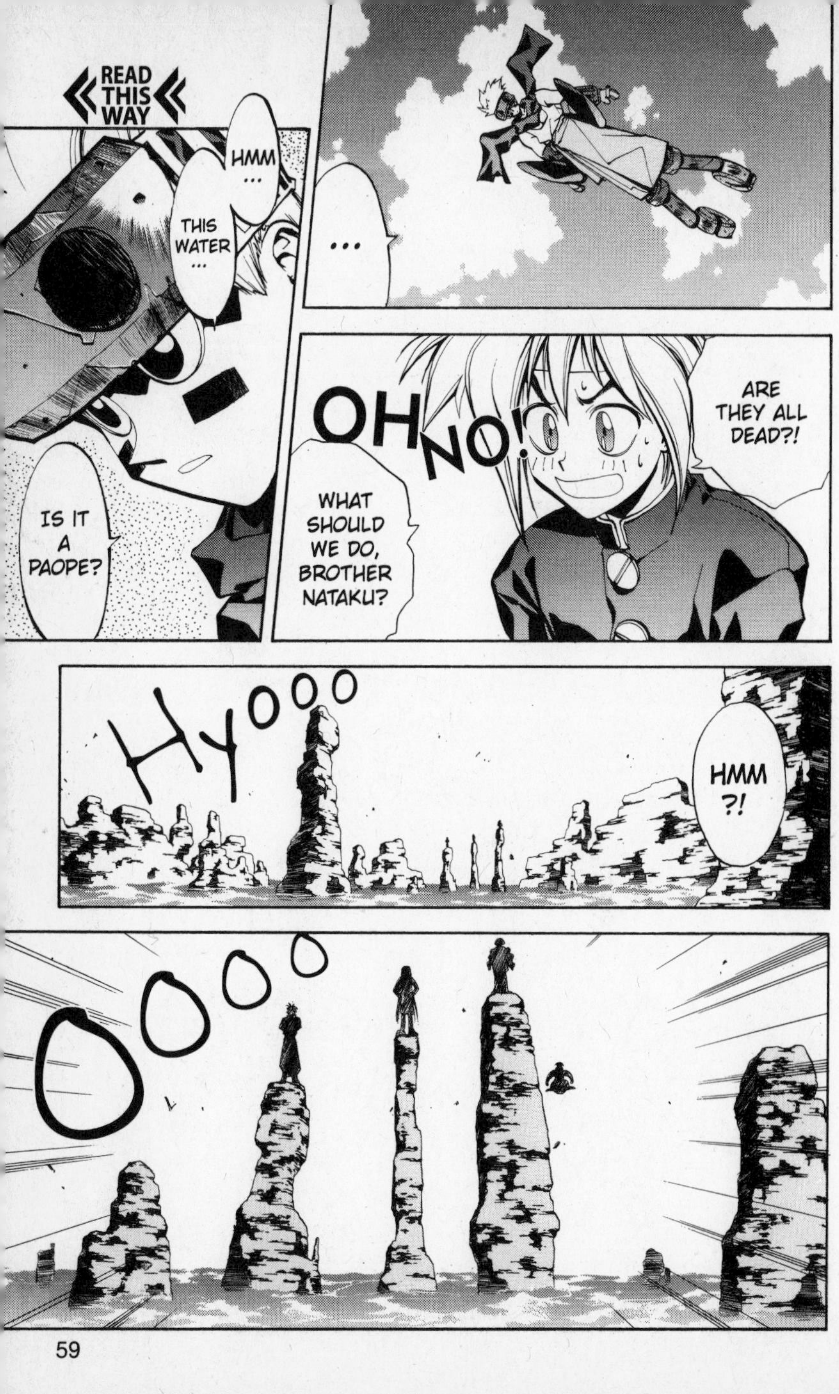

...
ARE THEY ALL DEAD?!
OH NO!
WHAT SHOULD WE DO, BROTHER NATAKU?
HMM ...
THIS WATER ...
IS IT A PAOPE?
HMM ?!
HYOOO
OOOO

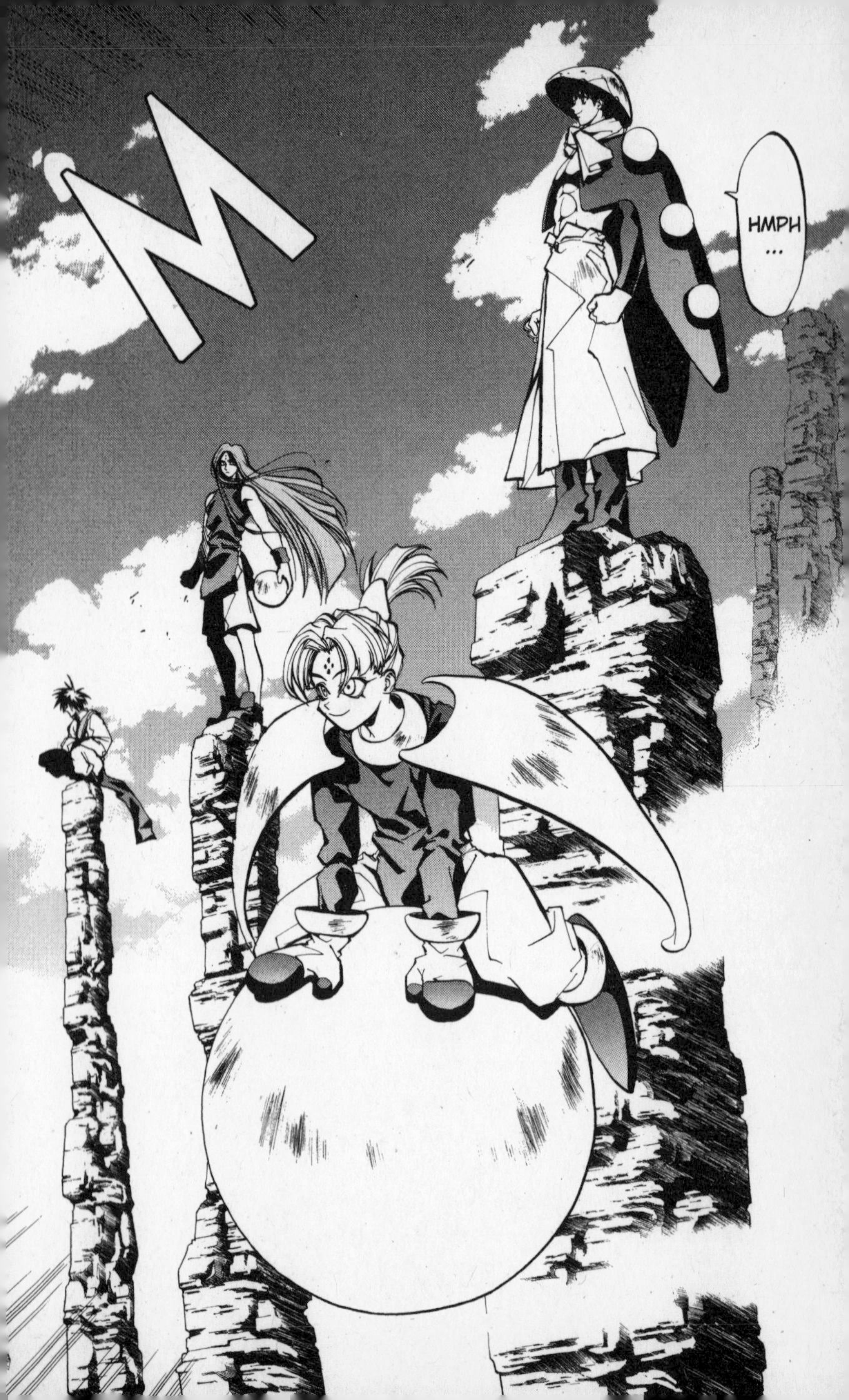
HMPH ...
M

READ THIS WAY

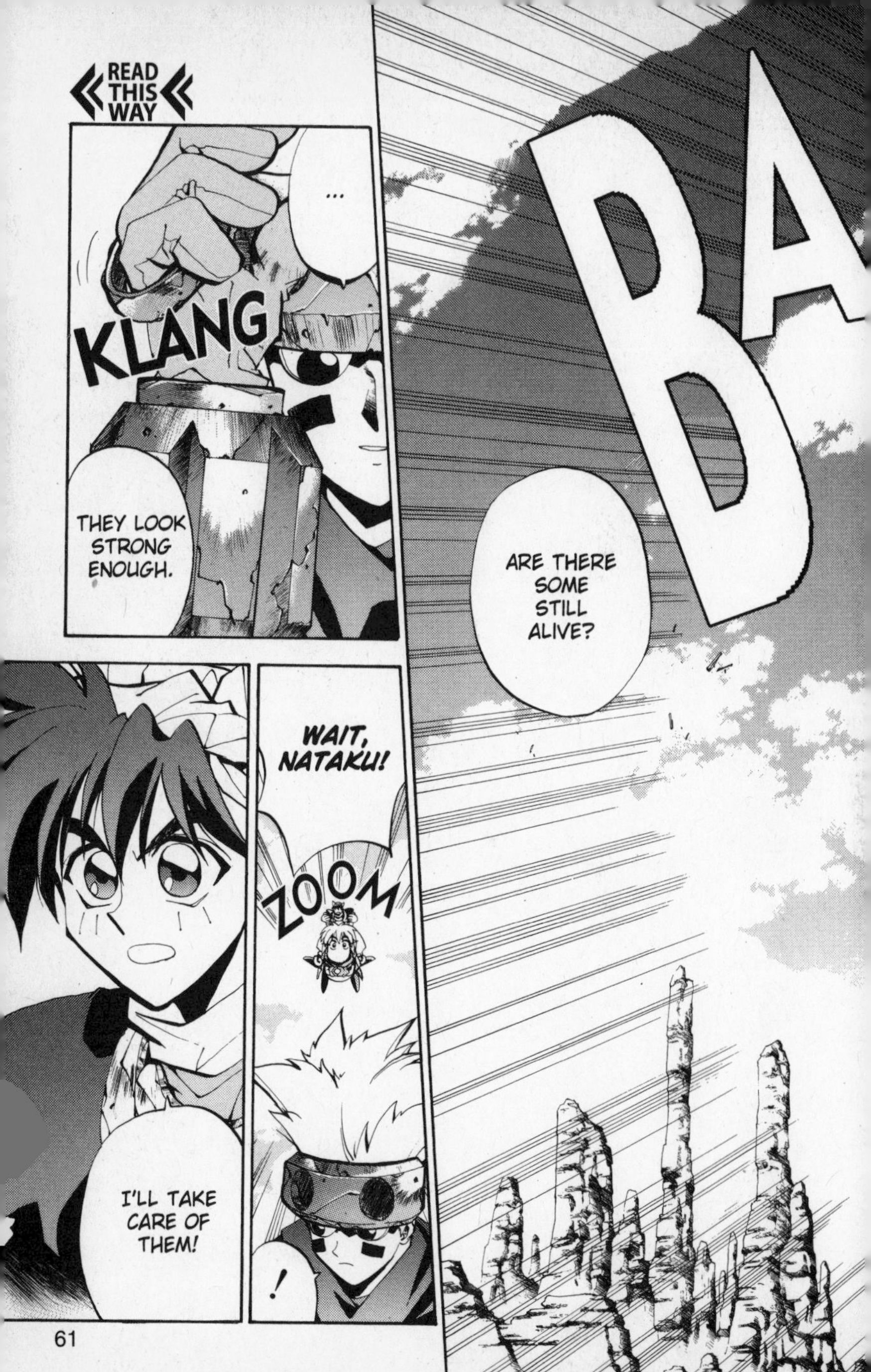
BA
ARE THERE SOME STILL ALIVE?
...
KLANG
THEY LOOK STRONG ENOUGH.
WAIT, NATAKU!
ZOOM
!
I'LL TAKE CARE OF THEM!

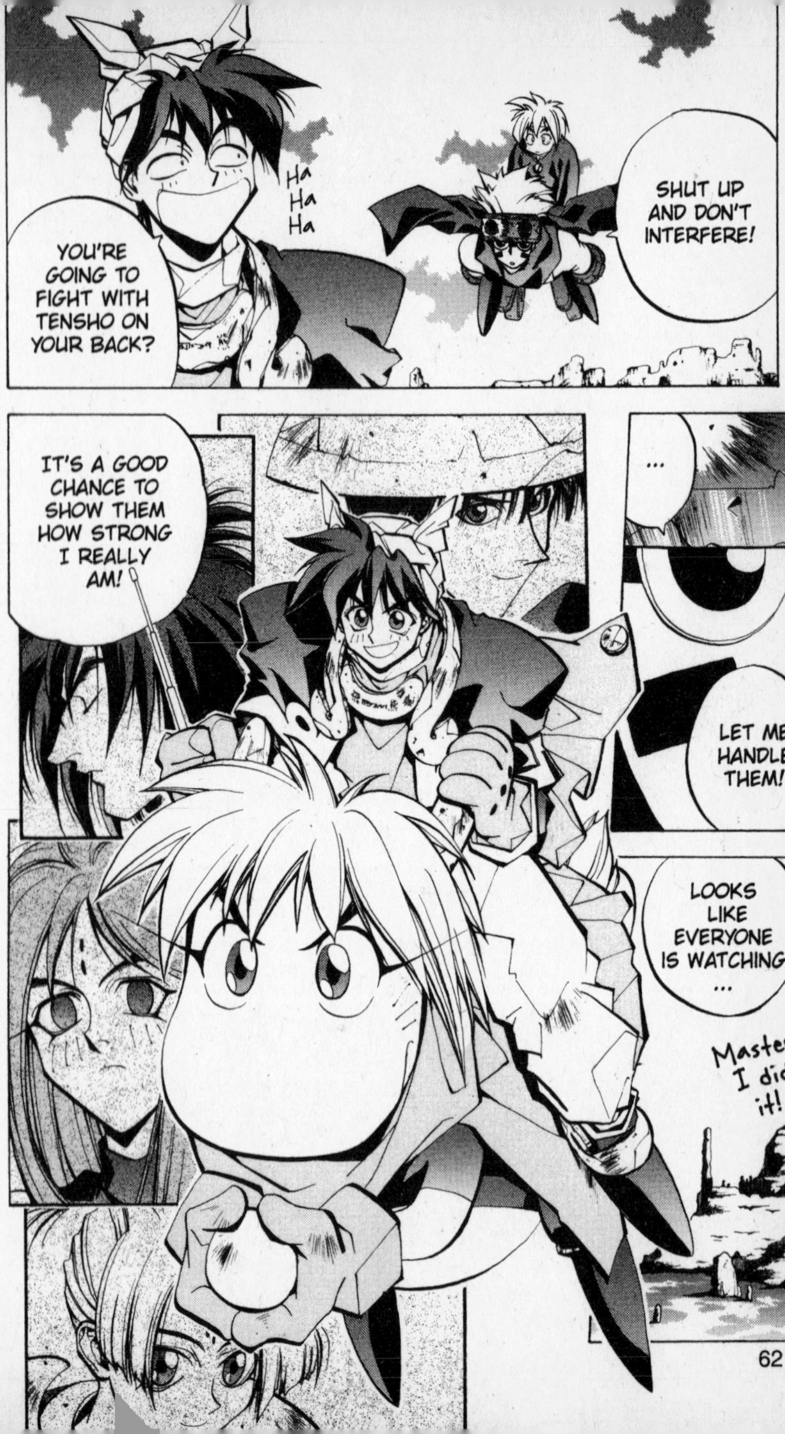
YOU'RE GOING TO FIGHT WITH TENSHO ON YOUR BACK?
Ha Ha Ha
SHUT UP AND DON'T INTERFERE!
...
LET ME HANDLE THEM!
IT'S A GOOD CHANCE TO SHOW THEM HOW STRONG I REALLY AM!
LOOKS LIKE EVERYONE IS WATCHING ...
Master, I did it!

READ THIS WAY

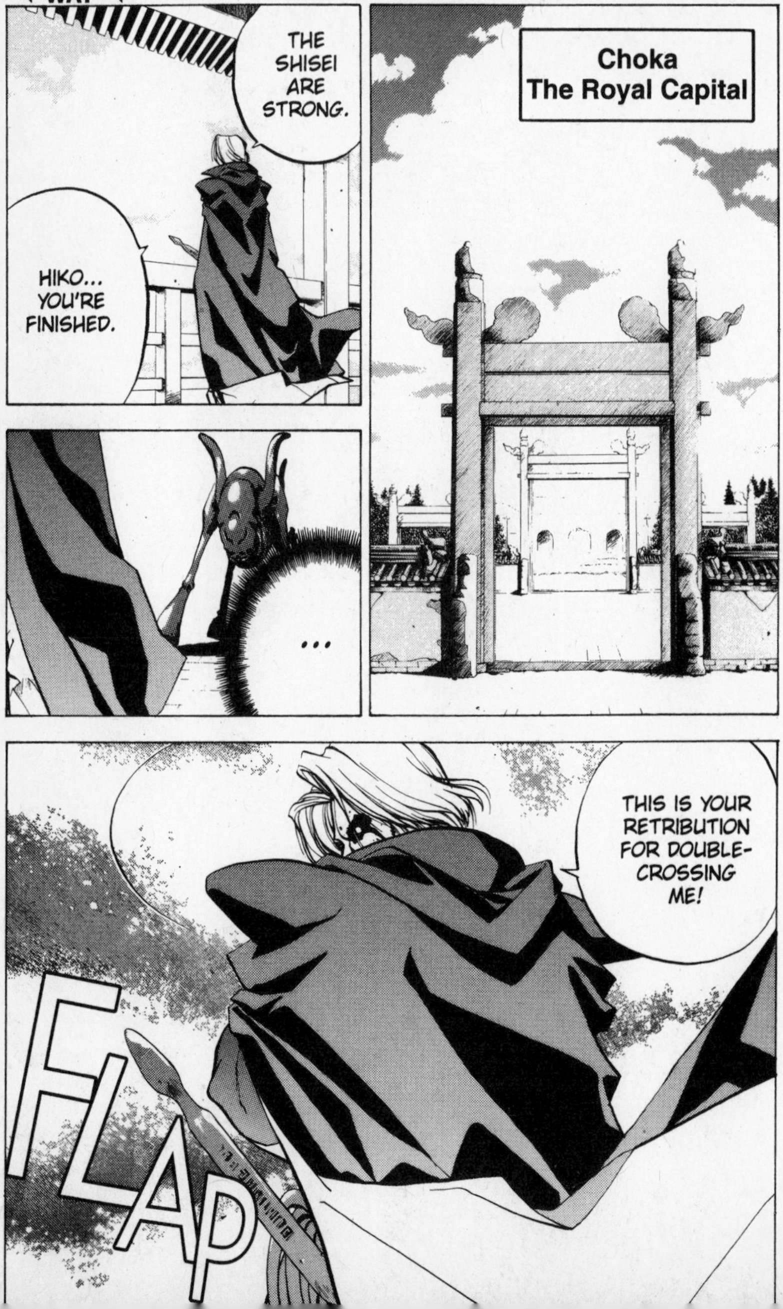

Choka
The Royal Capital
THE SHISEI ARE STRONG.
HIKO... YOU'RE FINISHED.
...
THIS IS YOUR RETRIBUTION FOR DOUBLE-CROSSING ME!
FLAP

封神演義

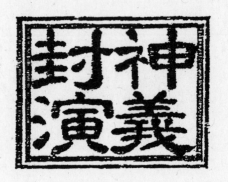

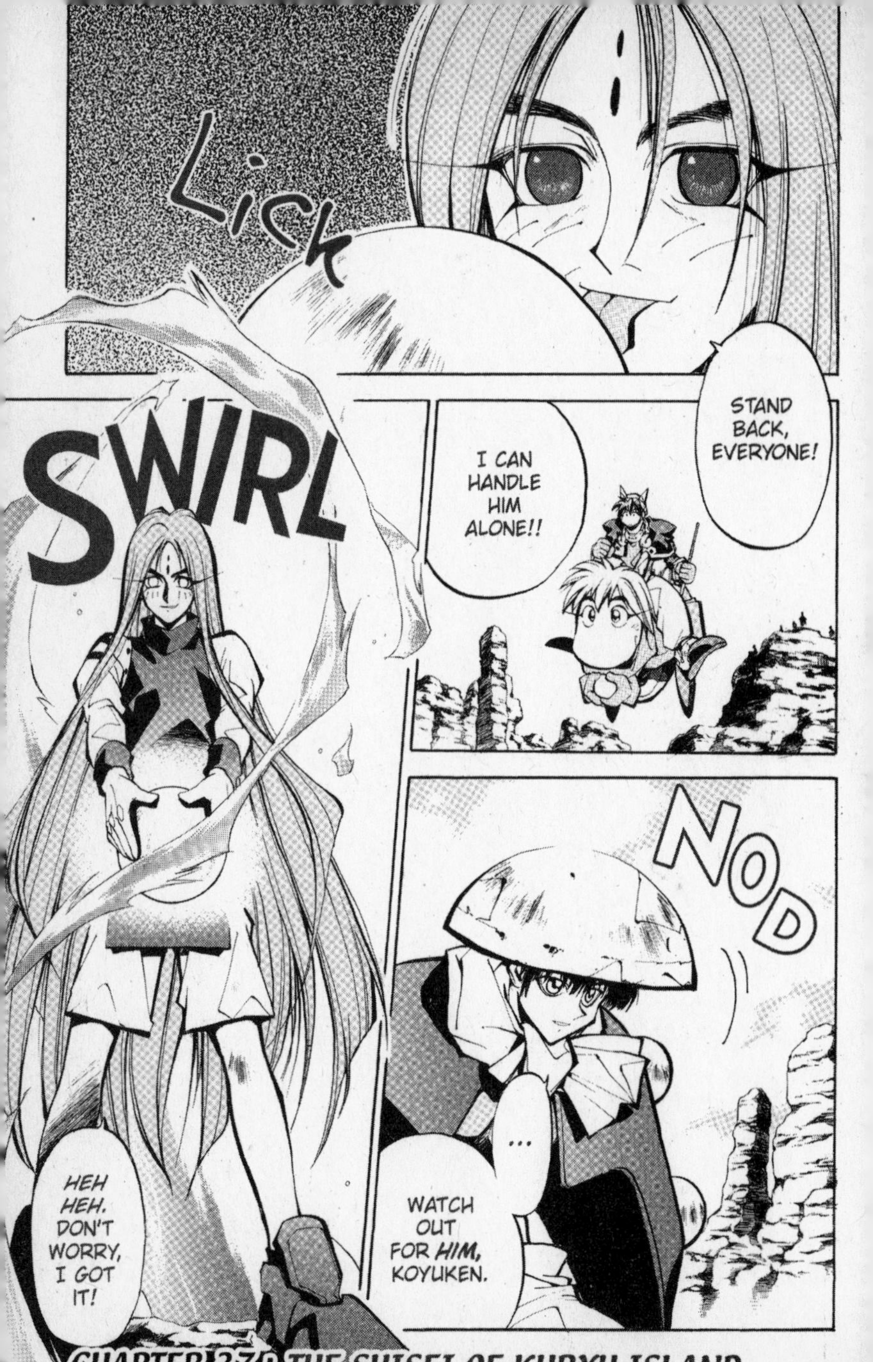
LICK
STAND BACK, EVERYONE!
I CAN HANDLE HIM ALONE!!
NOD
...
WATCH OUT FOR *HIM*, KOYUKEN.
SWIRL
HEH HEH. DON'T WORRY, I GOT IT!

CHAPTER 37 : THE SHISEI OF KURYU ISLAND, PART 2 – THE SHISEI'S PAST

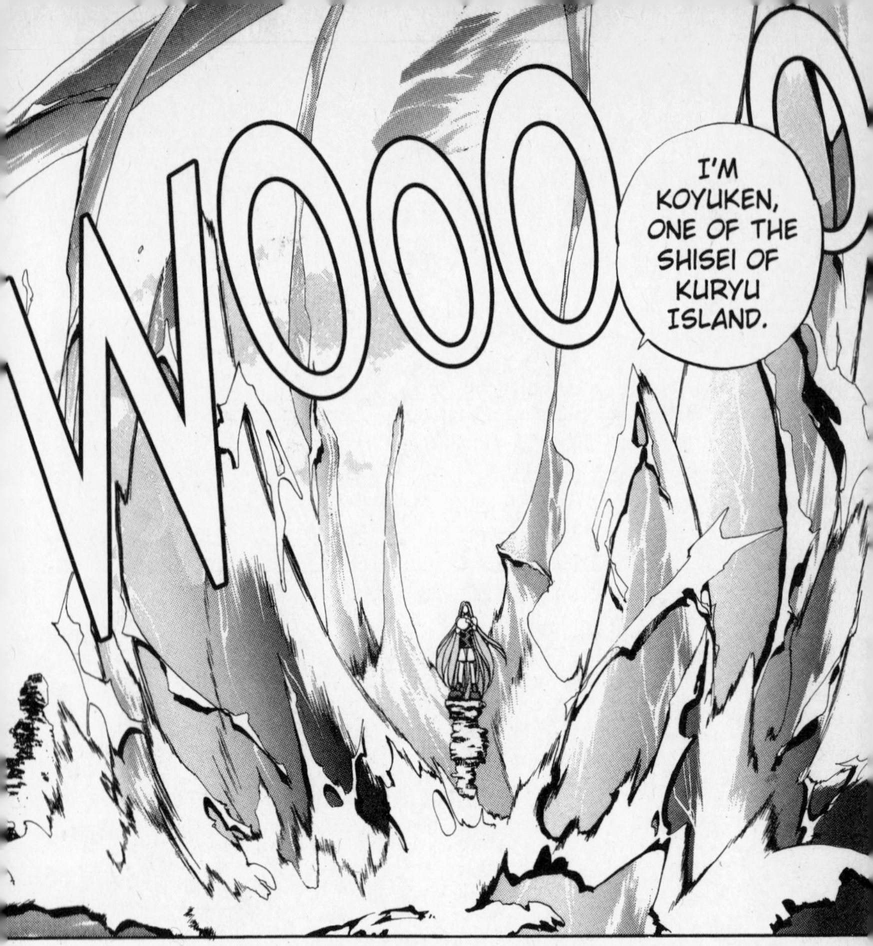
I'M KOYUKEN, ONE OF THE SHISEI OF KURYU ISLAND.
WOOOOO

THE SHISEI'S PAST

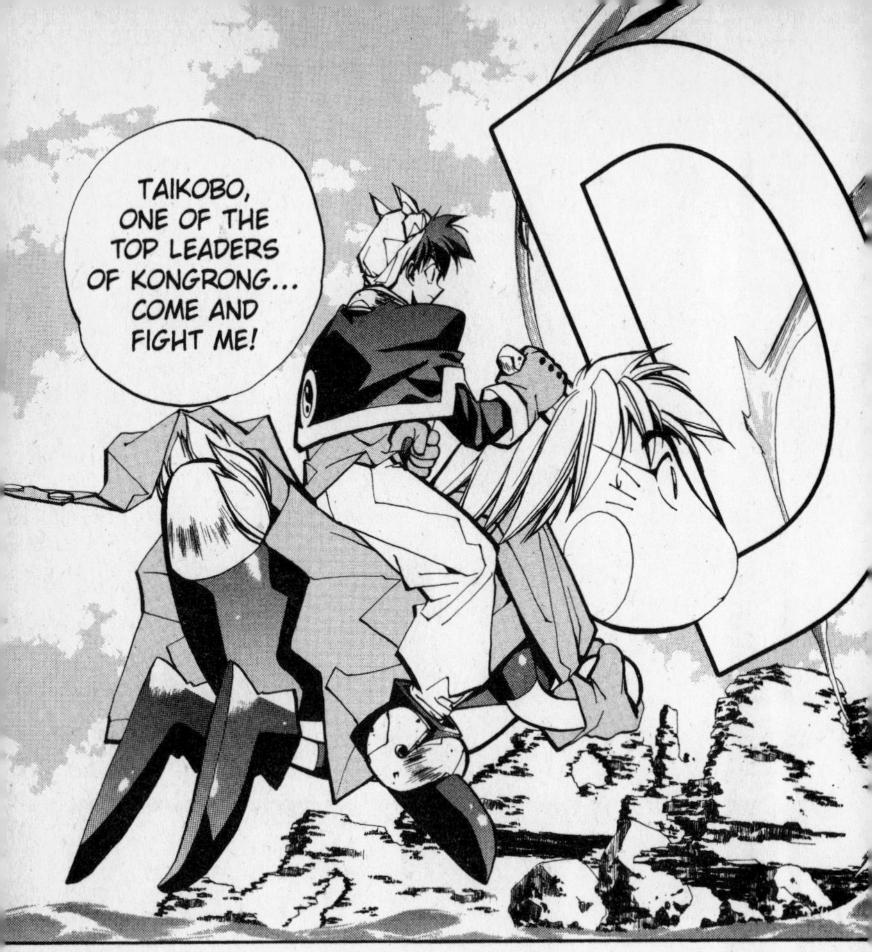
TAIKOBO, ONE OF THE TOP LEADERS OF KONGRONG... COME AND FIGHT ME!

Chapter 37

THE SHISEI OF KURYU ISLAND, PART 2

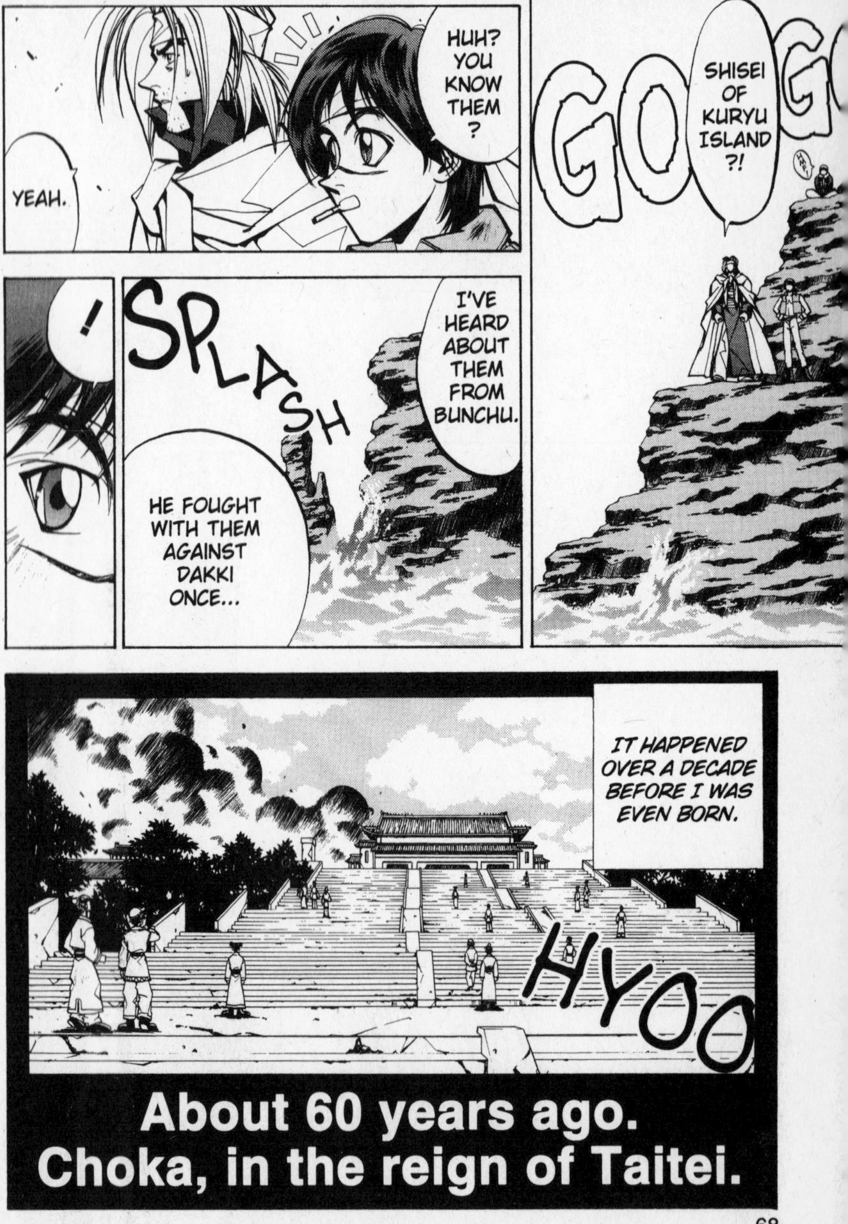
GO GO
SHISEI OF KURYU ISLAND ?!
HUH? YOU KNOW THEM ?
YEAH.
I'VE HEARD ABOUT THEM FROM BUNCHU.
SPLASH
HE FOUGHT WITH THEM AGAINST DAKKI ONCE...
!
IT HAPPENED OVER A DECADE BEFORE I WAS EVEN BORN.
HYOO
About 60 years ago.
Choka, in the reign of Taitei.

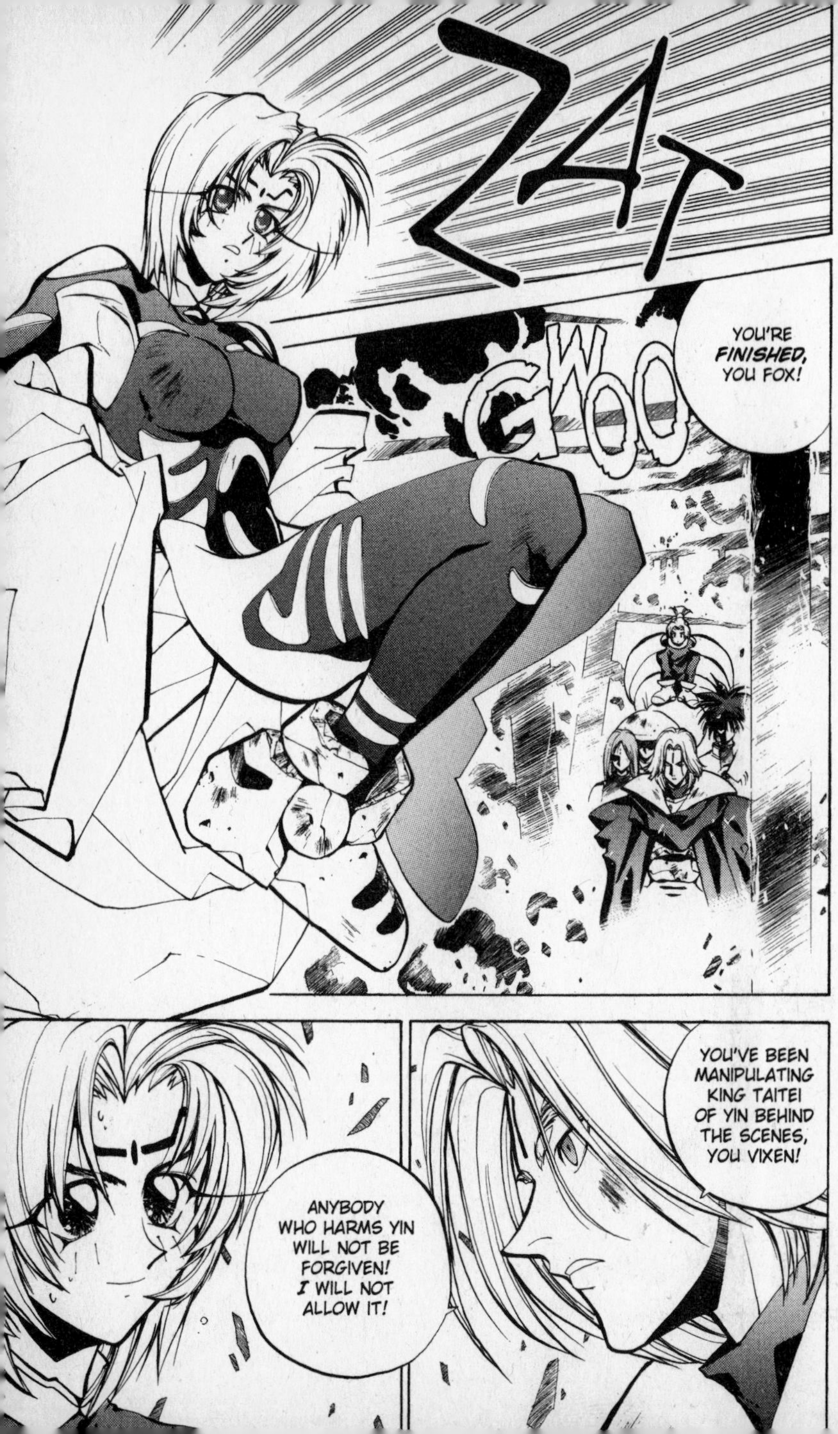
ZAT
YOU'RE FINISHED, YOU FOX!
GWOO
YOU'VE BEEN MANIPULATING KING TAITEI OF YIN BEHIND THE SCENES, YOU VIXEN!
ANYBODY WHO HARMS YIN WILL NOT BE FORGIVEN! I WILL NOT ALLOW IT!

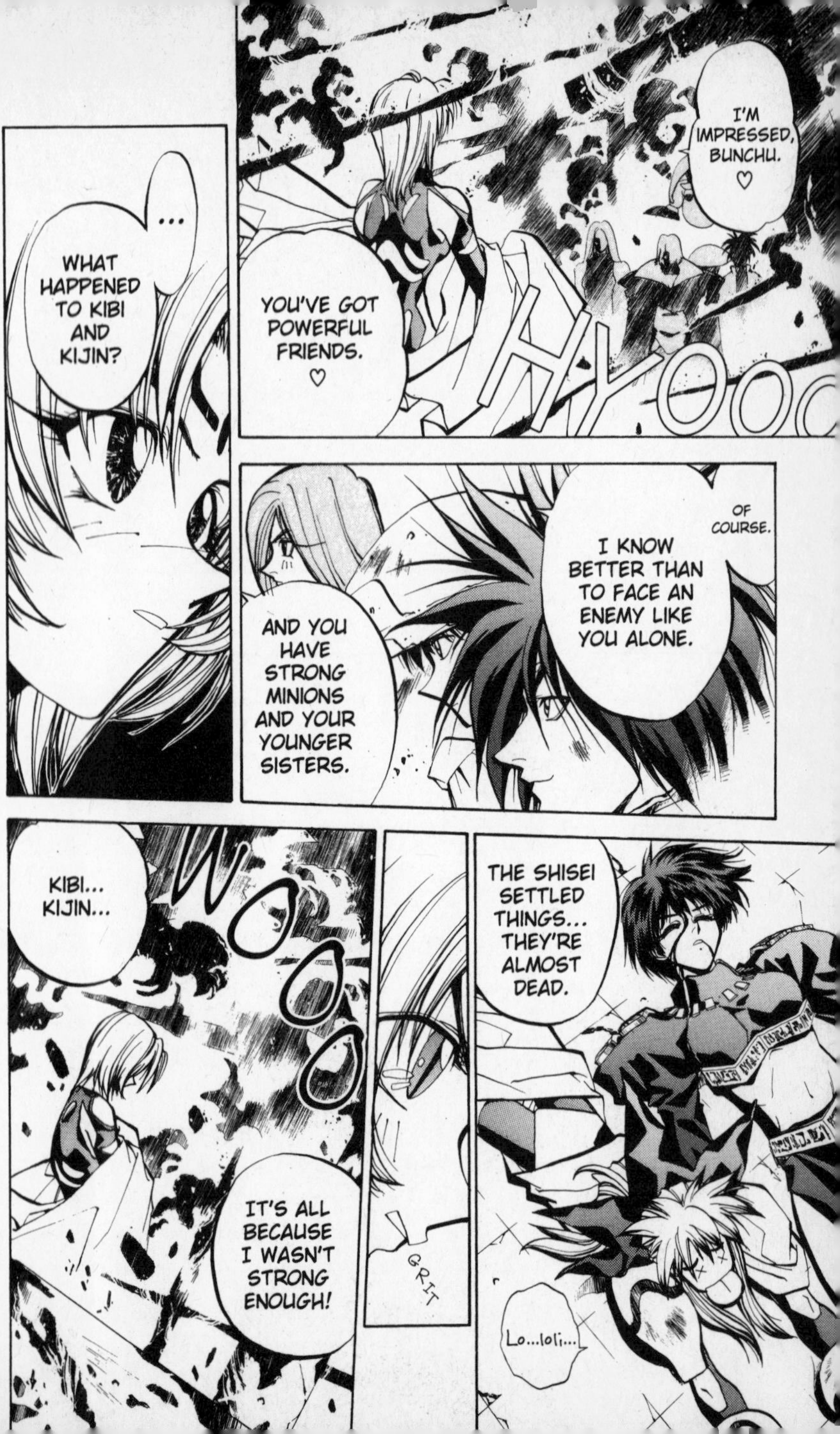
I'M IMPRESSED, BUNCHU. ♡
YOU'VE GOT POWERFUL FRIENDS. ♡
HYOOO
OF COURSE.
I KNOW BETTER THAN TO FACE AN ENEMY LIKE YOU ALONE.
AND YOU HAVE STRONG MINIONS AND YOUR YOUNGER SISTERS.
...
WHAT HAPPENED TO KIBI AND KIJIN?
THE SHISEI SETTLED THINGS... THEY'RE ALMOST DEAD.
Lo...loli...
GRIT
KIBI... KIJIN...
WOOOO
IT'S ALL BECAUSE I WASN'T STRONG ENOUGH!

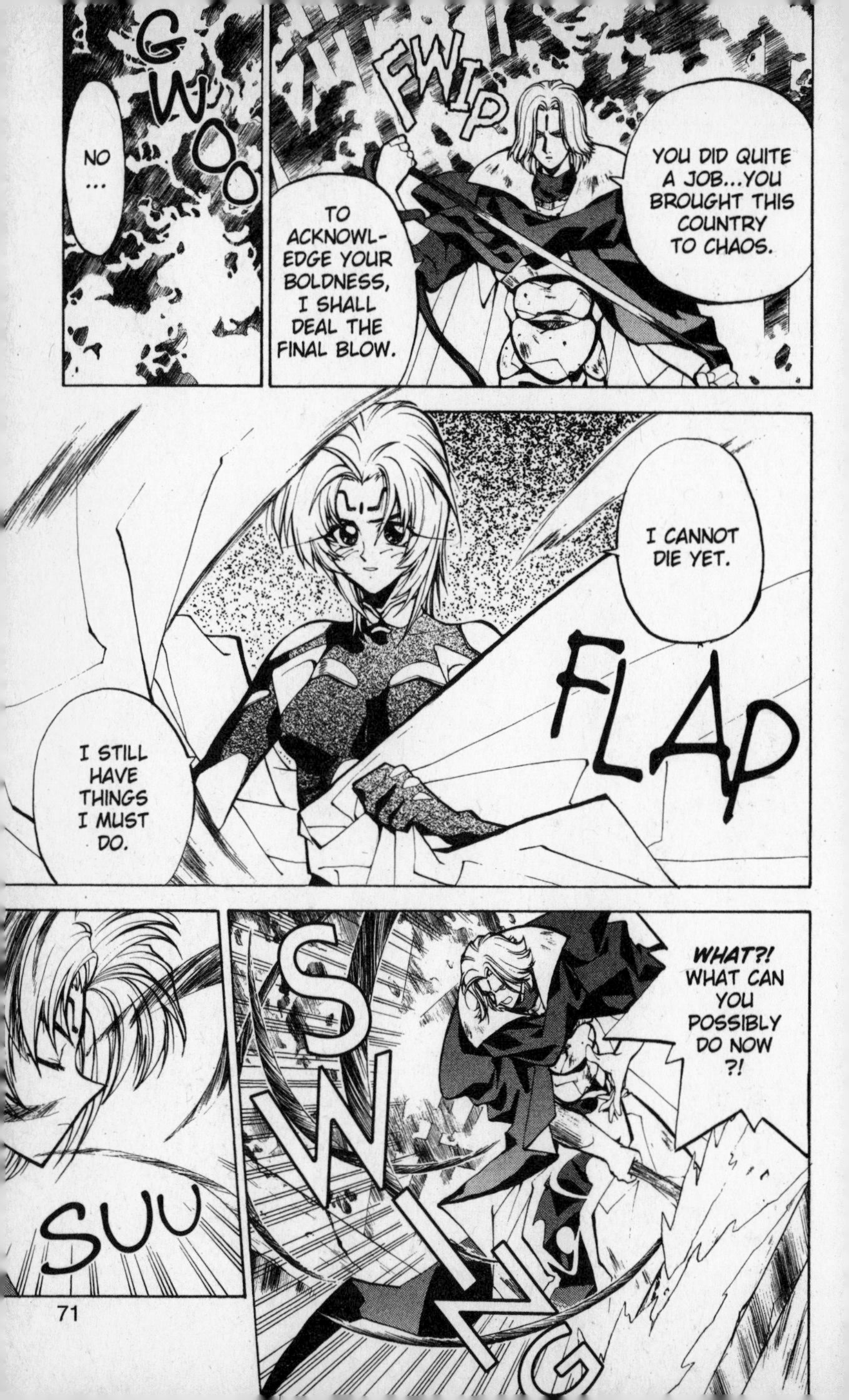
FWIP
YOU DID QUITE A JOB...YOU BROUGHT THIS COUNTRY TO CHAOS.
TO ACKNOWL-EDGE YOUR BOLDNESS, I SHALL DEAL THE FINAL BLOW.
GWOOO
NO ...
I CANNOT DIE YET.
FLAP
I STILL HAVE THINGS I MUST DO.
WHAT?! WHAT CAN YOU POSSIBLY DO NOW ?!
SWING
SUU

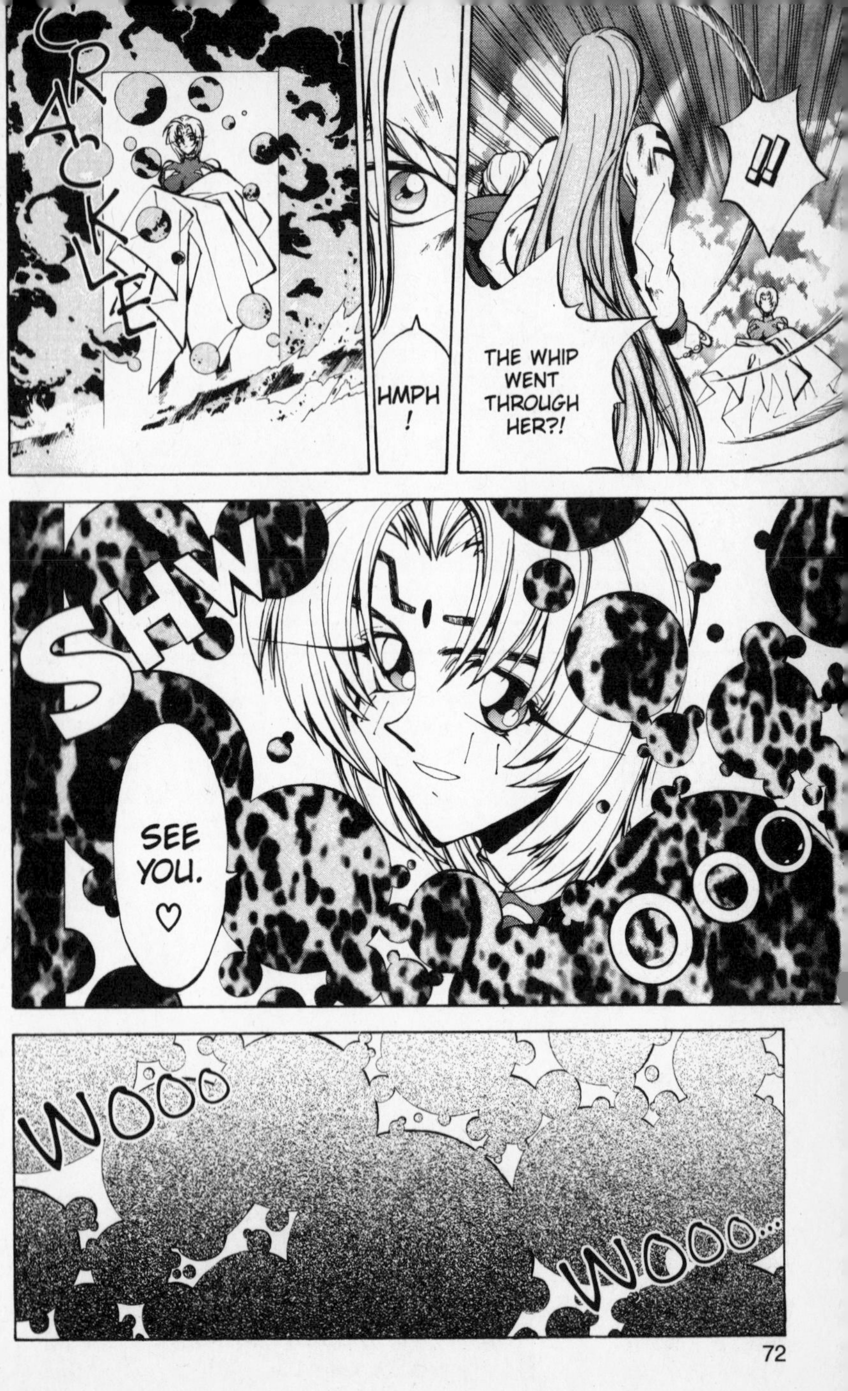
!!
THE WHIP WENT THROUGH HER?!
HMPH!
CRACKLE
SHW
OOOO
SEE YOU. ♡
WOOO
WOOO...

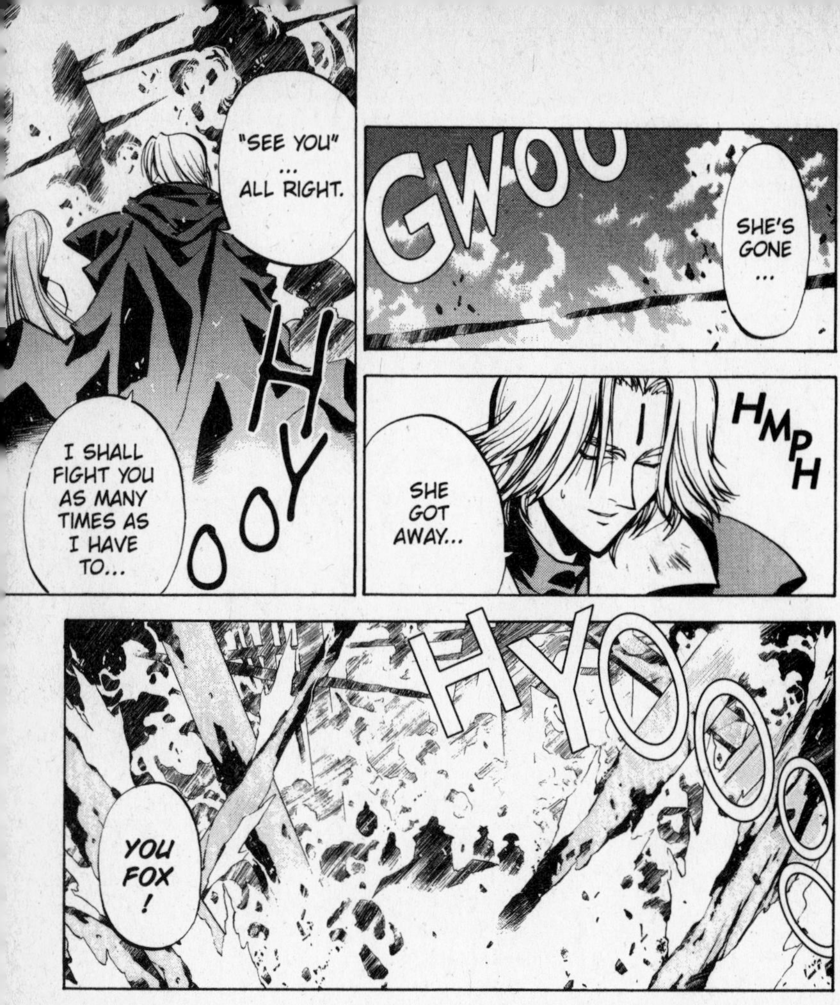
GWOO
SHE'S GONE...
SHE GOT AWAY...
HMPH
"SEE YOU" ... ALL RIGHT.
HYOO
I SHALL FIGHT YOU AS MANY TIMES AS I HAVE TO...
HYOOOOO
YOU FOX!

KOKIBI AND OKIJIN WERE GONE, TOO.

DAKKI PROBABLY TOOK THEM AWAY WITH HER.

AFTERWARDS, EVEN THE SENNIN WORLD WAS TALKING ABOUT BUNCHU AND THE SHISEI, WHO DEFEATED DAKKI AND HER TWO SISTERS...

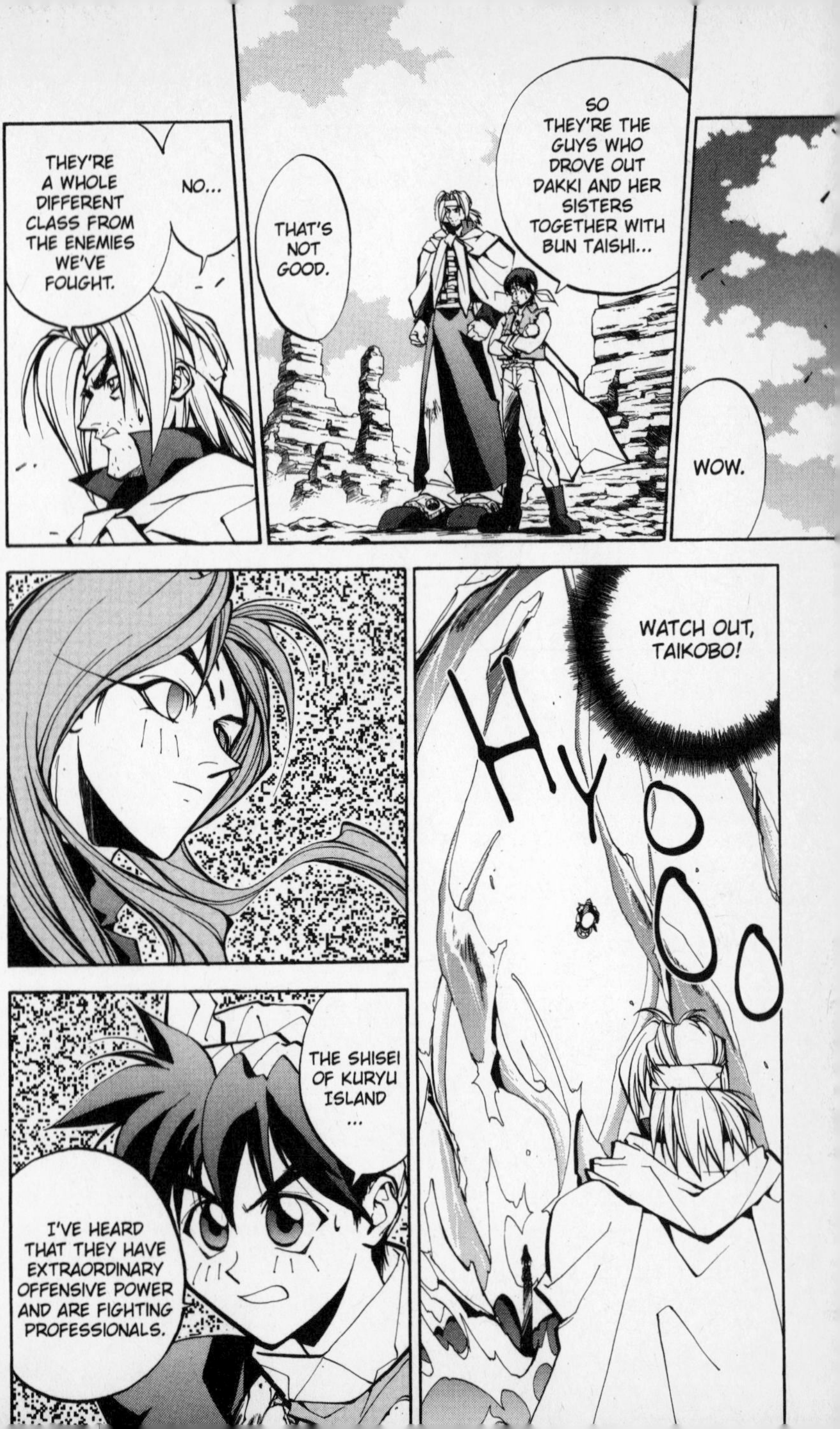
WOW.
SO THEY'RE THE GUYS WHO DROVE OUT DAKKI AND HER SISTERS TOGETHER WITH BUN TAISHI...
THAT'S NOT GOOD.
NO...
THEY'RE A WHOLE DIFFERENT CLASS FROM THE ENEMIES WE'VE FOUGHT.
WATCH OUT, TAIKOBO!
HYOOO
THE SHISEI OF KURYU ISLAND ...
I'VE HEARD THAT THEY HAVE EXTRAORDINARY OFFENSIVE POWER AND ARE FIGHTING PROFESSIONALS.

READ THIS WAY

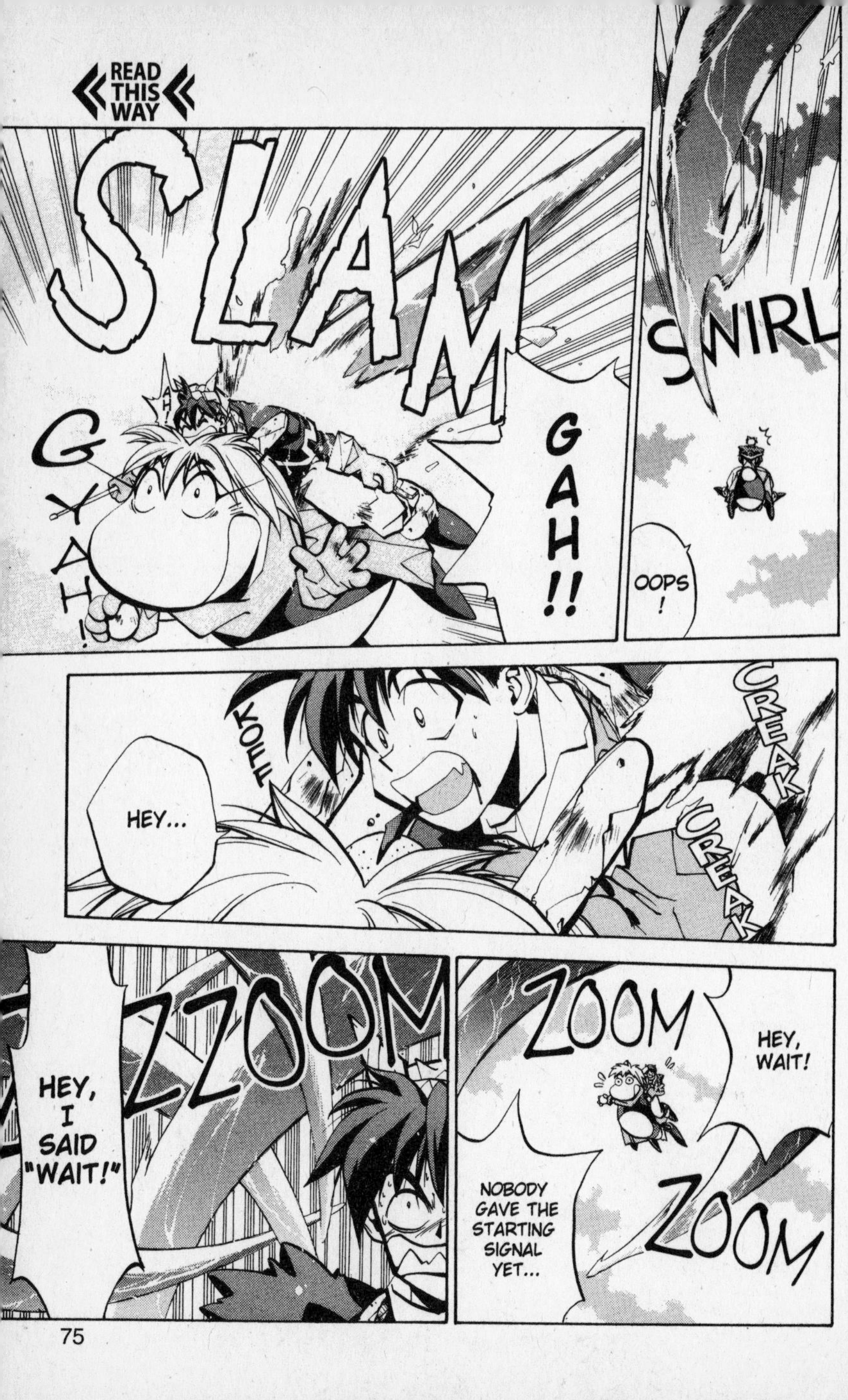
SWIRL
OOPS!
SLAM
GAH!!
AH!
GYAH!
CREAK
CREAK
KOFF
HEY...
ZOOM
HEY, WAIT!
NOBODY GAVE THE STARTING SIGNAL YET...
ZOOM
ZZOOM
HEY, I SAID "WAIT!"

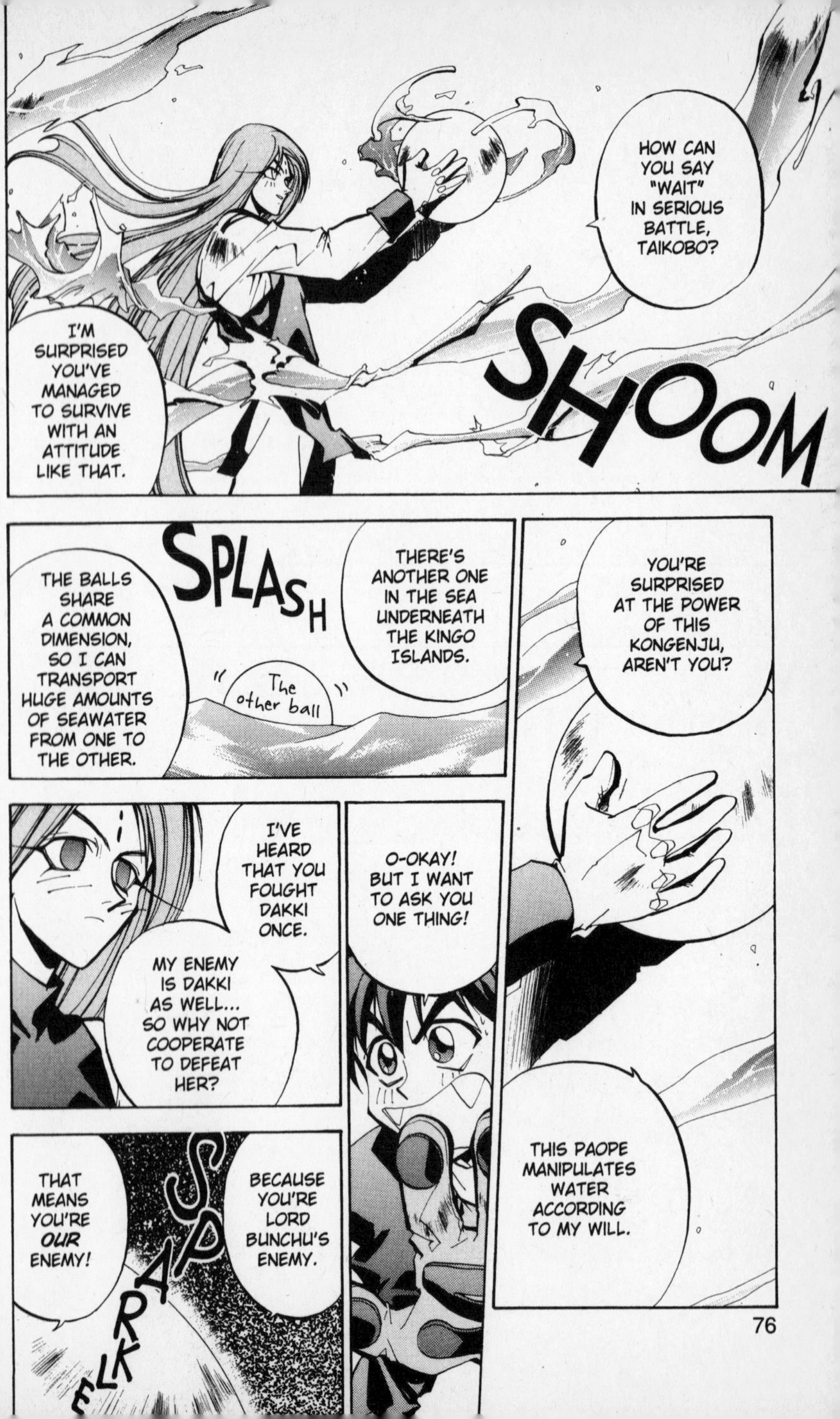
HOW CAN YOU SAY "WAIT" IN SERIOUS BATTLE, TAIKOBO?
SHOOM
I'M SURPRISED YOU'VE MANAGED TO SURVIVE WITH AN ATTITUDE LIKE THAT.
YOU'RE SURPRISED AT THE POWER OF THIS KONGENJU, AREN'T YOU?
THIS PAOPE MANIPULATES WATER ACCORDING TO MY WILL.
THERE'S ANOTHER ONE IN THE SEA UNDERNEATH THE KINGO ISLANDS.
SPLASH
"The other ball"
THE BALLS SHARE A COMMON DIMENSION, SO I CAN TRANSPORT HUGE AMOUNTS OF SEAWATER FROM ONE TO THE OTHER.
O-OKAY! BUT I WANT TO ASK YOU ONE THING!
I'VE HEARD THAT YOU FOUGHT DAKKI ONCE.
MY ENEMY IS DAKKI AS WELL... SO WHY NOT COOPERATE TO DEFEAT HER?
BECAUSE YOU'RE LORD BUNCHU'S ENEMY.
SPARKLE
THAT MEANS YOU'RE *OUR* ENEMY!

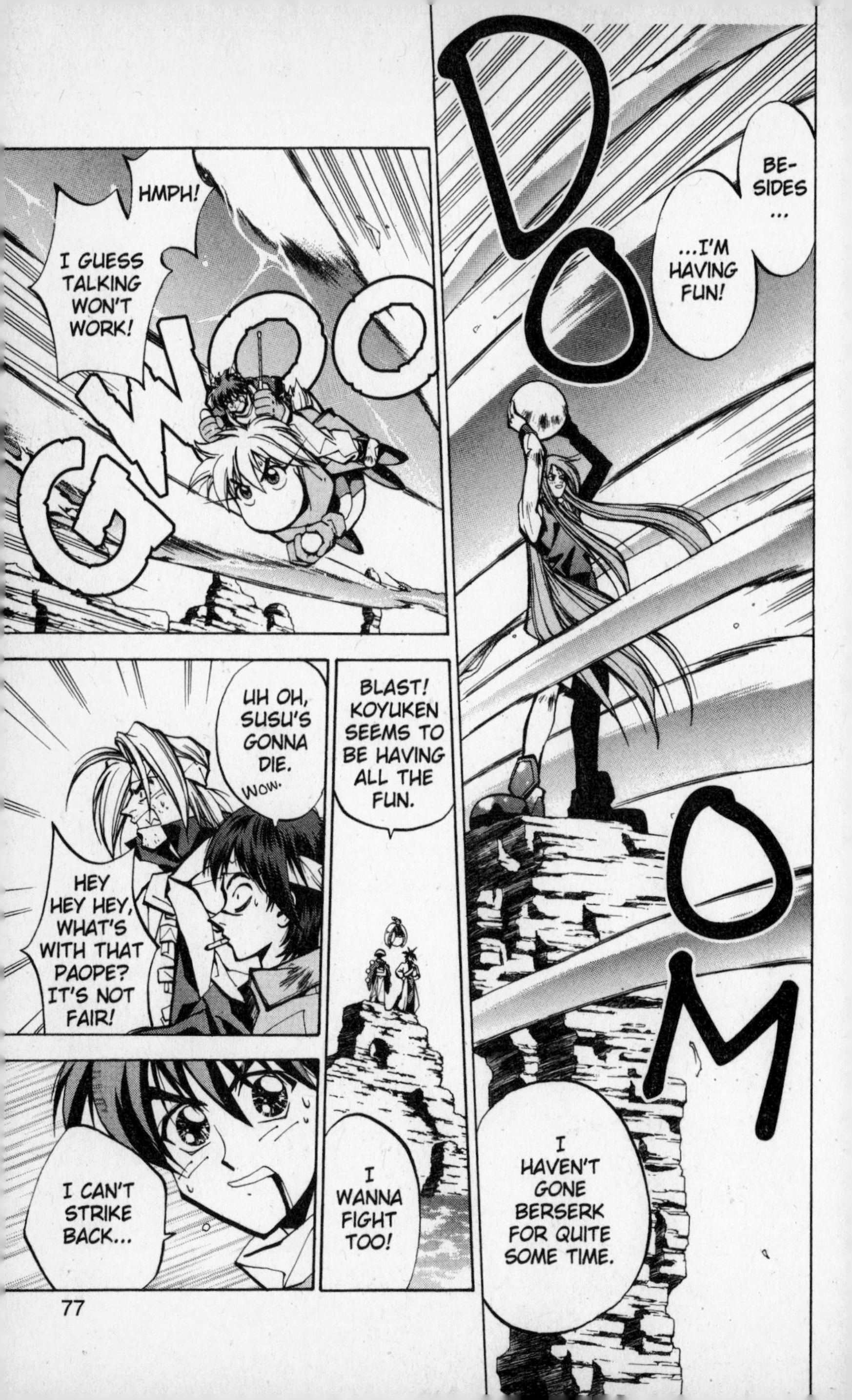
DOO
BESIDES...
...I'M HAVING FUN!
OM
I HAVEN'T GONE BERSERK FOR QUITE SOME TIME.
HMPH!
I GUESS TALKING WON'T WORK!
GWOO
BLAST! KOYUKEN SEEMS TO BE HAVING ALL THE FUN.
I WANNA FIGHT TOO!
UH OH, SUSU'S GONNA DIE.
WOW.
HEY HEY HEY, WHAT'S WITH THAT PAOPE? IT'S NOT FAIR!
I CAN'T STRIKE BACK...

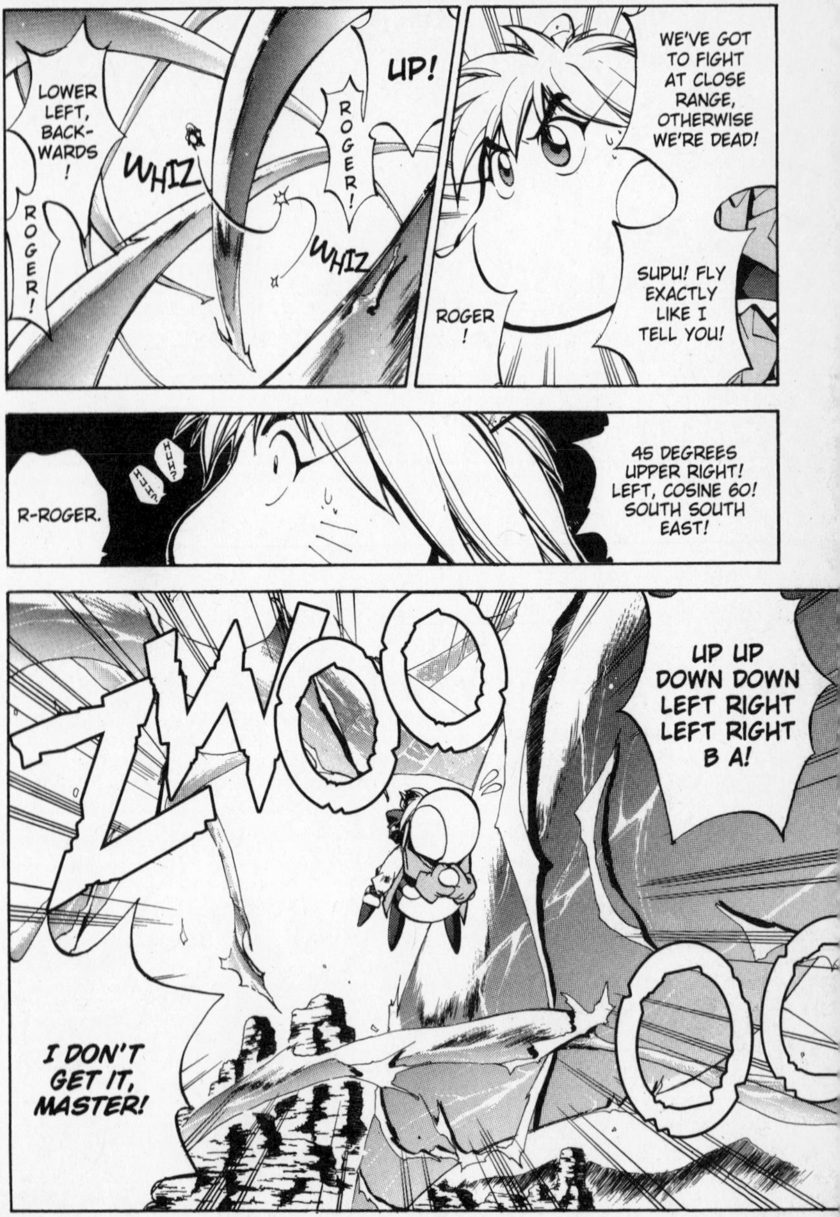
WE'VE GOT TO FIGHT AT CLOSE RANGE, OTHERWISE WE'RE DEAD!
SUPU! FLY EXACTLY LIKE I TELL YOU!
ROGER!
UP!
ROGER!
WHIZ
LOWER LEFT, BACK-WARDS!
WHIZ
ROGER!
45 DEGREES UPPER RIGHT! LEFT, COSINE 60! SOUTH SOUTH EAST!
HUH?
R-ROGER.
UP UP DOWN DOWN LEFT RIGHT LEFT RIGHT B A!
ZWOOOO
I DON'T GET IT, MASTER!

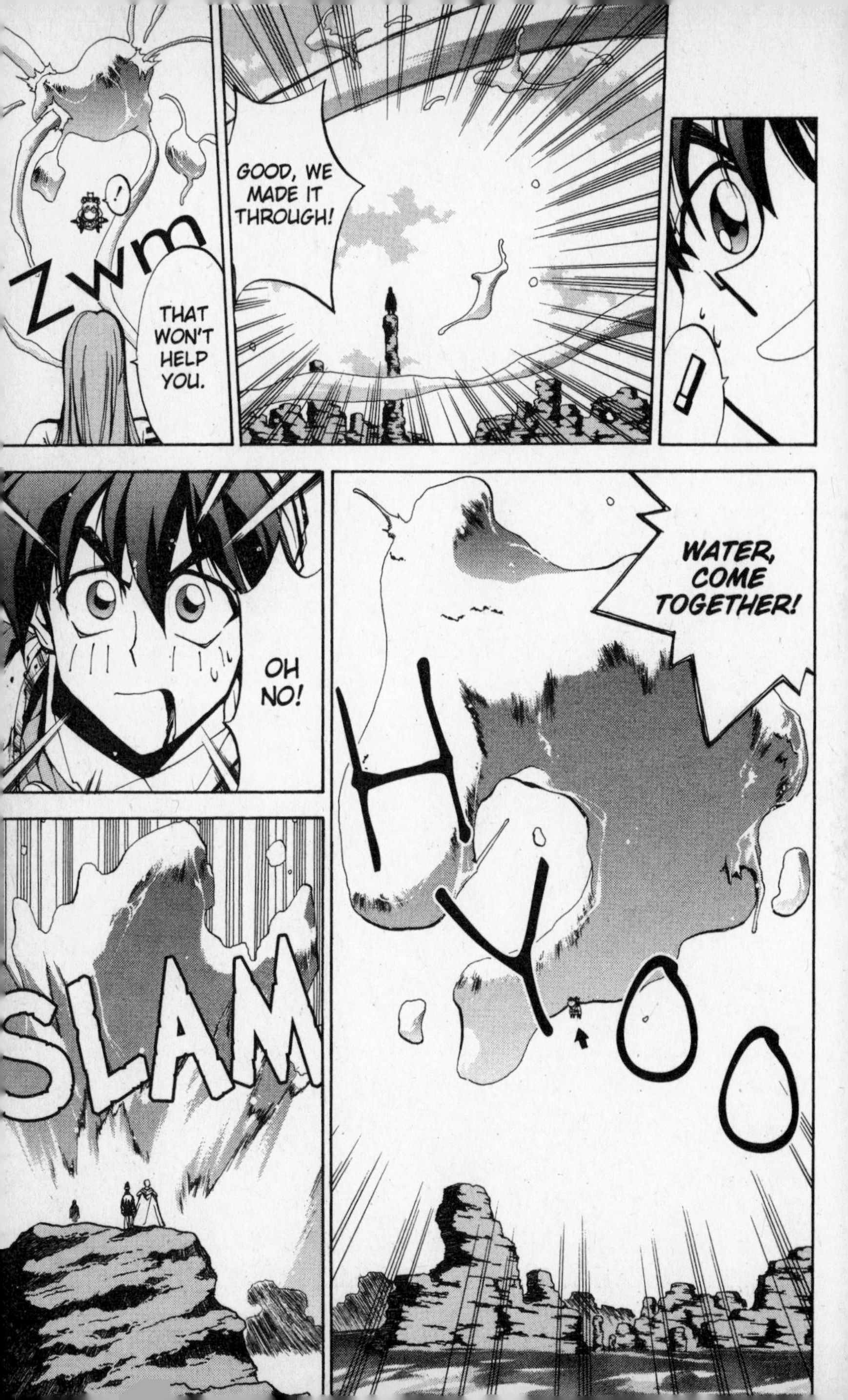
!
GOOD, WE MADE IT THROUGH!
!
Zwm
THAT WON'T HELP YOU.
WATER, COME TOGETHER!
HYOO
OH NO!
SLAM

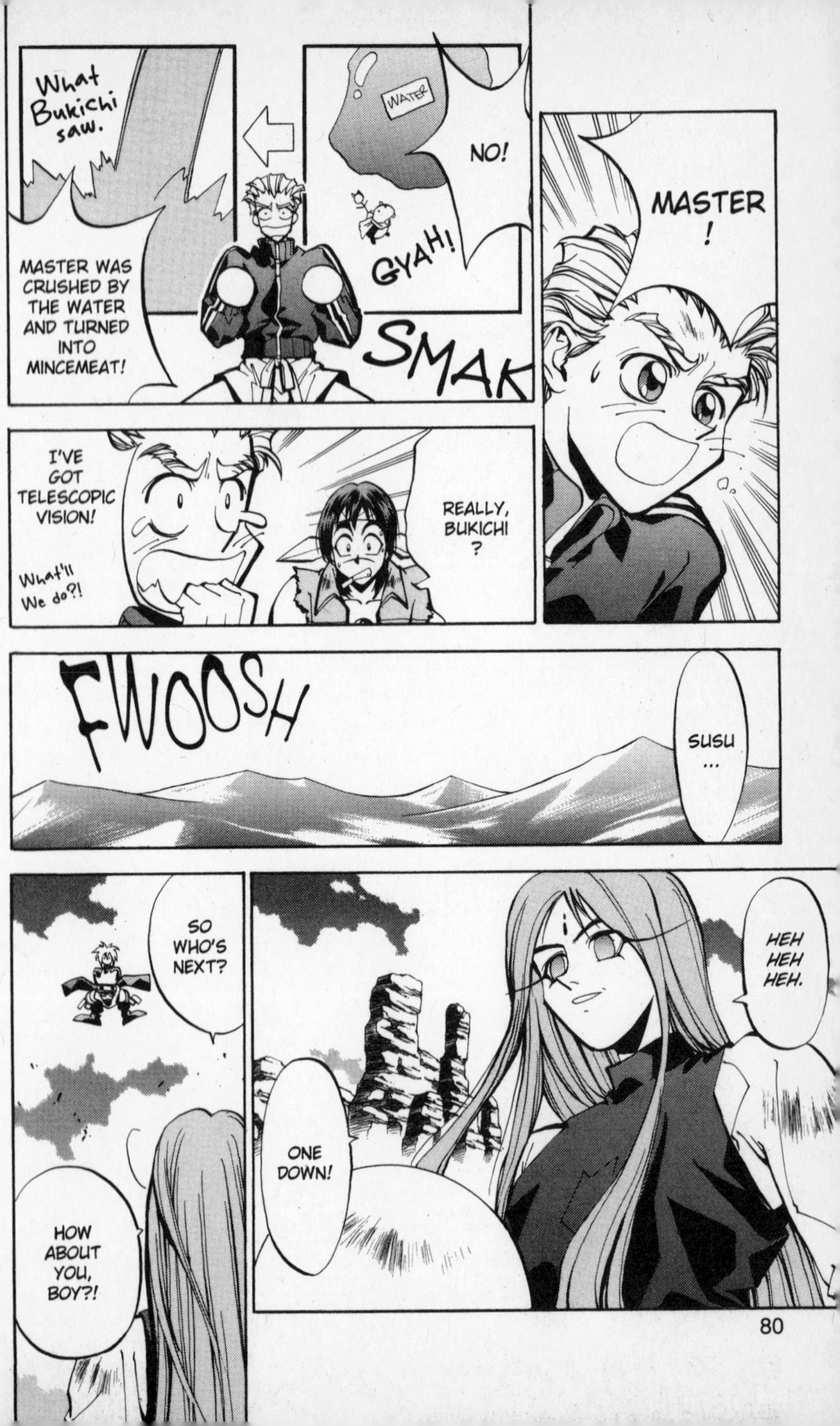
NO!
WATER
GYAH!
SMAK
MASTER!
What Bukichi saw.
MASTER WAS CRUSHED BY THE WATER AND TURNED INTO MINCEMEAT!
REALLY, BUKICHI?
I'VE GOT TELESCOPIC VISION!
What'll We do?!
FWOOSH
SUSU ...
HEH HEH HEH.
ONE DOWN!
SO WHO'S NEXT?
HOW ABOUT YOU, BOY?!

READ THIS WAY

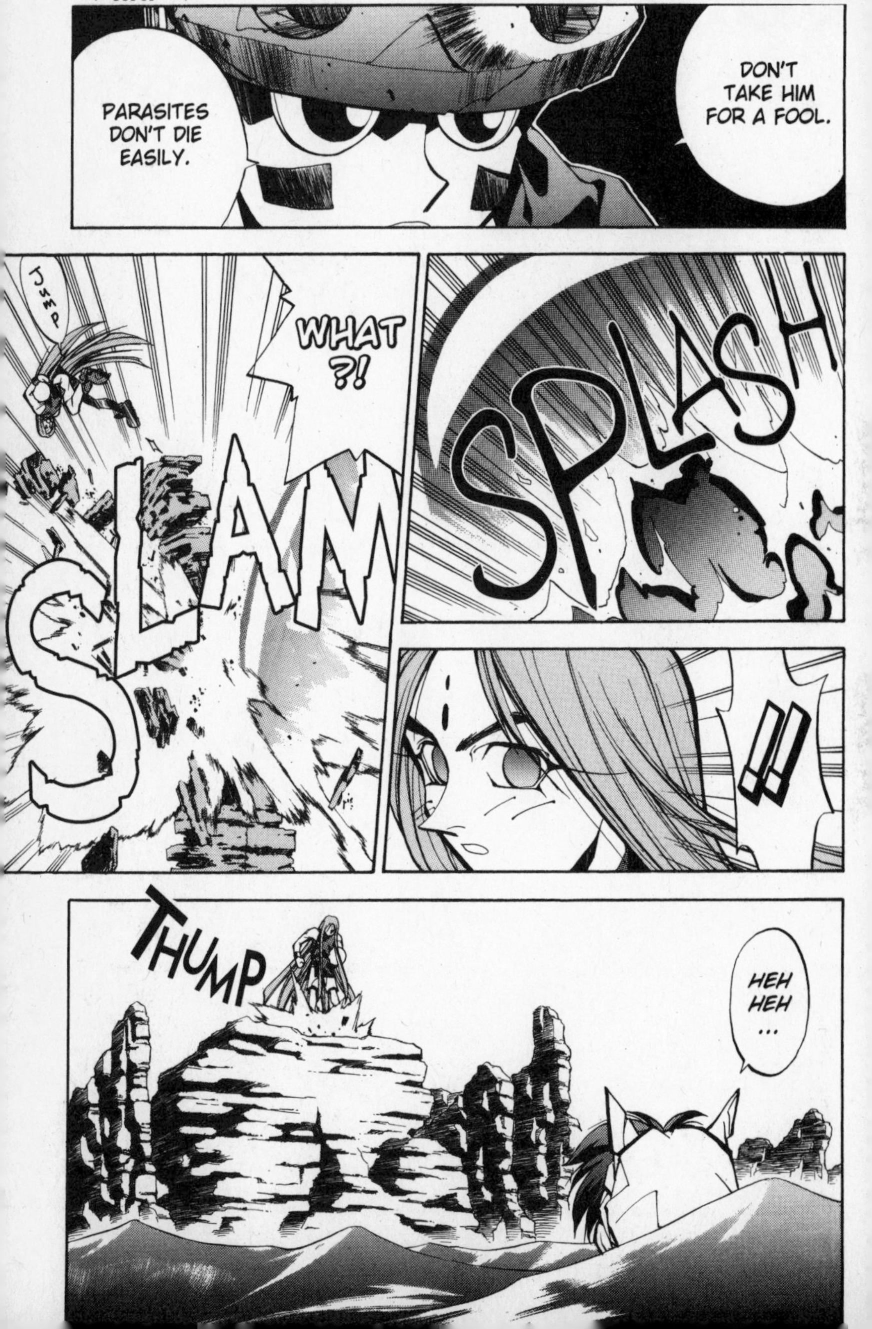
DON'T TAKE HIM FOR A FOOL.
PARASITES DON'T DIE EASILY.
SPLASH
!!
Jump
WHAT ?!
SLAM
THUMP
HEH HEH ...

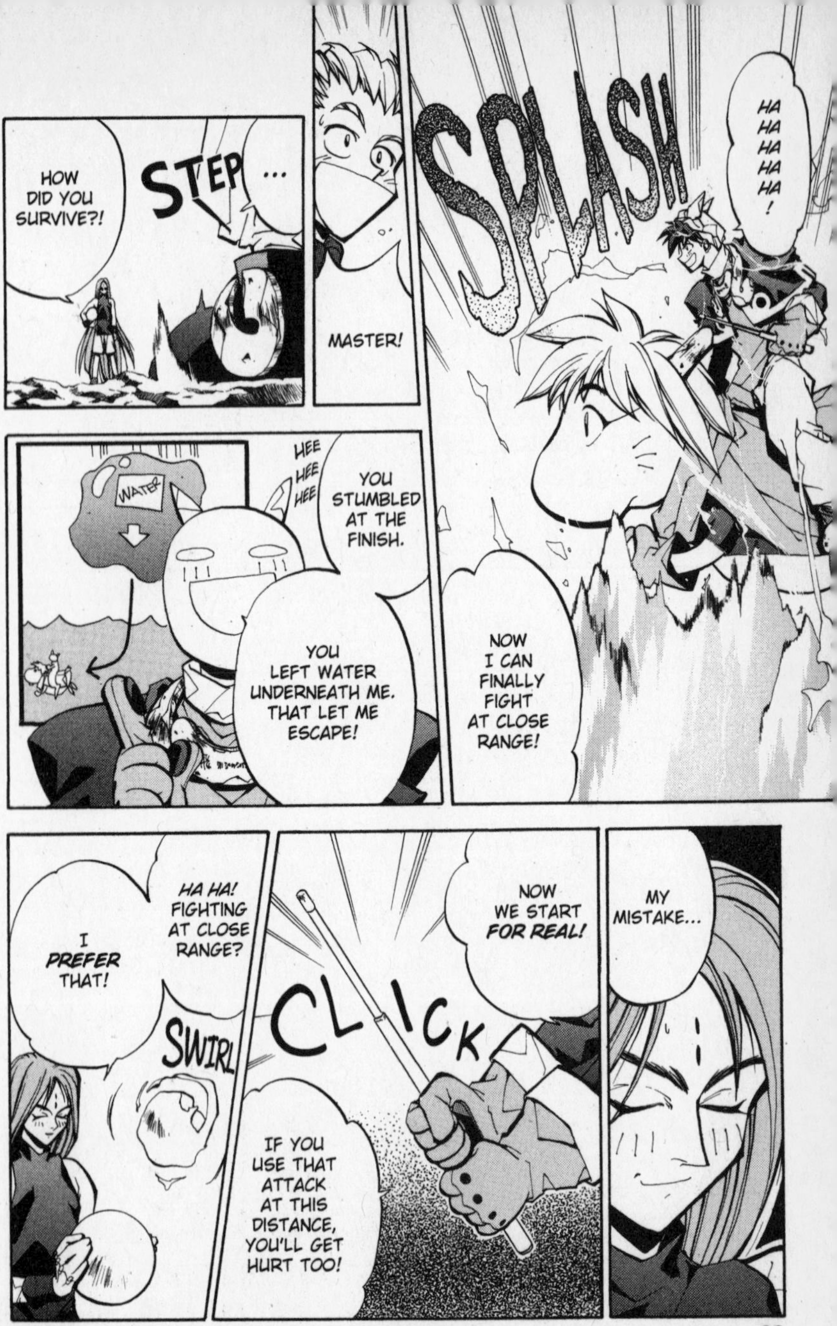

HA HA HA HA HA!
SPLASH
NOW I CAN FINALLY FIGHT AT CLOSE RANGE!
MASTER!
...
STEP
HOW DID YOU SURVIVE?!
HEE HEE HEE
YOU STUMBLED AT THE FINISH.
WATER
YOU LEFT WATER UNDERNEATH ME. THAT LET ME ESCAPE!
MY MISTAKE...
NOW WE START FOR REAL!
CLICK
IF YOU USE THAT ATTACK AT THIS DISTANCE, YOU'LL GET HURT TOO!
HA HA! FIGHTING AT CLOSE RANGE?
I PREFER THAT!
SWIRL

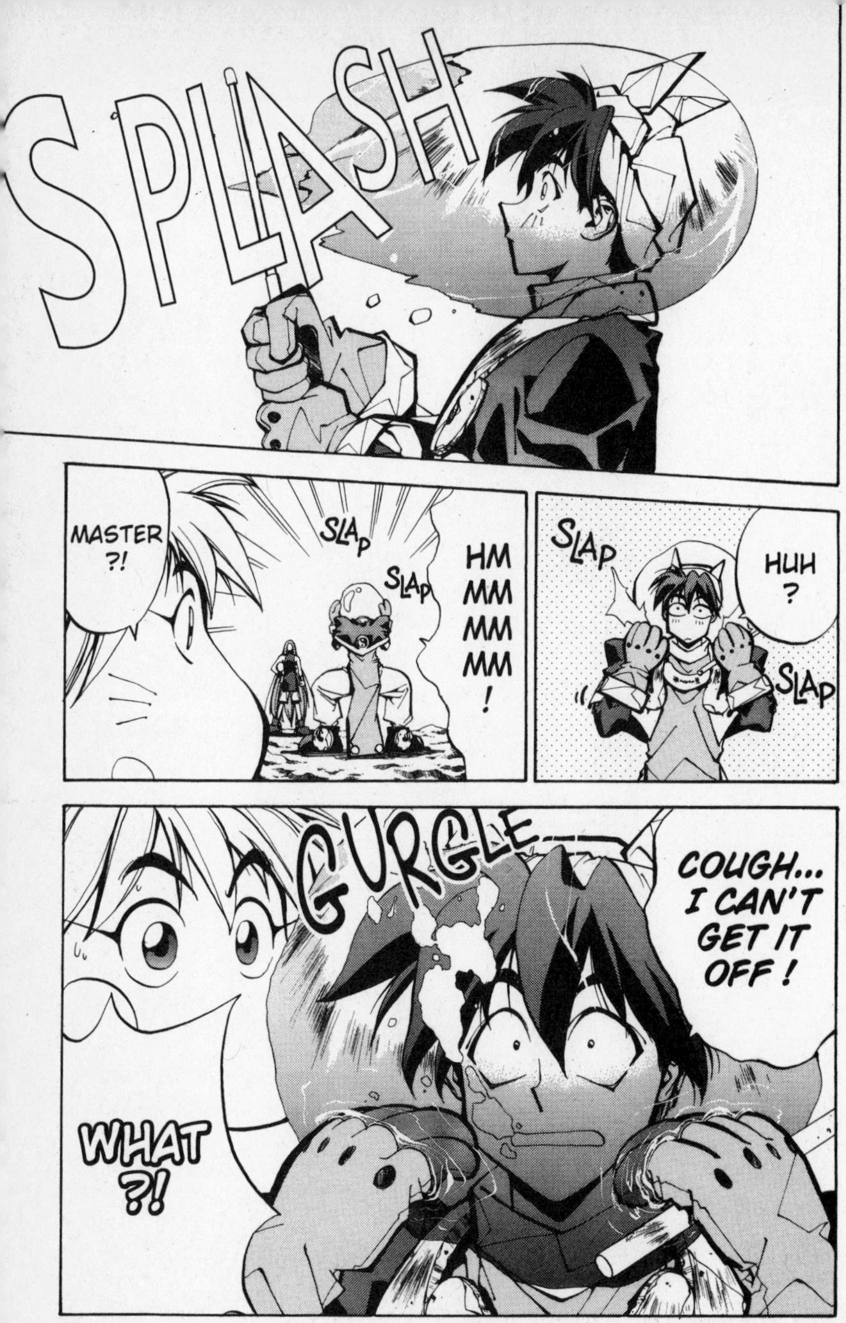
SPLASH
SLAP
HUH?
SLAP
HMMMMMMMM!
SLAP
SLAP
MASTER?!
COUGH... I CAN'T GET IT OFF!
GURGLE
WHAT?!

封神演義

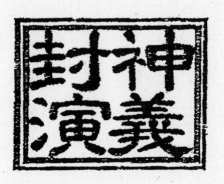

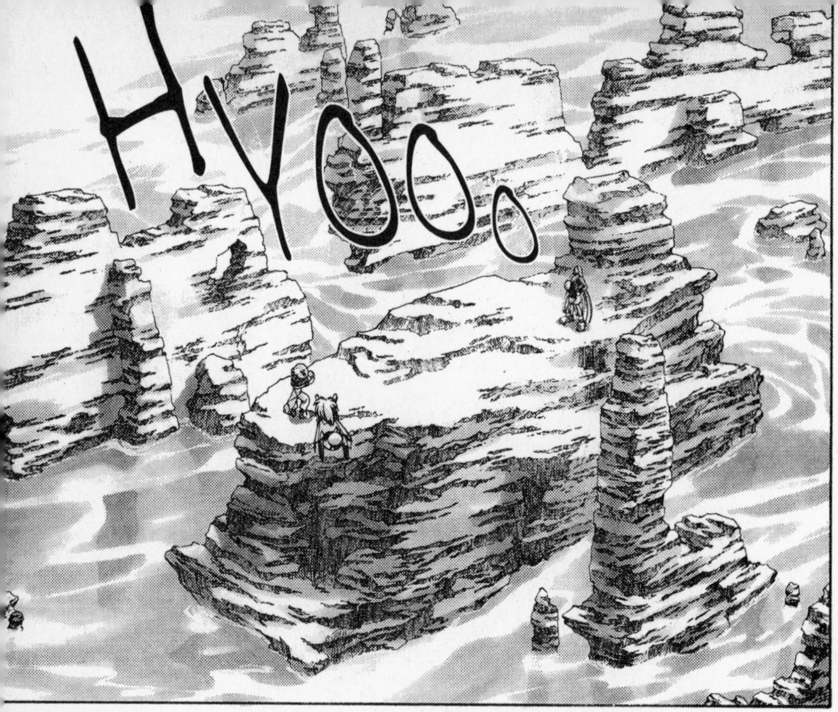
HYOOO

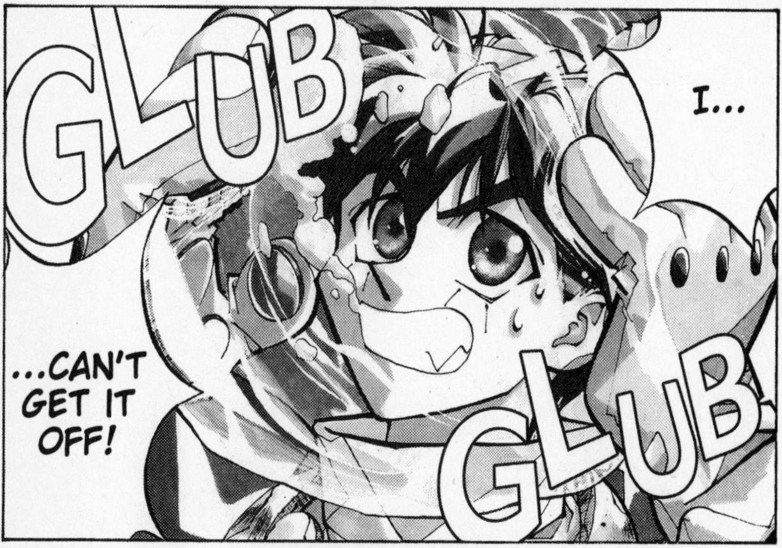
I...
GLUB
...CAN'T GET IT OFF!
GLUB

CHAPTER 38 :
THE SHISEI OF KURYU ISLAND, PART 3
THE DRINKING MATCH

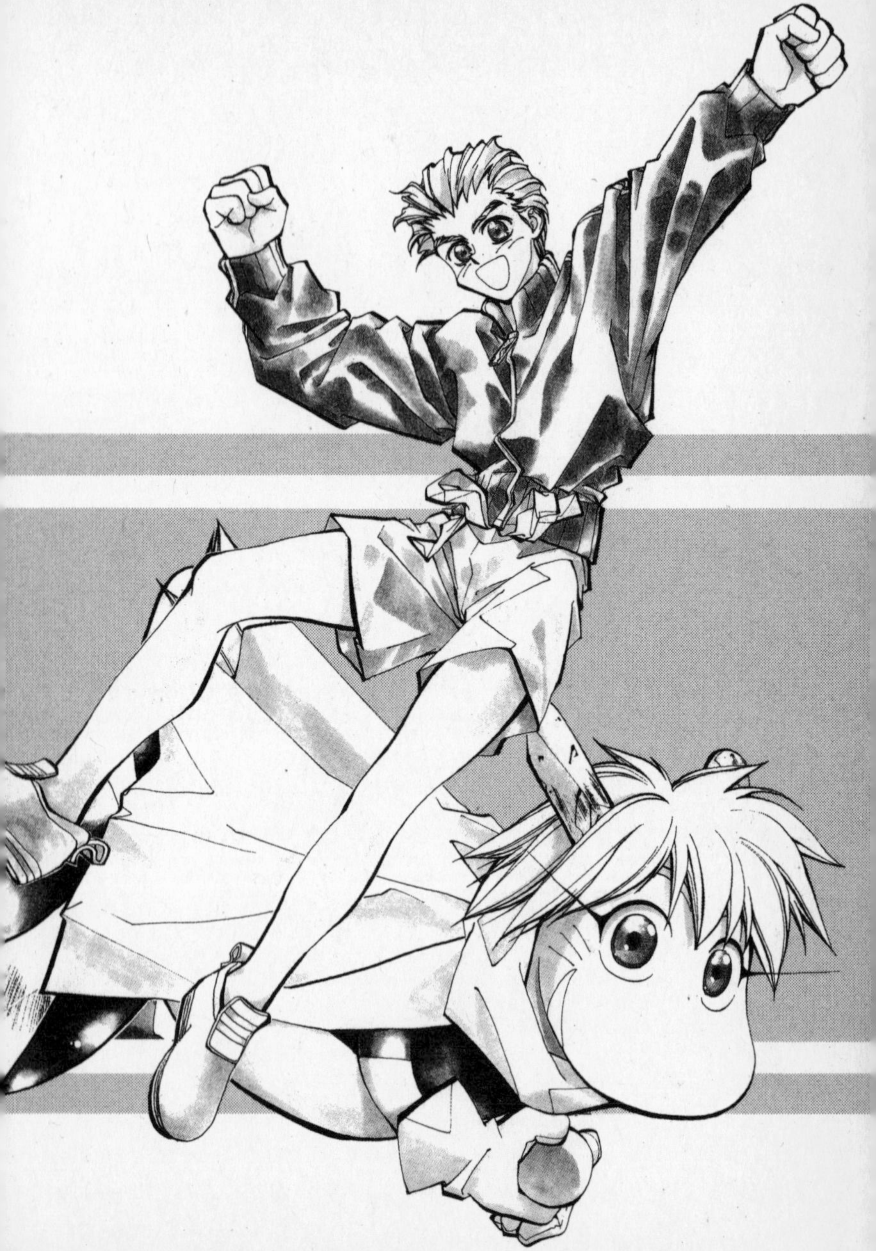

Chapter 38

THE SHISEI OF KURYU ISLAND, PART 3 THE DRINKING MATCH

YOU DON'T HAVE TO READ IT, BUT SINCE THERE'S AN EXTRA PAGE:

HACK WRITING III

△ I KNOW CIGARETTES ARE BAD FOR MY HEALTH, BUT I CAN'T STOP SMOKING.

△ I SAY THAT BECAUSE I QUIT SMOKING ONCE, AND I DIDN'T DO TOO WELL AFTER THAT.

△ I HAD NO HEALTH PROBLEMS. BUT MAYBE BECAUSE MY BRAIN CELLS INCREASED TOO MUCH, I THOUGHT ABOUT THINGS TOO DEEPLY. AND THAT INFLUENCED MY MANGA. I CRAMMED TOO MANY SERIOUS THEMES INTO ONE MANGA, AND I SPENT FOUR MONTHS ON THE STORYBOARDS FOR A ONE-SHOT MANGA. THIS WASN'T GOOD.

△ I STARTED SMOKING 1-MG CIGARETTES AGAIN. THEN I GOT MY STORYBOARDS DONE IN NO TIME. STRANGE.

△ YOU'RE PROBABLY THINKING "THAT'S THE EXCUSE OF A NICOTINE ADDICT!" BUT TO ME, IT'S NOT AN EXCUSE. THAT WAS THE WAY *IT WAS*, SO I CAN'T HELP IT.

△ SO I CONTINUE TO SMOKE LOTS OF CIGARETTES. THIS IS WHY I APPLAUDED WHEN PRIME MINISTER HASHIMOTO SAID "I WON'T QUIT SMOKING!!"

△ BY THE WAY, I STARTED SMOKING ON MY 20TH BIRTHDAY (REALLY).

△ THERE WERE RUMORS THAT YOU'LL STOP GROWING TALLER IF YOU TAKE IN POISON BY SMOKING DURING YOUR GROWTH PERIOD. I HAD THE IMAGE THAT INSTEAD OF BECOMING AN "ADULT" WHEN YOU'RE 20, YOU TURN INTO A "POISONED HUMAN."

△ TO EVERYBODY— SMOKE AFTER YOU'VE TURNED 20. UNTIL THEN, DRINK MILK FOR YOUR HEIGHT.

END OF HACK WRITING

READ THIS WAY

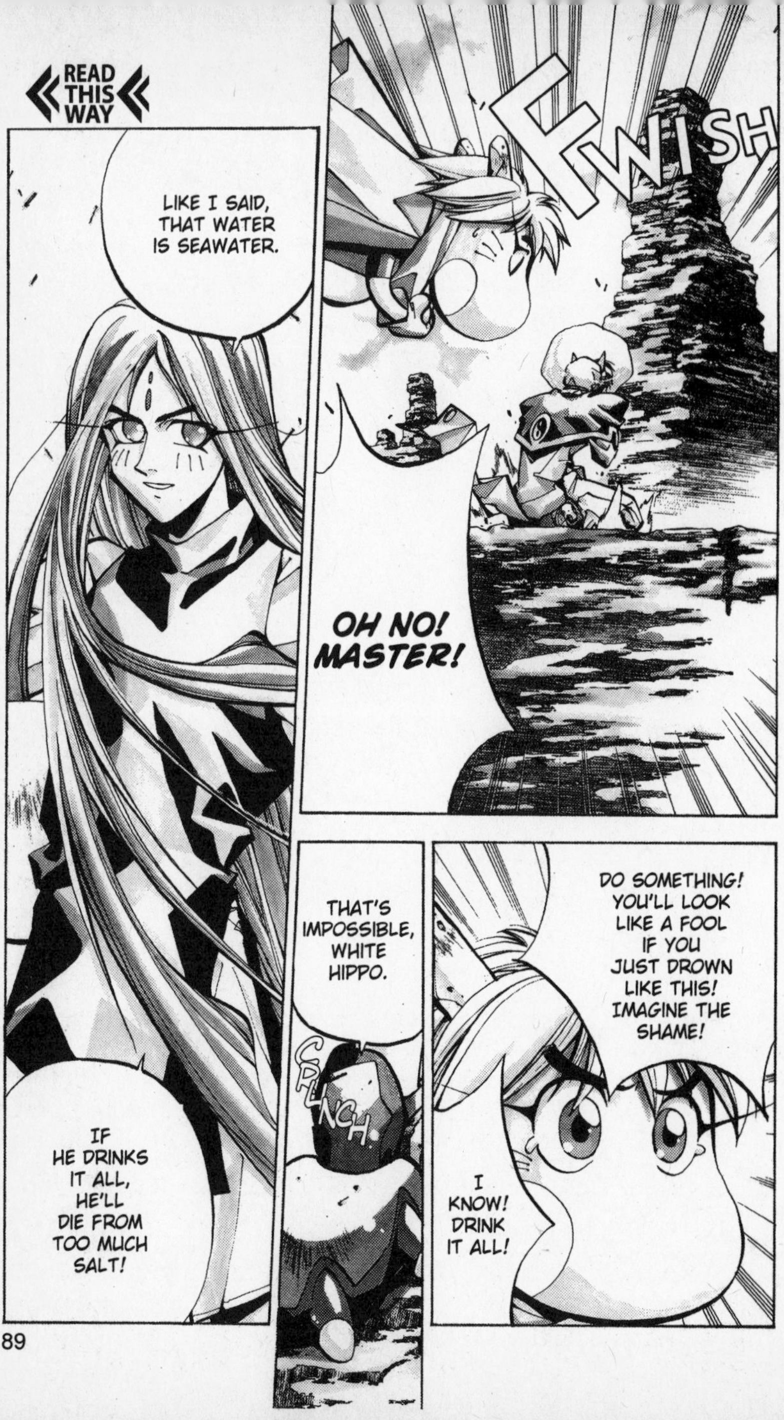

FWISH
OH NO! MASTER!
DO SOMETHING! YOU'LL LOOK LIKE A FOOL IF YOU JUST DROWN LIKE THIS! IMAGINE THE SHAME!
I KNOW! DRINK IT ALL!
THAT'S IMPOSSIBLE, WHITE HIPPO.
CPLUNCH
LIKE I SAID, THAT WATER IS SEAWATER.
IF HE DRINKS IT ALL, HE'LL DIE FROM TOO MUCH SALT!

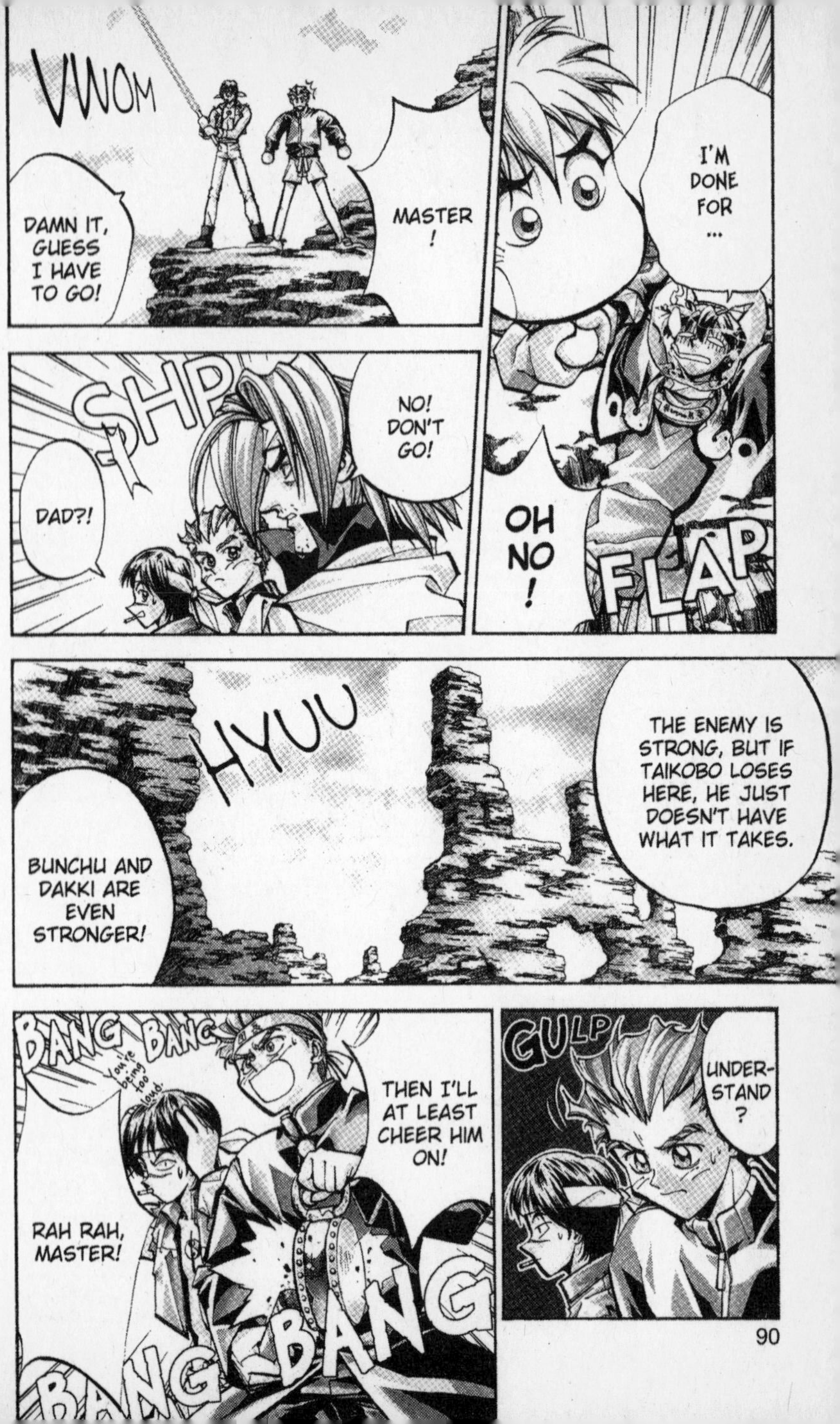
I'M DONE FOR ...
OH NO !
FLAP
MASTER !
VWOM
DAMN IT, GUESS I HAVE TO GO!
NO! DON'T GO!
SHP
DAD?!
THE ENEMY IS STRONG, BUT IF TAIKOBO LOSES HERE, HE JUST DOESN'T HAVE WHAT IT TAKES.
HYUU
BUNCHU AND DAKKI ARE EVEN STRONGER!
GULP
UNDERSTAND ?
THEN I'LL AT LEAST CHEER HIM ON!
BANG BANG
You're being too loud.
RAH RAH, MASTER!
BANG BANG

READ THIS WAY

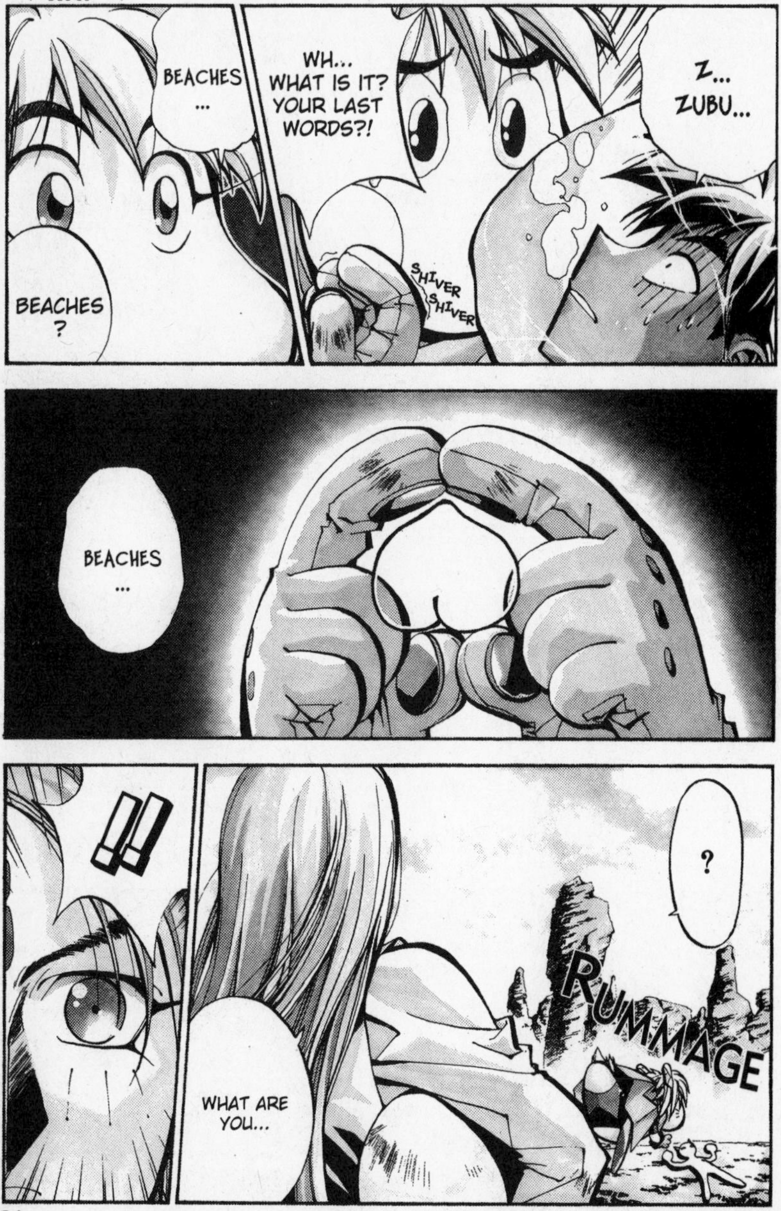

Z... ZUBU...
WH... WHAT IS IT? YOUR LAST WORDS?!
SHIVER SHIVER
BEACHES ...
BEACHES ?
BEACHES ...
?
RUMMAGE
WHAT ARE YOU...
!!

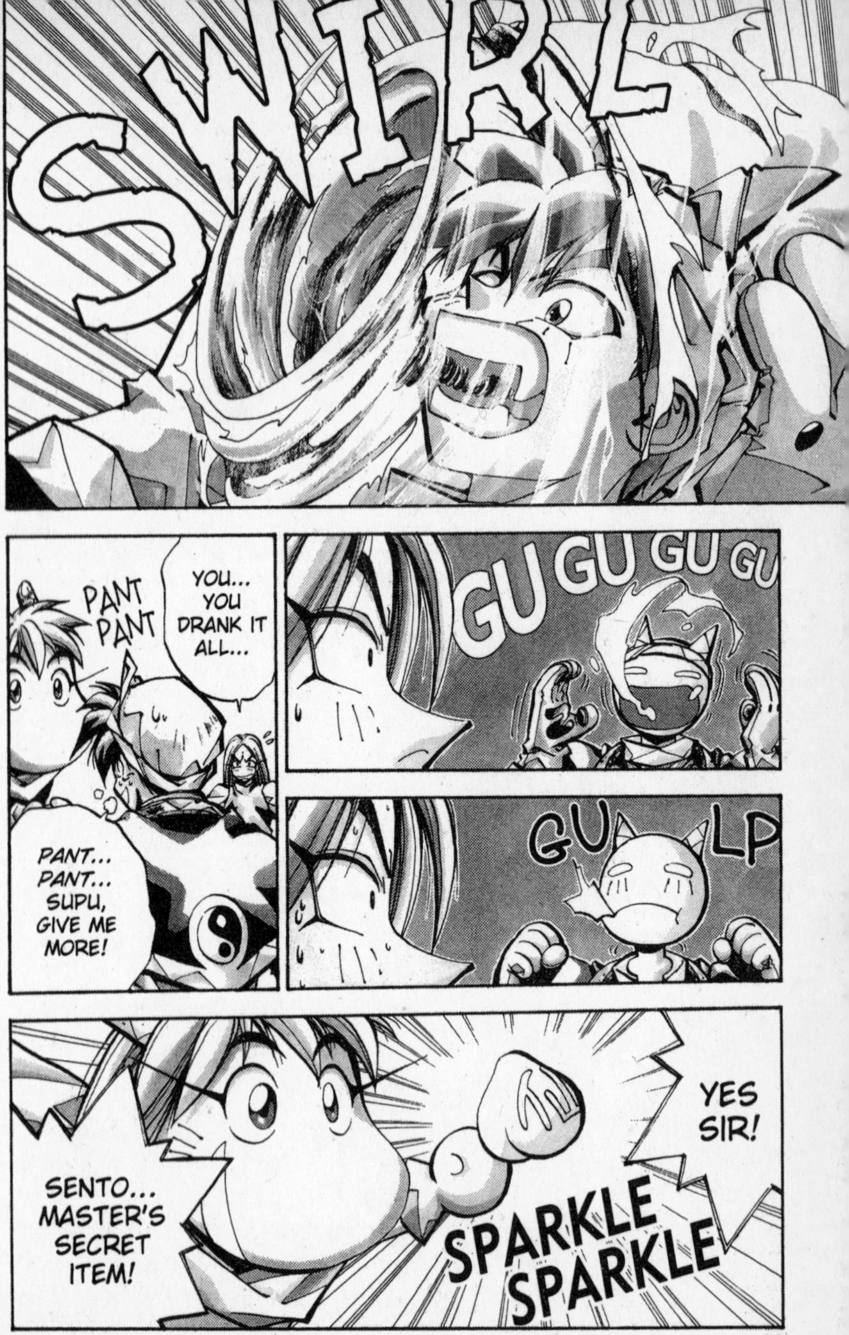
SWIRL
GU GU GU GU
GULP
YOU... YOU DRANK IT ALL...
PANT PANT
PANT... PANT... SUPU, GIVE ME MORE!
YES SIR!
SPARKLE SPARKLE
SENTO... MASTER'S SECRET ITEM!

READ THIS WAY

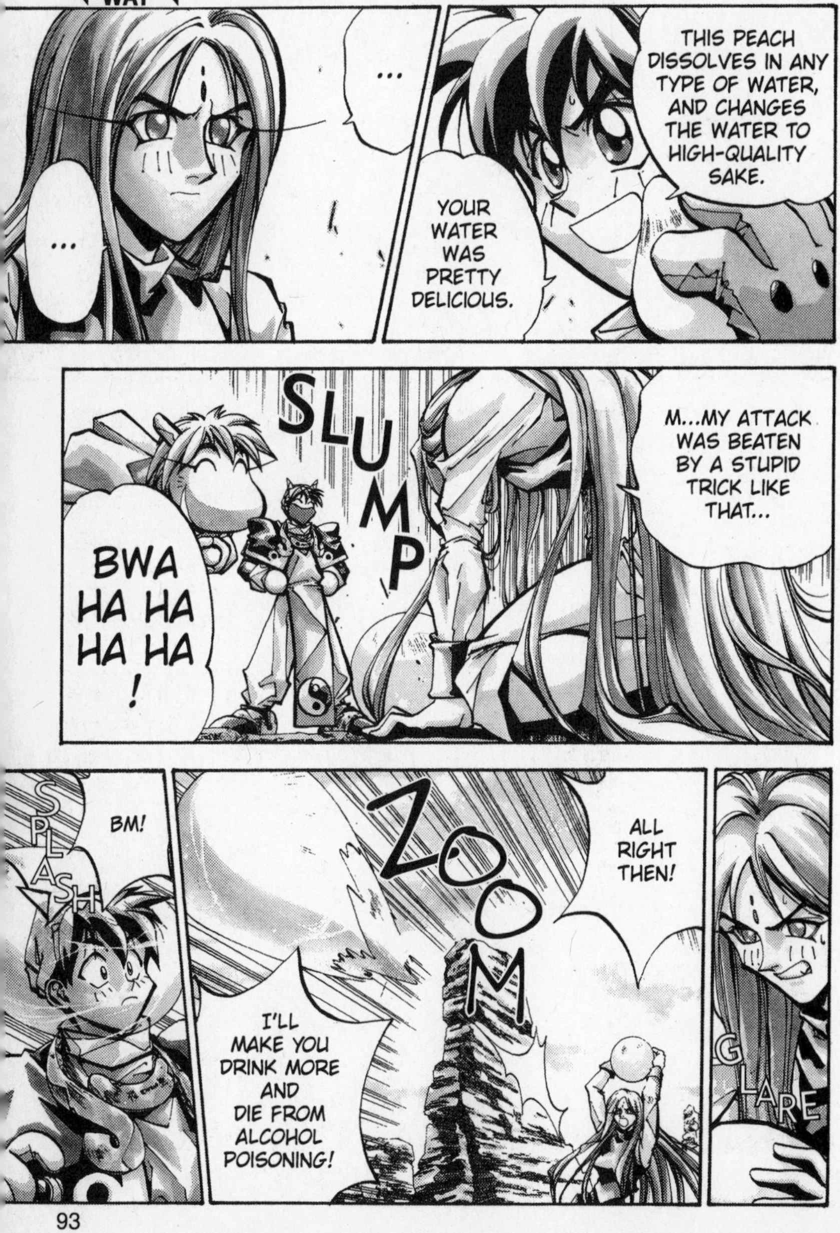
THIS PEACH DISSOLVES IN ANY TYPE OF WATER, AND CHANGES THE WATER TO HIGH-QUALITY SAKE.
YOUR WATER WAS PRETTY DELICIOUS.
...
...
M...MY ATTACK WAS BEATEN BY A STUPID TRICK LIKE THAT...
SLUMP
BWA HA HA HA HA!
GLARE
ALL RIGHT THEN!
ZOOM
I'LL MAKE YOU DRINK MORE AND DIE FROM ALCOHOL POISONING!
BM!
SPLASH

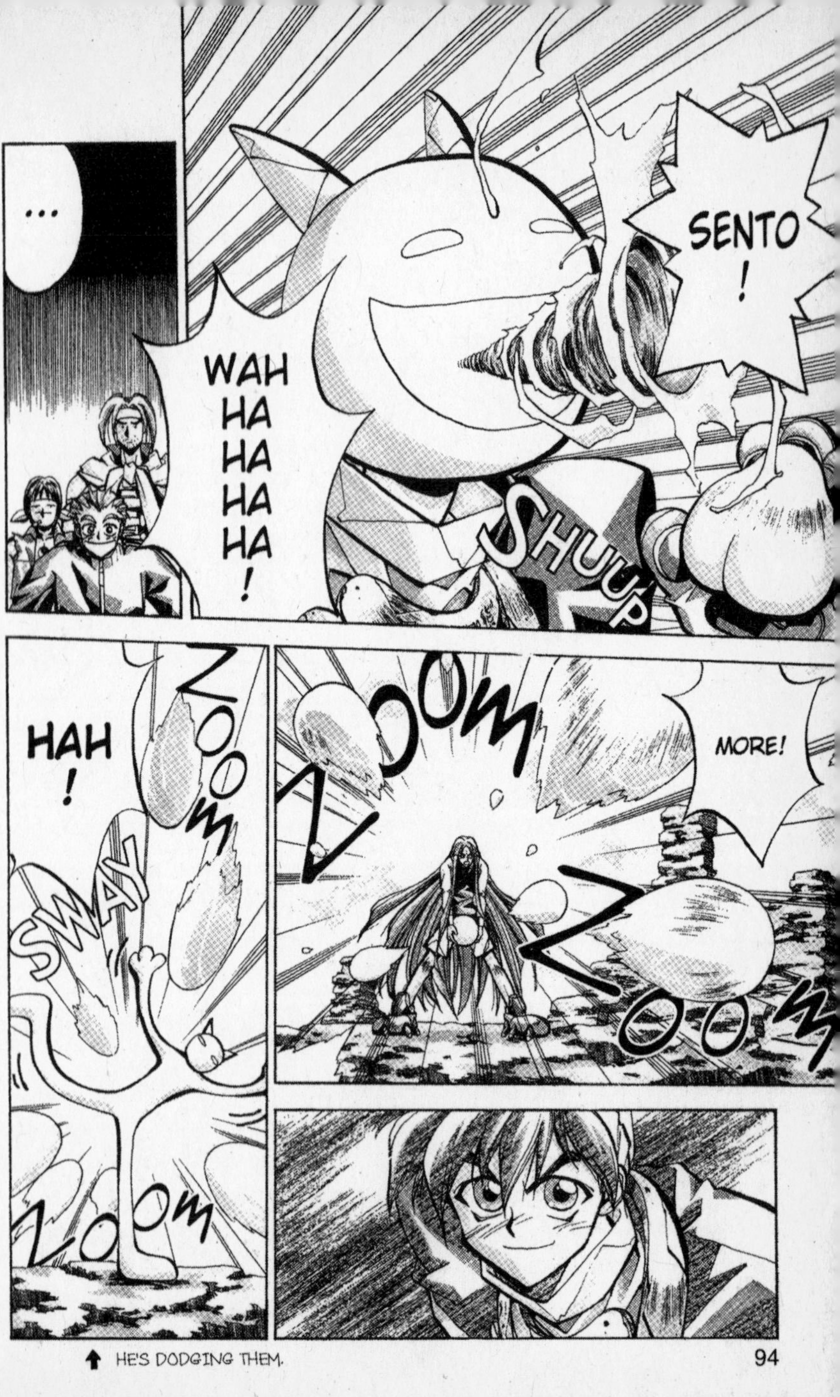
SENTO!
WAH HA HA HA HA!
SHUUP
...
MORE!
ZOOM
ZOOM
HAH!
ZOOM
SWAY
ZOOM

↑ HE'S DODGING THEM.

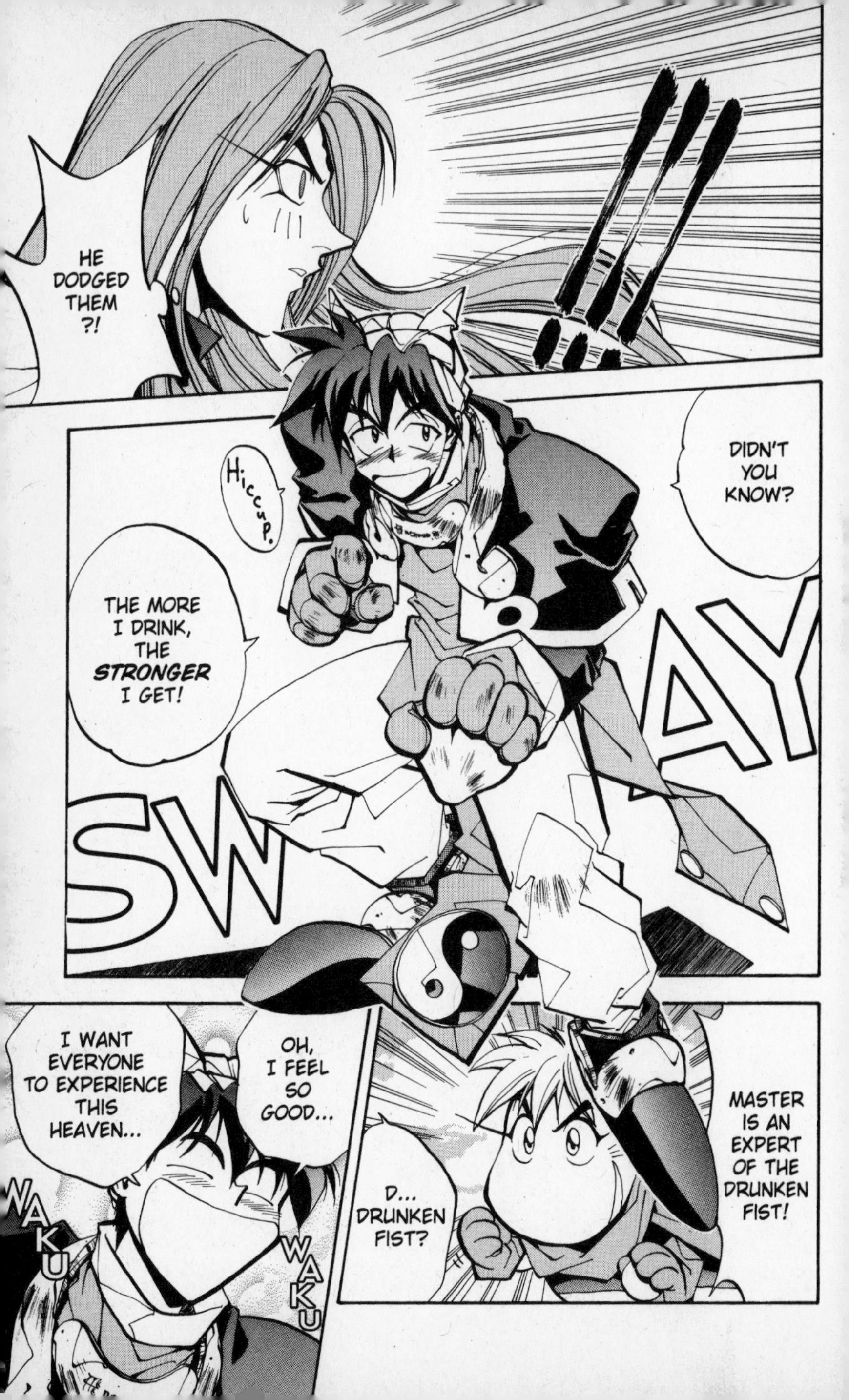
HE DODGED THEM ?!
DIDN'T YOU KNOW?
Hiccup.
THE MORE I DRINK, THE STRONGER I GET!
SWAY
MASTER IS AN EXPERT OF THE DRUNKEN FIST!
D... DRUNKEN FIST?
OH, I FEEL SO GOOD...
I WANT EVERYONE TO EXPERIENCE THIS HEAVEN...
WAKU
WAKU

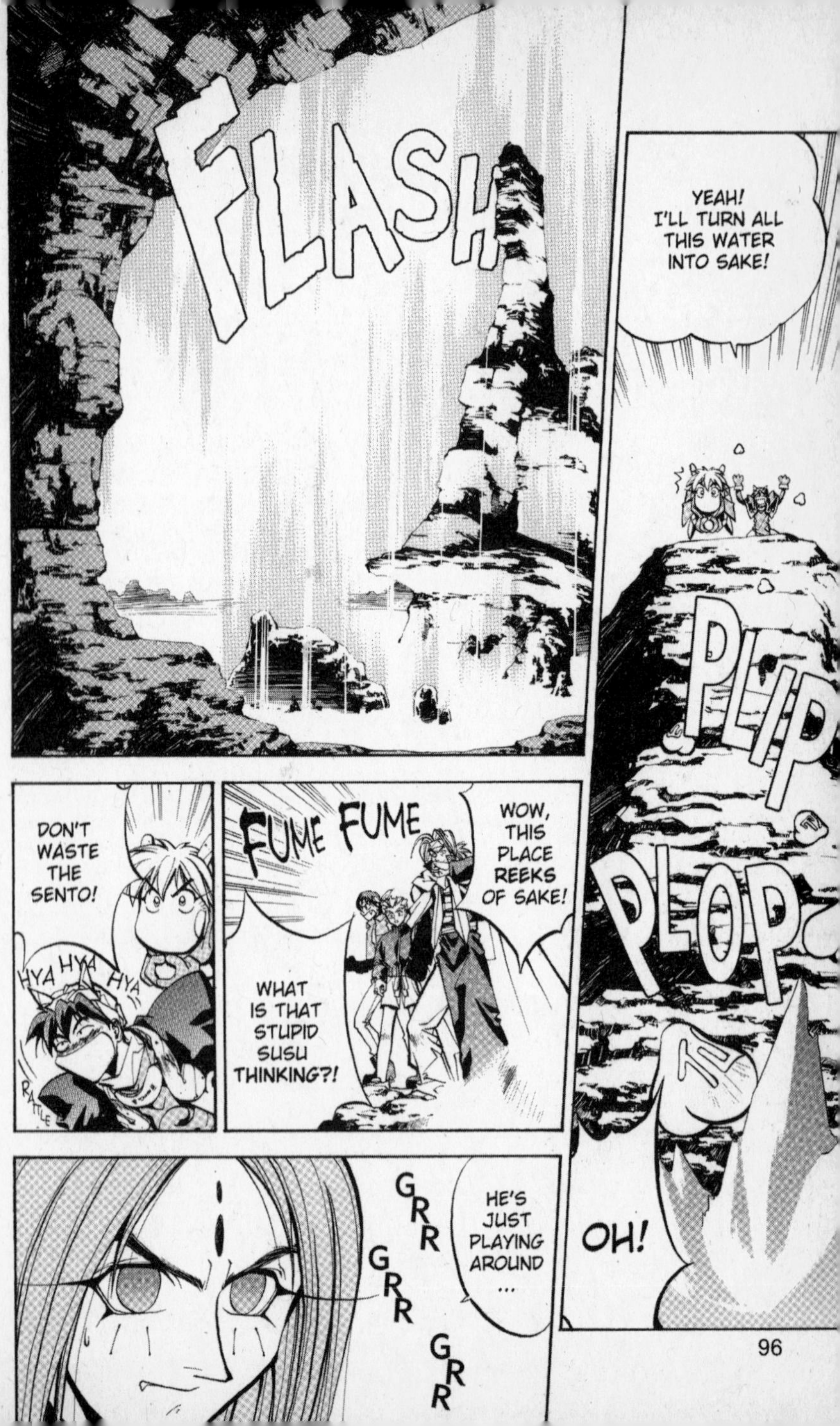
YEAH! I'LL TURN ALL THIS WATER INTO SAKE!
PLIP
PLOP
OH!
FLASH
WOW, THIS PLACE REEKS OF SAKE!
FUME FUME
WHAT IS THAT STUPID SUSU THINKING?!
DON'T WASTE THE SENTO!
HYA HYA HYA
RATTLE
HE'S JUST PLAYING AROUND ...
GRR GRR GRR

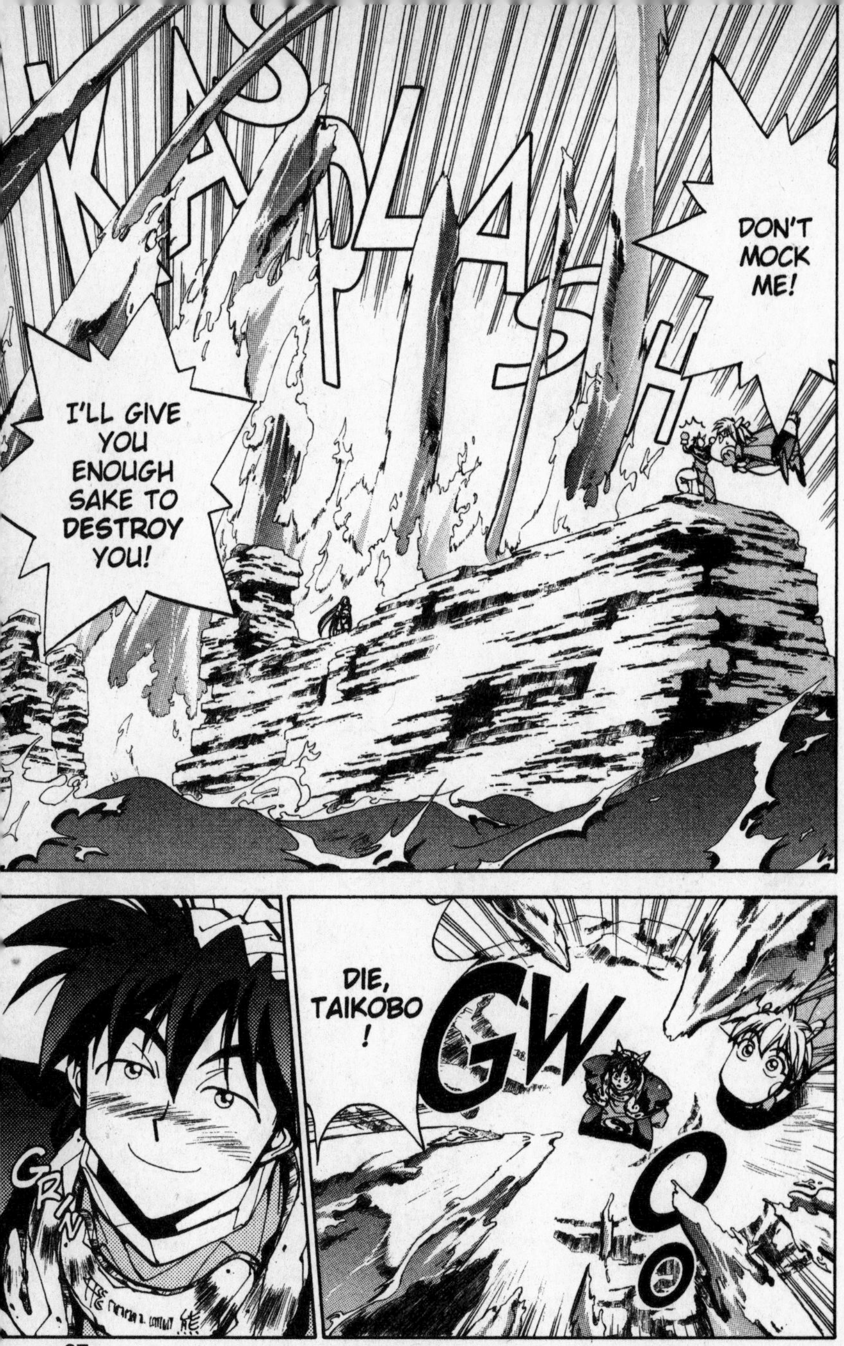
KASPLASH
DON'T MOCK ME!
I'LL GIVE YOU ENOUGH SAKE TO DESTROY YOU!
DIE, TAIKOBO!
GRIN

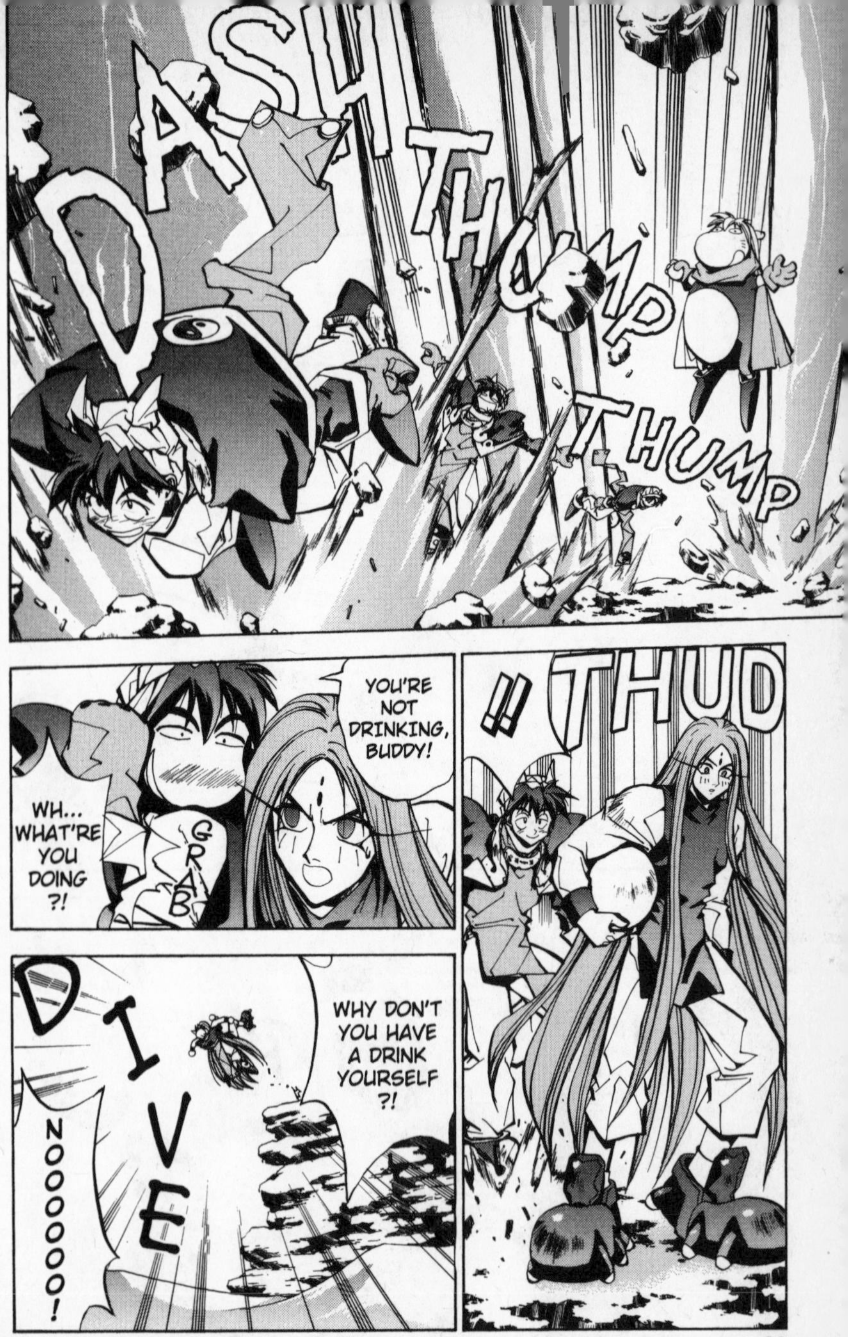
DASH
THUMP
THUMP
!!
THUD
YOU'RE NOT DRINKING, BUDDY!
WH... WHAT'RE YOU DOING ?!
GRAB
WHY DON'T YOU HAVE A DRINK YOURSELF ?!
DIVE
NOOOOOOO!

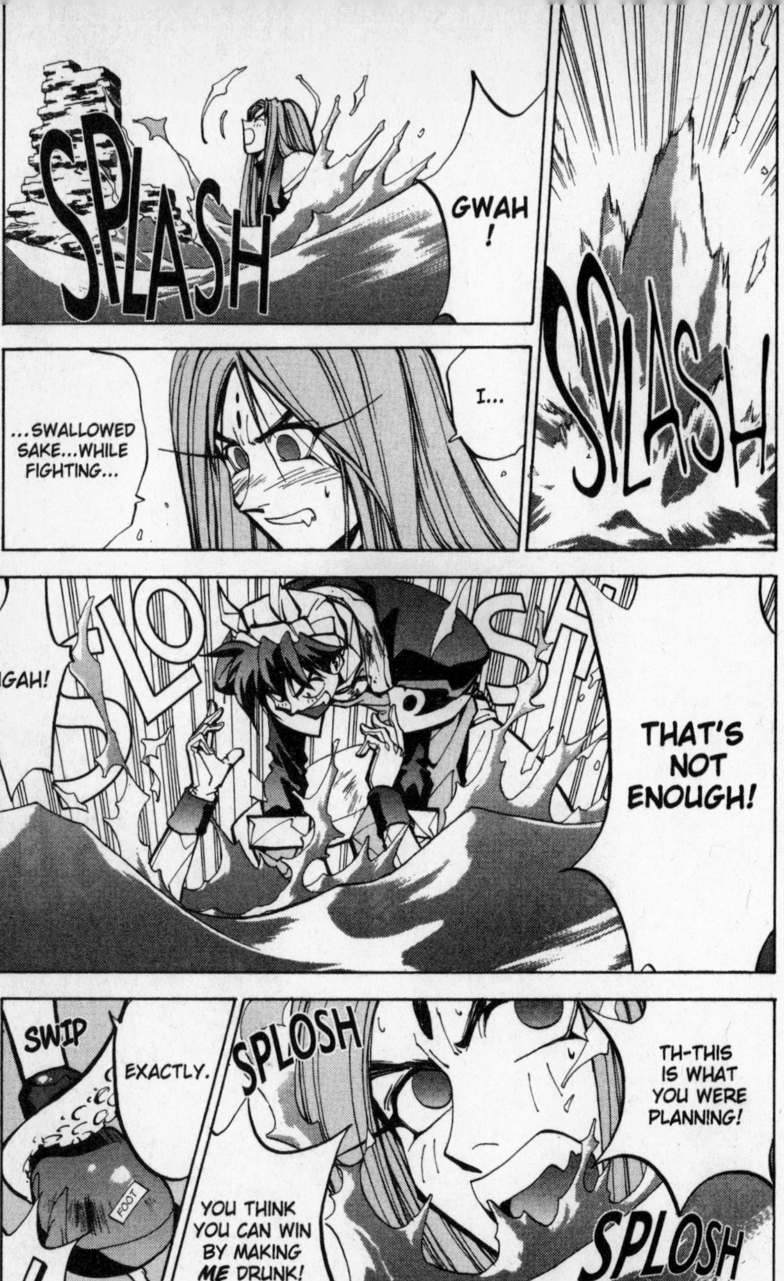
SPLASH
GWAH!
SPLASH
I...
...SWALLOWED SAKE...WHILE FIGHTING...
THAT'S NOT ENOUGH!
UGAH!
TH-THIS IS WHAT YOU WERE PLANNING!
SPLOSH
SPLOSH
YOU THINK YOU CAN WIN BY MAKING *ME* DRUNK!
SWIP
EXACTLY.
FOOT
!
SWIP

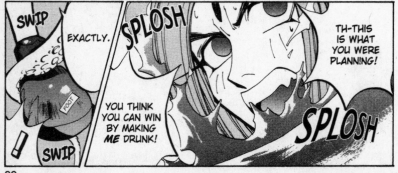

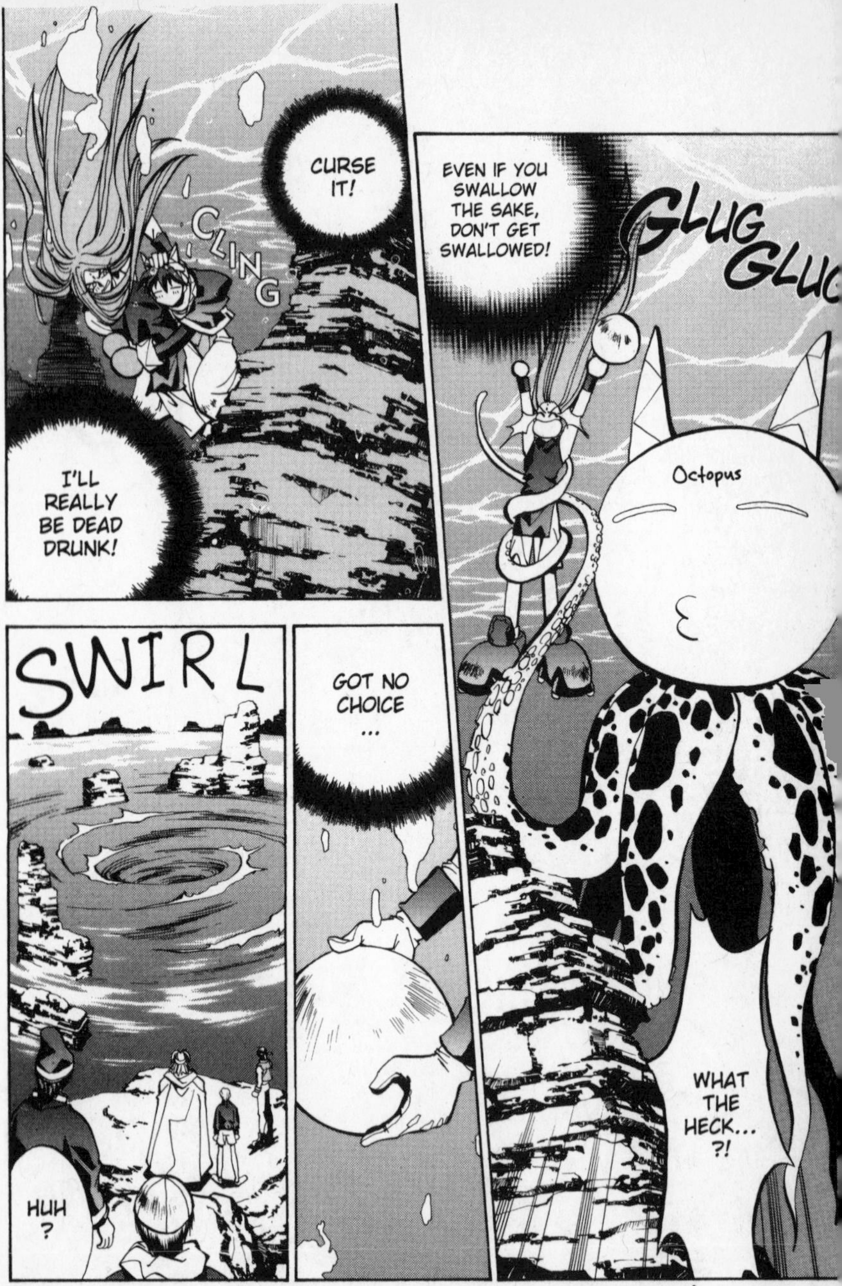
CURSE IT!
CLING
I'LL REALLY BE DEAD DRUNK!
EVEN IF YOU SWALLOW THE SAKE, DON'T GET SWALLOWED!
GLUG GLUC
Octopus
WHAT THE HECK... ?!
GOT NO CHOICE ...
SWIRL
HUH ?

READ THIS WAY

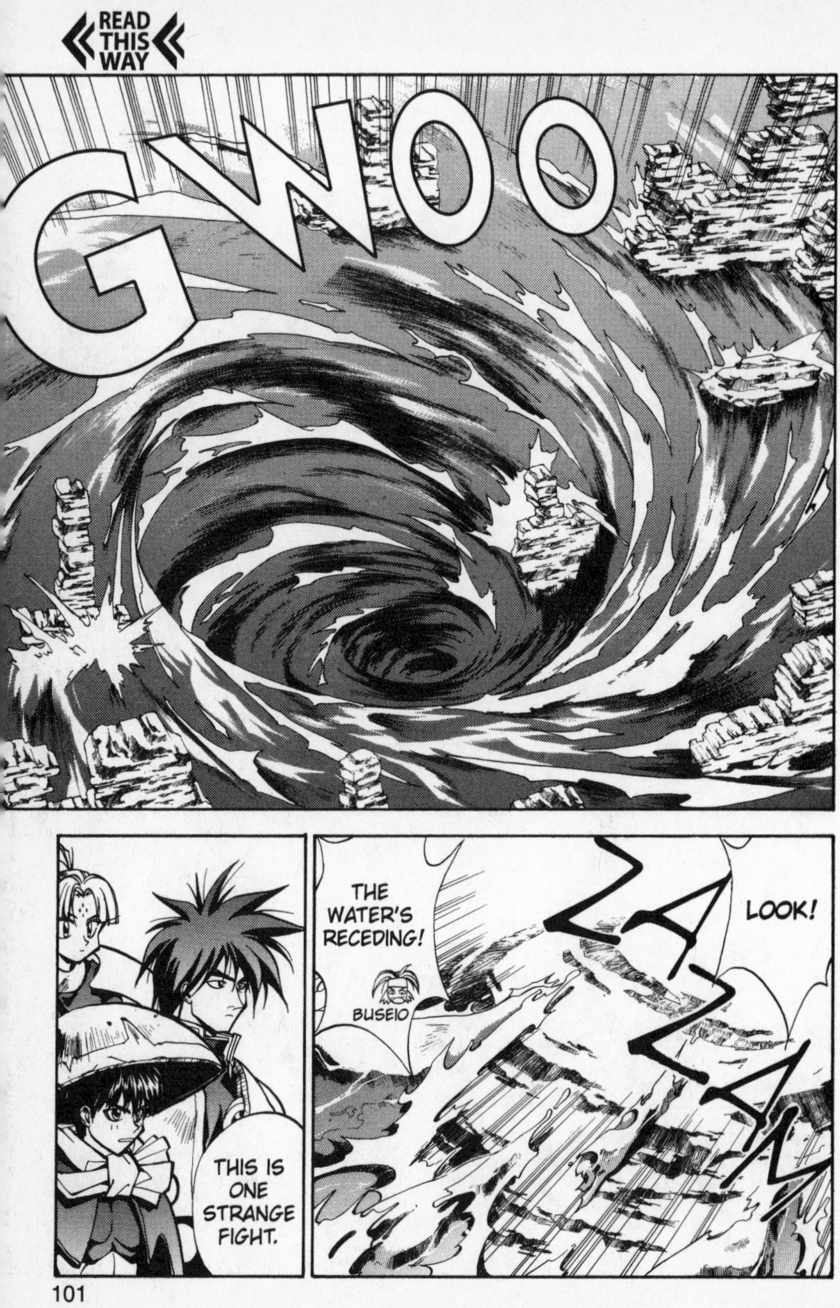
GWOO
LOOK!
THE WATER'S RECEDING!
BUSEIO
ZAZAM
THIS IS ONE STRANGE FIGHT.

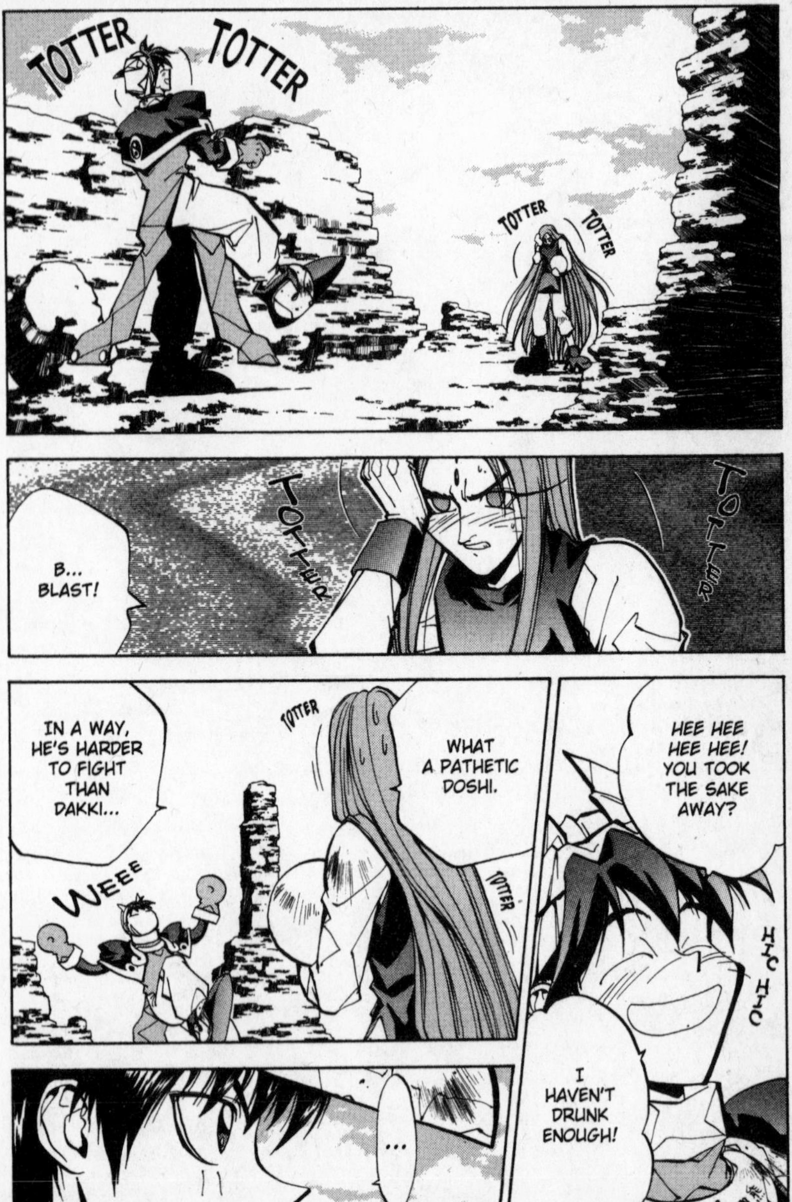
TOTTER
TOTTER
TOTTER
TOTTER
TOTTER
TOTTER
B...
BLAST!
HEE HEE
HEE HEE!
YOU TOOK
THE SAKE
AWAY?
HIC HIC
I
HAVEN'T
DRUNK
ENOUGH!
WHAT
A PATHETIC
DOSHI.
TOTTER
TOTTER
IN A WAY,
HE'S HARDER
TO FIGHT
THAN
DAKKI...
WEEE
...

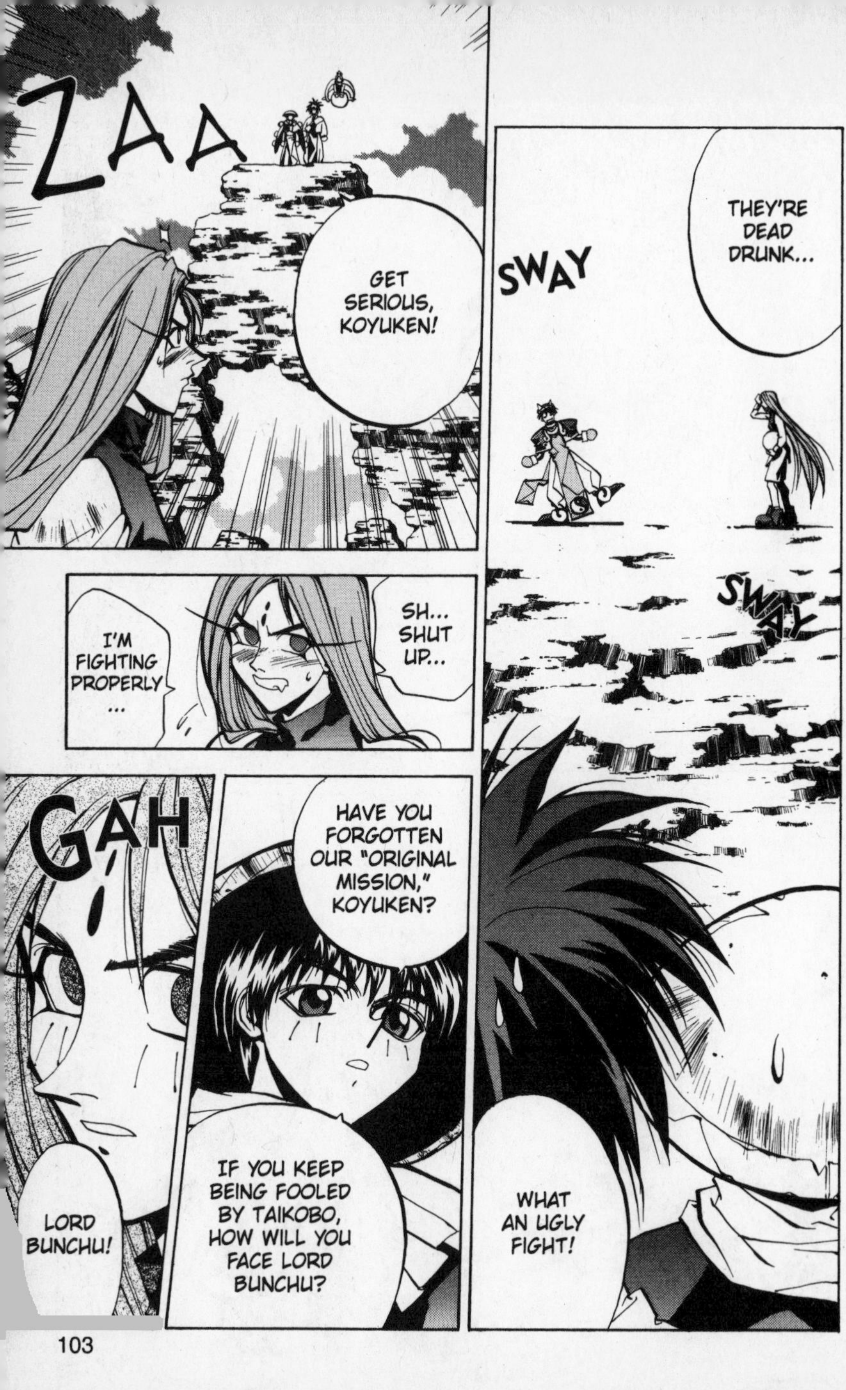
THEY'RE DEAD DRUNK...
SWAY
SWAY
WHAT AN UGLY FIGHT!
ZAA
GET SERIOUS, KOYUKEN!
SH... SHUT UP...
I'M FIGHTING PROPERLY...
HAVE YOU FORGOTTEN OUR "ORIGINAL MISSION," KOYUKEN?
IF YOU KEEP BEING FOOLED BY TAIKOBO, HOW WILL YOU FACE LORD BUNCHU?
GAH
LORD BUNCHU!

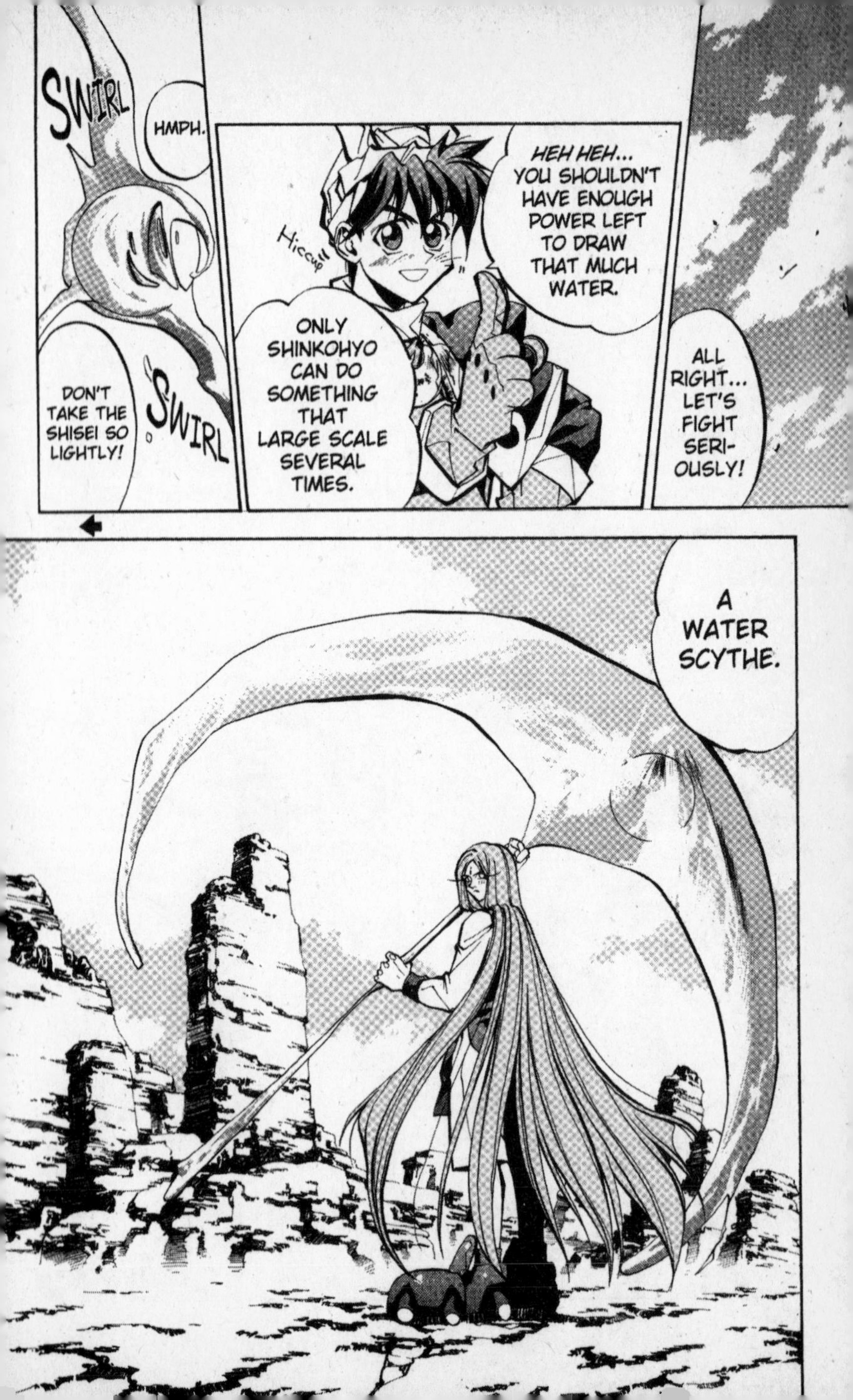
ALL RIGHT... LET'S FIGHT SERIOUSLY!
HEH HEH... YOU SHOULDN'T HAVE ENOUGH POWER LEFT TO DRAW THAT MUCH WATER.
Hiccup
ONLY SHINKOHYO CAN DO SOMETHING THAT LARGE SCALE SEVERAL TIMES.
SWIRL
HMPH.
DON'T TAKE THE SHISEI SO LIGHTLY!
SWIRL
A WATER SCYTHE.

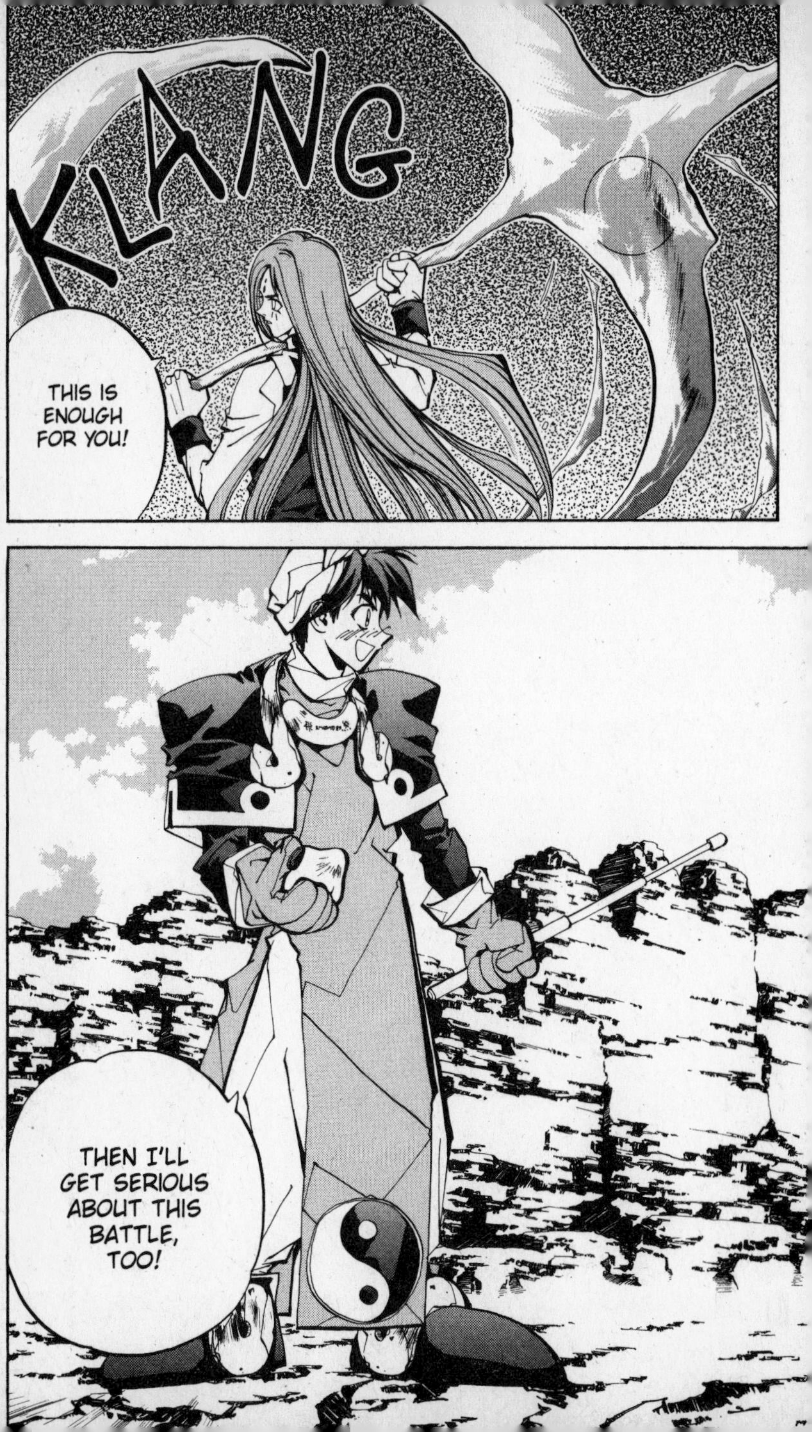
KLANG
THIS IS ENOUGH FOR YOU!
THEN I'LL GET SERIOUS ABOUT THIS BATTLE, TOO!

封神演義

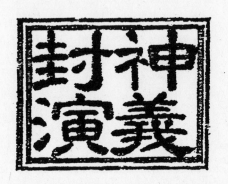

CHAPTER 39 :
THE SHISEI OF KURYU ISLAND, PART 4
THE SHISEI GO TO SEIKI

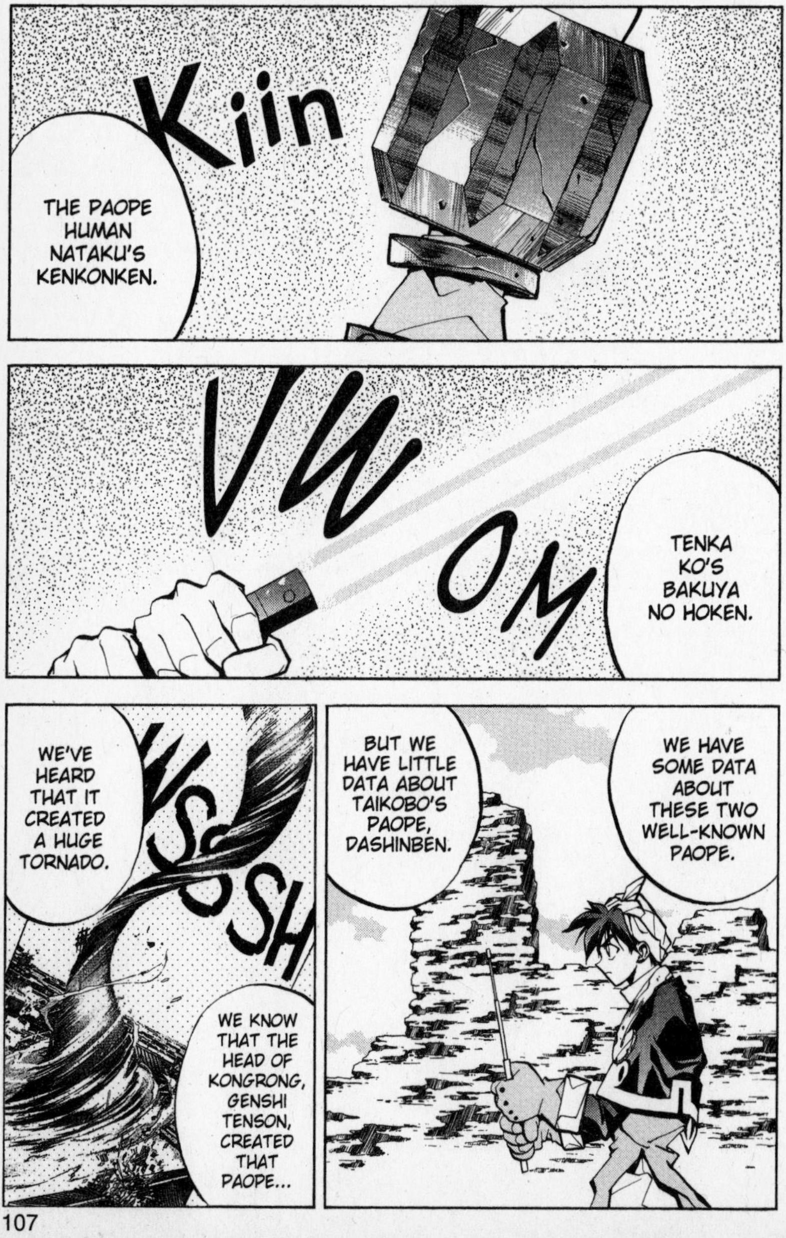
Kiin
THE PAOPE HUMAN NATAKU'S KENKONKEN.
VWOM
TENKA KO'S BAKUYA NO HOKEN.
WE HAVE SOME DATA ABOUT THESE TWO WELL-KNOWN PAOPE.
BUT WE HAVE LITTLE DATA ABOUT TAIKOBO'S PAOPE, DASHINBEN.
WE'VE HEARD THAT IT CREATED A HUGE TORNADO.
WSSSH
WE KNOW THAT THE HEAD OF KONGRONG, GENSHI TENSON, CREATED THAT PAOPE...

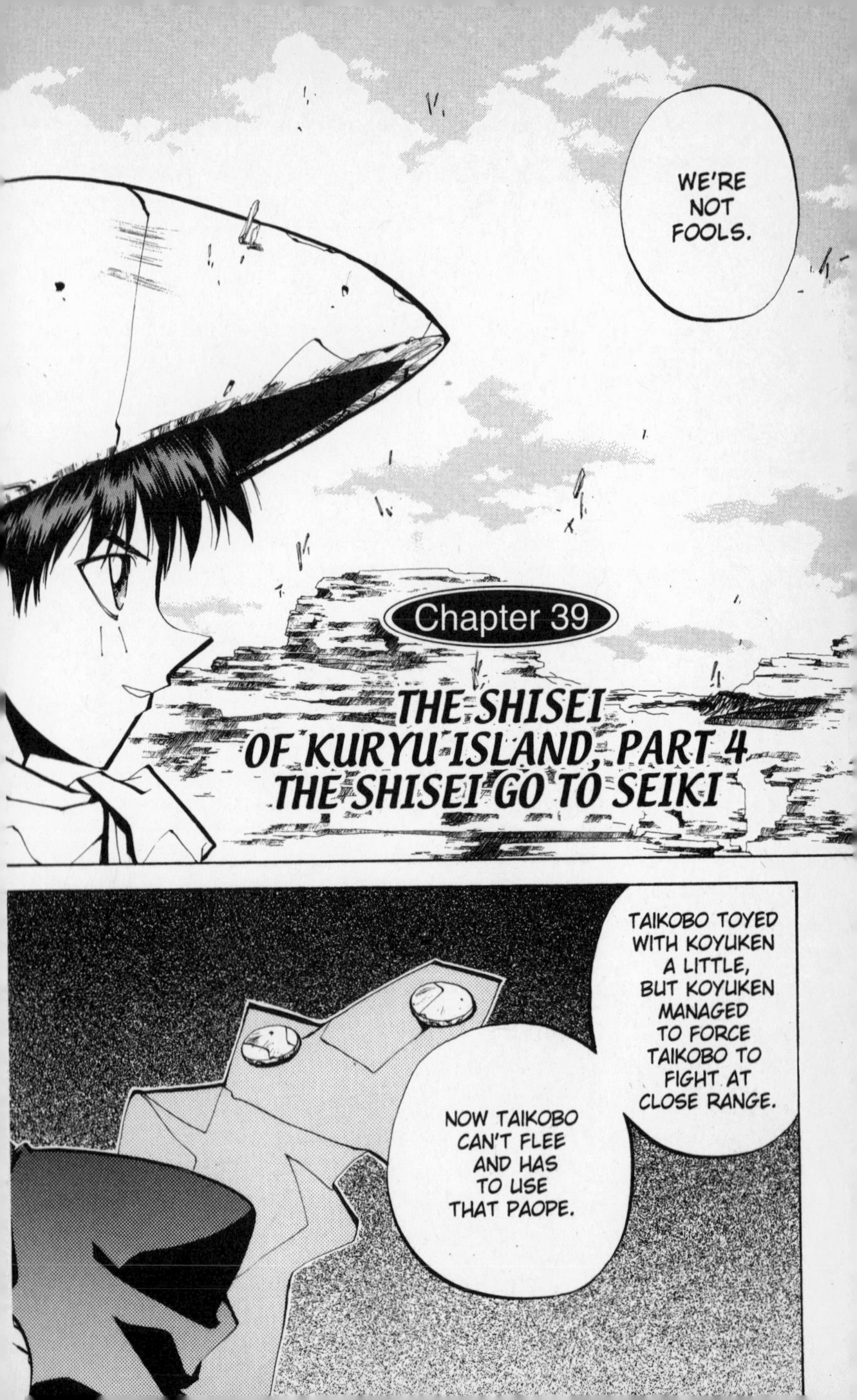
WE'RE NOT FOOLS.
Chapter 39
THE SHISEI OF KURYU ISLAND, PART 4
THE SHISEI GO TO SEIKI
TAIKOBO TOYED WITH KOYUKEN A LITTLE, BUT KOYUKEN MANAGED TO FORCE TAIKOBO TO FIGHT AT CLOSE RANGE.
NOW TAIKOBO CAN'T FLEE AND HAS TO USE THAT PAOPE.

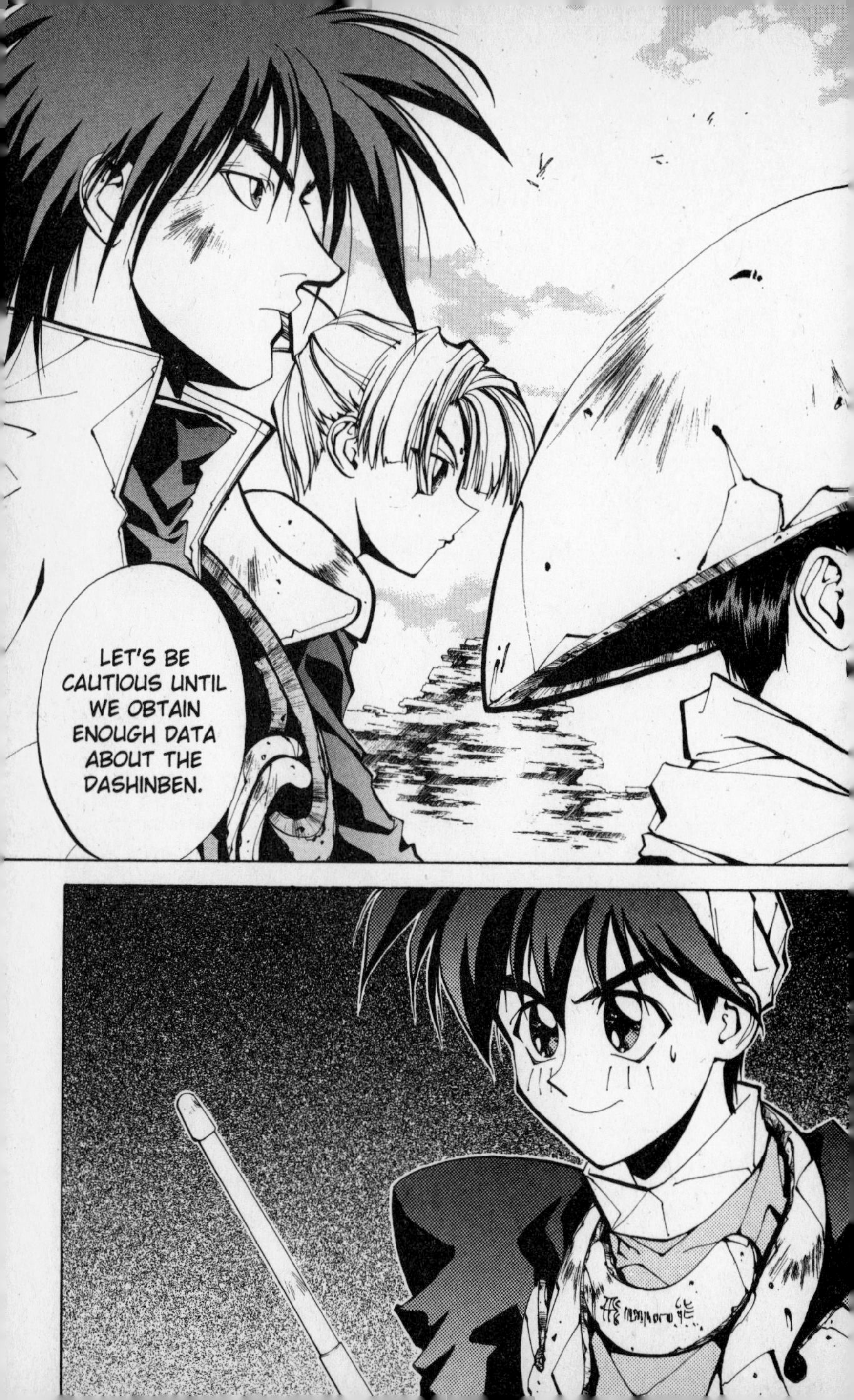
LET'S BE CAUTIOUS UNTIL WE OBTAIN ENOUGH DATA ABOUT THE DASHINBEN.

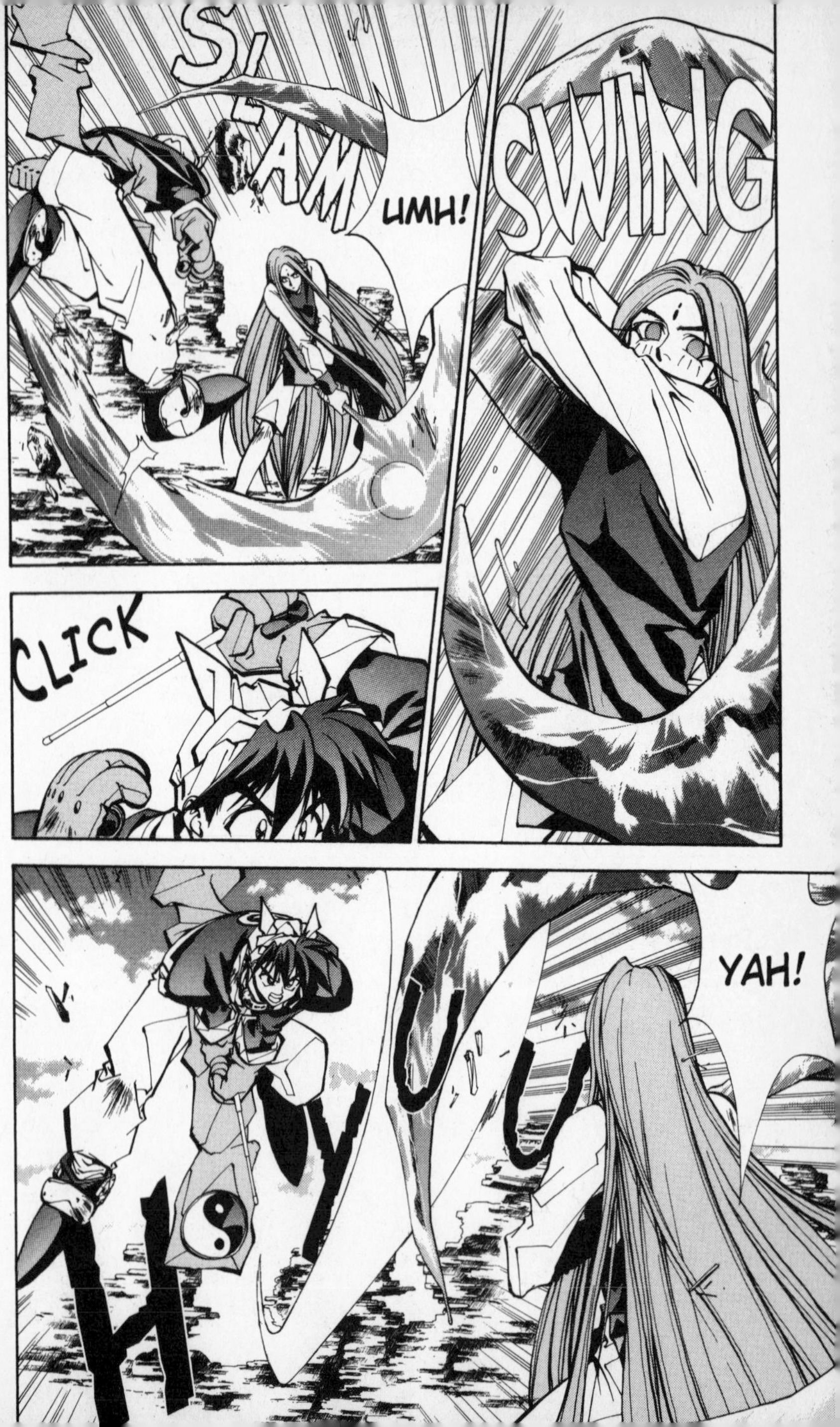
SWING
SLAM
UMH!
CLICK
YAH!
HYUUU

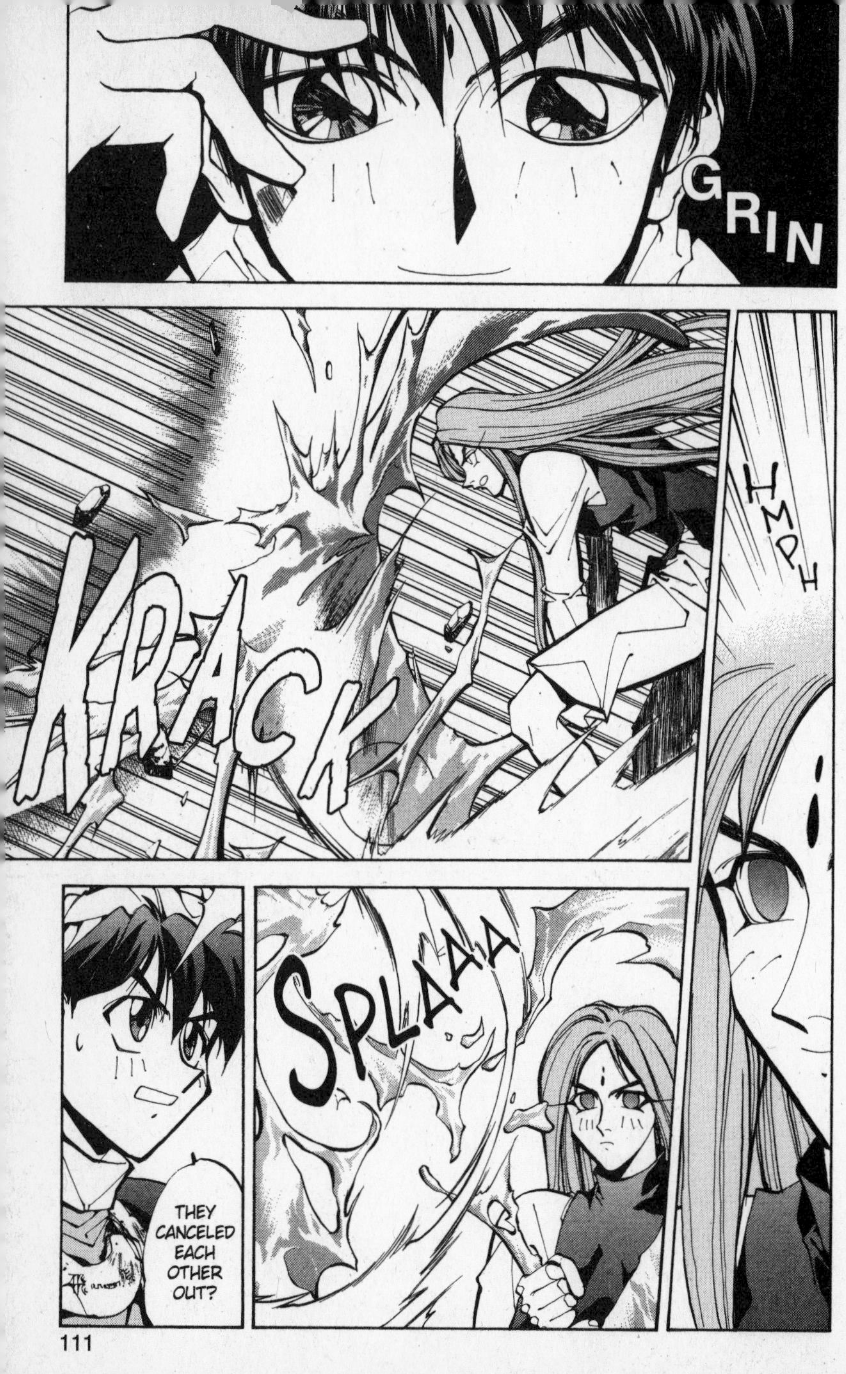
GRIN
HMPH
KRACK
SPLAAA
THEY CANCELED EACH OTHER OUT?

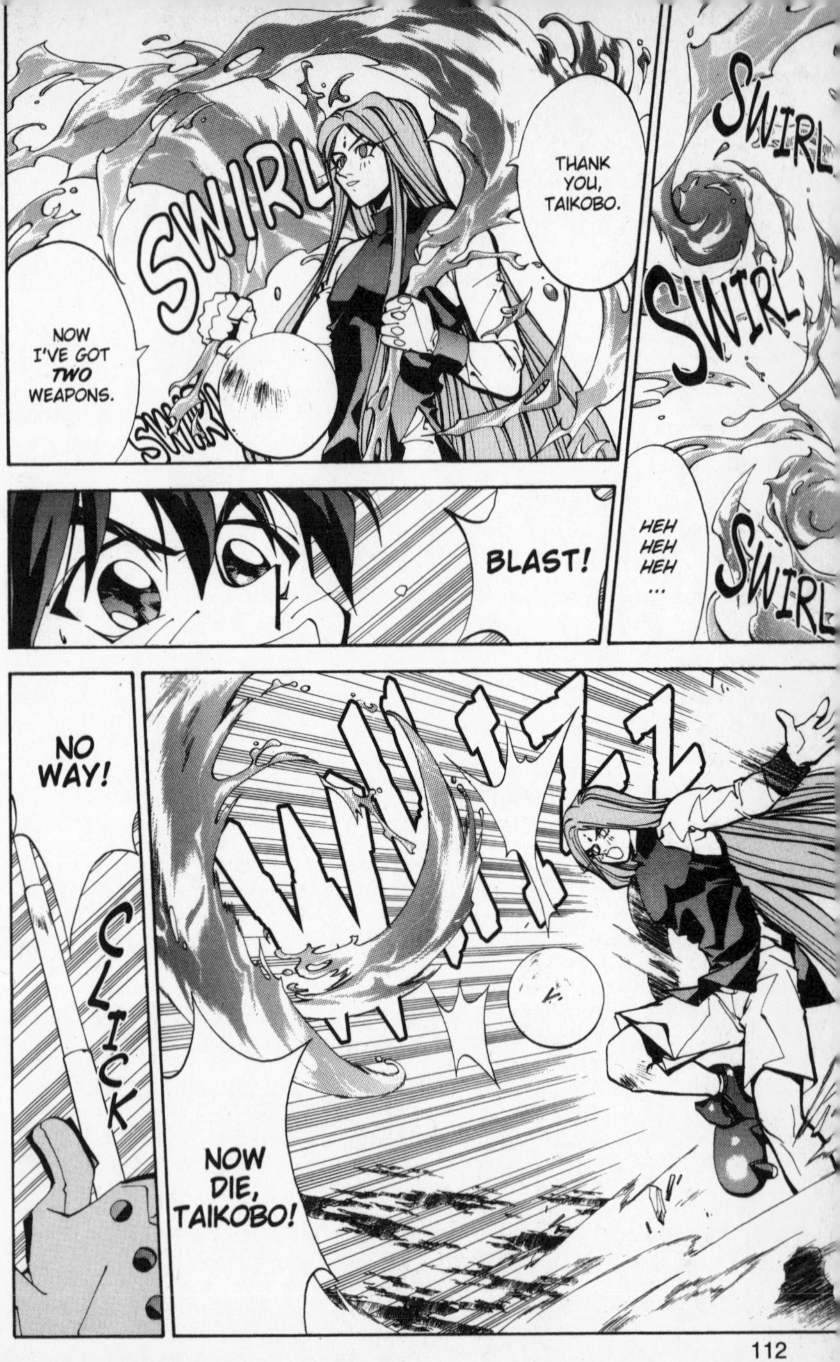
SWIRL
SWIRL
HEH HEH HEH ...
SWIRL
SWIRL
THANK YOU, TAIKOBO.
NOW I'VE GOT *TWO* WEAPONS.
BLAST!
NOW DIE, TAIKOBO!
NO WAY!
CLICK

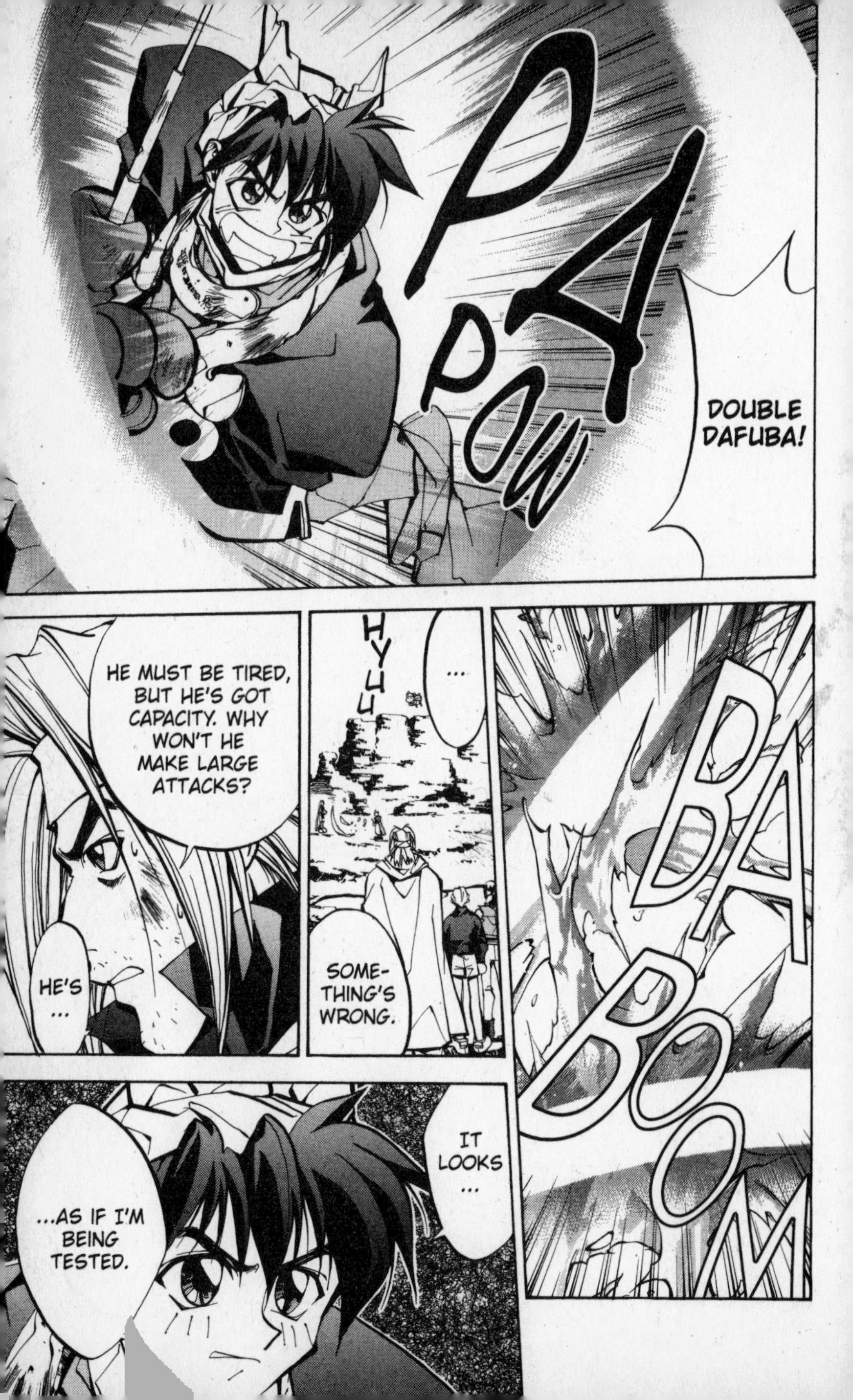
DOUBLE DAFUBA!
PA
POW
DA
BOOM
HYUU
...
SOME-THING'S WRONG.
HE MUST BE TIRED, BUT HE'S GOT CAPACITY. WHY WON'T HE MAKE LARGE ATTACKS?
HE'S ...
IT LOOKS ...
...AS IF I'M BEING TESTED.

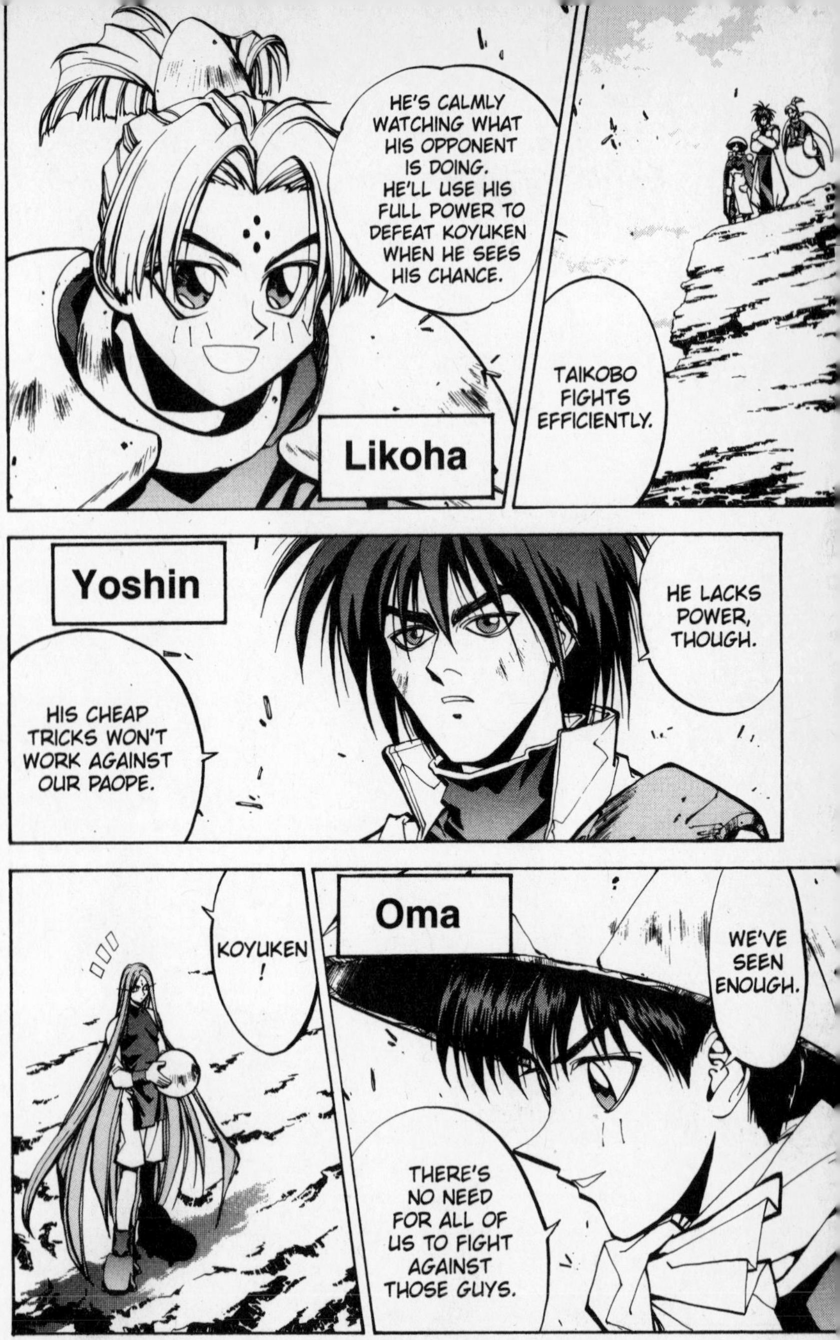
TAIKOBO FIGHTS EFFICIENTLY.
HE'S CALMLY WATCHING WHAT HIS OPPONENT IS DOING. HE'LL USE HIS FULL POWER TO DEFEAT KOYUKEN WHEN HE SEES HIS CHANCE.
Likoha
HE LACKS POWER, THOUGH.
Yoshin
HIS CHEAP TRICKS WON'T WORK AGAINST OUR PAOPE.
WE'VE SEEN ENOUGH.
Oma
THERE'S NO NEED FOR ALL OF US TO FIGHT AGAINST THOSE GUYS.
KOYUKEN!

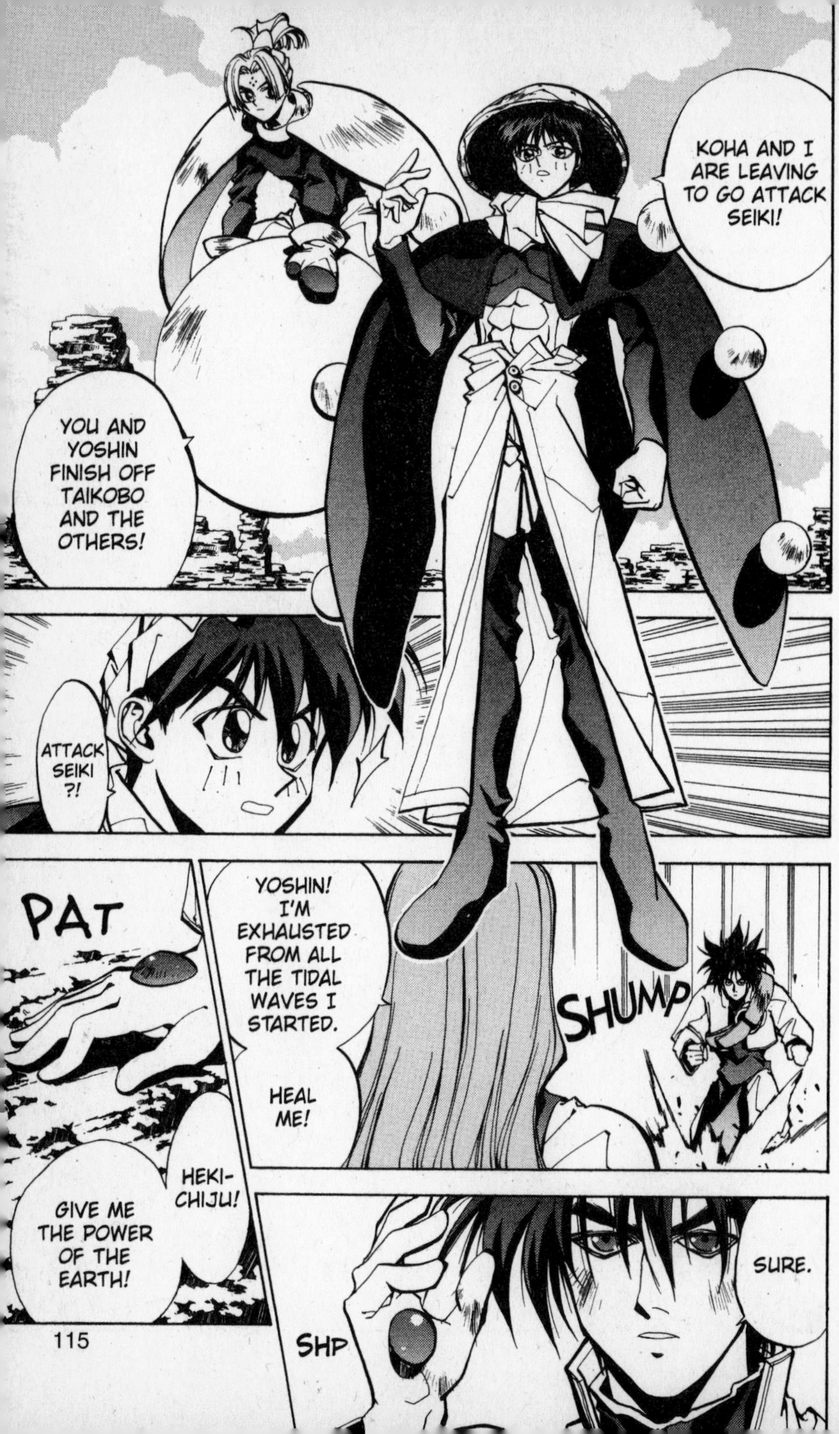

KOHA AND I ARE LEAVING TO GO ATTACK SEIKI!
YOU AND YOSHIN FINISH OFF TAIKOBO AND THE OTHERS!
ATTACK SEIKI?!
SHUMP
YOSHIN! I'M EXHAUSTED FROM ALL THE TIDAL WAVES I STARTED.
HEAL ME!
SURE.
SHP
PAT
HEKI-CHIJU!
GIVE ME THE POWER OF THE EARTH!

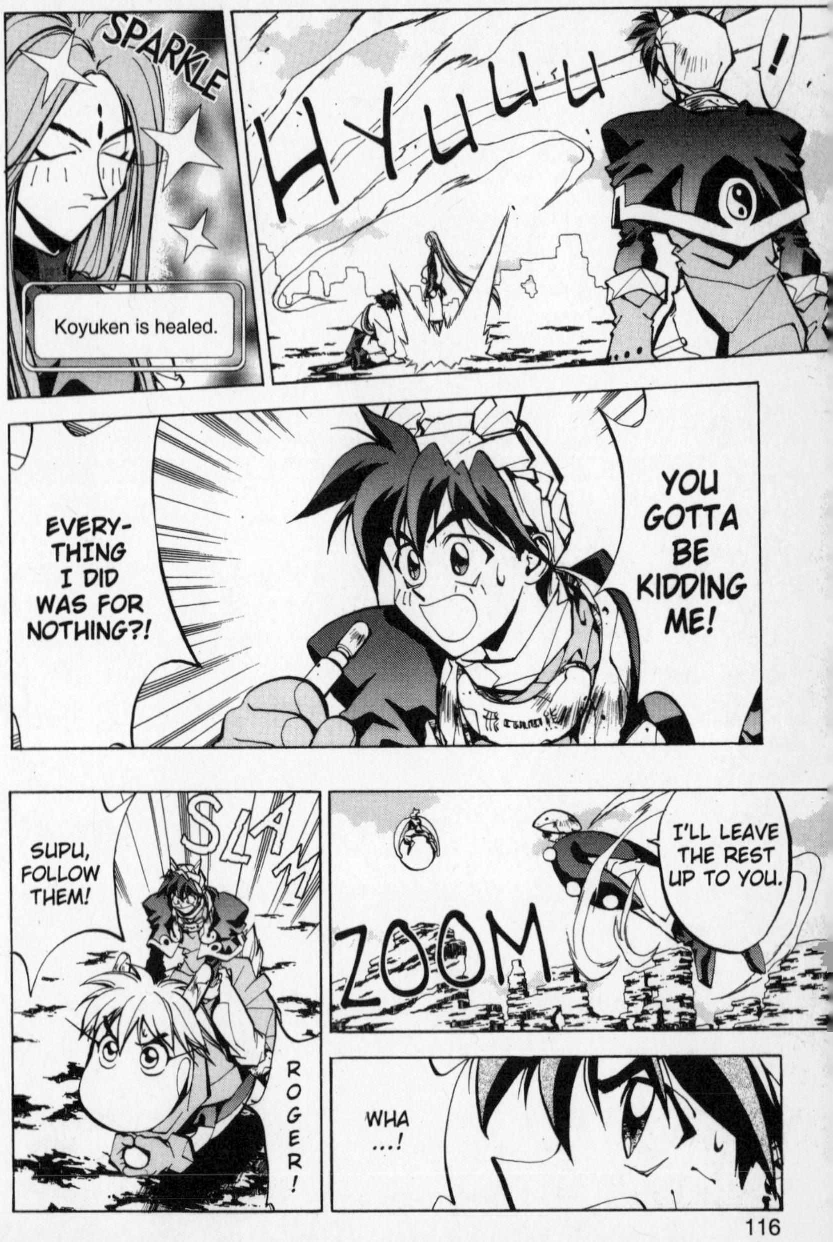
HYuuuu
!
SPARKLE
Koyuken is healed.
YOU GOTTA BE KIDDING ME!
EVERY-THING I DID WAS FOR NOTHING?!
I'LL LEAVE THE REST UP TO YOU.
ZOOM
WHA ...!
SLAM
SUPU, FOLLOW THEM!
ROGER!

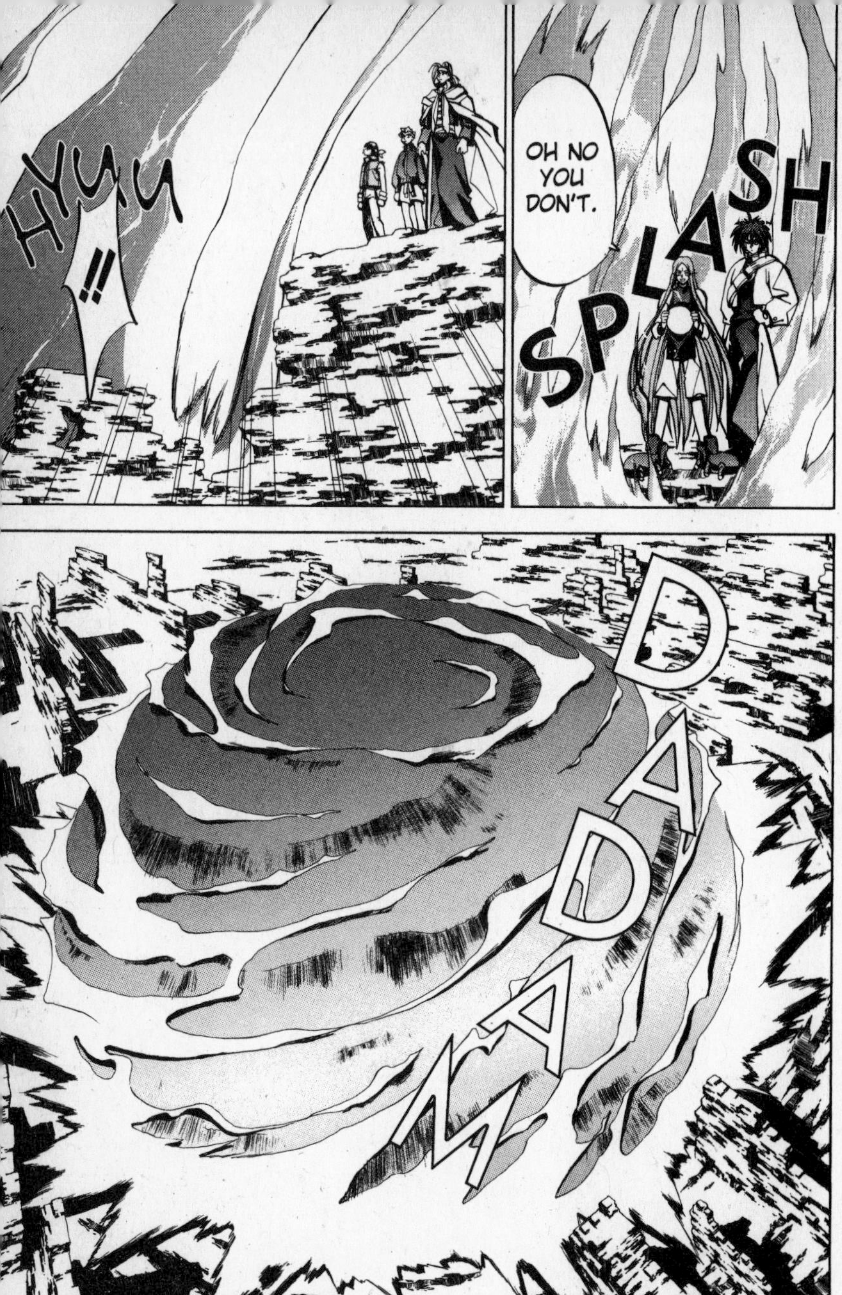
OH NO YOU DON'T.
SPLASH
HYUUU!!
DADAM

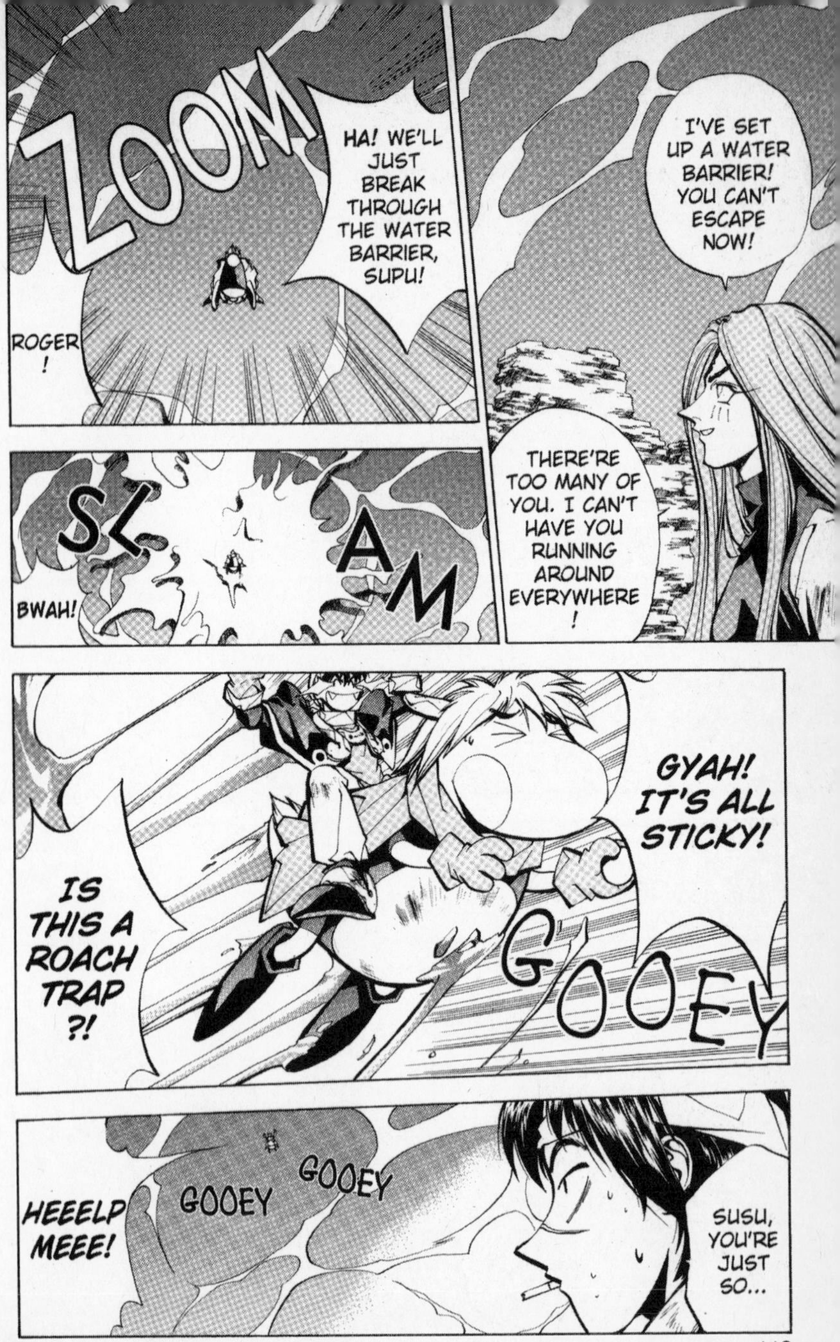
I'VE SET UP A WATER BARRIER! YOU CAN'T ESCAPE NOW!
THERE'RE TOO MANY OF YOU. I CAN'T HAVE YOU RUNNING AROUND EVERYWHERE!
HA! WE'LL JUST BREAK THROUGH THE WATER BARRIER, SUPU!
ZOOM
ROGER!
SLAM
BWAH!
GYAH! IT'S ALL STICKY!
GOOEY
IS THIS A ROACH TRAP?!
SUSU, YOU'RE JUST SO...
GOOEY
GOOEY
HEEELP MEEE!

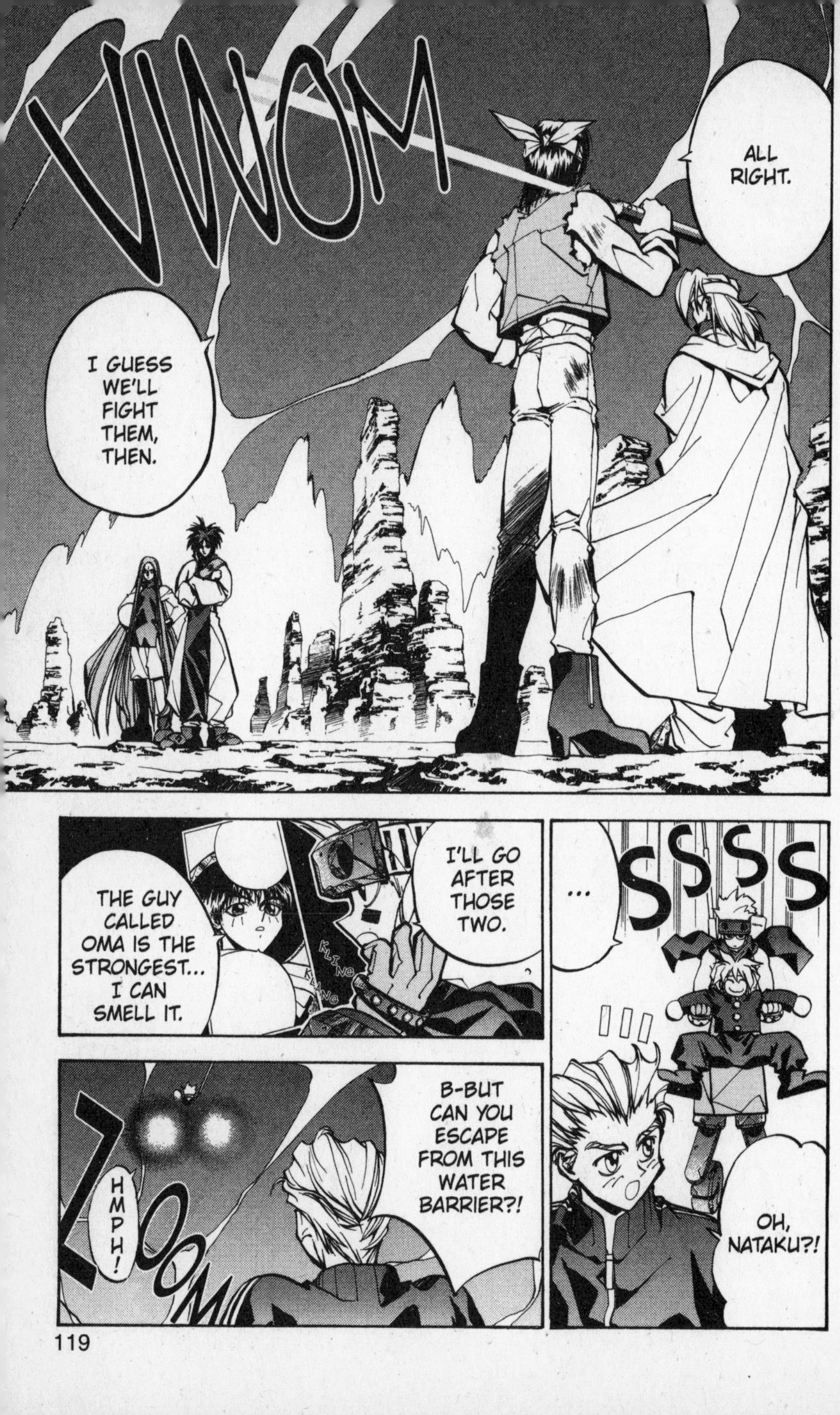
ALL RIGHT.
VWOM
I GUESS WE'LL FIGHT THEM, THEN.
...
SSSS
OH, NATAKU?!
I'LL GO AFTER THOSE TWO.
KLINe
KLANe
THE GUY CALLED OMA IS THE STRONGEST... I CAN SMELL IT.
B-BUT CAN YOU ESCAPE FROM THIS WATER BARRIER?!
HMPH!
ZOOM

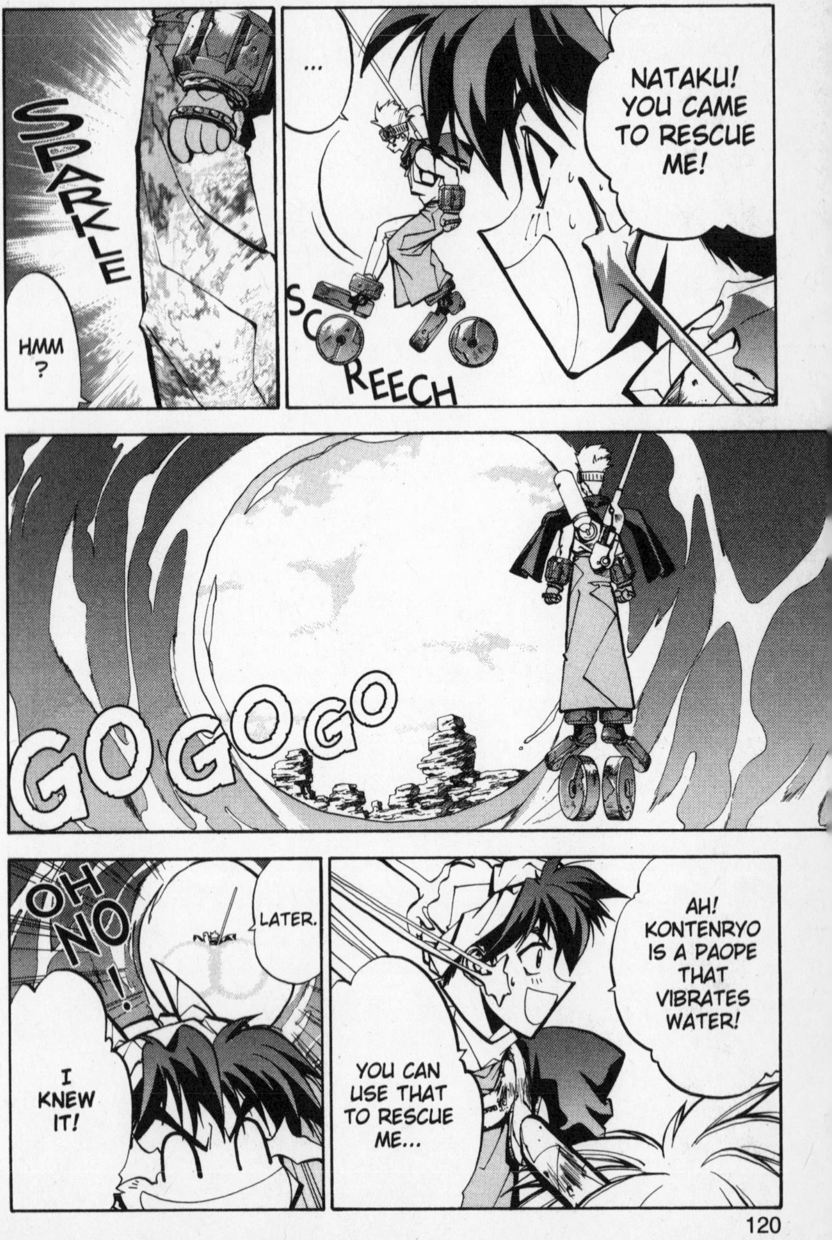
NATAKU! YOU CAME TO RESCUE ME!
...
SCREECH
SPARKLE
HMM ?
GOGOGO
AH! KONTENRYO IS A PAOPE THAT VIBRATES WATER!
YOU CAN USE THAT TO RESCUE ME...
LATER.
OH NO!
I KNEW IT!

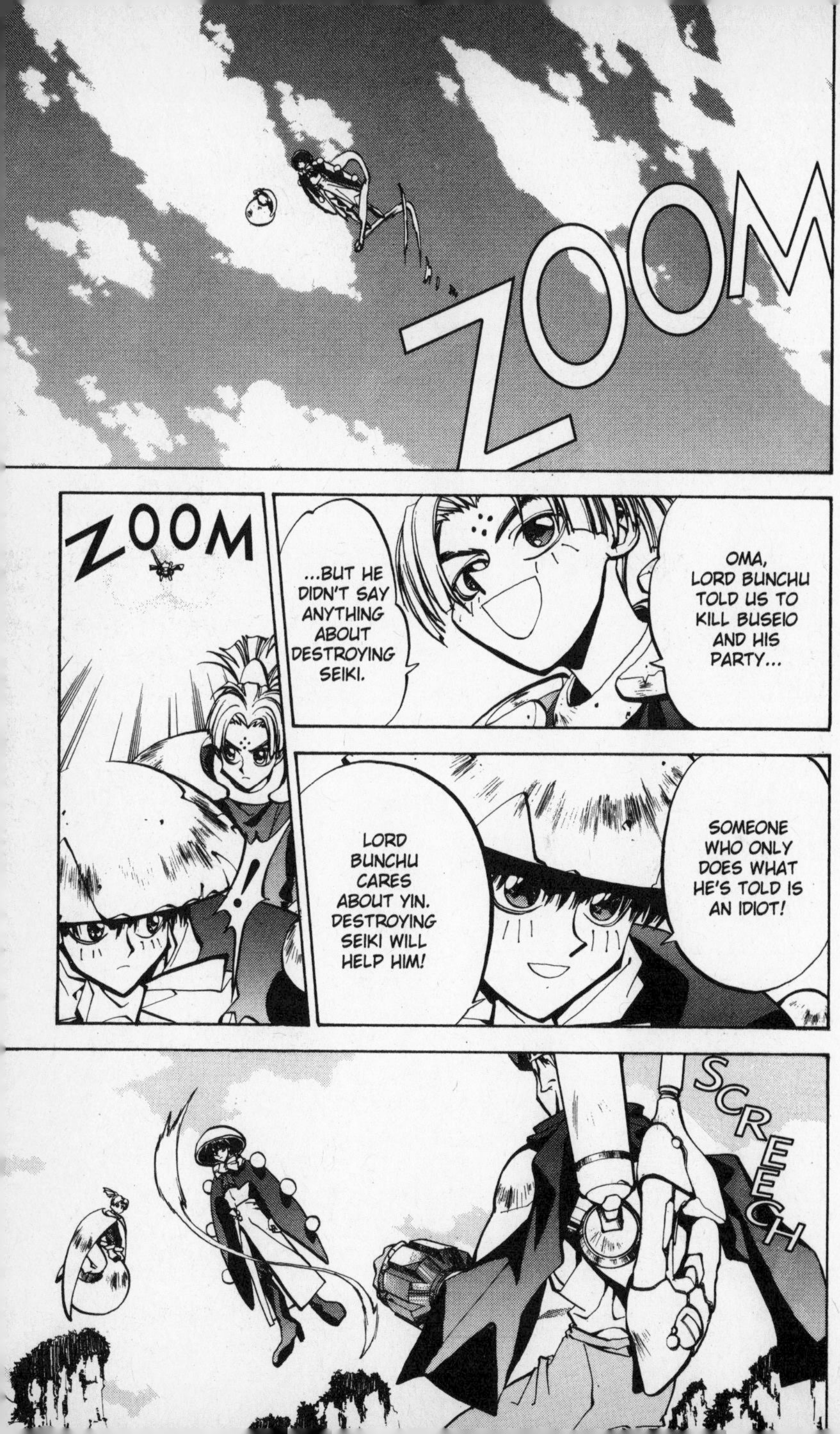
ZOOM
OMA, LORD BUNCHU TOLD US TO KILL BUSEIO AND HIS PARTY...
...BUT HE DIDN'T SAY ANYTHING ABOUT DESTROYING SEIKI.
ZOOM
SOMEONE WHO ONLY DOES WHAT HE'S TOLD IS AN IDIOT!
LORD BUNCHU CARES ABOUT YIN. DESTROYING SEIKI WILL HELP HIM!
!
SCREECH

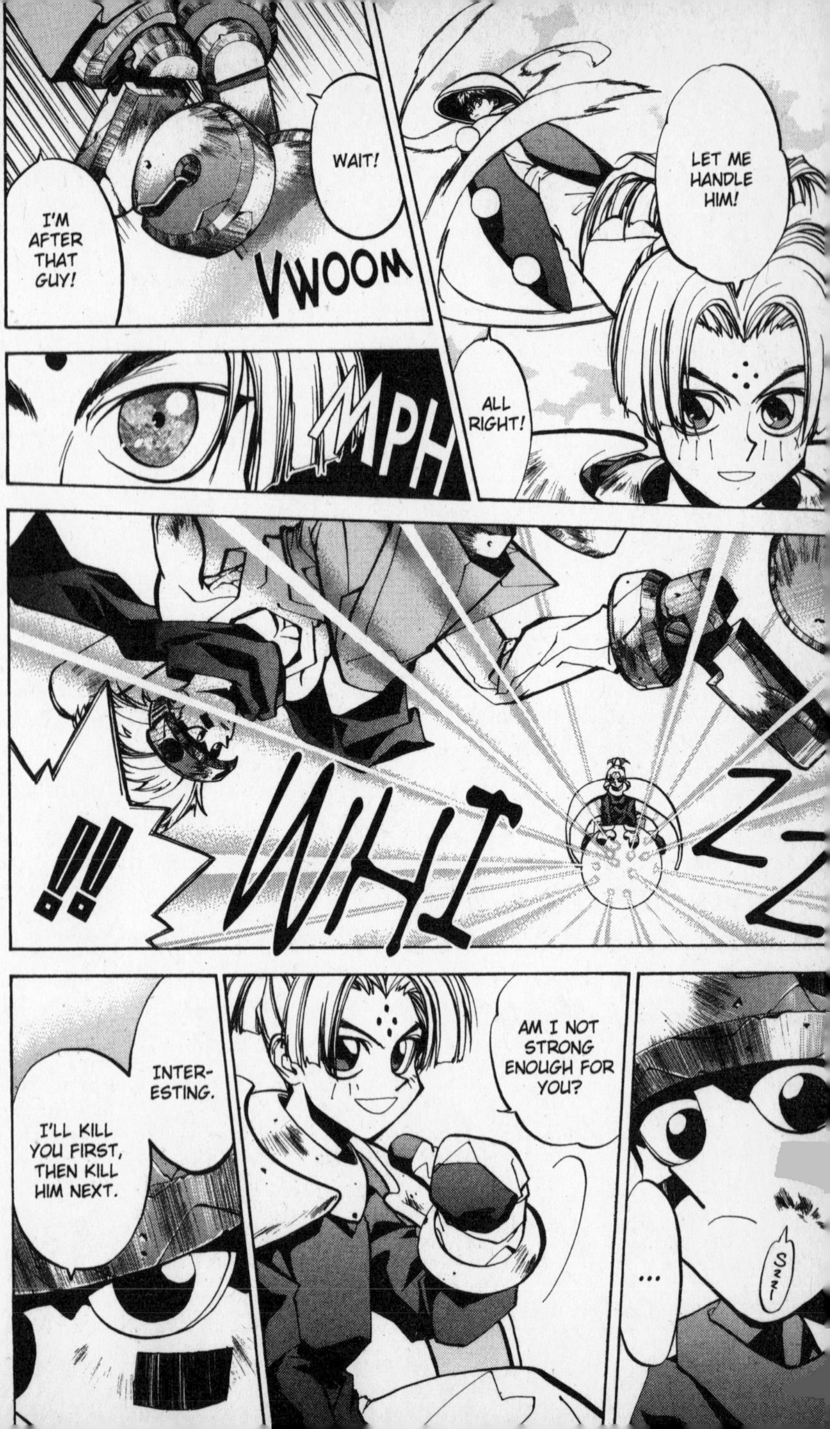
LET ME HANDLE HIM!
ALL RIGHT!
WAIT!
I'M AFTER THAT GUY!
VWOOM
MPH
!!
WHIZZ
...
SZZ
AM I NOT STRONG ENOUGH FOR YOU?
INTER-ESTING.
I'LL KILL YOU FIRST, THEN KILL HIM NEXT.

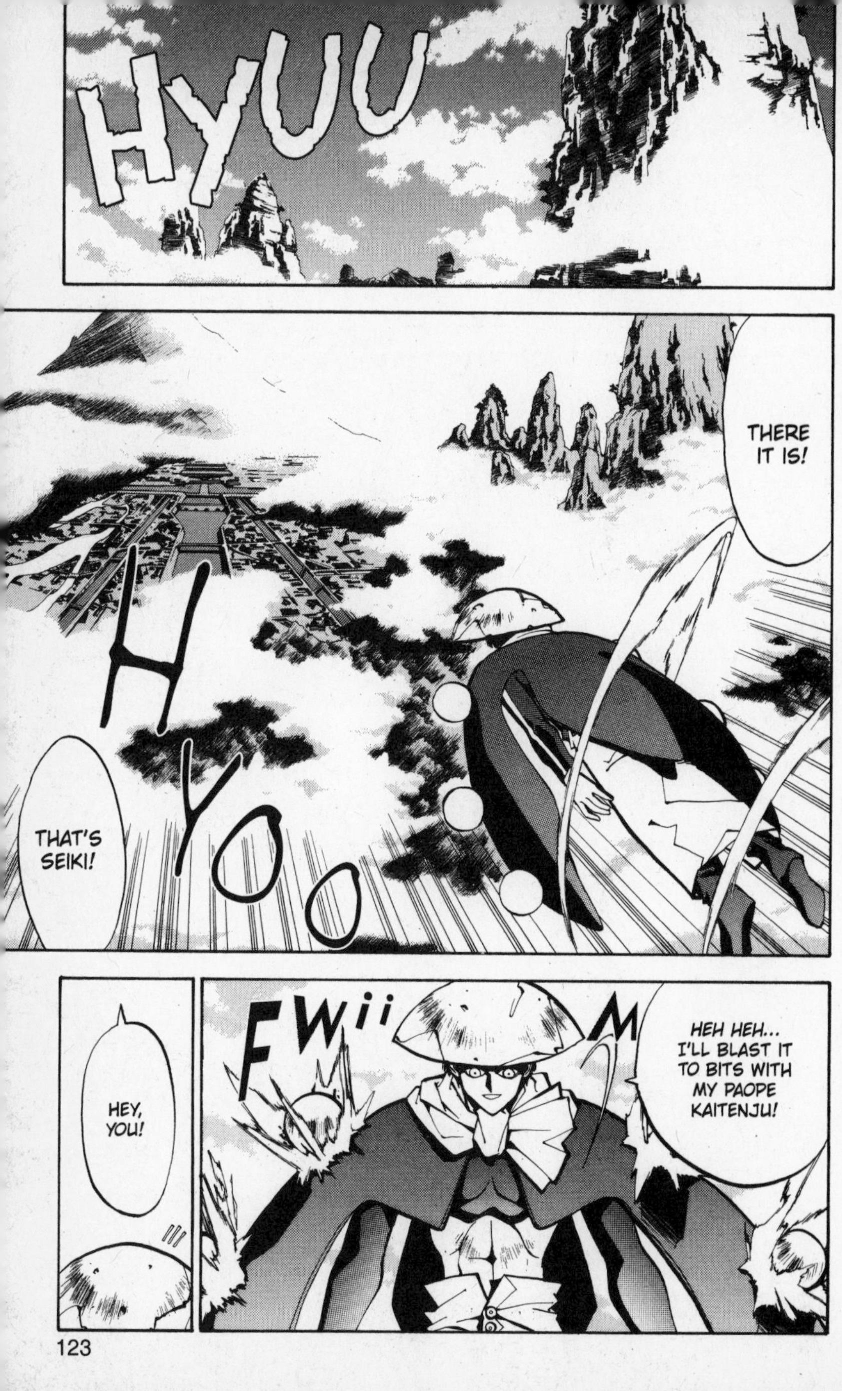
HYUU
THERE IT IS!
HYOOO
THAT'S SEIKI!
FWiiM
HEH HEH... I'LL BLAST IT TO BITS WITH MY PAOPE KAITENJU!
HEY, YOU!
!!!

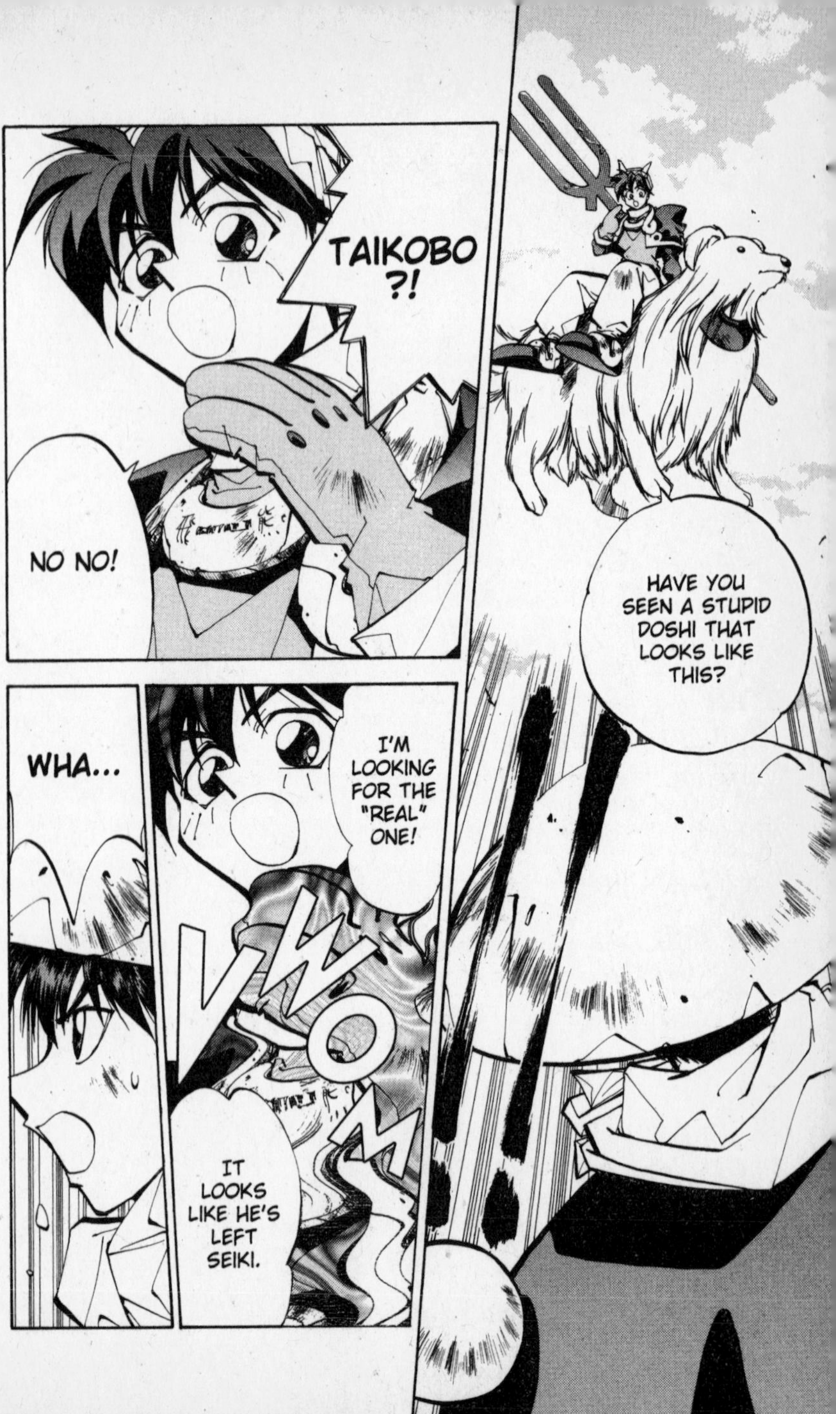
HAVE YOU SEEN A STUPID DOSHI THAT LOOKS LIKE THIS?
TAIKOBO ?!
NO NO!
I'M LOOKING FOR THE "REAL" ONE!
VWOM
IT LOOKS LIKE HE'S LEFT SEIKI.
WHA...

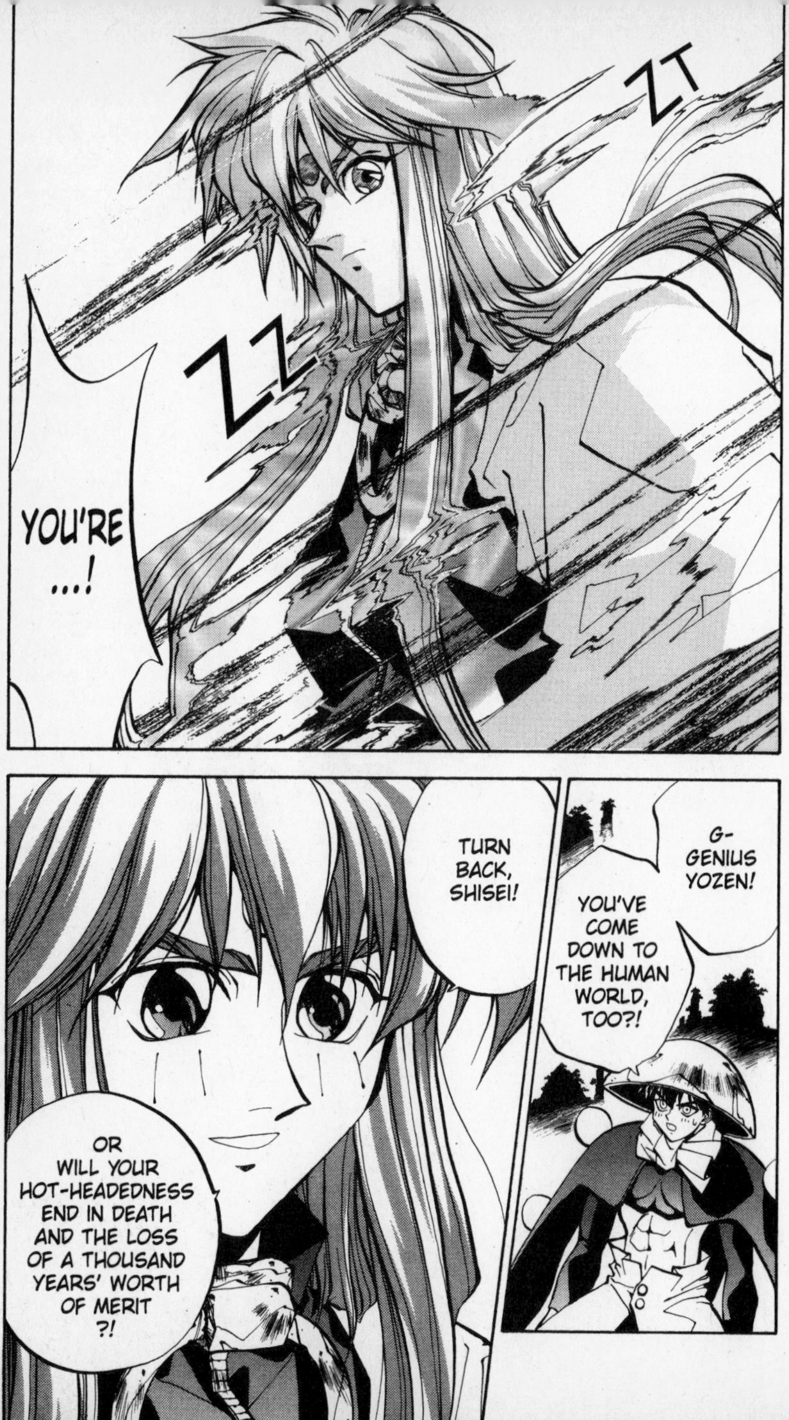
ZT
ZZ
YOU'RE ...!
G- GENIUS YOZEN!
YOU'VE COME DOWN TO THE HUMAN WORLD, TOO?!
TURN BACK, SHISEI!
OR WILL YOUR HOT-HEADEDNESS END IN DEATH AND THE LOSS OF A THOUSAND YEARS' WORTH OF MERIT ?!

封神演義

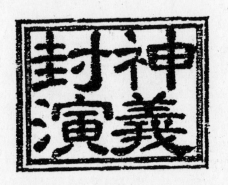

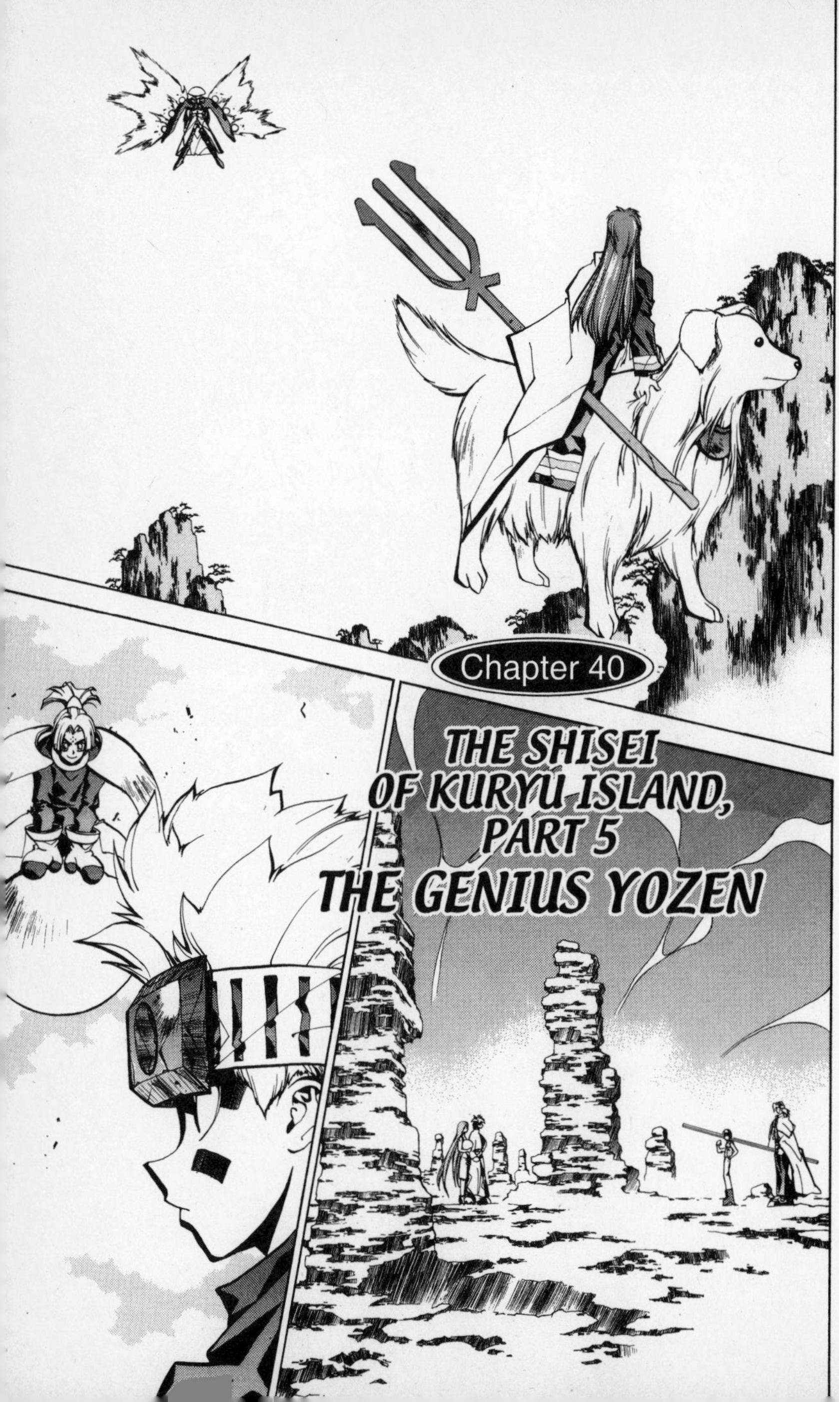
Chapter 40
THE SHISEI OF KURYU ISLAND, PART 5
THE GENIUS YOZEN

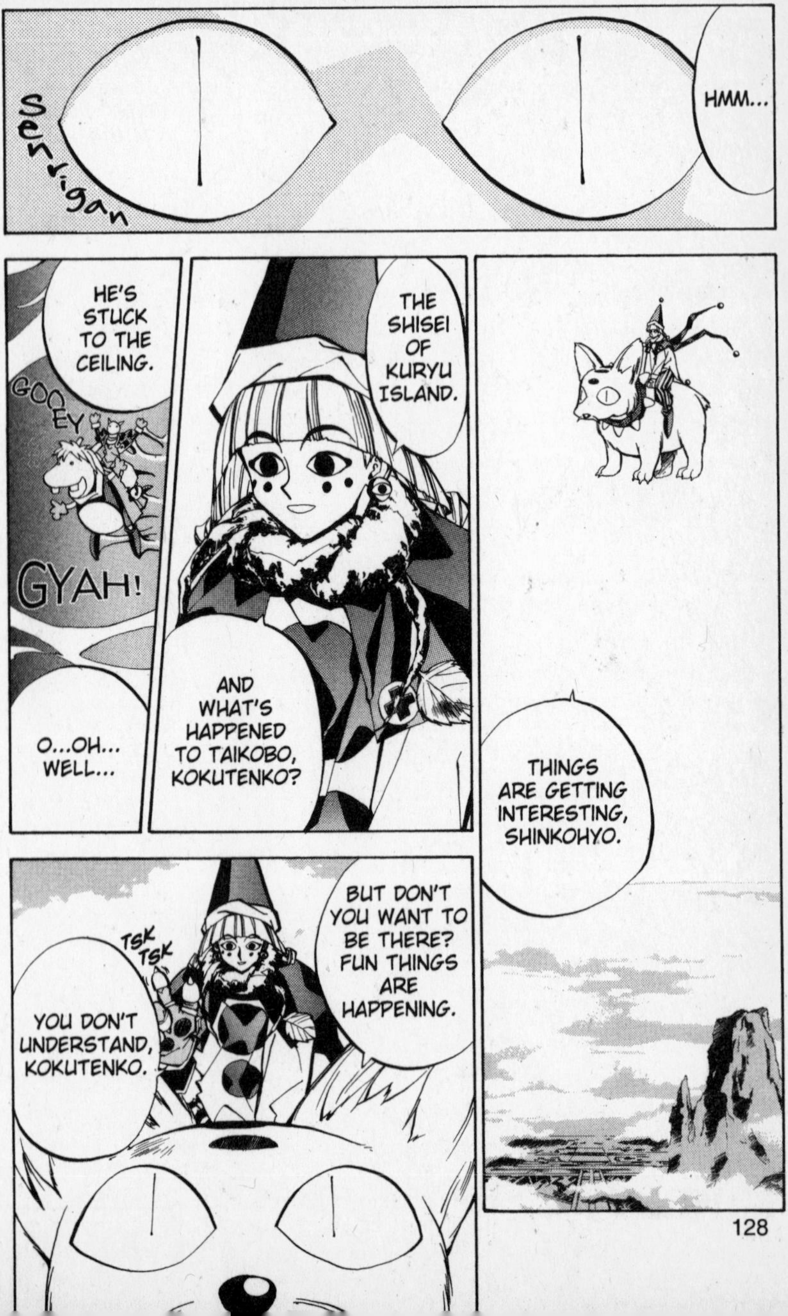
HMM...
Senrigan
THINGS ARE GETTING INTERESTING, SHINKOHYO.
THE SHISEI OF KURYU ISLAND.
AND WHAT'S HAPPENED TO TAIKOBO, KOKUTENKO?
HE'S STUCK TO THE CEILING.
GOOEY
GYAH!
O...OH... WELL...
BUT DON'T YOU WANT TO BE THERE? FUN THINGS ARE HAPPENING.
TSK TSK
YOU DON'T UNDERSTAND, KOKUTENKO.

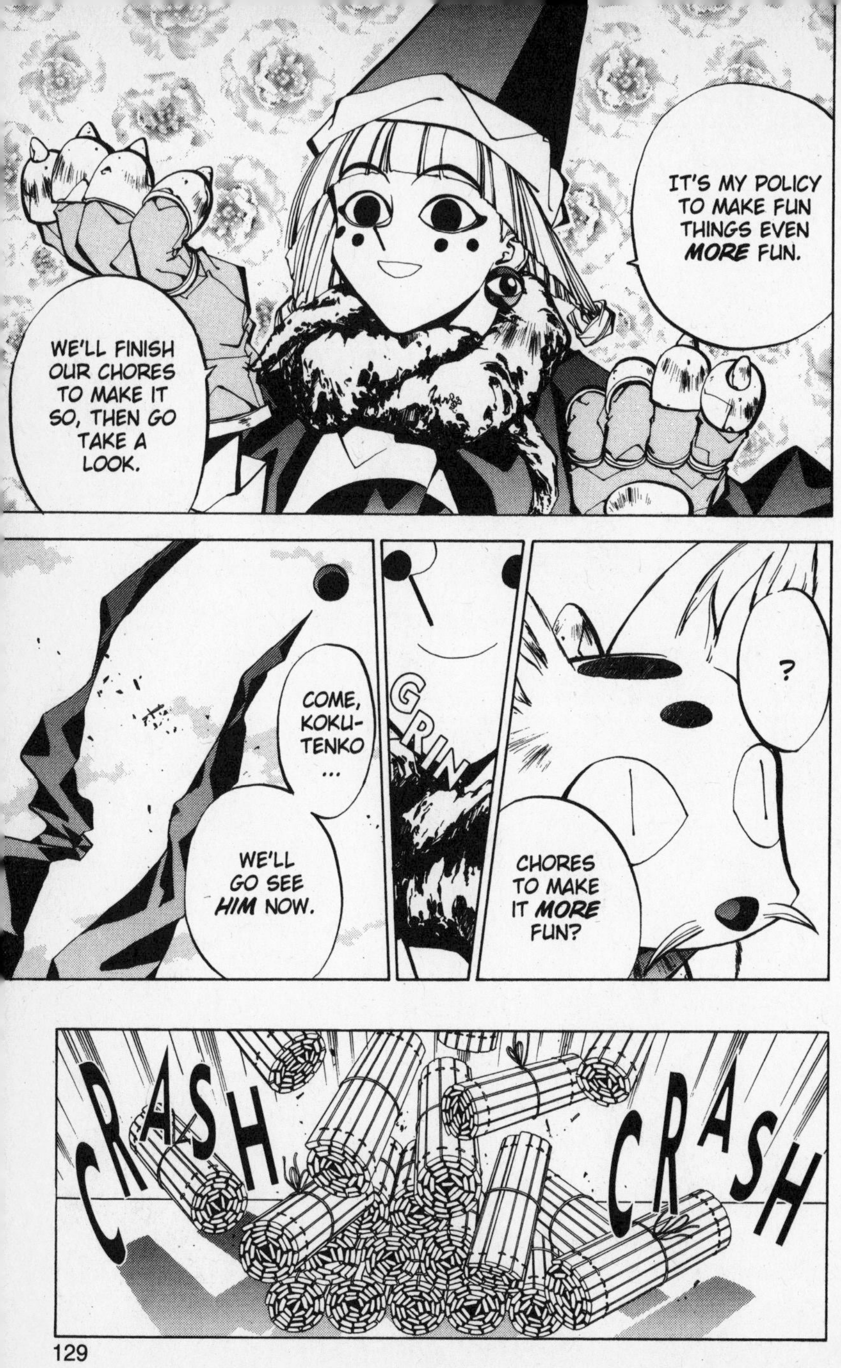
IT'S MY POLICY TO MAKE FUN THINGS EVEN MORE FUN.
WE'LL FINISH OUR CHORES TO MAKE IT SO, THEN GO TAKE A LOOK.
?
CHORES TO MAKE IT MORE FUN?
GRIN
COME, KOKU-TENKO...
WE'LL GO SEE HIM NOW.
CRASH
CRASH

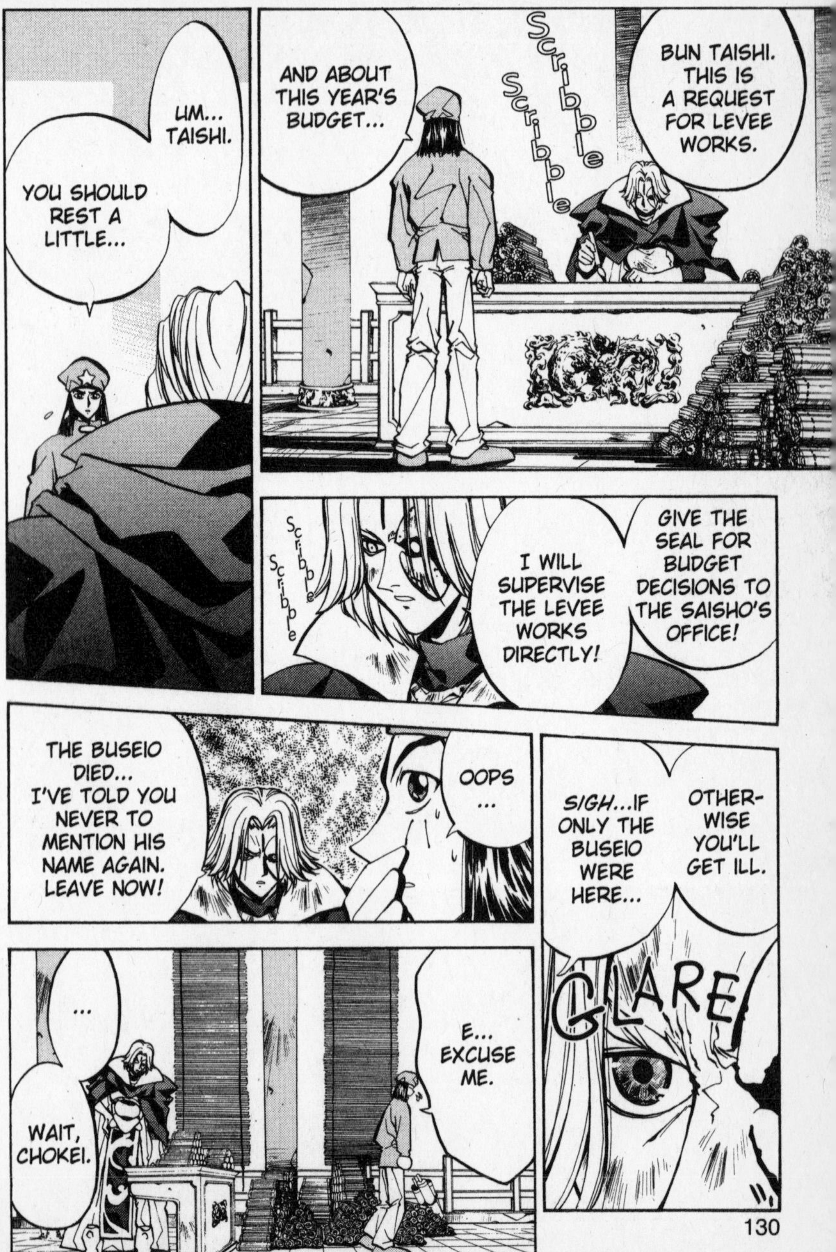

BUN TAISHI. THIS IS A REQUEST FOR LEVEE WORKS.
Scribble Scribble
AND ABOUT THIS YEAR'S BUDGET...
Scribble Scribble
GIVE THE SEAL FOR BUDGET DECISIONS TO THE SAISHO'S OFFICE!
I WILL SUPERVISE THE LEVEE WORKS DIRECTLY!
UM... TAISHI.
YOU SHOULD REST A LITTLE...
OTHER-WISE YOU'LL GET ILL.
SIGH...IF ONLY THE BUSEIO WERE HERE...
GLARE
OOPS ...
THE BUSEIO DIED... I'VE TOLD YOU NEVER TO MENTION HIS NAME AGAIN. LEAVE NOW!
E... EXCUSE ME.
...
WAIT, CHOKEI.

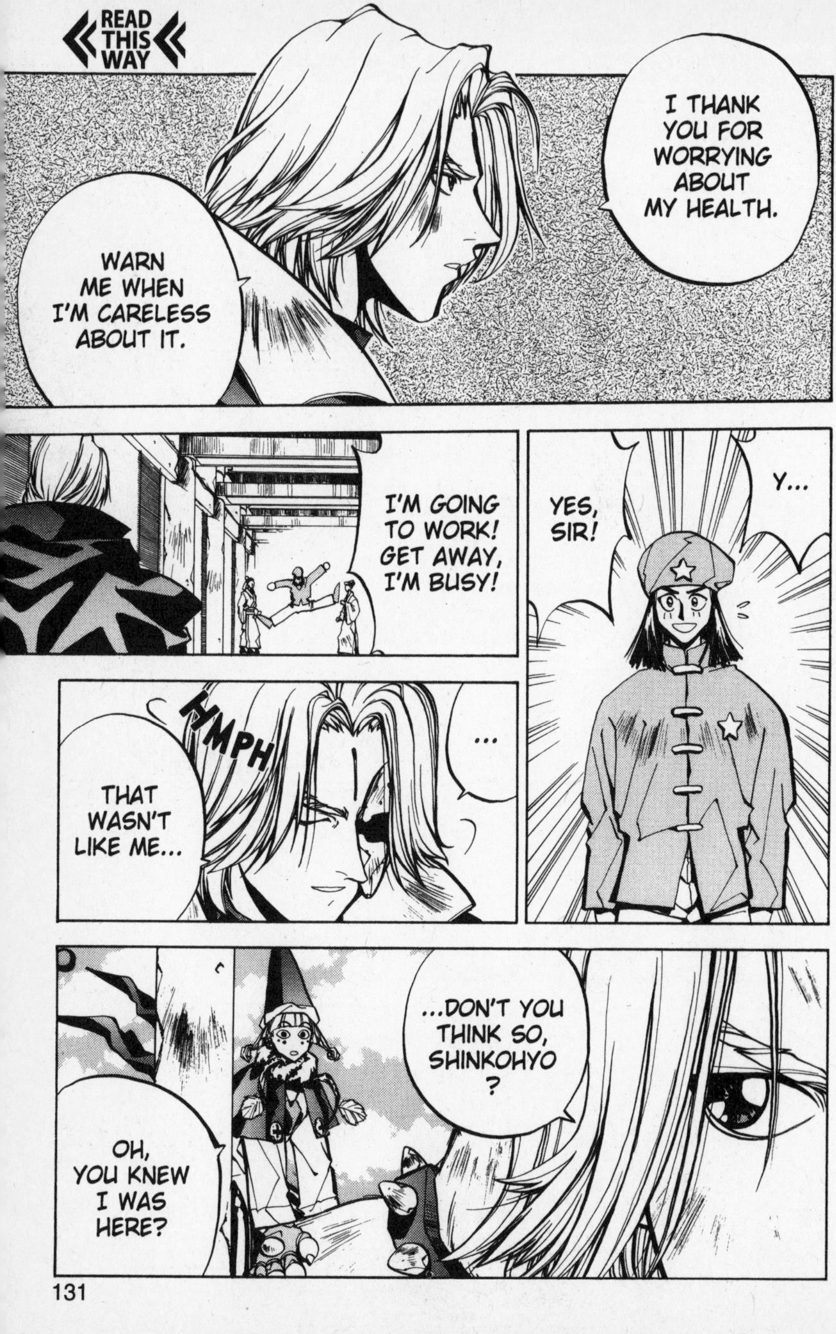
READ THIS WAY
I THANK YOU FOR WORRYING ABOUT MY HEALTH.
WARN ME WHEN I'M CARELESS ABOUT IT.
Y...
YES, SIR!
I'M GOING TO WORK! GET AWAY, I'M BUSY!
...
HMPH
THAT WASN'T LIKE ME...
...DON'T YOU THINK SO, SHINKOHYO?
OH, YOU KNEW I WAS HERE?

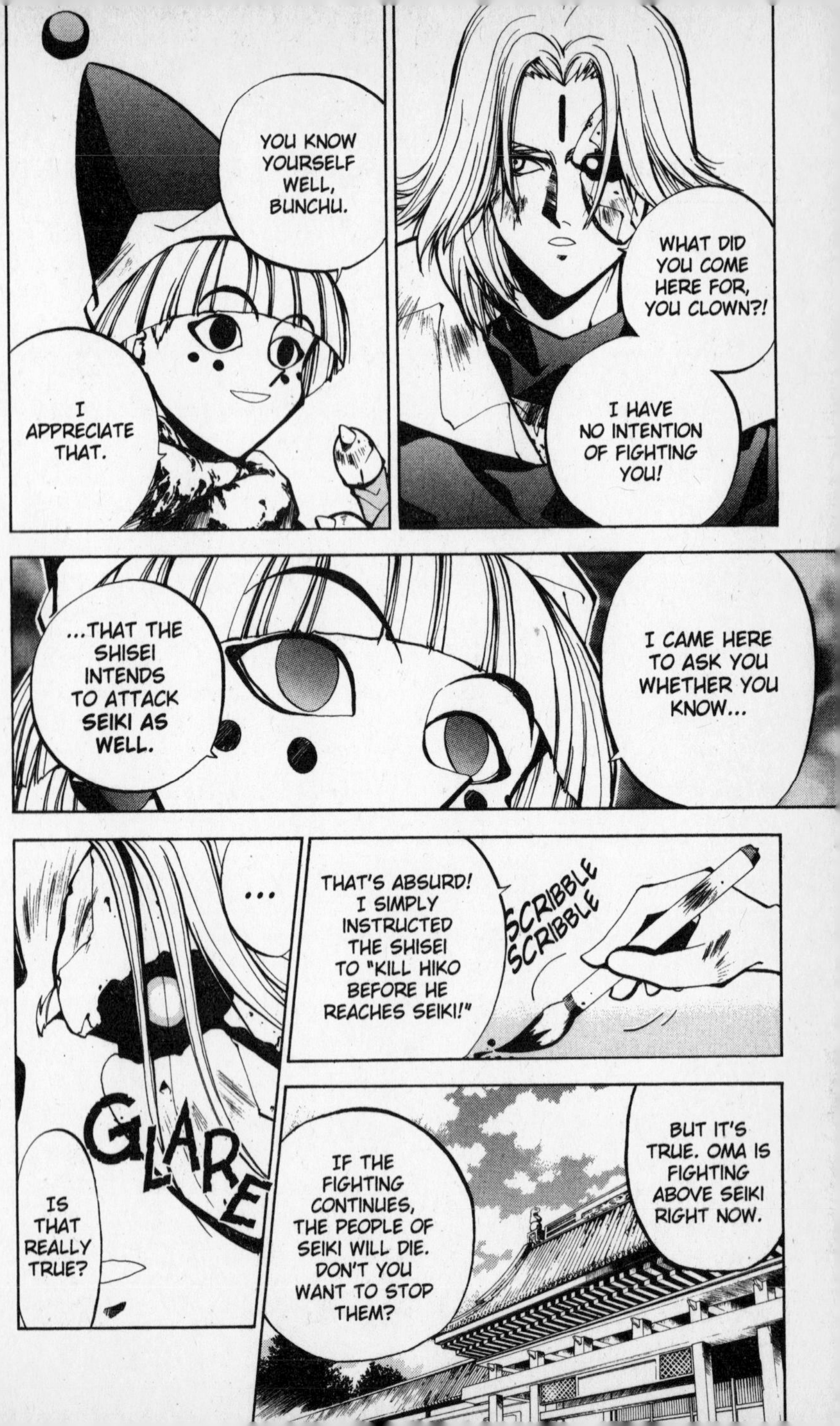
WHAT DID YOU COME HERE FOR, YOU CLOWN?!
I HAVE NO INTENTION OF FIGHTING YOU!
YOU KNOW YOURSELF WELL, BUNCHU.
I APPRECIATE THAT.
I CAME HERE TO ASK YOU WHETHER YOU KNOW...
...THAT THE SHISEI INTENDS TO ATTACK SEIKI AS WELL.
SCRIBBLE SCRIBBLE
THAT'S ABSURD! I SIMPLY INSTRUCTED THE SHISEI TO "KILL HIKO BEFORE HE REACHES SEIKI!"
BUT IT'S TRUE. OMA IS FIGHTING ABOVE SEIKI RIGHT NOW.
IF THE FIGHTING CONTINUES, THE PEOPLE OF SEIKI WILL DIE. DON'T YOU WANT TO STOP THEM?
...
GLARE
IS THAT REALLY TRUE?

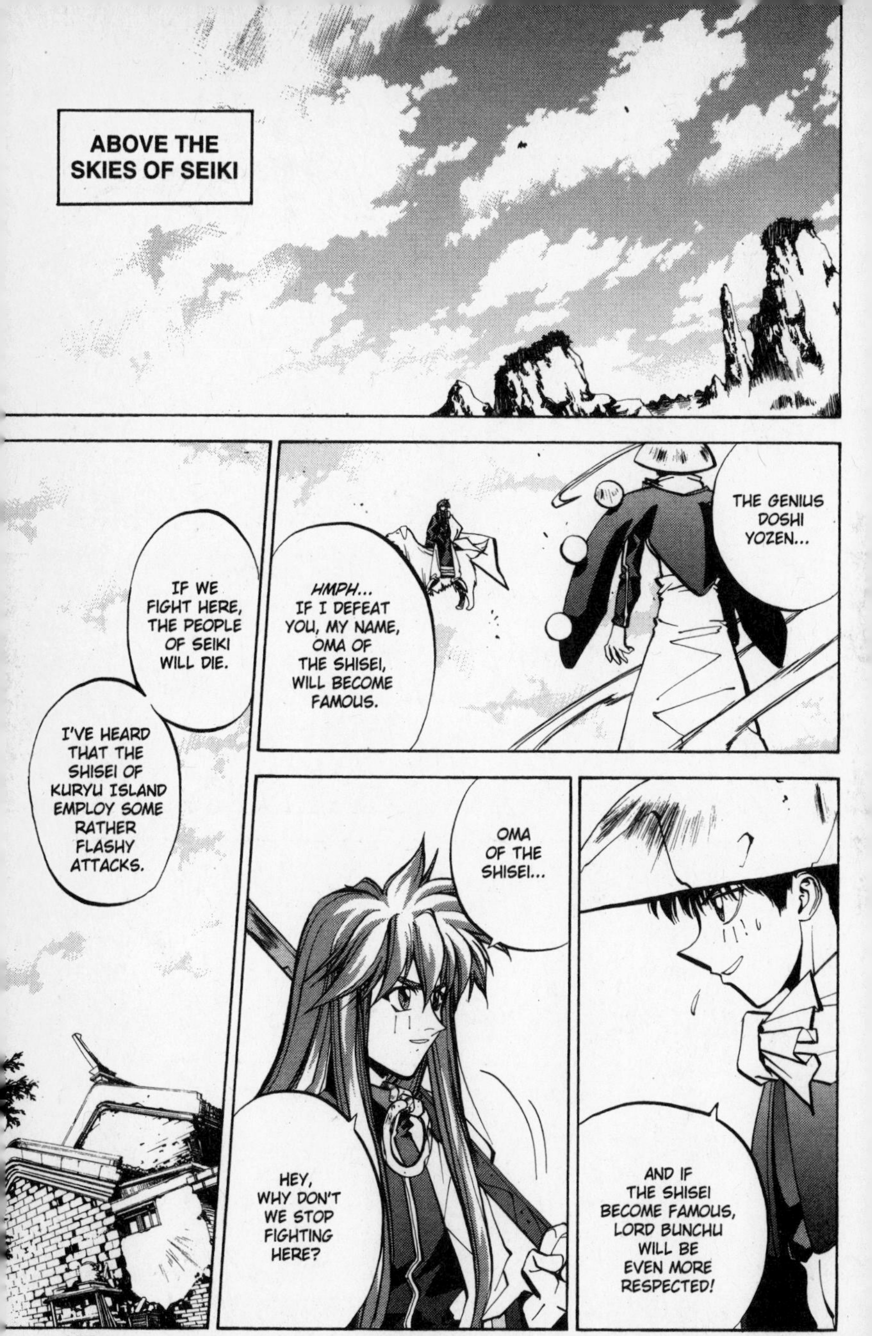
ABOVE THE SKIES OF SEIKI
THE GENIUS DOSHI YOZEN...
HMPH... IF I DEFEAT YOU, MY NAME, OMA OF THE SHISEI, WILL BECOME FAMOUS.
AND IF THE SHISEI BECOME FAMOUS, LORD BUNCHU WILL BE EVEN MORE RESPECTED!
OMA OF THE SHISEI...
HEY, WHY DON'T WE STOP FIGHTING HERE?
IF WE FIGHT HERE, THE PEOPLE OF SEIKI WILL DIE.
I'VE HEARD THAT THE SHISEI OF KURYU ISLAND EMPLOY SOME RATHER FLASHY ATTACKS.

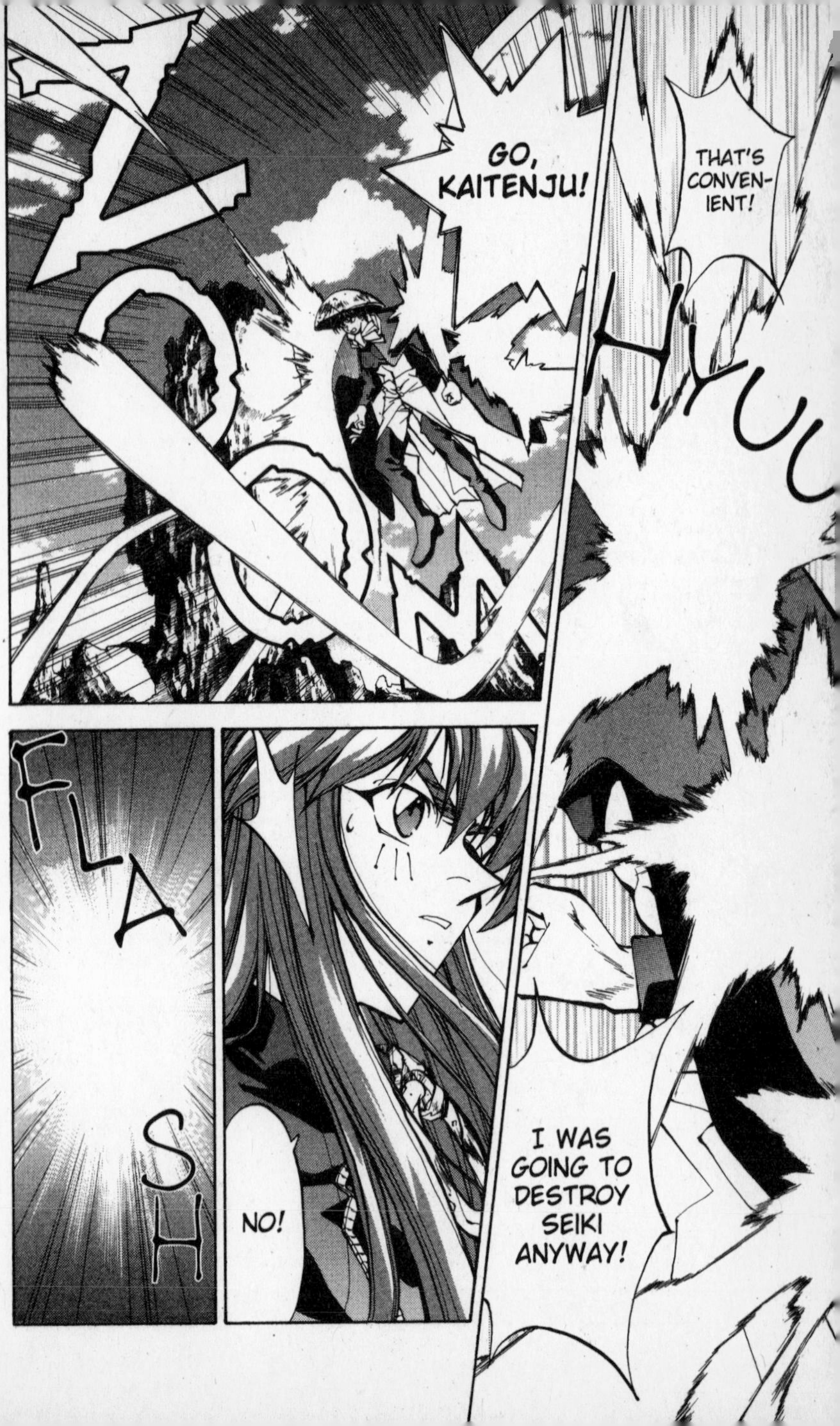
THAT'S CONVENIENT!
HYUU
I WAS GOING TO DESTROY SEIKI ANYWAY!
GO, KAITENJU!
NO!
FLASH

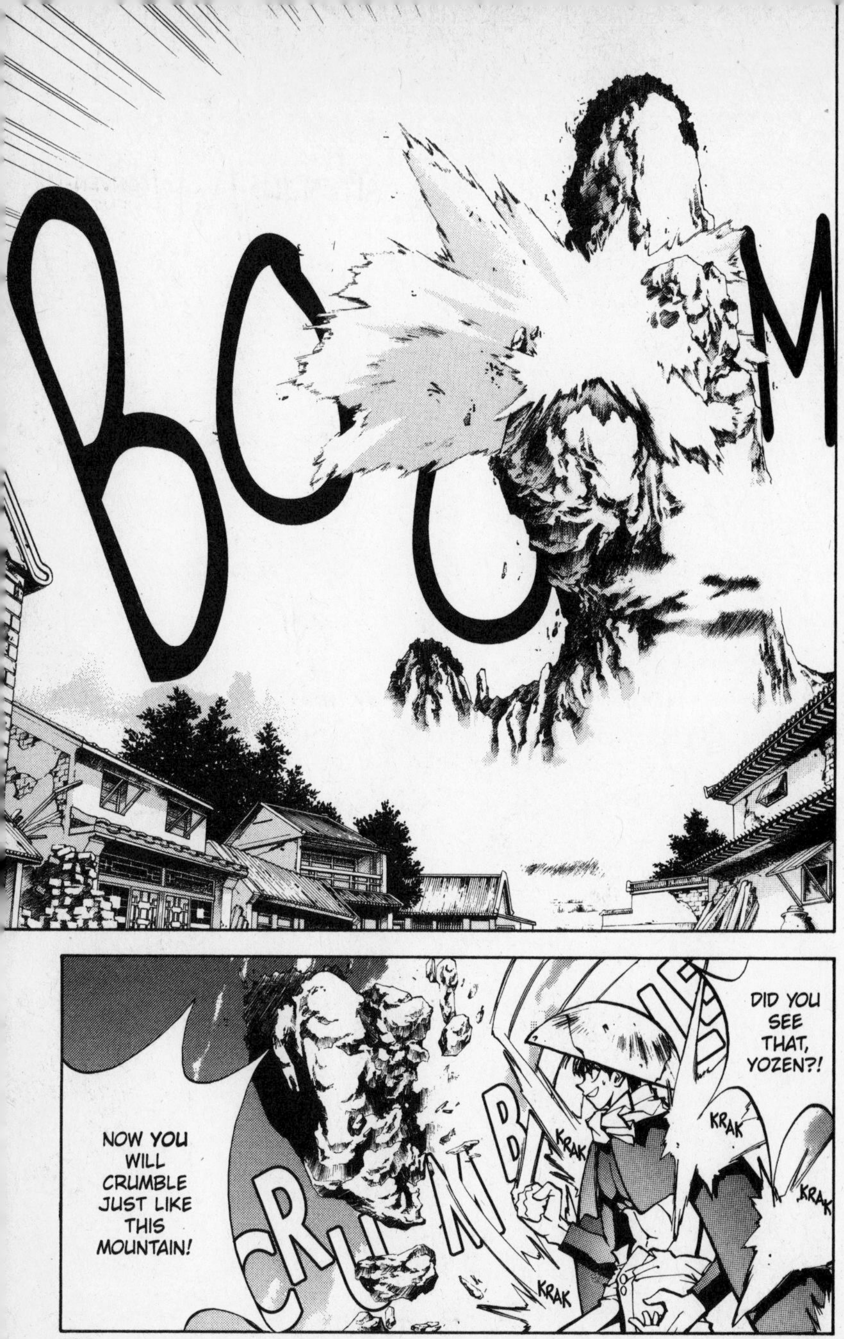
BOOM
DID YOU SEE THAT, YOZEN?!
KRAK
KRAK
KRAK
KRAK
NOW YOU WILL CRUMBLE JUST LIKE THIS MOUNTAIN!

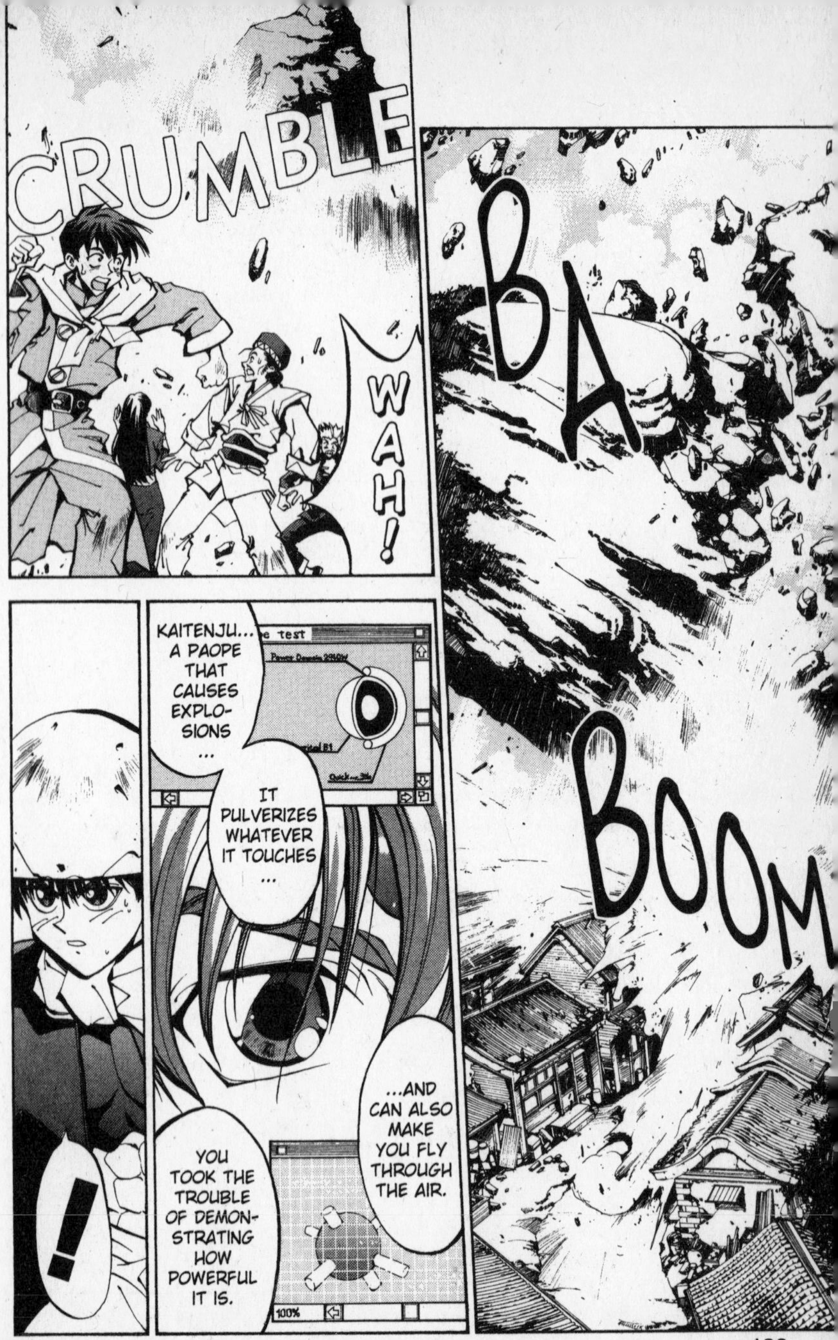
BA BOOM
CRUMBLE
WAH!
KAITENJU... A PAOPE THAT CAUSES EXPLOSIONS...
IT PULVERIZES WHATEVER IT TOUCHES...
...AND CAN ALSO MAKE YOU FLY THROUGH THE AIR.
YOU TOOK THE TROUBLE OF DEMONSTRATING HOW POWERFUL IT IS.
!

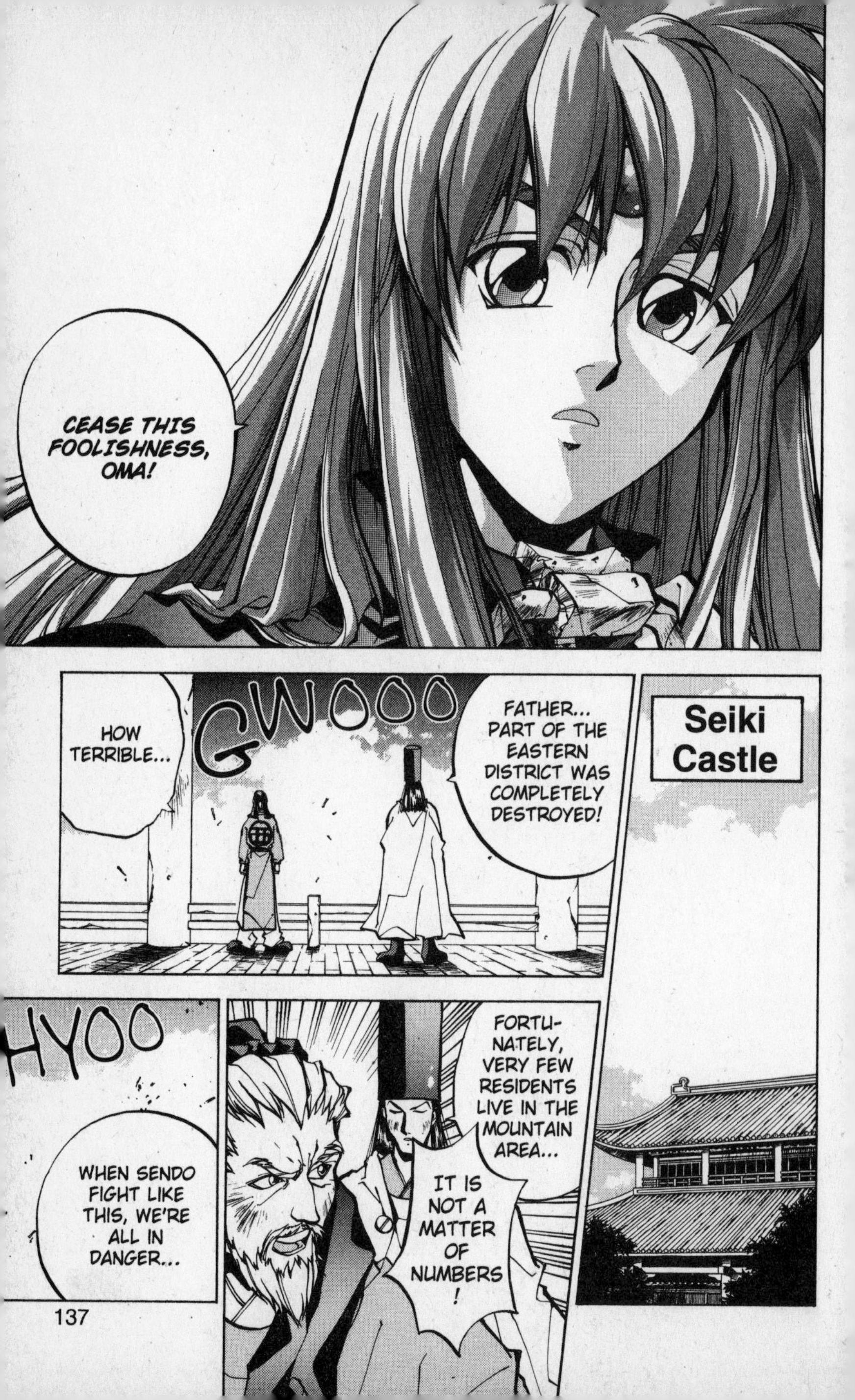
CEASE THIS FOOLISHNESS, OMA!
Seiki Castle
FATHER... PART OF THE EASTERN DISTRICT WAS COMPLETELY DESTROYED!
GWOOO
HOW TERRIBLE...
FORTU-NATELY, VERY FEW RESIDENTS LIVE IN THE MOUNTAIN AREA...
IT IS NOT A MATTER OF NUMBERS!
HYOO
WHEN SENDO FIGHT LIKE THIS, WE'RE ALL IN DANGER...

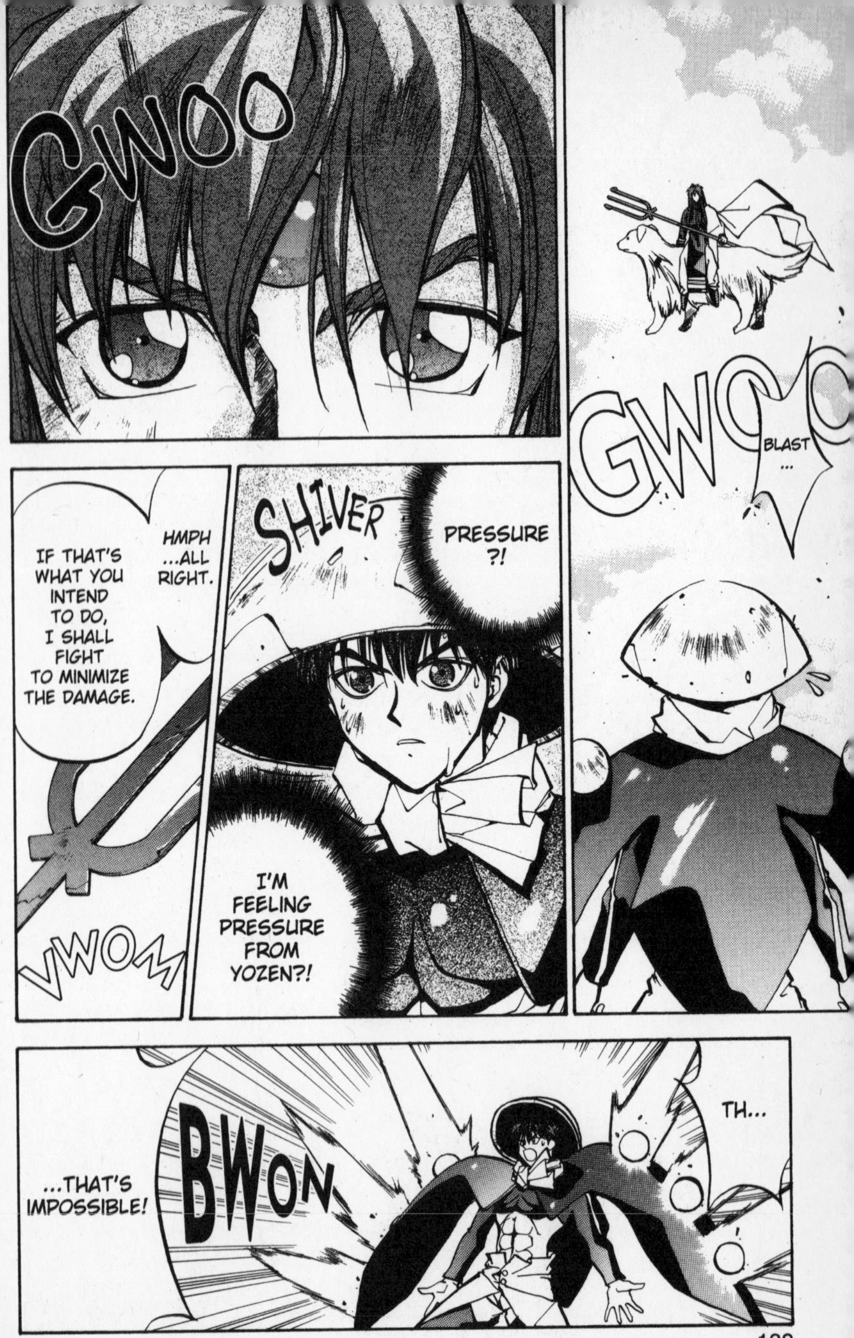

GWOO
BLAST ...
GWOO
SHIVER
PRESSURE ?!
I'M FEELING PRESSURE FROM YOZEN?!
HMPH ...ALL RIGHT.
IF THAT'S WHAT YOU INTEND TO DO, I SHALL FIGHT TO MINIMIZE THE DAMAGE.
VWOM
TH...
BWON
...THAT'S IMPOSSIBLE!

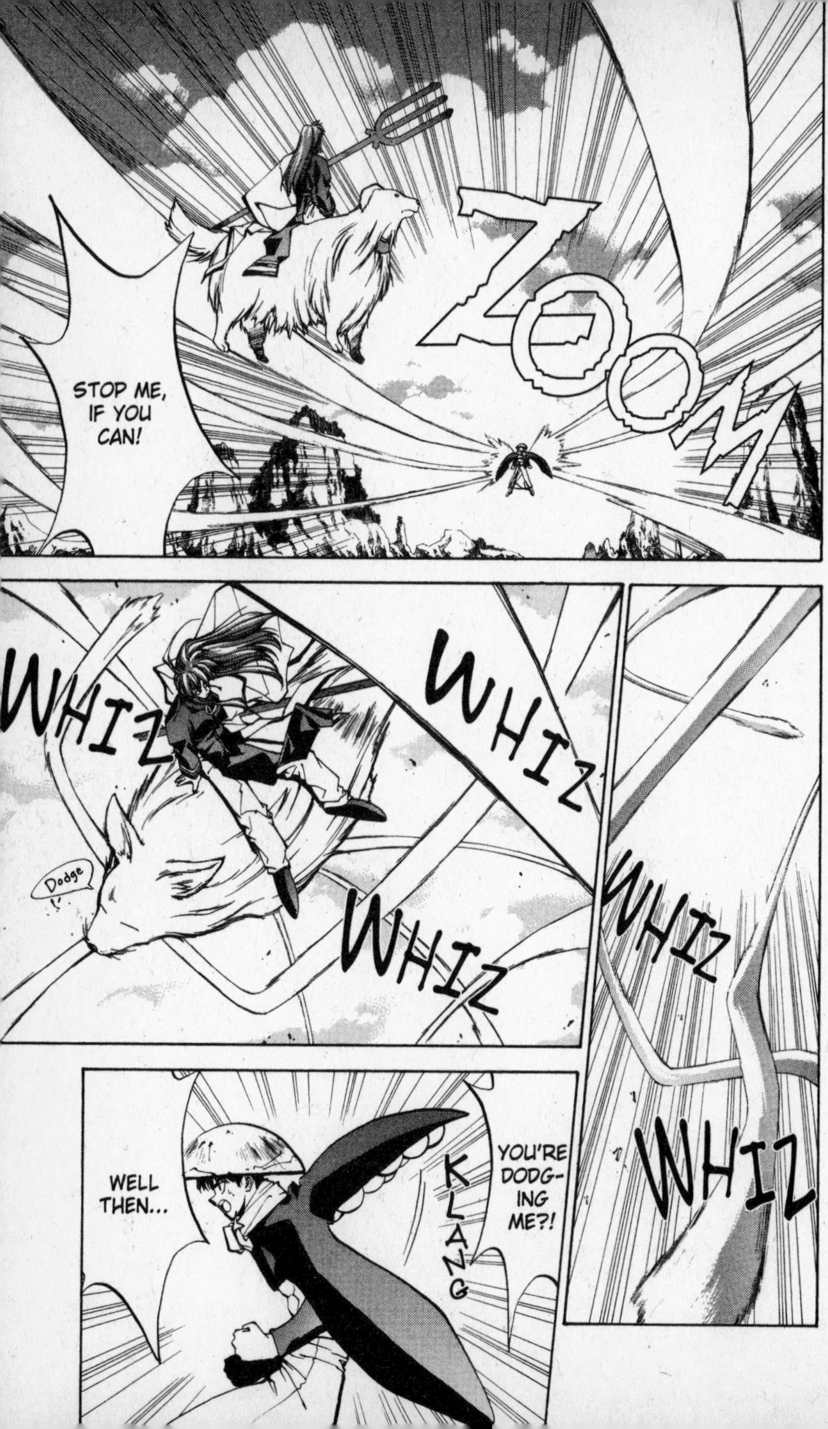
ZOOM
STOP ME, IF YOU CAN!
WHIZ
WHIZ
WHIZ
WHIZ
Dodge
WHIZ
YOU'RE DODG-ING ME?!
KLANG
WELL THEN...

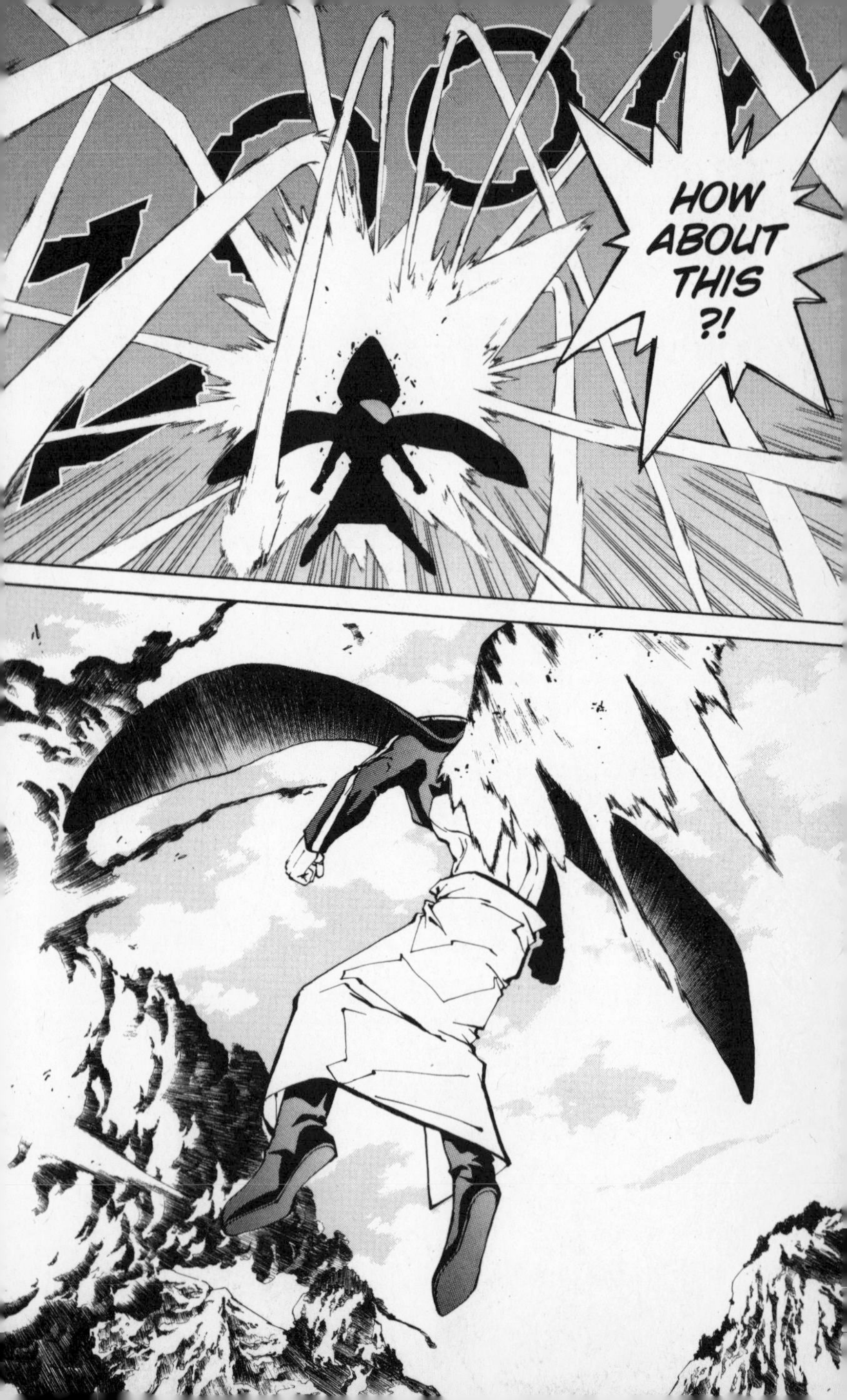
HOW ABOUT THIS ?!

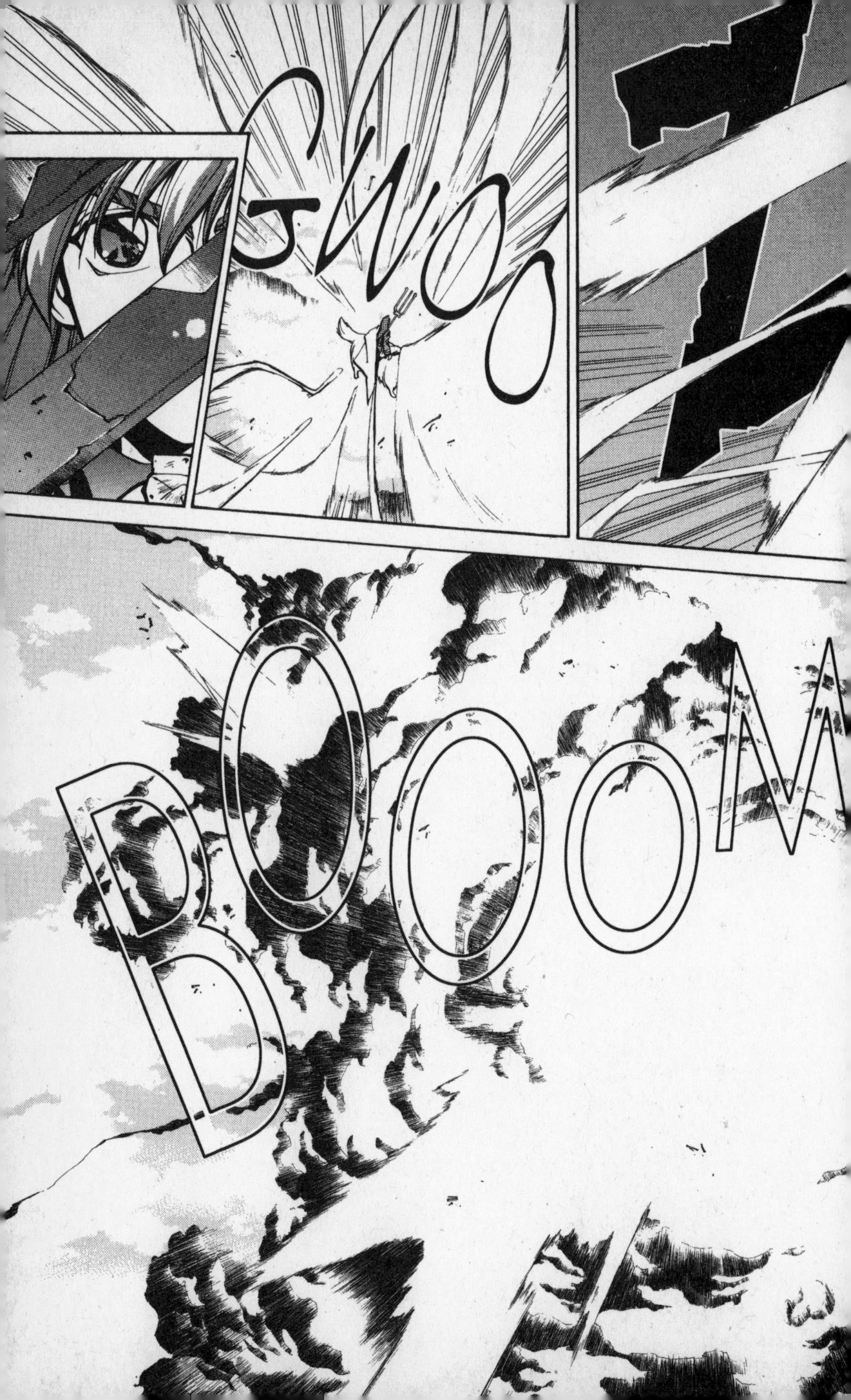
GWOO
BOOOM

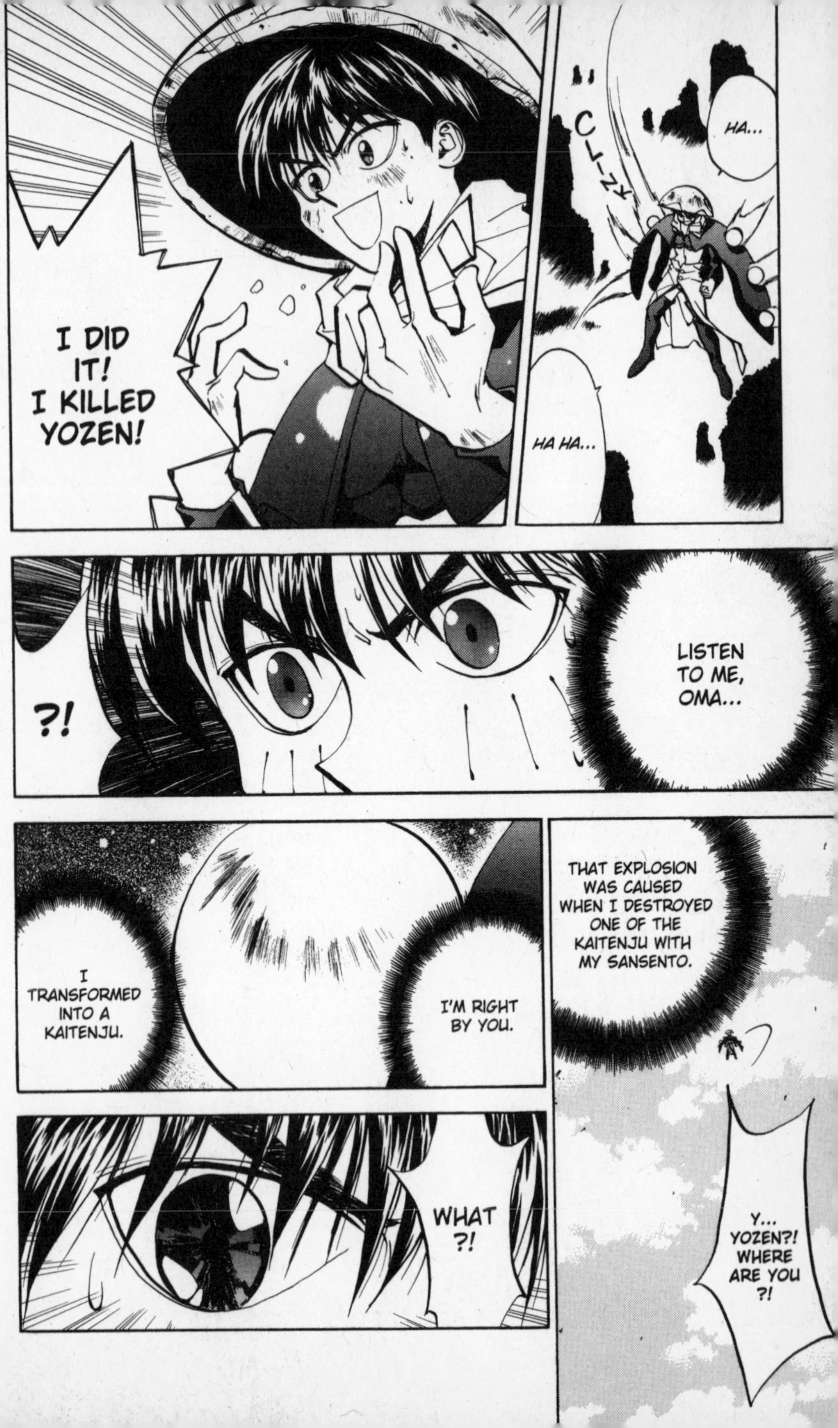
HA...
HA HA...
I DID IT! I KILLED YOZEN!
LISTEN TO ME, OMA...
?!
THAT EXPLOSION WAS CAUSED WHEN I DESTROYED ONE OF THE KAITENJU WITH MY SANSENTO.
Y... YOZEN?! WHERE ARE YOU ?!
I'M RIGHT BY YOU.
I TRANSFORMED INTO A KAITENJU.
WHAT ?!

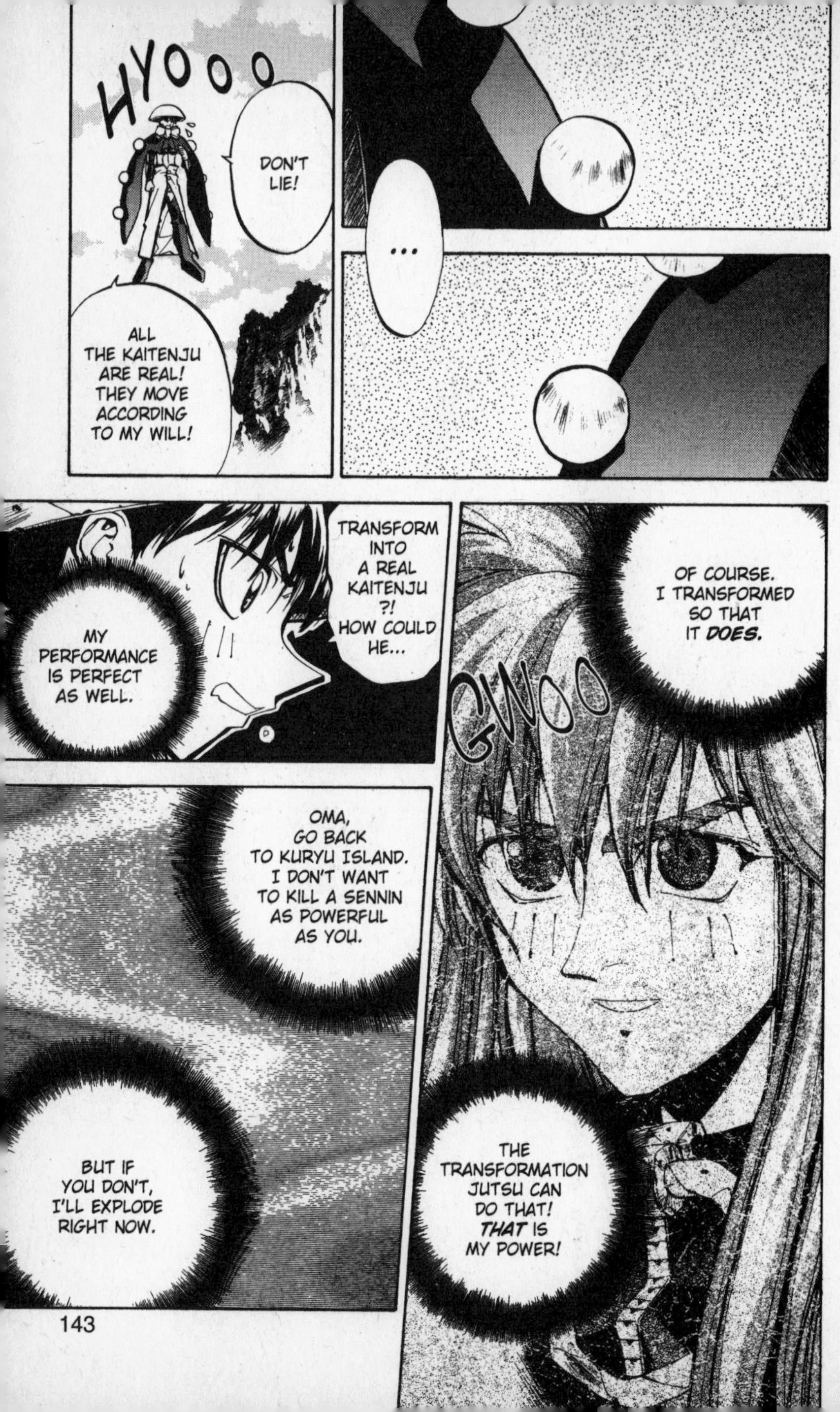
...
HYOOO
DON'T LIE!
ALL THE KAITENJU ARE REAL! THEY MOVE ACCORDING TO MY WILL!
OF COURSE. I TRANSFORMED SO THAT IT *DOES.*
GWOO
THE TRANSFORMATION JUTSU CAN DO THAT! *THAT* IS MY POWER!
TRANSFORM INTO A REAL KAITENJU ?! HOW COULD HE...
MY PERFORMANCE IS PERFECT AS WELL.
OMA, GO BACK TO KURYU ISLAND. I DON'T WANT TO KILL A SENNIN AS POWERFUL AS YOU.
BUT IF YOU DON'T, I'LL EXPLODE RIGHT NOW.

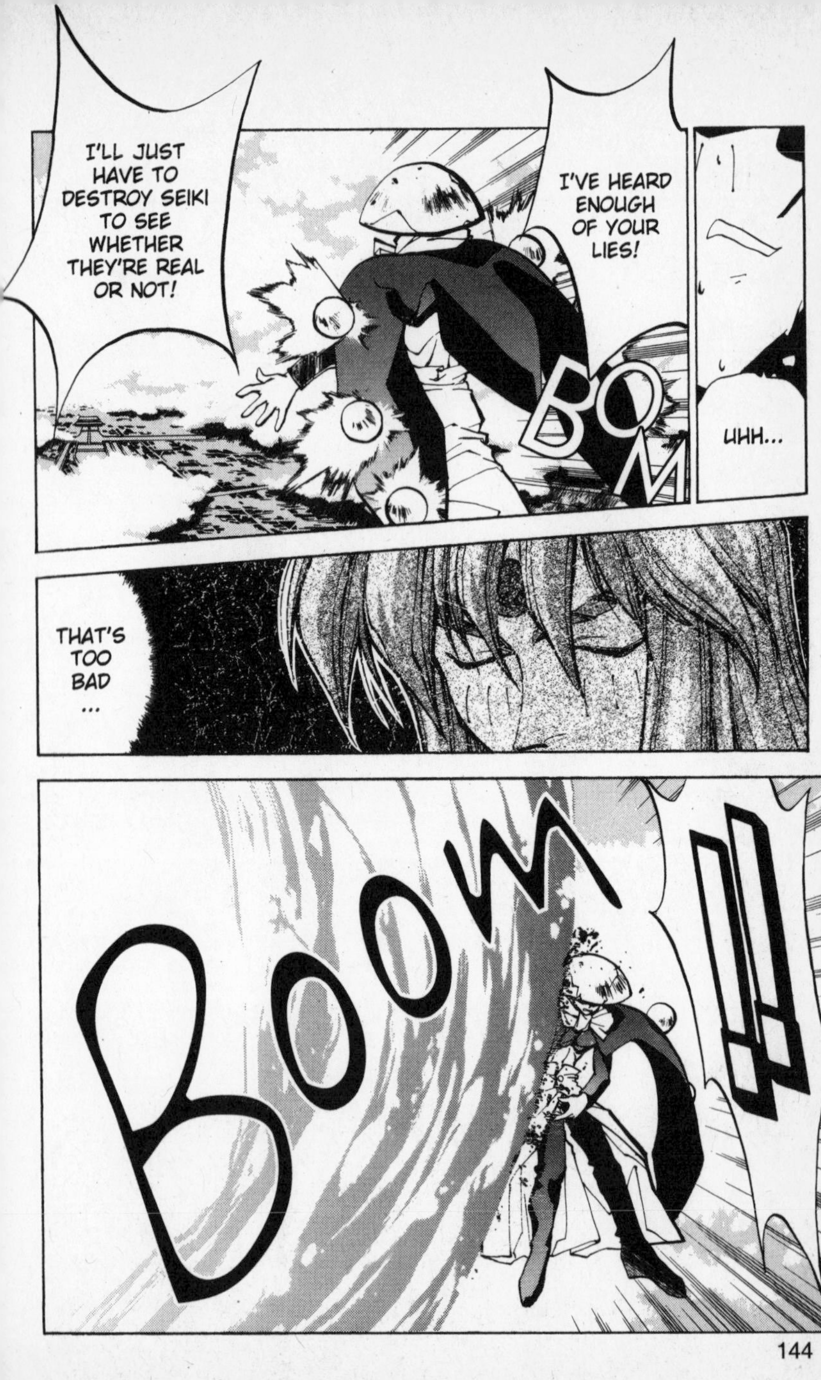
UHH...
I'VE HEARD ENOUGH OF YOUR LIES!
I'LL JUST HAVE TO DESTROY SEIKI TO SEE WHETHER THEY'RE REAL OR NOT!
BOOM
THAT'S TOO BAD ...
BOOM!!

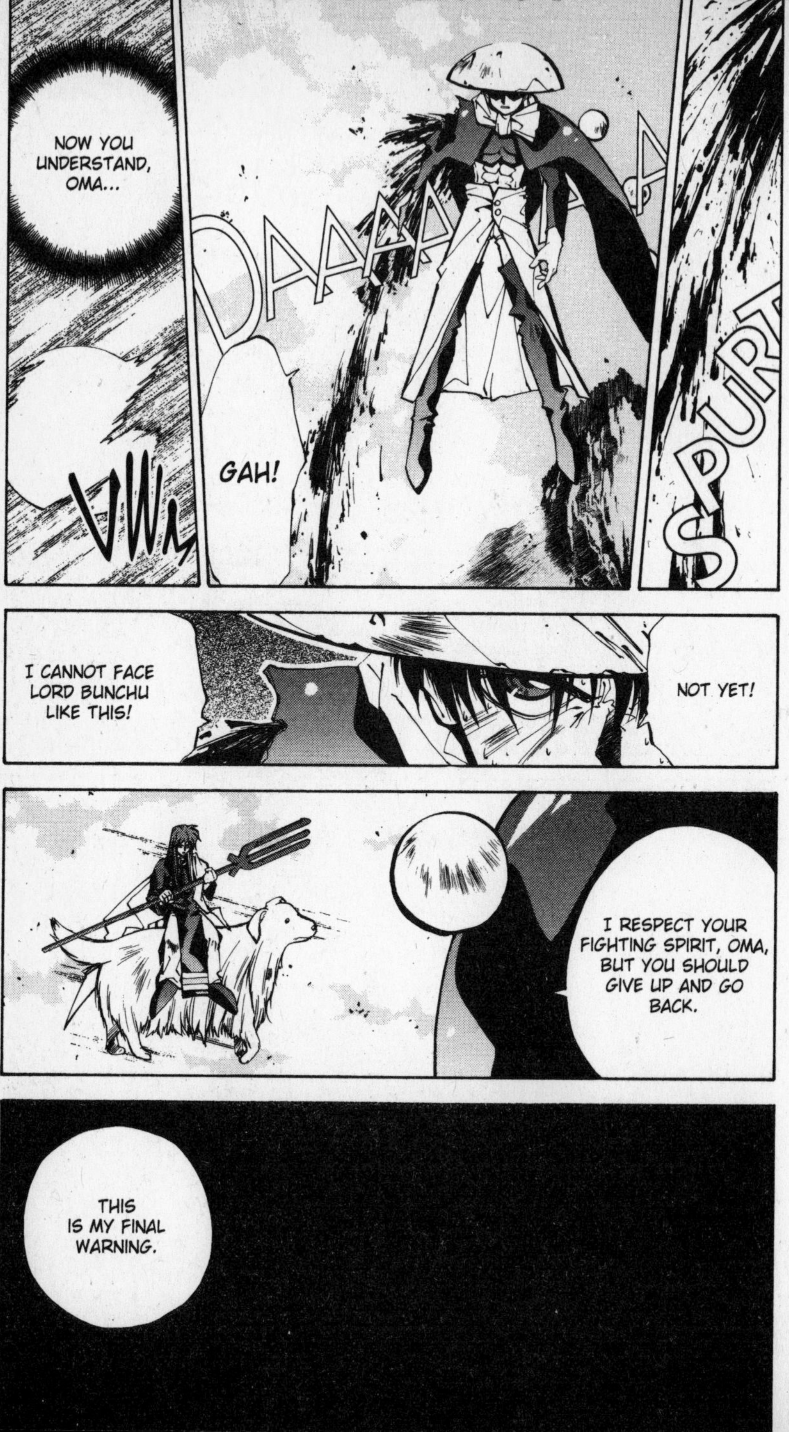
SPURT
DAAAA
GAH!
NOW YOU UNDERSTAND, OMA...
VWM
NOT YET!
I CANNOT FACE LORD BUNCHU LIKE THIS!
I RESPECT YOUR FIGHTING SPIRIT, OMA, BUT YOU SHOULD GIVE UP AND GO BACK.
THIS IS MY FINAL WARNING.

封神演義

CHAPTER 41
THE SHISEI OF KURYU ISLAND, PART 6 - NATAKU THE CRUSHER

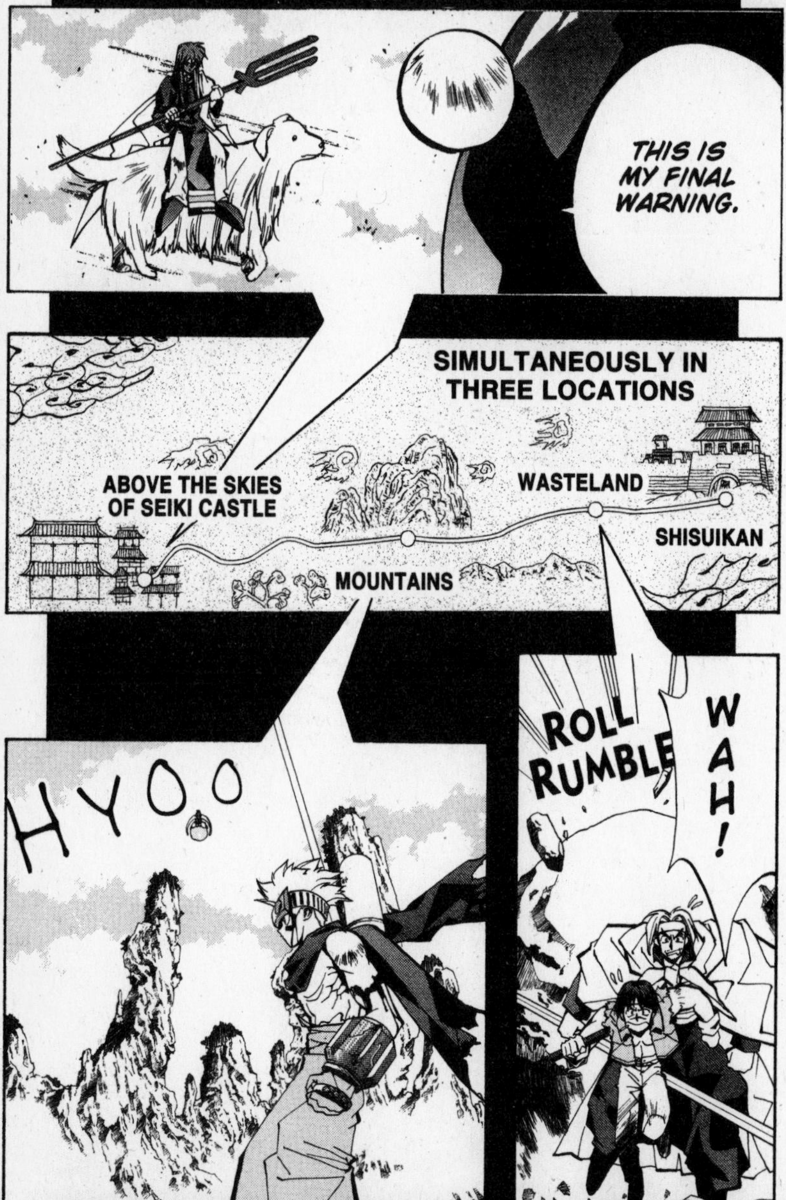
THIS IS MY FINAL WARNING.
SIMULTANEOUSLY IN THREE LOCATIONS
SHISUIKAN
WASTELAND
MOUNTAINS
ABOVE THE SKIES OF SEIKI CASTLE
ROLL RUMBLE
WAH!
HYOOO

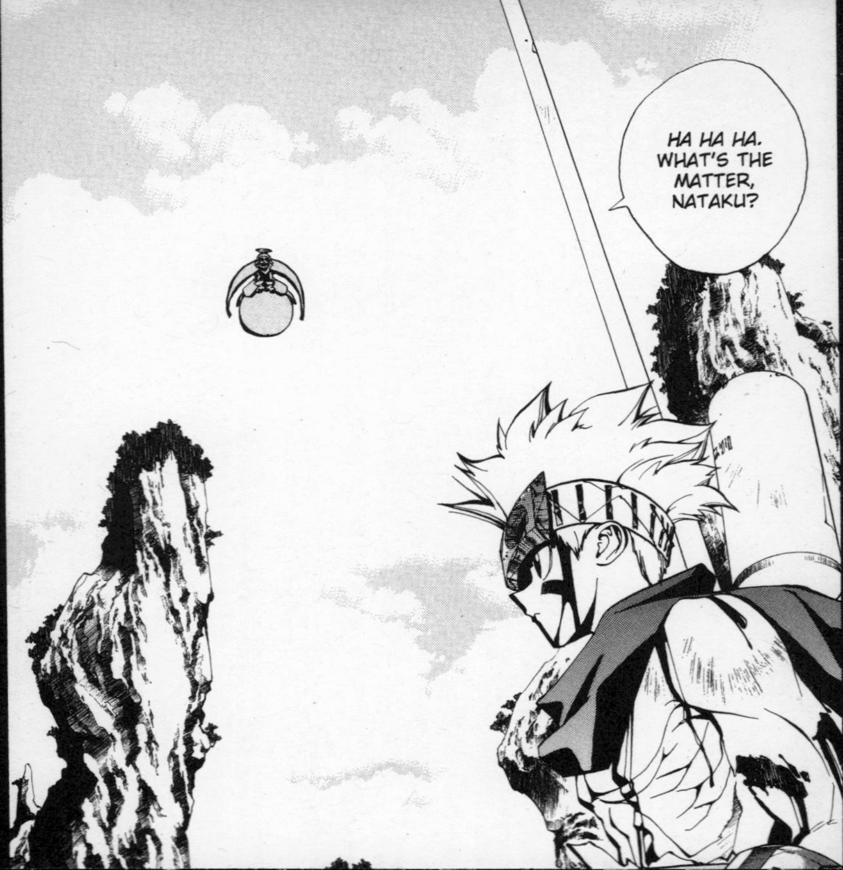
HA HA HA. WHAT'S THE MATTER, NATAKU?

Chapter 41

THE SHISEI OF KURYU ISLAND, PART 6

NATAKU THE CRUSHER

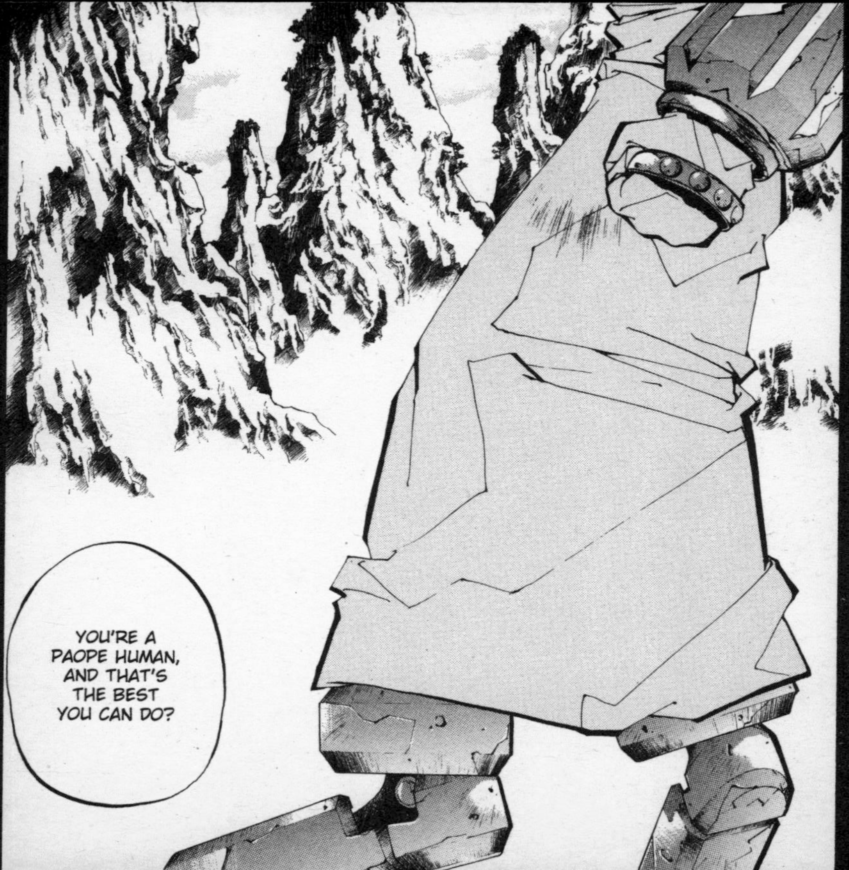
YOU'RE A PAOPE HUMAN, AND THAT'S THE BEST YOU CAN DO?

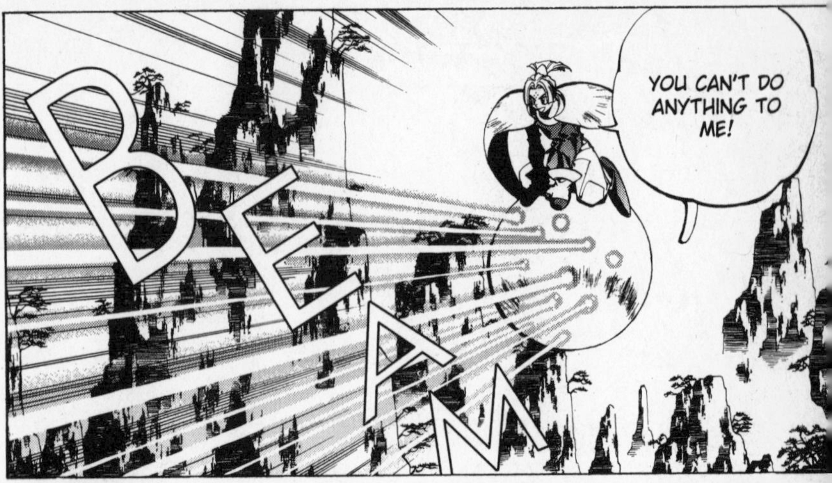
YOU CAN'T DO ANYTHING TO ME!
BEAM
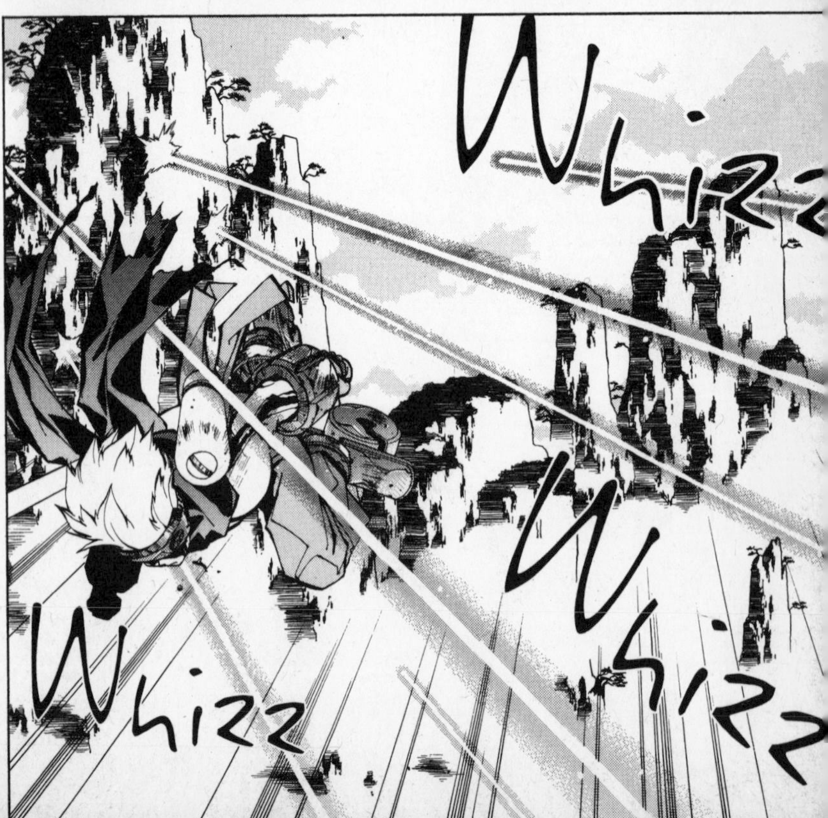
WHIZZ
WHIZZ
WHIZZ

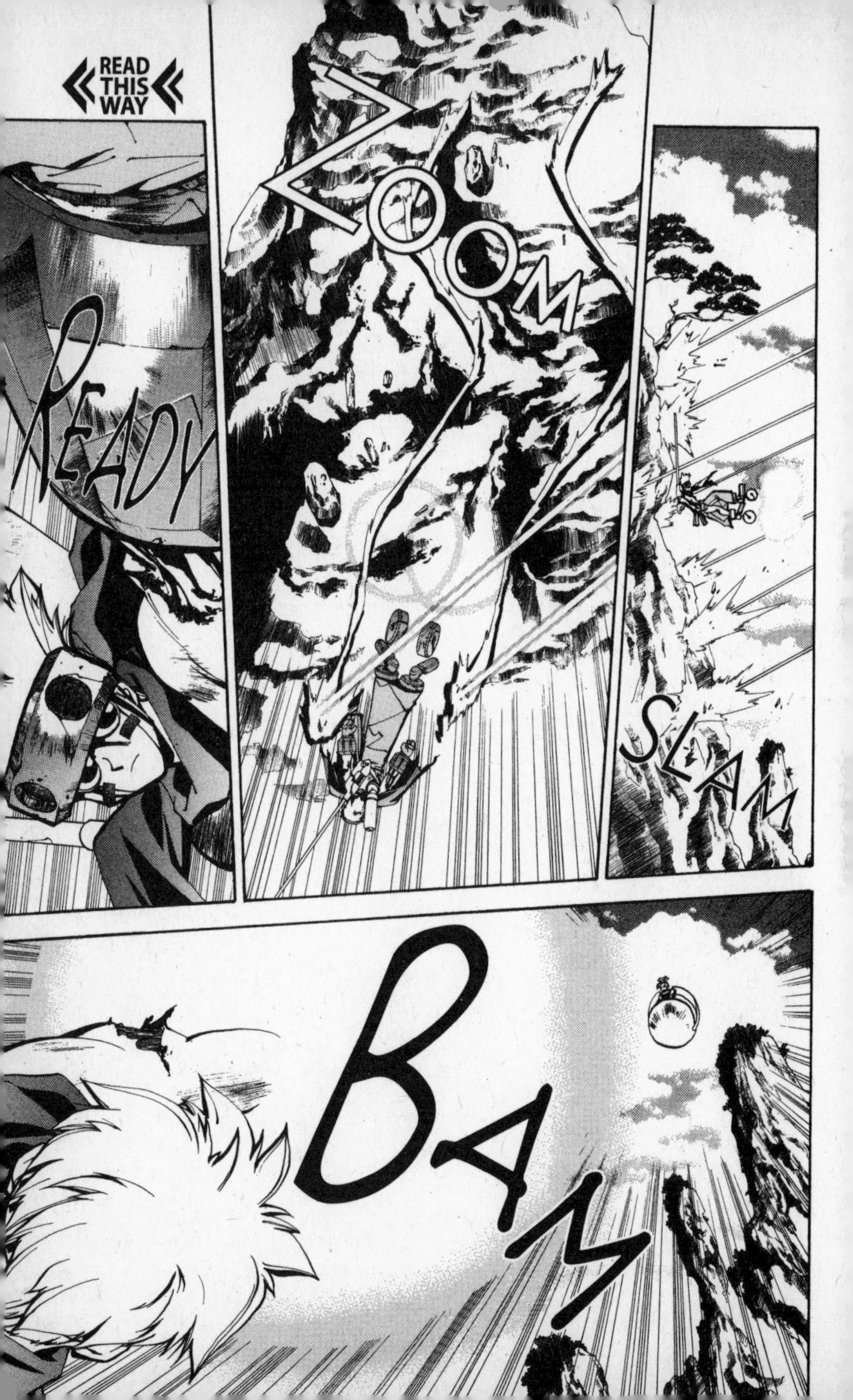
READ THIS WAY
SLAM
ZOOM
READY
BAM

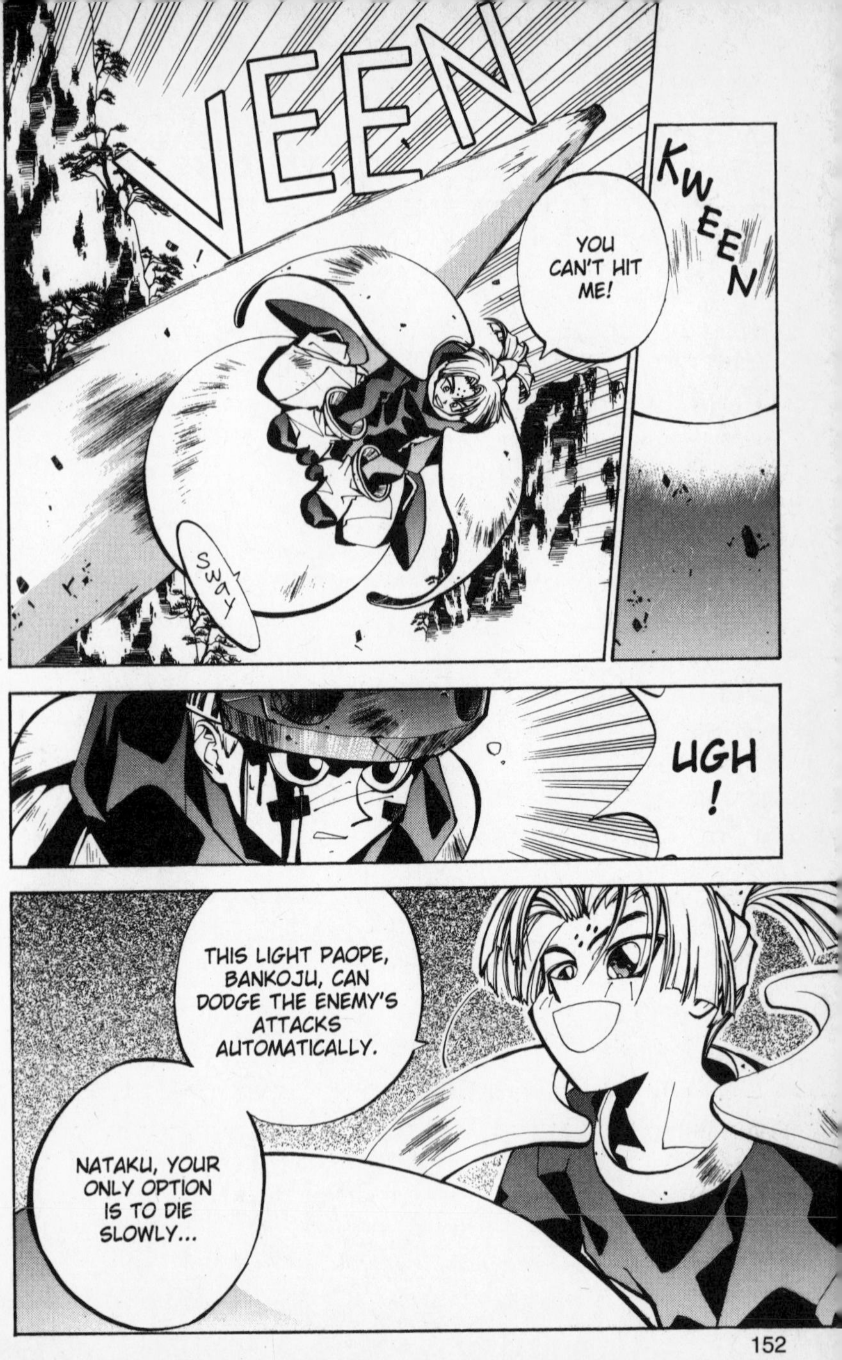
KWEEN
VEEN
YOU CAN'T HIT ME!
SWAY
UGH!
THIS LIGHT PAOPE, BANKOJU, CAN DODGE THE ENEMY'S ATTACKS AUTOMATICALLY.
NATAKU, YOUR ONLY OPTION IS TO DIE SLOWLY...

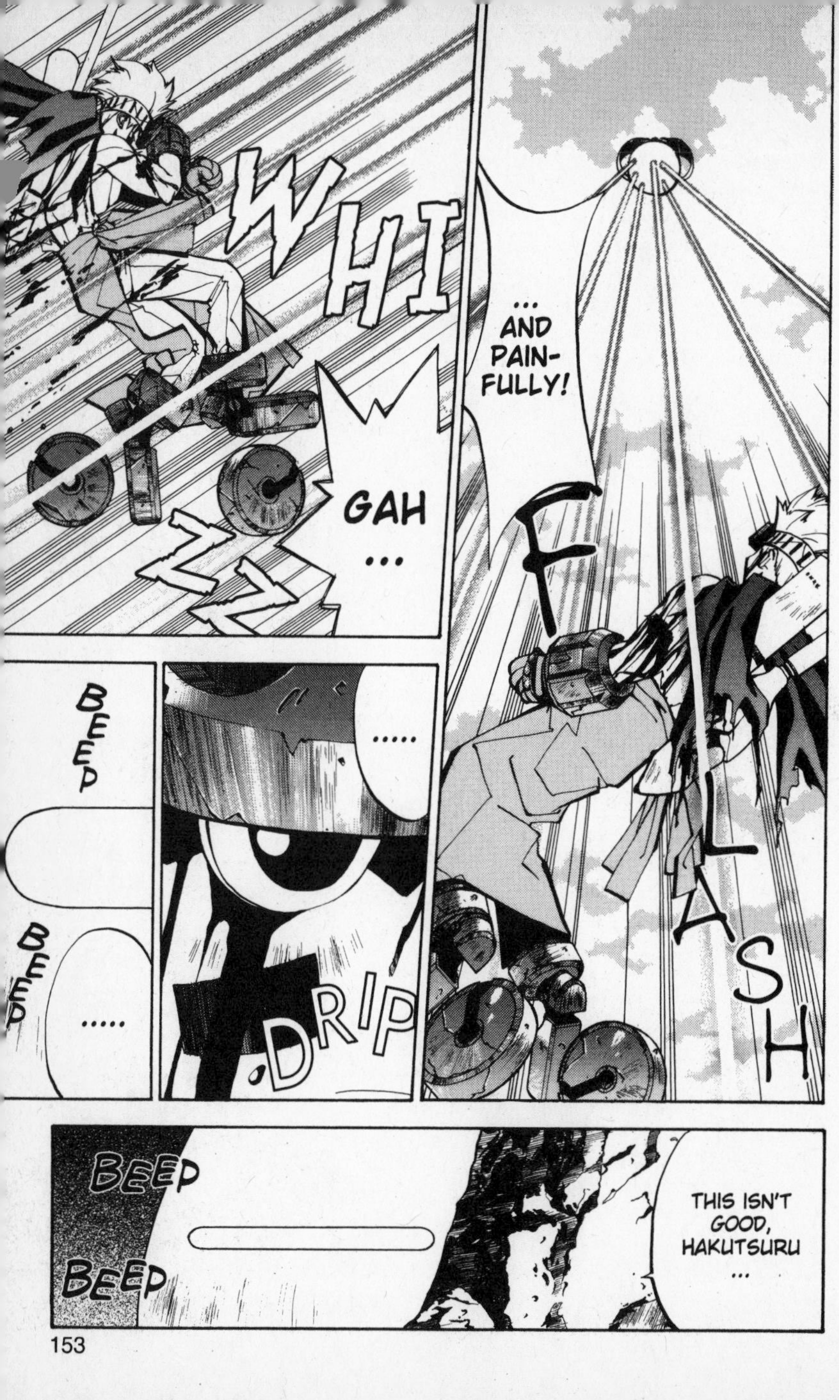
... AND PAIN-FULLY!
FLASH
WHIZZ
GAH ...
.....
DRIP
BEEP
BEEP
.....
THIS ISN'T GOOD, HAKUTSURU ...
BEEP
BEEP

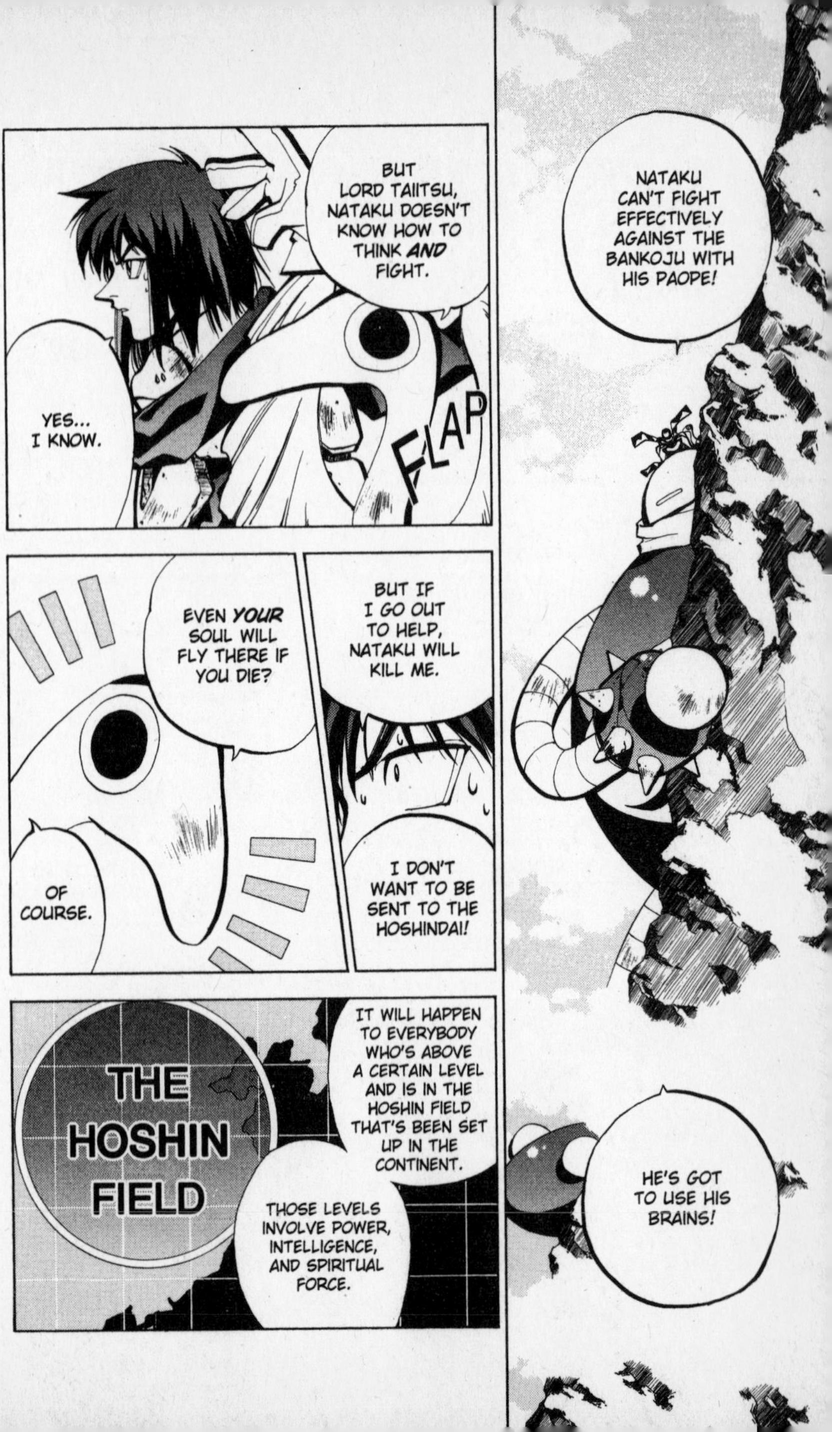
NATAKU CAN'T FIGHT EFFECTIVELY AGAINST THE BANKOJU WITH HIS PAOPE!
HE'S GOT TO USE HIS BRAINS!
BUT LORD TAIITSU, NATAKU DOESN'T KNOW HOW TO THINK *AND* FIGHT.
YES... I KNOW.
FLAP
BUT IF I GO OUT TO HELP, NATAKU WILL KILL ME.
I DON'T WANT TO BE SENT TO THE HOSHINDAI!
EVEN *YOUR* SOUL WILL FLY THERE IF YOU DIE?
OF COURSE.
IT WILL HAPPEN TO EVERYBODY WHO'S ABOVE A CERTAIN LEVEL AND IS IN THE HOSHIN FIELD THAT'S BEEN SET UP IN THE CONTINENT.
THOSE LEVELS INVOLVE POWER, INTELLIGENCE, AND SPIRITUAL FORCE.
THE HOSHIN FIELD

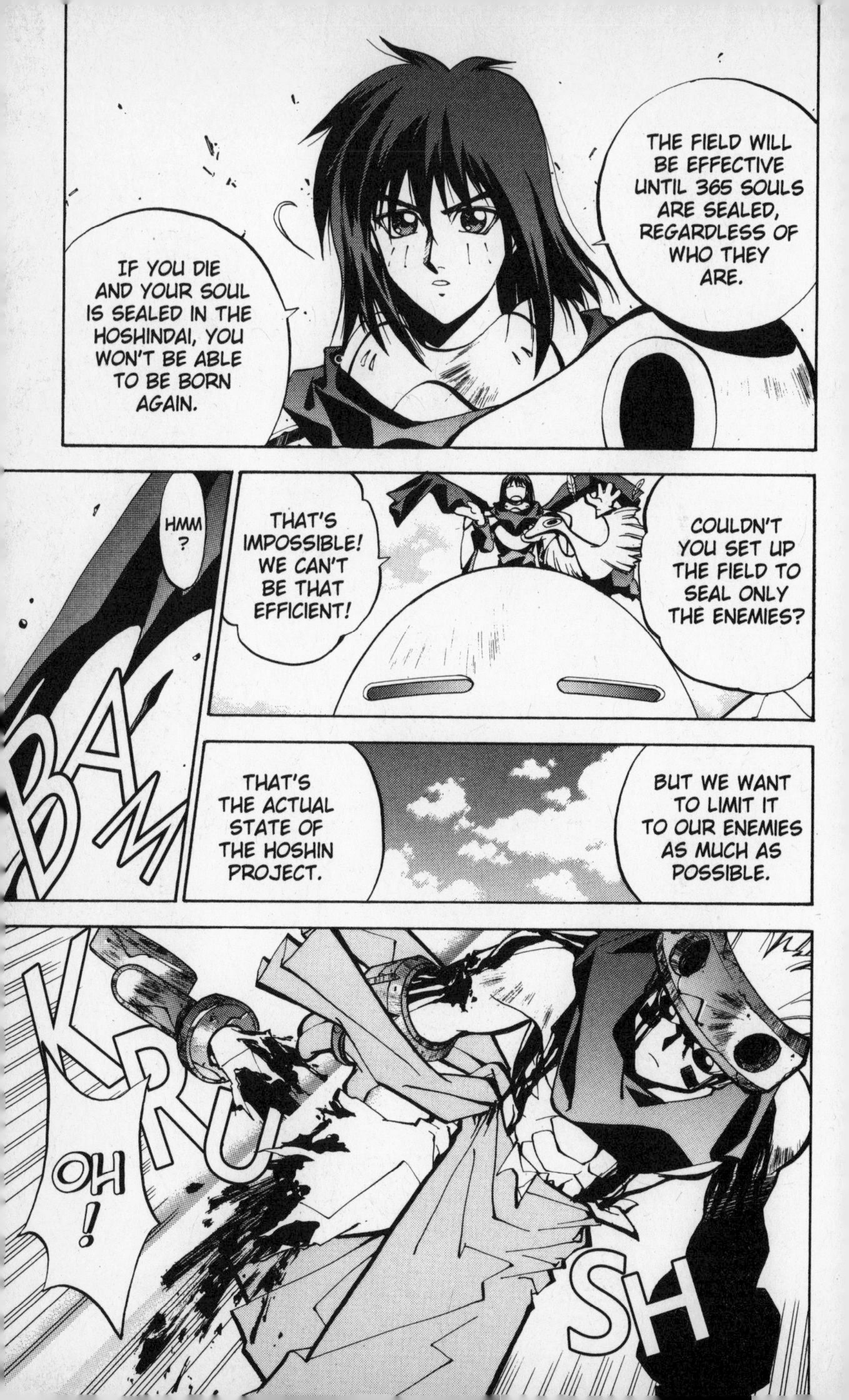
THE FIELD WILL BE EFFECTIVE UNTIL 365 SOULS ARE SEALED, REGARDLESS OF WHO THEY ARE.
IF YOU DIE AND YOUR SOUL IS SEALED IN THE HOSHINDAI, YOU WON'T BE ABLE TO BE BORN AGAIN.
COULDN'T YOU SET UP THE FIELD TO SEAL ONLY THE ENEMIES?
THAT'S IMPOSSIBLE! WE CAN'T BE THAT EFFICIENT!
BUT WE WANT TO LIMIT IT TO OUR ENEMIES AS MUCH AS POSSIBLE.
THAT'S THE ACTUAL STATE OF THE HOSHIN PROJECT.
HMM?
BAM
KRUSH
OH!

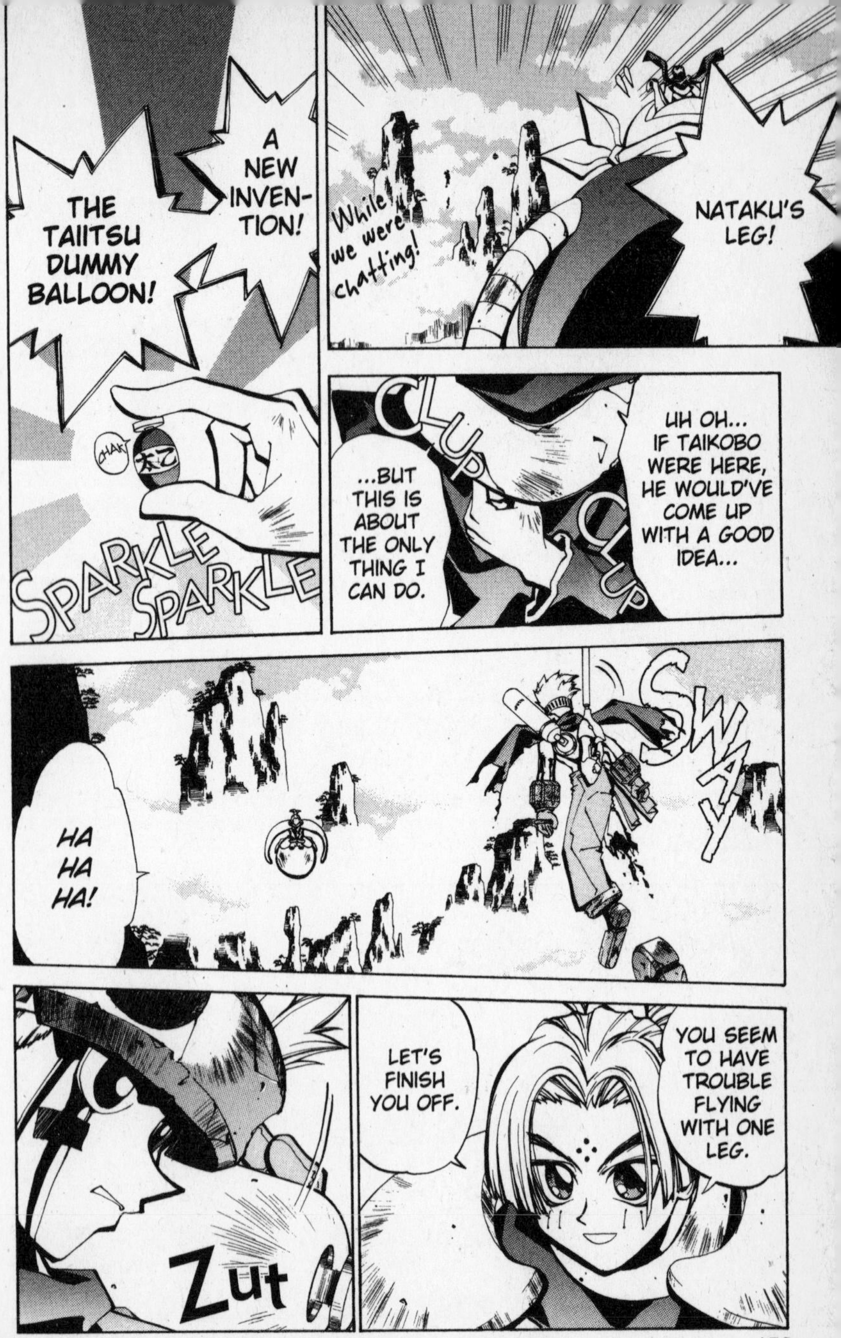
NATAKU'S LEG!
While we were chatting!
UH OH... IF TAIKOBO WERE HERE, HE WOULD'VE COME UP WITH A GOOD IDEA...
CLUP CLUP
...BUT THIS IS ABOUT THE ONLY THING I CAN DO.
A NEW INVENTION!
THE TAIITSU DUMMY BALLOON!
CHAK
SPARKLE SPARKLE
SWAY
HA HA HA!
YOU SEEM TO HAVE TROUBLE FLYING WITH ONE LEG.
LET'S FINISH YOU OFF.
Zut

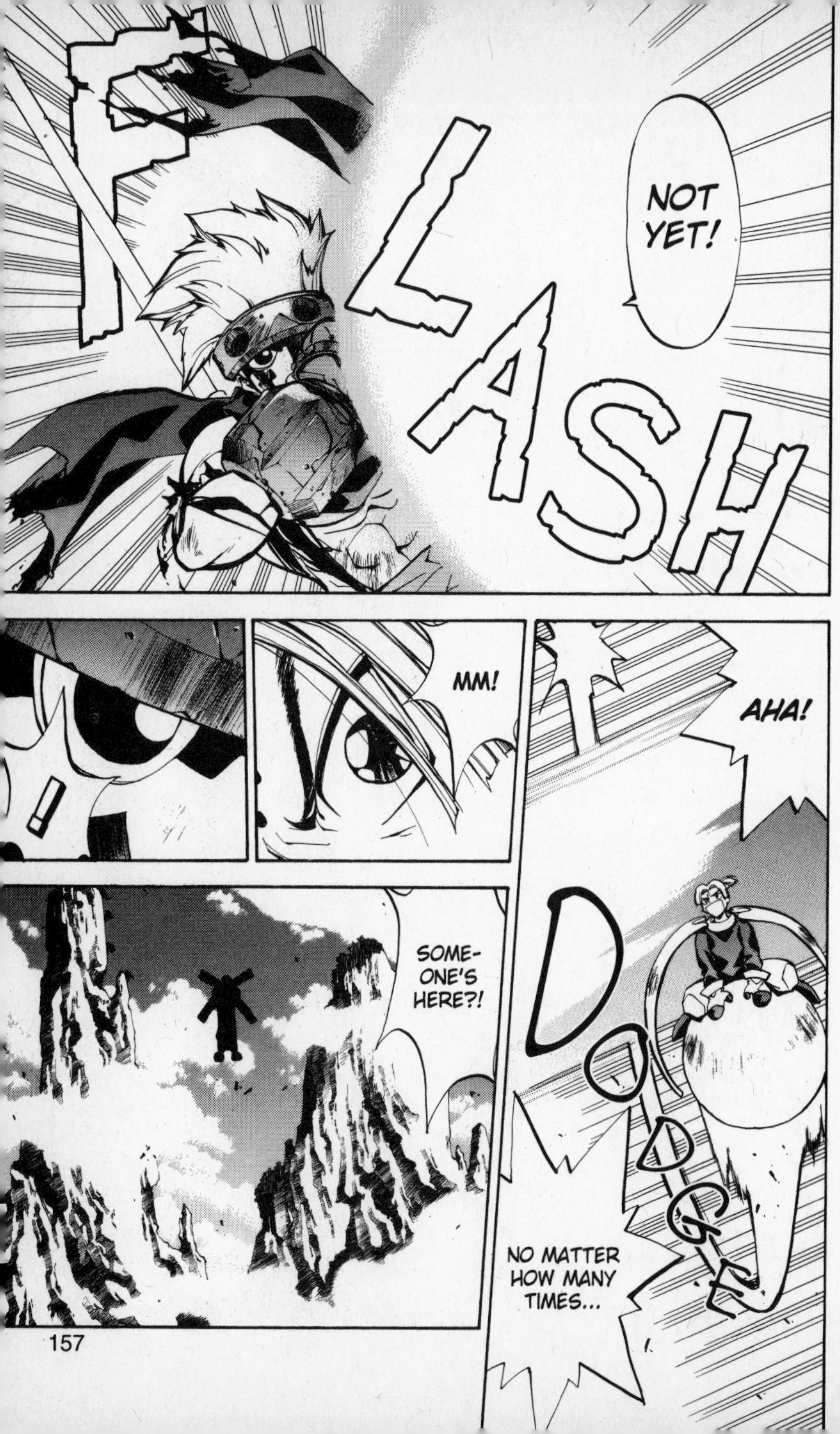
NOT YET!
FLASH
AHA!
DODGE
NO MATTER HOW MANY TIMES...
MM!
!
SOME-ONE'S HERE?!

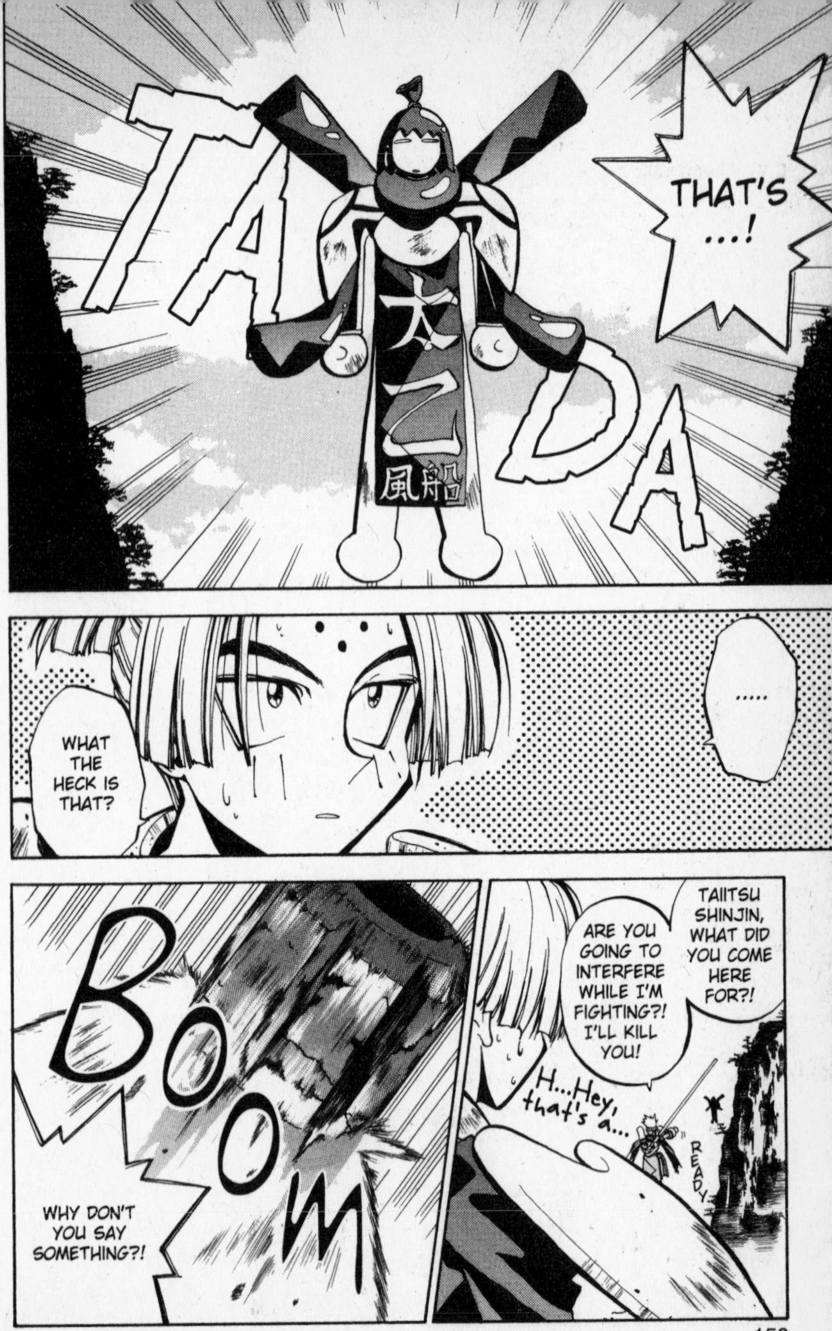
TA DA
THAT'S ...!
太乙
風船
.....
WHAT THE HECK IS THAT?
TAIITSU SHINJIN, WHAT DID YOU COME HERE FOR?!
ARE YOU GOING TO INTERFERE WHILE I'M FIGHTING?! I'LL KILL YOU!
H...Hey, that's a...
READY
BOOM
WHY DON'T YOU SAY SOMETHING?!

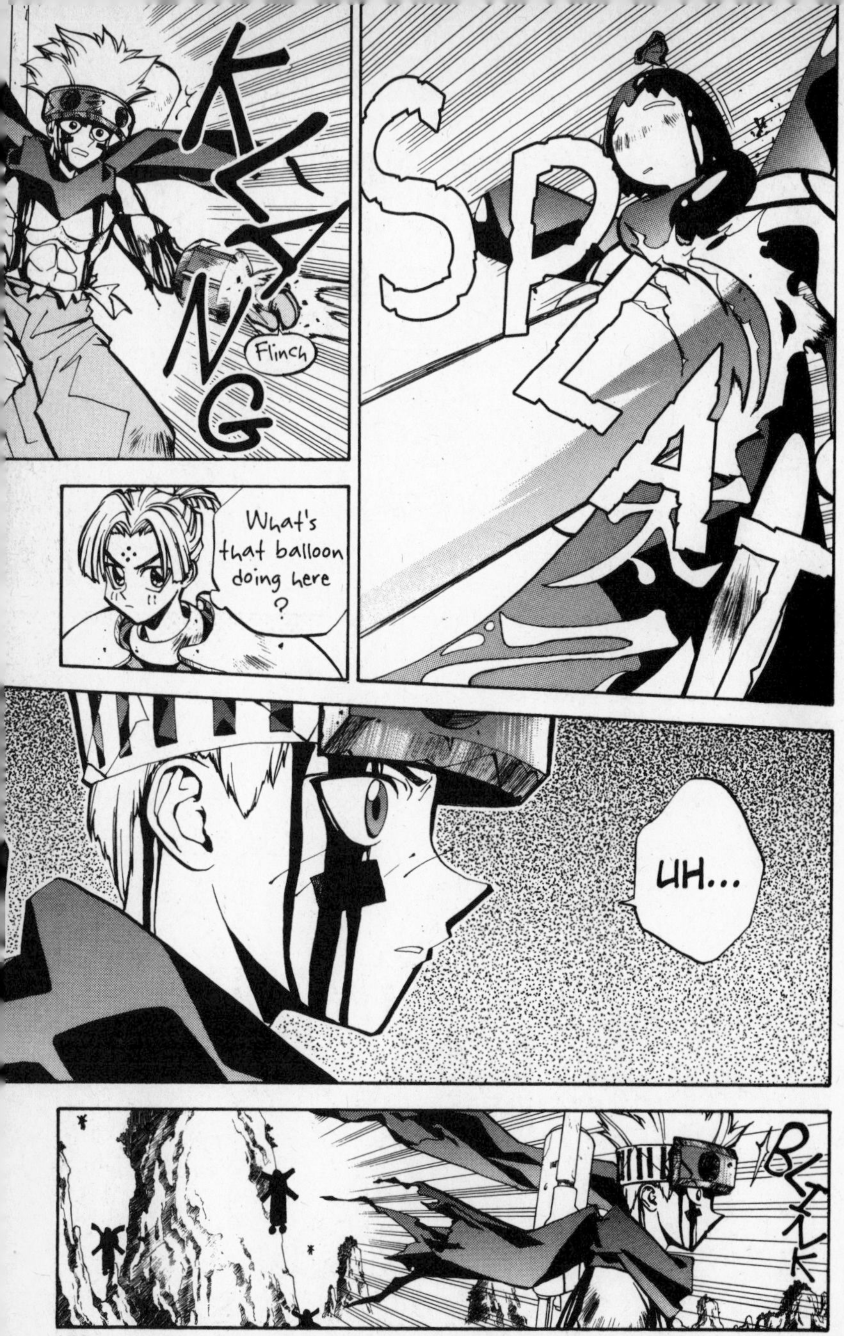
SPLAT
KLANG
Flinch
What's that balloon doing here?
UH...
BLINK

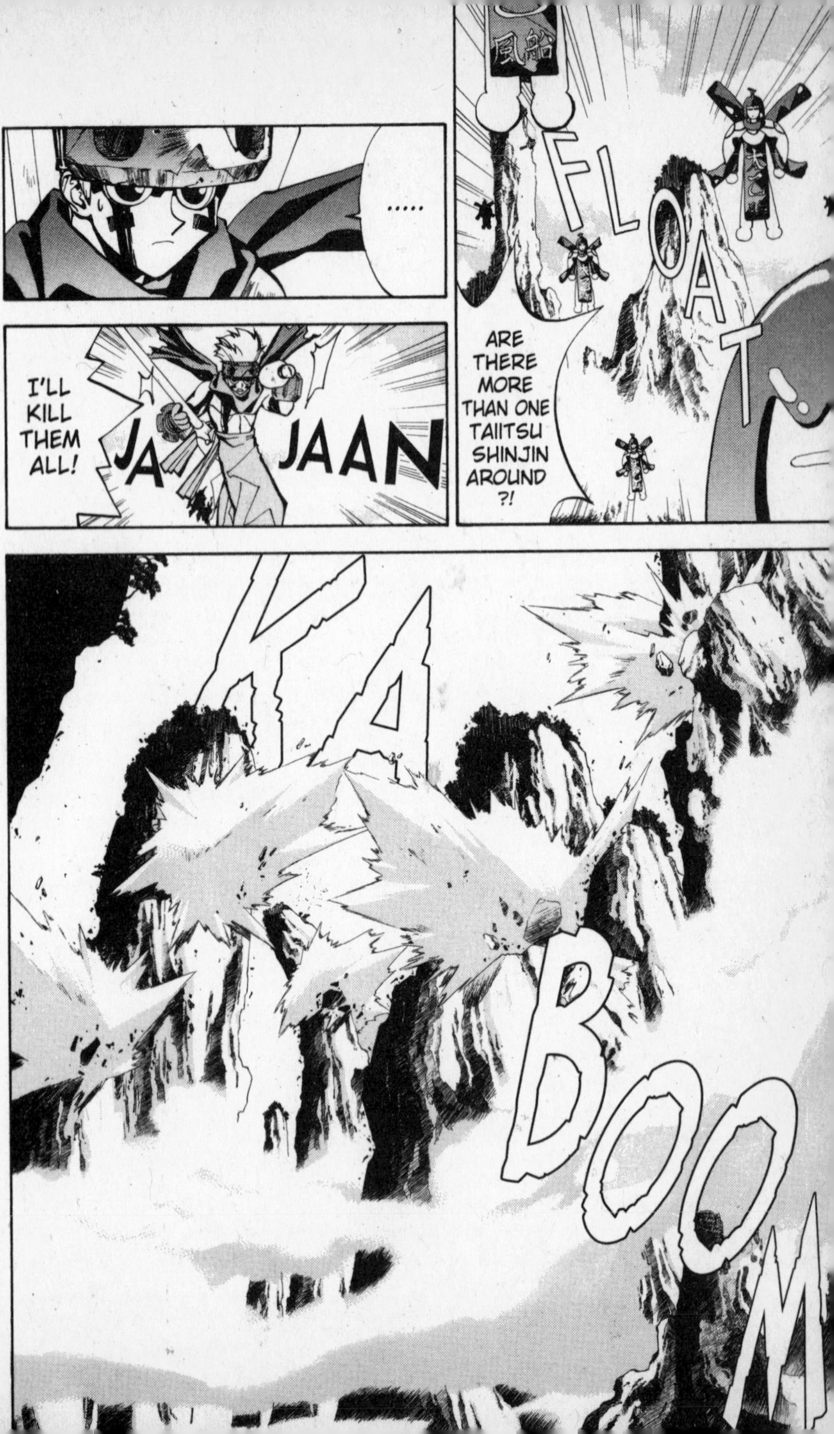
風船
FLOAT
ARE THERE MORE THAN ONE TAIITSU SHINJIN AROUND?!
......
I'LL KILL THEM ALL!
JA JAAN
KA BOOM

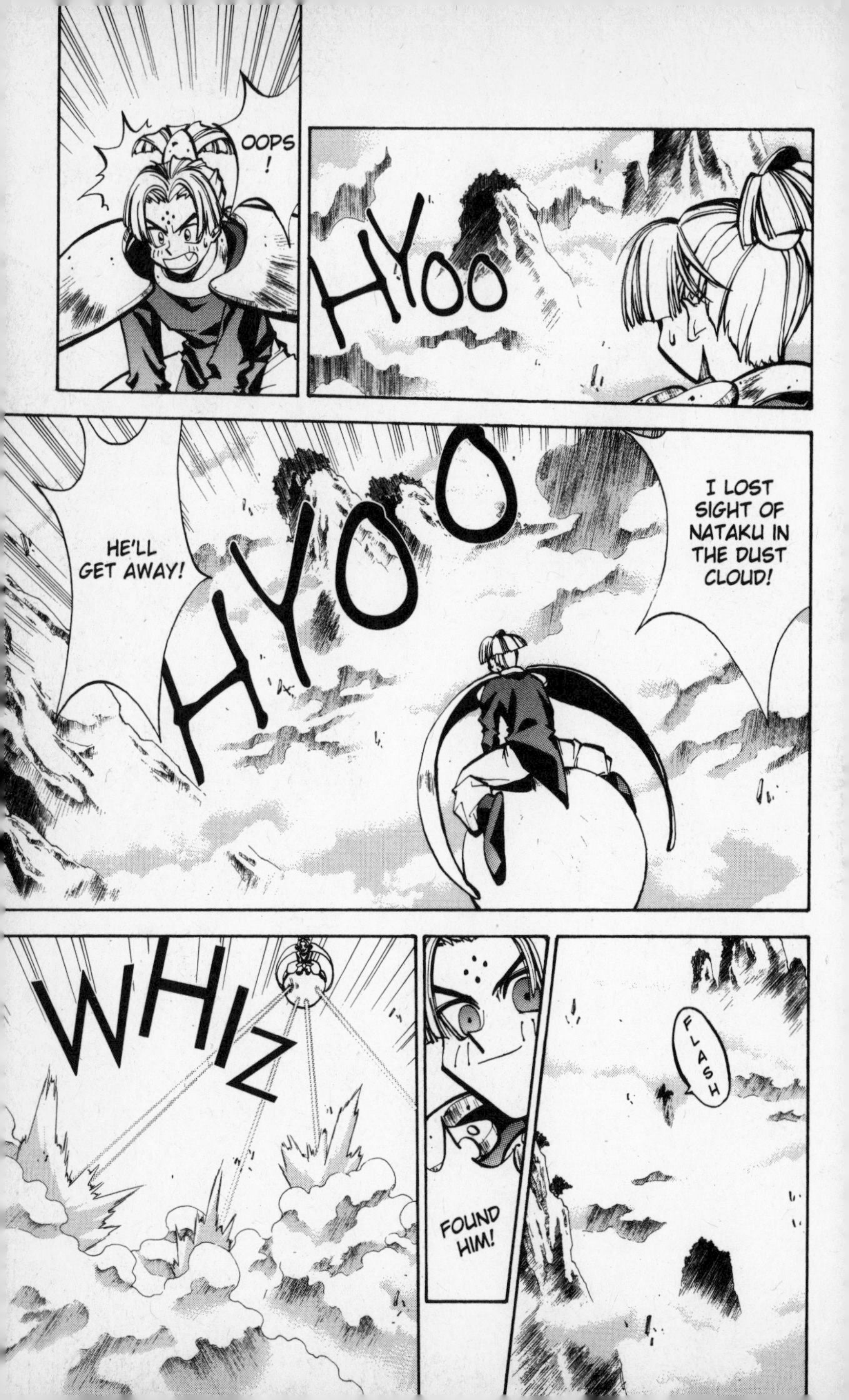
HYOO
OOPS!
I LOST SIGHT OF NATAKU IN THE DUST CLOUD!
HYOO
HE'LL GET AWAY!
FLASH
FOUND HIM!
WHIZ

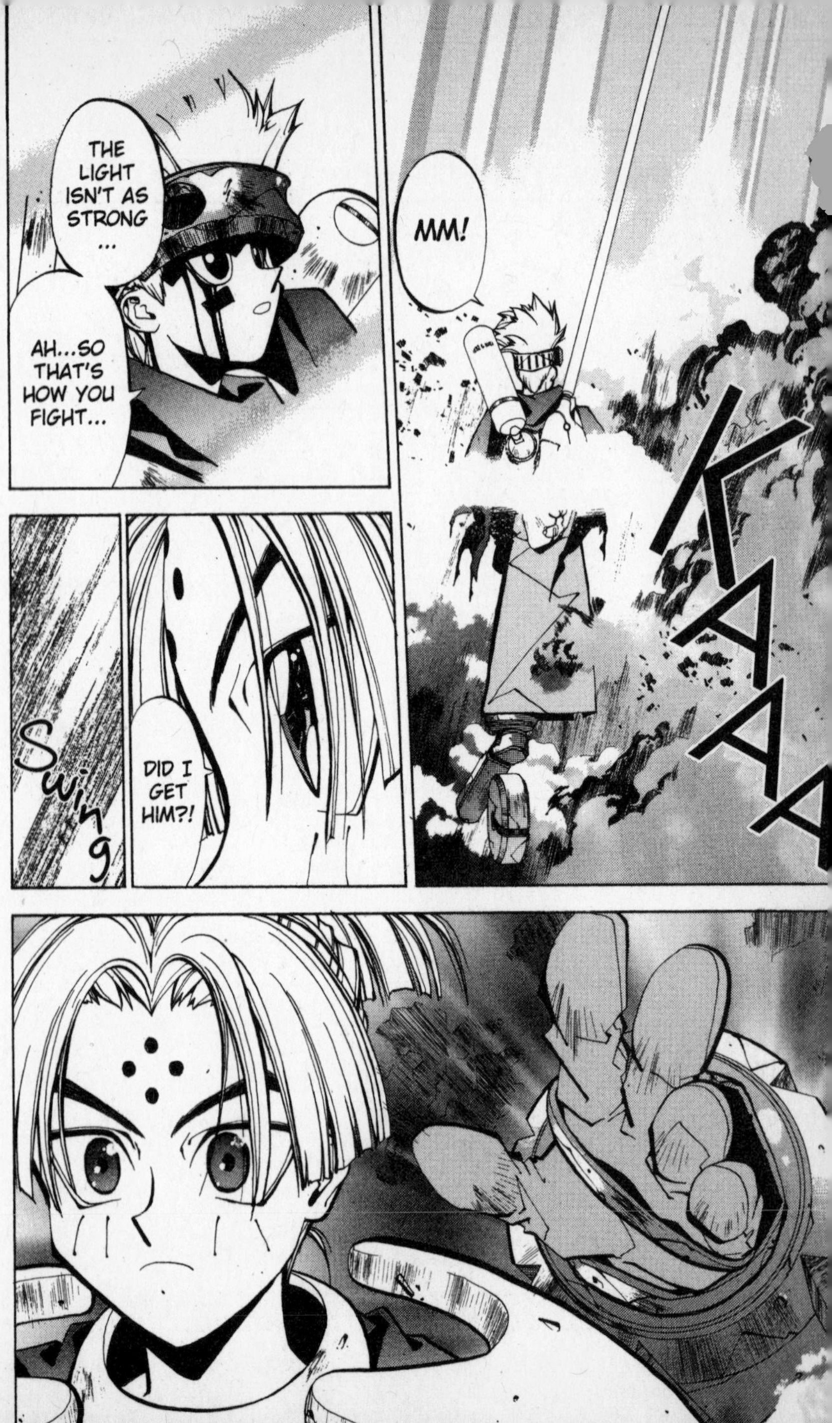
MM!
KAAAA
THE LIGHT ISN'T AS STRONG ...
AH...SO THAT'S HOW YOU FIGHT...
DID I GET HIM?!
Swing

READ THIS WAY

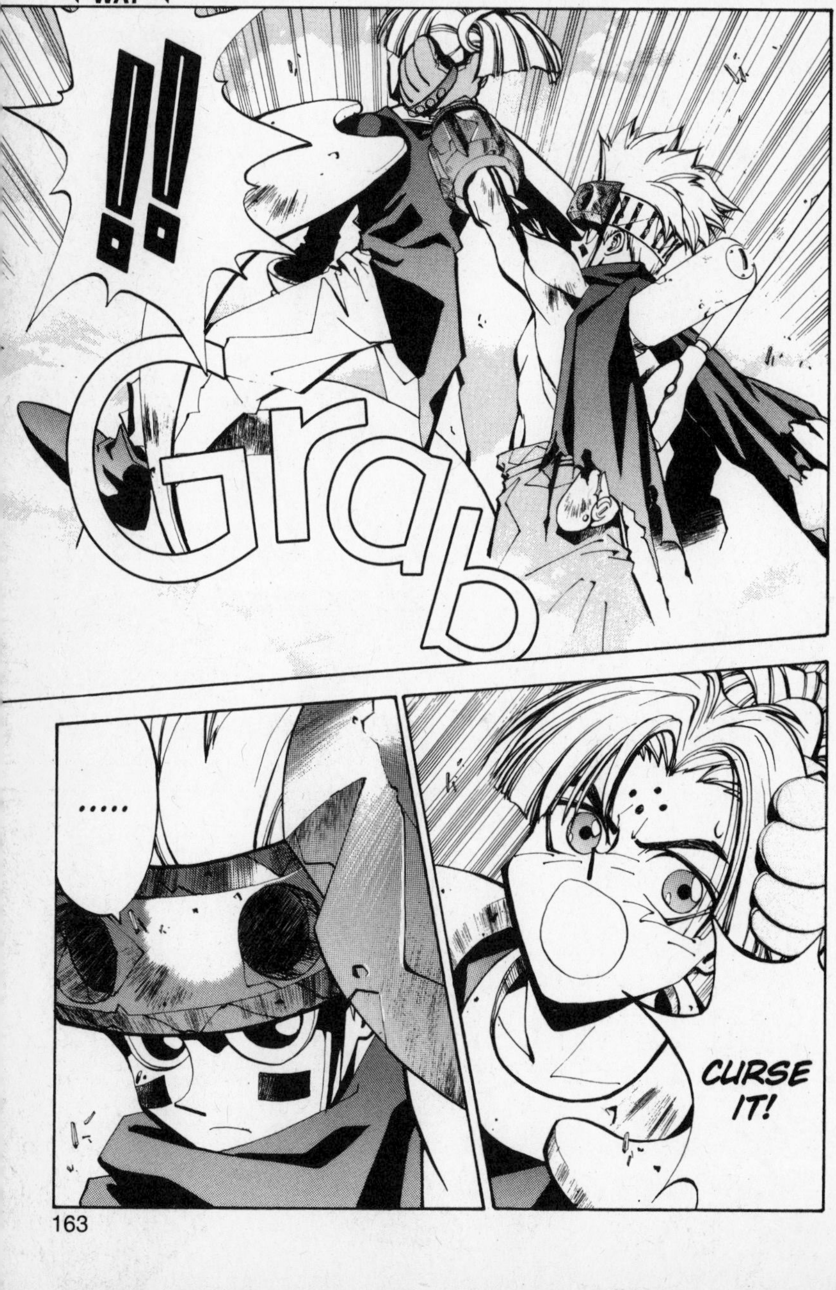

!!
Grab
CURSE IT!
.....

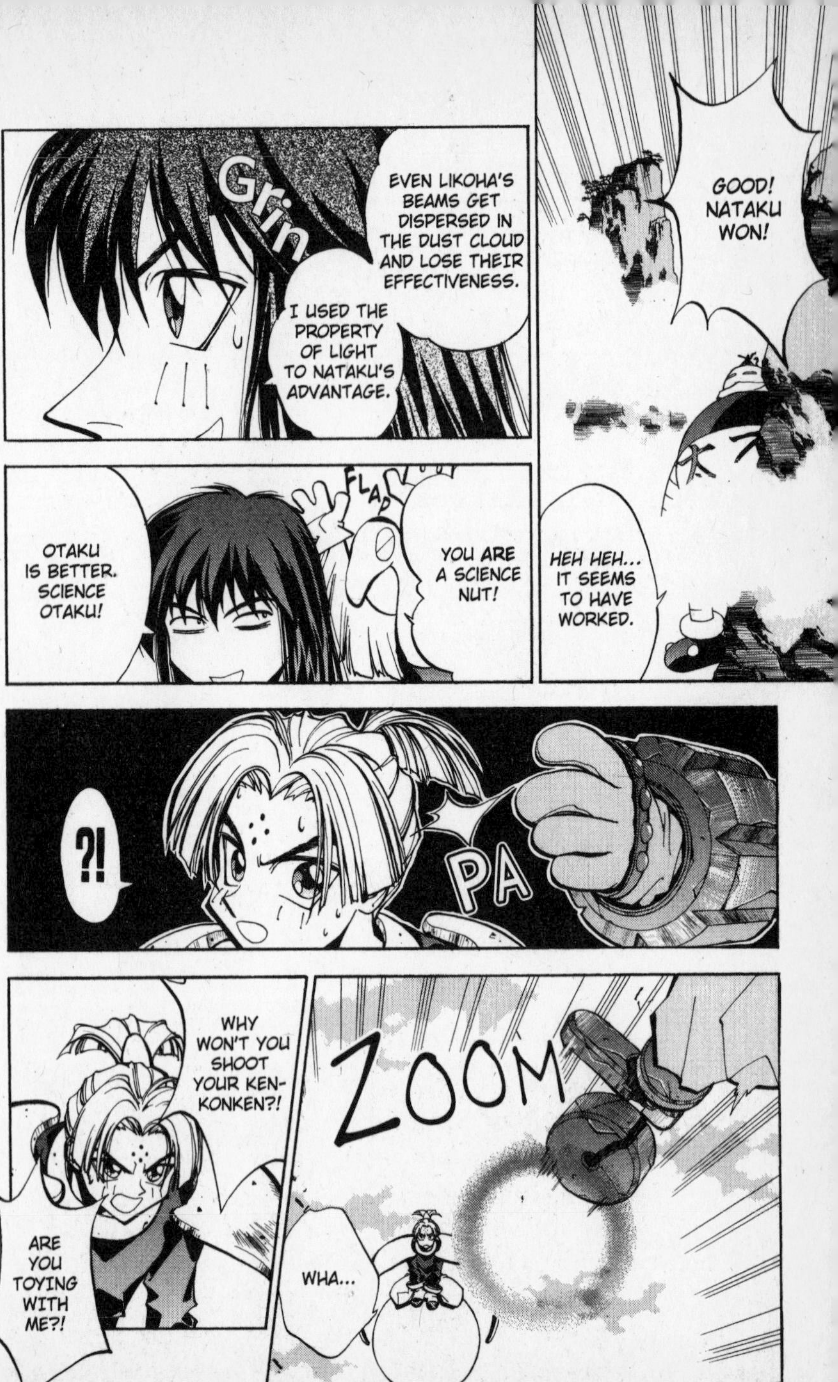
GOOD! NATAKU WON!
HEH HEH... IT SEEMS TO HAVE WORKED.
Grin
EVEN LIKOHA'S BEAMS GET DISPERSED IN THE DUST CLOUD AND LOSE THEIR EFFECTIVENESS.
I USED THE PROPERTY OF LIGHT TO NATAKU'S ADVANTAGE.
FLAP
YOU ARE A SCIENCE NUT!
OTAKU IS BETTER. SCIENCE OTAKU!
PA
?!
ZOOM
WHA...
WHY WON'T YOU SHOOT YOUR KEN-KONKEN?!
ARE YOU TOYING WITH ME?!

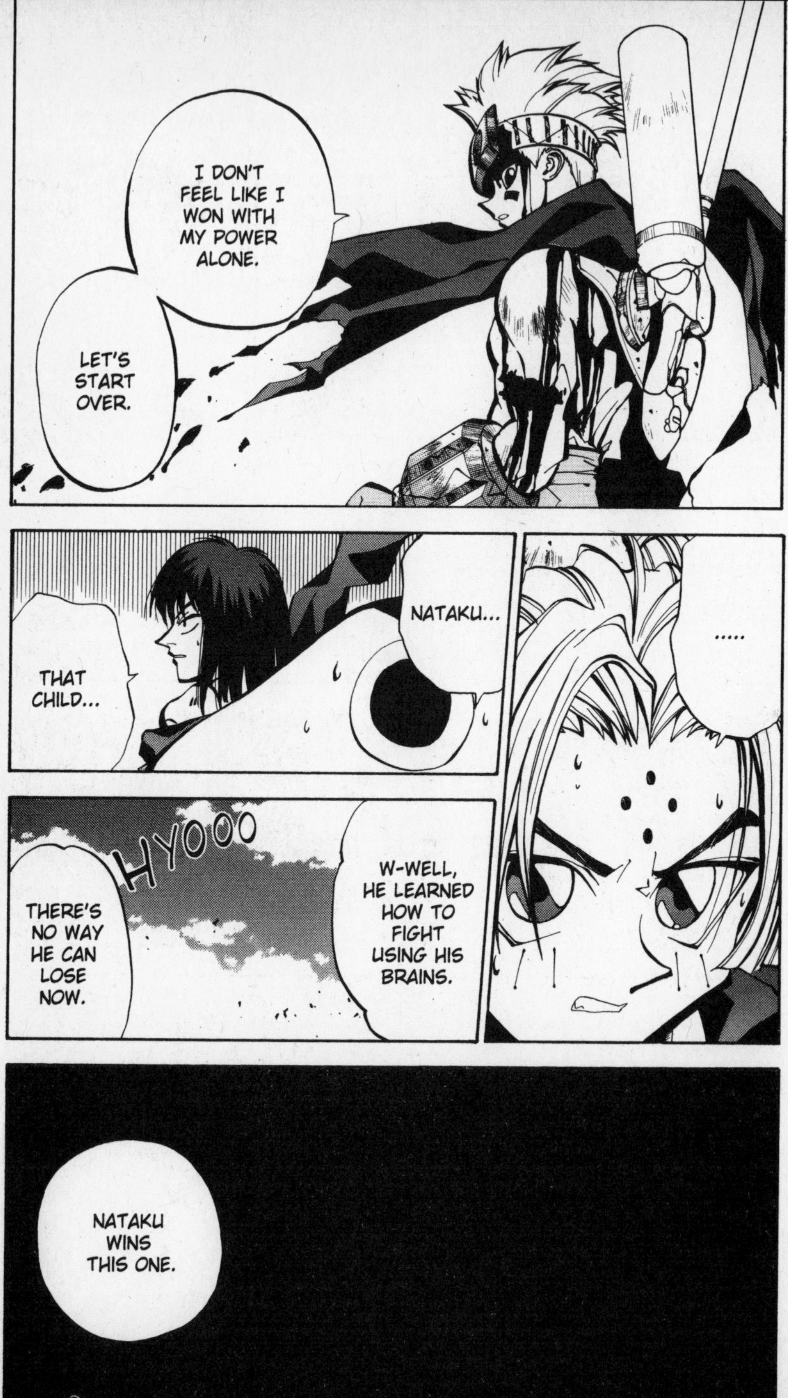
I DON'T FEEL LIKE I WON WITH MY POWER ALONE.
LET'S START OVER.
.....
NATAKU...
THAT CHILD...
W-WELL, HE LEARNED HOW TO FIGHT USING HIS BRAINS.
HYOOO
THERE'S NO WAY HE CAN LOSE NOW.
NATAKU WINS THIS ONE.

封神演義

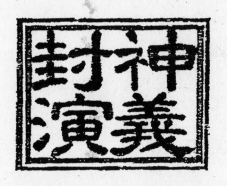

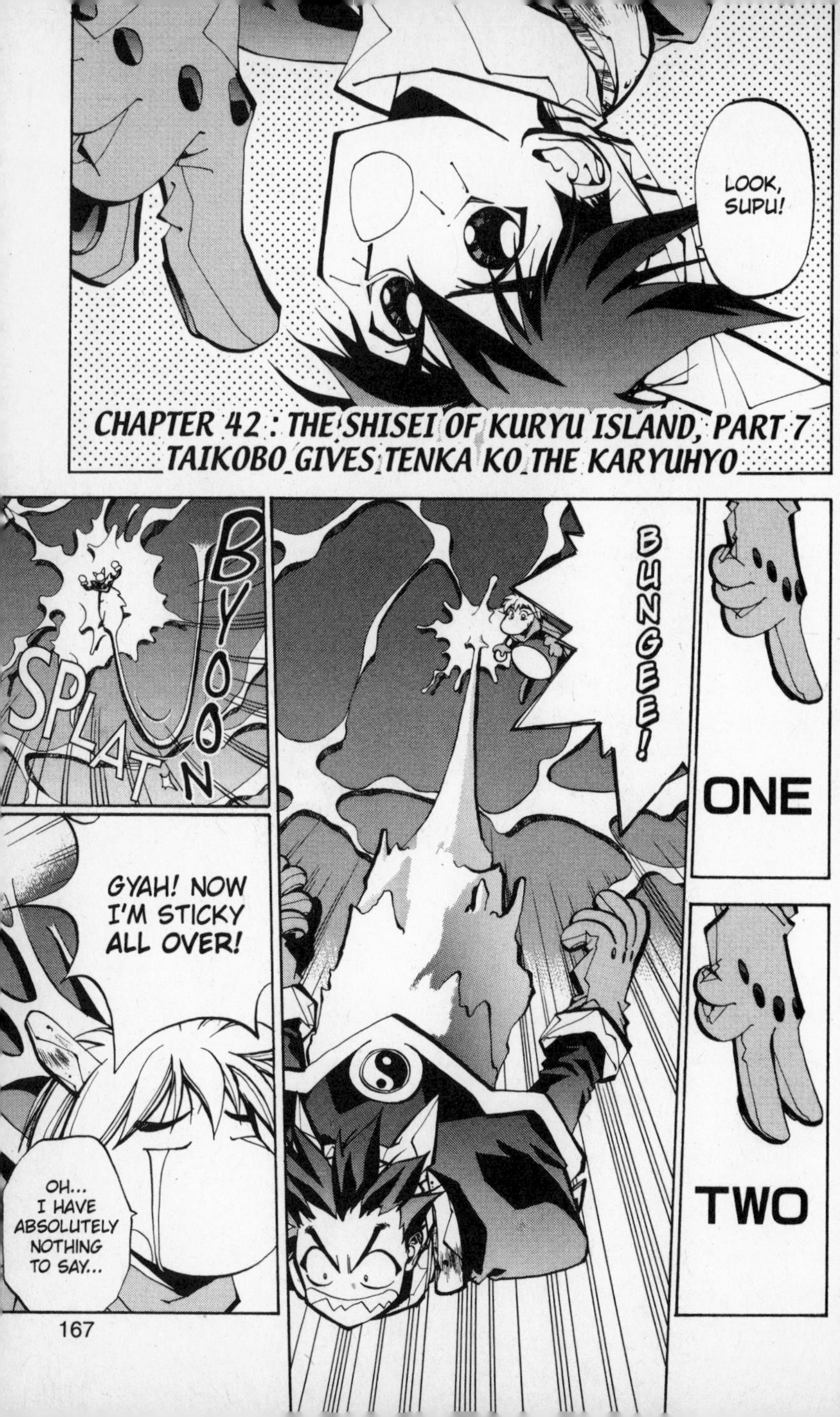
LOOK, SUPU!
CHAPTER 42 : THE SHISEI OF KURYU ISLAND, PART 7
TAIKOBO GIVES TENKA KO THE KARYUHYO
ONE
TWO
BUNGEE!
BYOOON
SPLAT
GYAH! NOW I'M STICKY ALL OVER!
OH... I HAVE ABSOLUTELY NOTHING TO SAY...

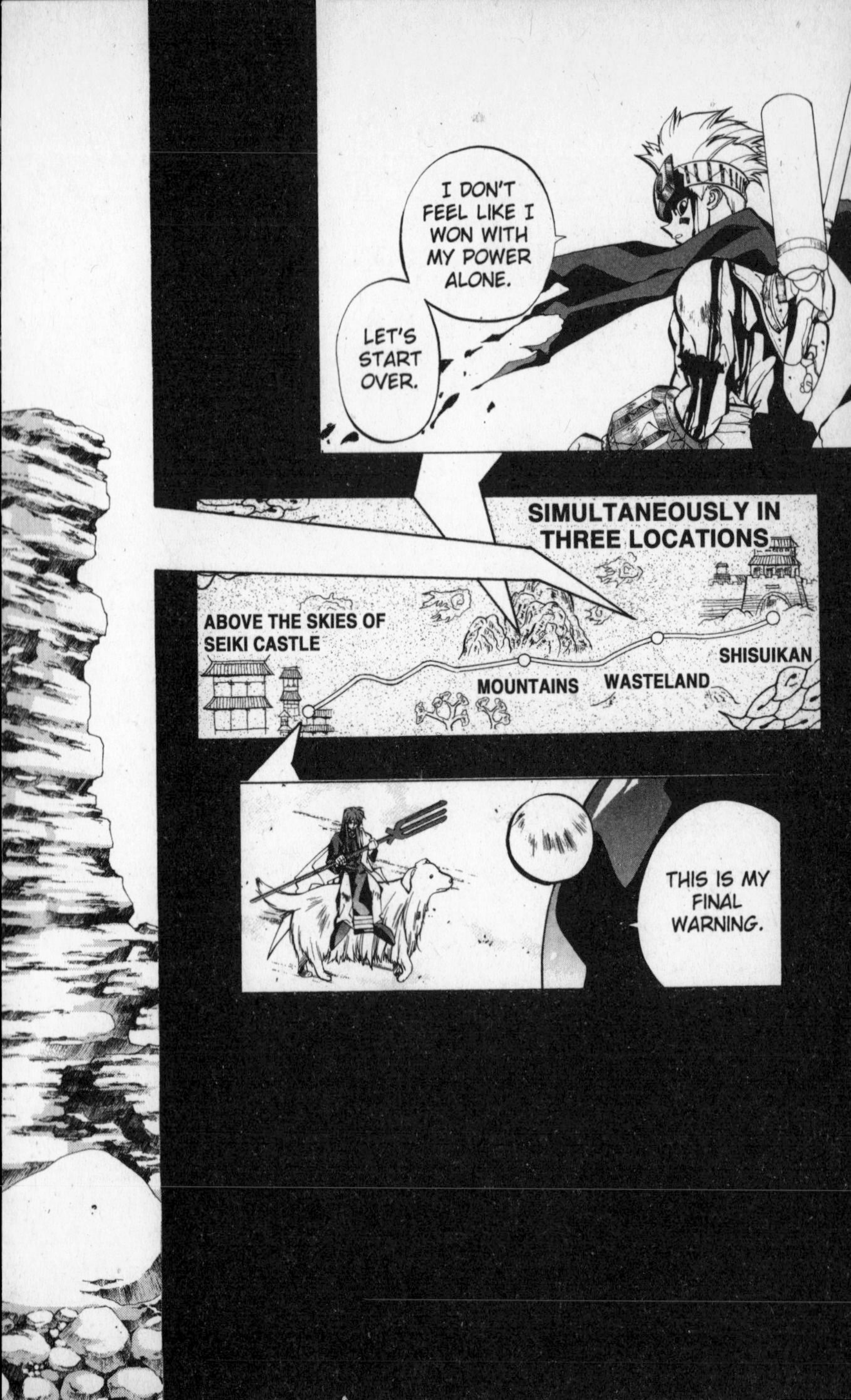
I DON'T FEEL LIKE I WON WITH MY POWER ALONE.
LET'S START OVER.
SIMULTANEOUSLY IN THREE LOCATIONS
SHISUIKAN
WASTELAND
MOUNTAINS
ABOVE THE SKIES OF SEIKI CASTLE
THIS IS MY FINAL WARNING.

Chapter 42

THE SHISEI OF KURYU ISLAND, PART 7

TAIKOBO GIVES TENKA KO THE KARYUHYO

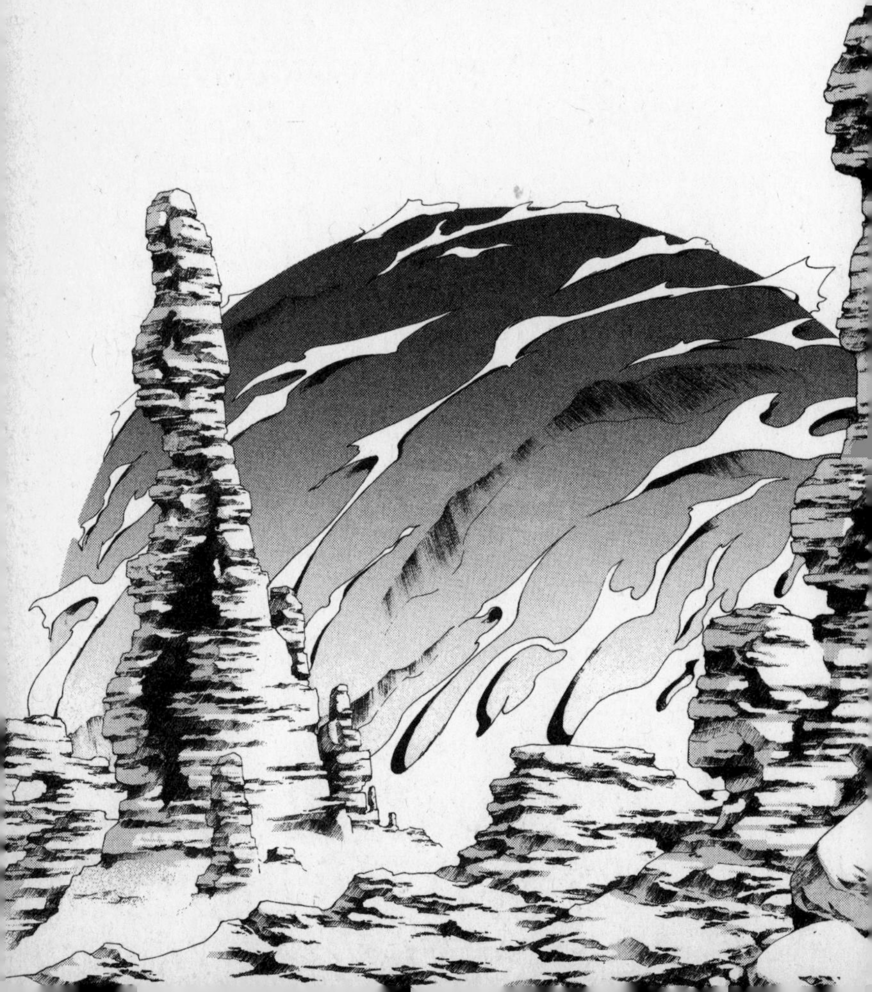

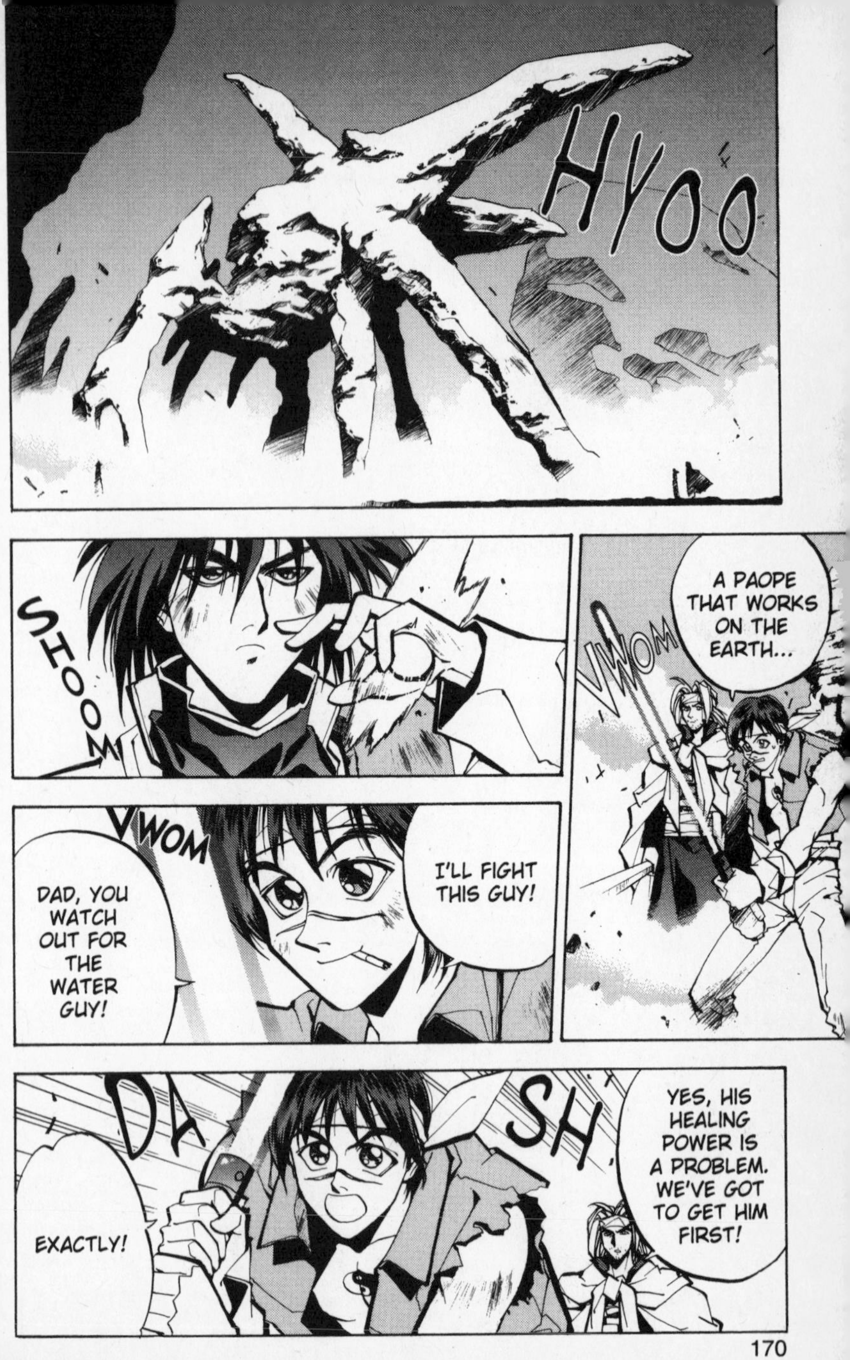
HYOO
A PAOPE THAT WORKS ON THE EARTH...
VWOM
SHOOM
I'LL FIGHT THIS GUY!
VWOM
DAD, YOU WATCH OUT FOR THE WATER GUY!
YES, HIS HEALING POWER IS A PROBLEM. WE'VE GOT TO GET HIM FIRST!
DASH
EXACTLY!

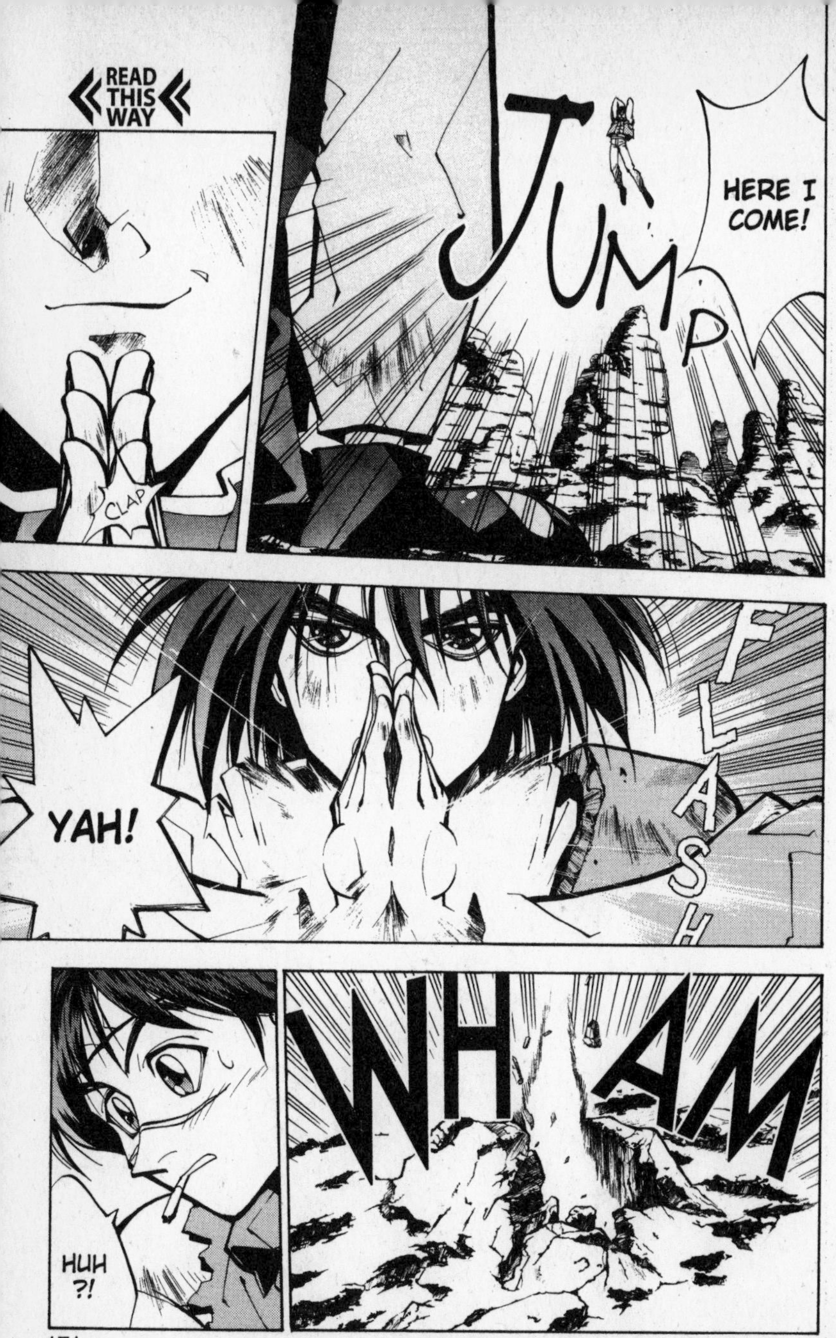
READ THIS WAY
HERE I COME!
JUMP
CLAP
FLASH
YAH!
WHAM
HUH ?!

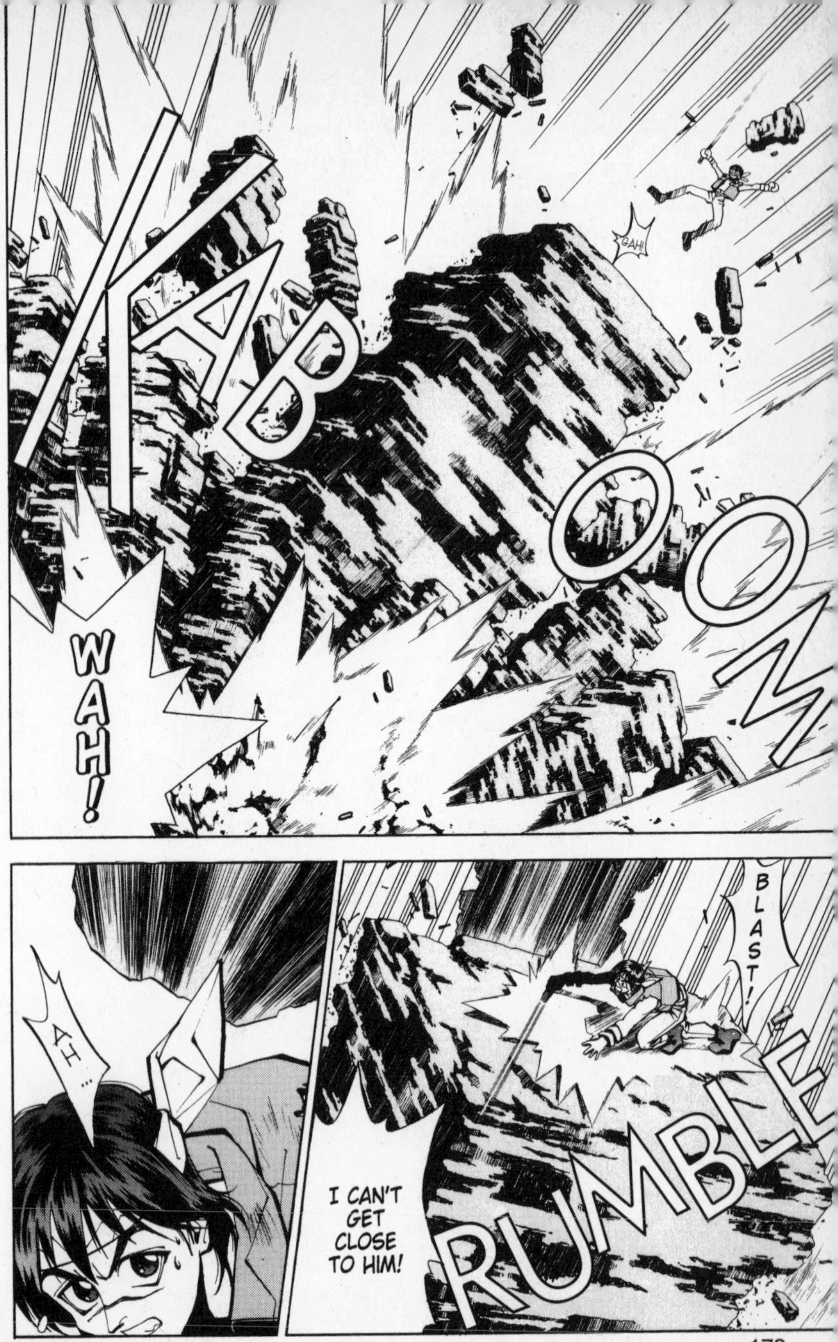
GAH!
KABOOOM
WAH!
BLAST!
RUMBLE
I CAN'T GET CLOSE TO HIM!
AH...

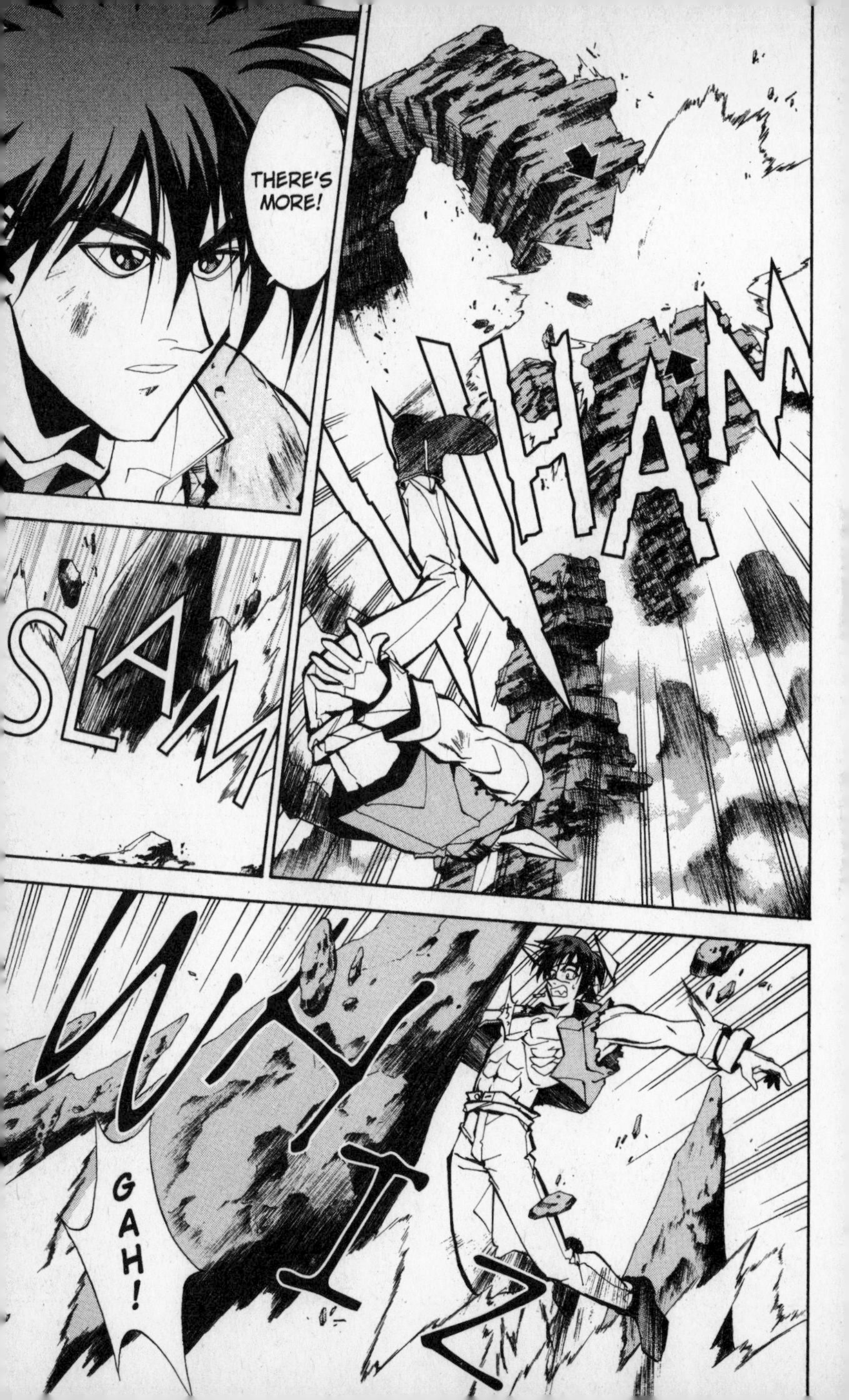
WHAM
THERE'S MORE!
SLAM
WHIZ
GAH!

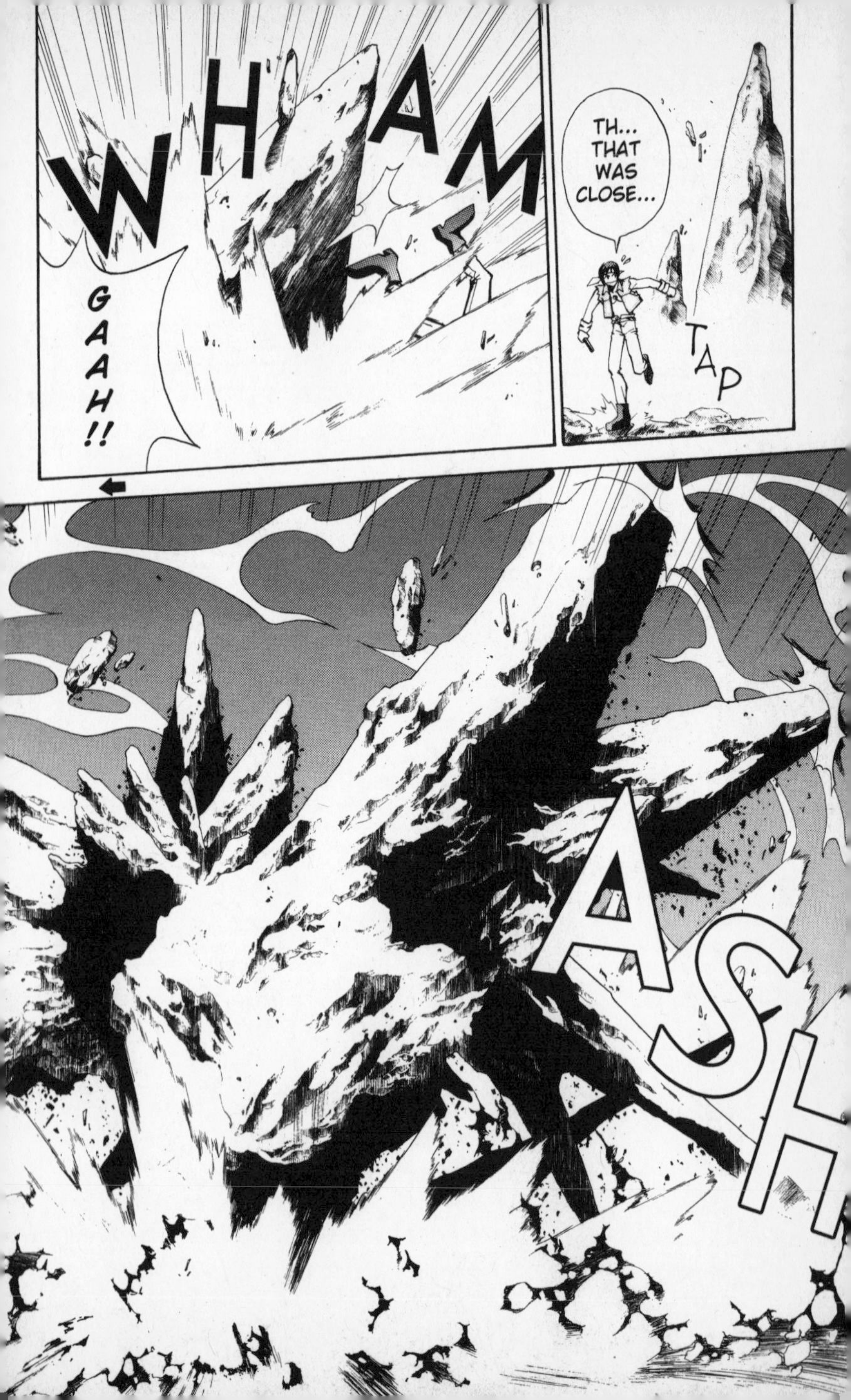
TH... THAT WAS CLOSE...
TAP
WHAM
GAAH!!
ASH

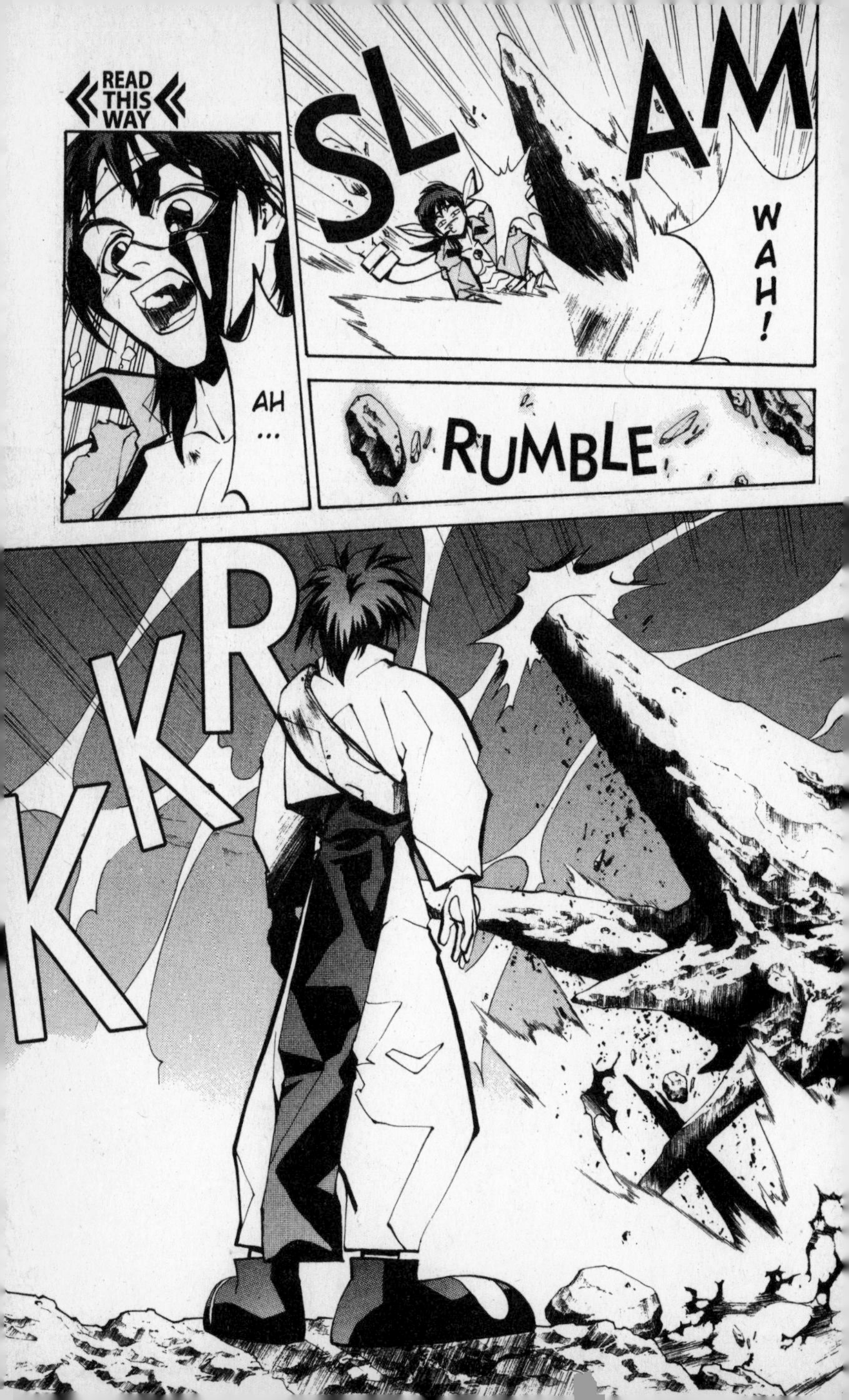
READ THIS WAY
SLAM
WAH!
RUMBLE
AH ...
KKR

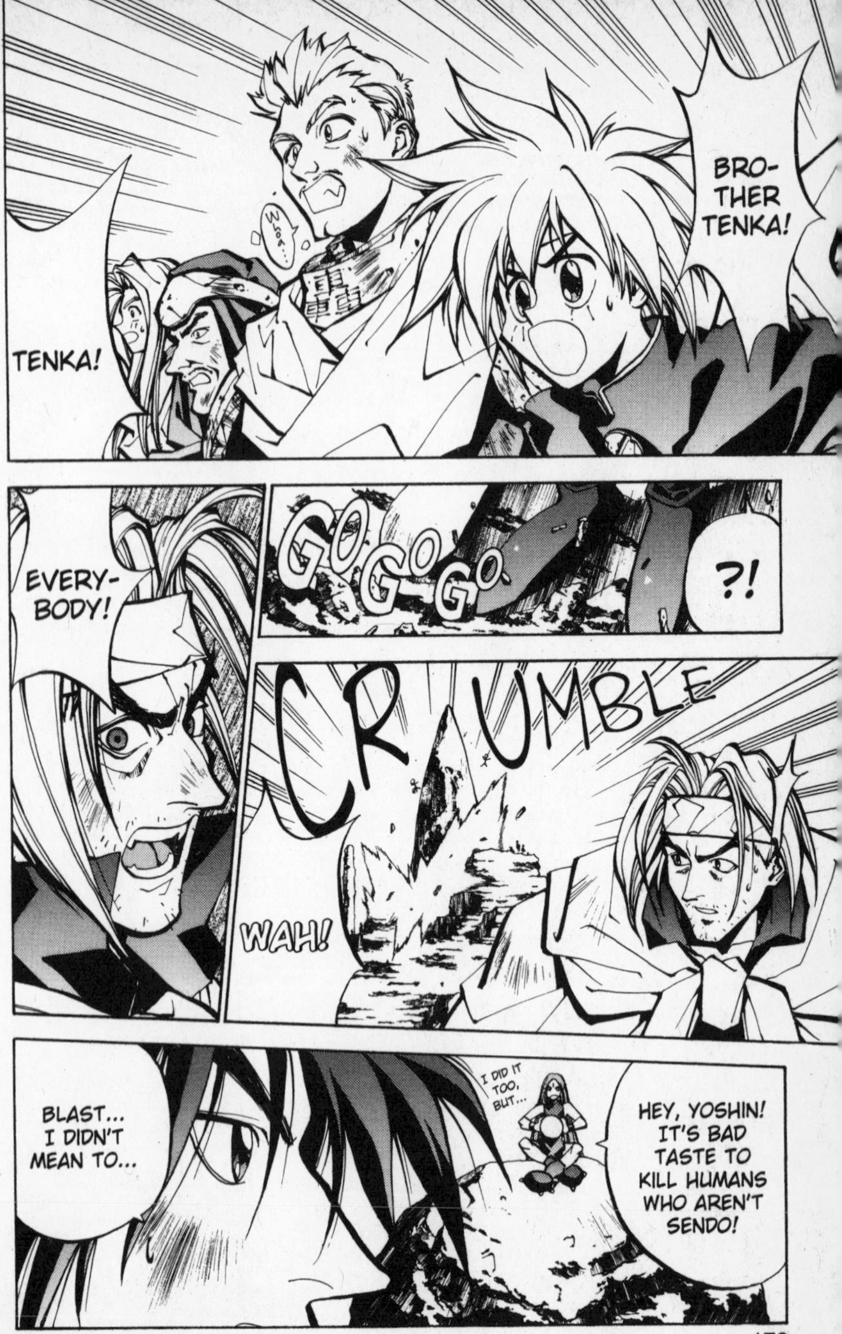
BRO-THER TENKA!
Whoa...
TENKA!
?!
GOGOGOGO
CRUMBLE
WAH!
EVERY-BODY!
HEY, YOSHIN! IT'S BAD TASTE TO KILL HUMANS WHO AREN'T SENDO!
I DID IT TOO, BUT...
BLAST... I DIDN'T MEAN TO...

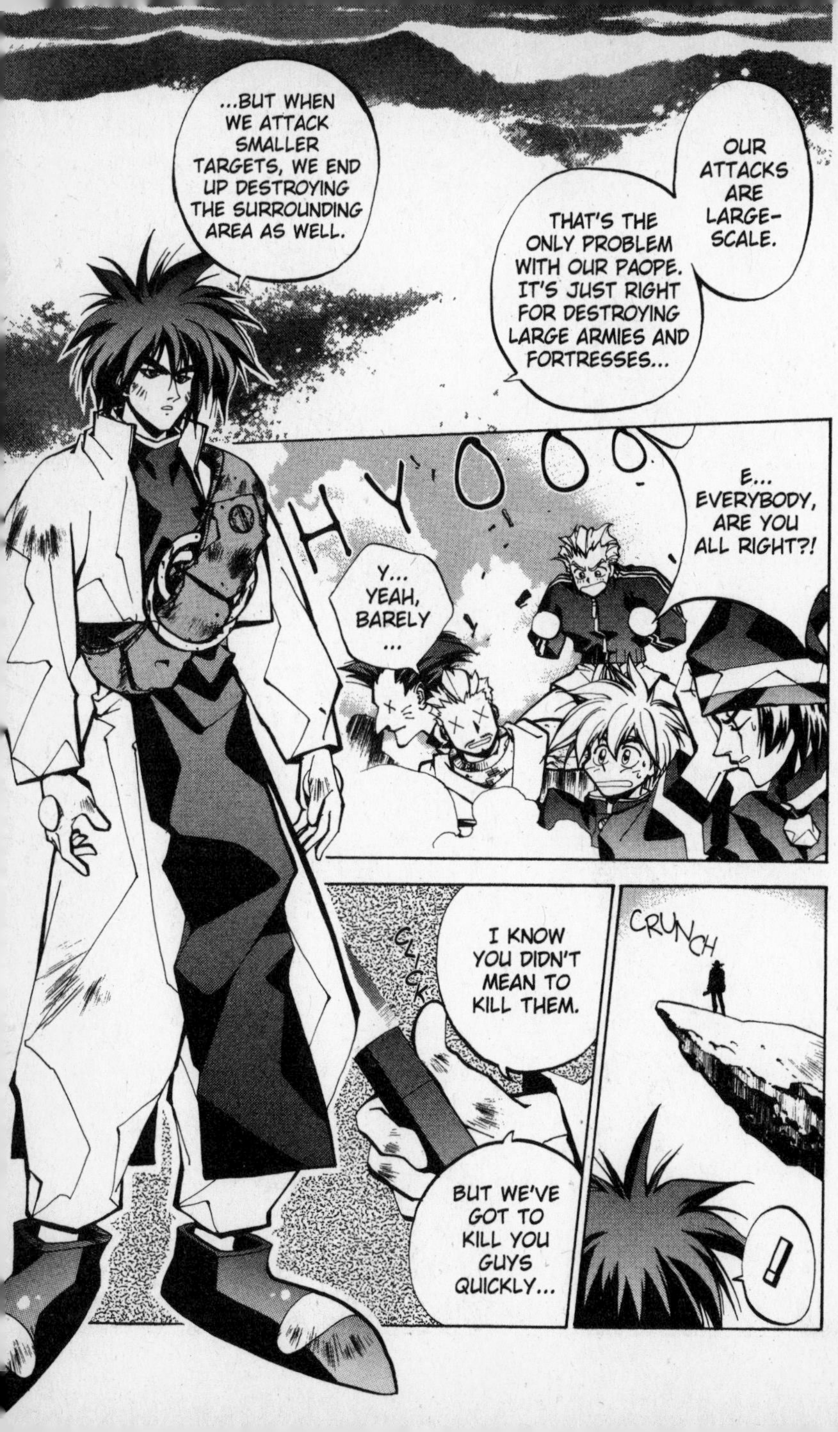
OUR ATTACKS ARE LARGE-SCALE.
THAT'S THE ONLY PROBLEM WITH OUR PAOPE. IT'S JUST RIGHT FOR DESTROYING LARGE ARMIES AND FORTRESSES...
...BUT WHEN WE ATTACK SMALLER TARGETS, WE END UP DESTROYING THE SURROUNDING AREA AS WELL.
HYOOO
E... EVERYBODY, ARE YOU ALL RIGHT?!
Y... YEAH, BARELY ...
CRUNCH
!
CLICK
I KNOW YOU DIDN'T MEAN TO KILL THEM.
BUT WE'VE GOT TO KILL YOU GUYS QUICKLY...

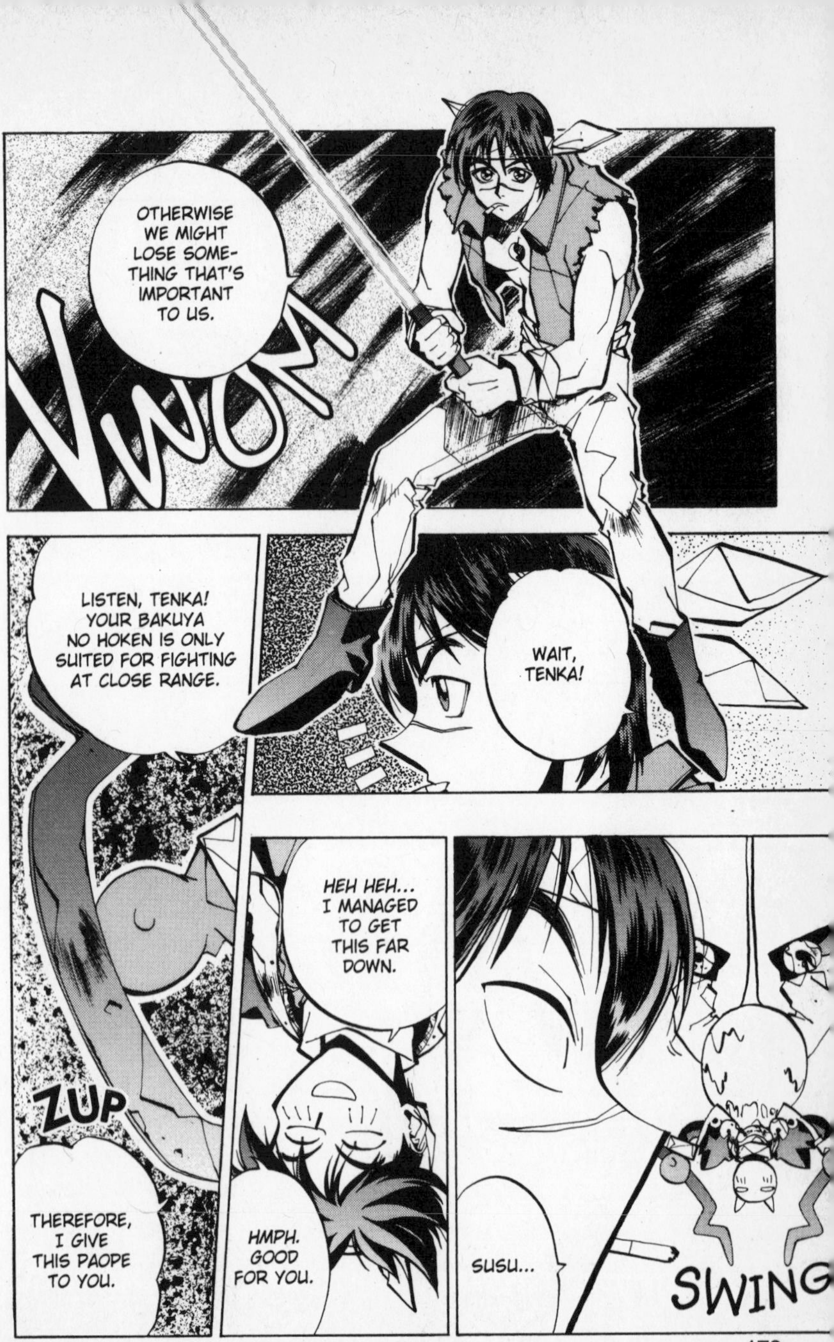
OTHERWISE WE MIGHT LOSE SOME-THING THAT'S IMPORTANT TO US.
VWOM
WAIT, TENKA!
SWING
SUSU...
HEH HEH... I MANAGED TO GET THIS FAR DOWN.
HMPH. GOOD FOR YOU.
LISTEN, TENKA! YOUR BAKUYA NO HOKEN IS ONLY SUITED FOR FIGHTING AT CLOSE RANGE.
ZUP
THEREFORE, I GIVE THIS PAOPE TO YOU.

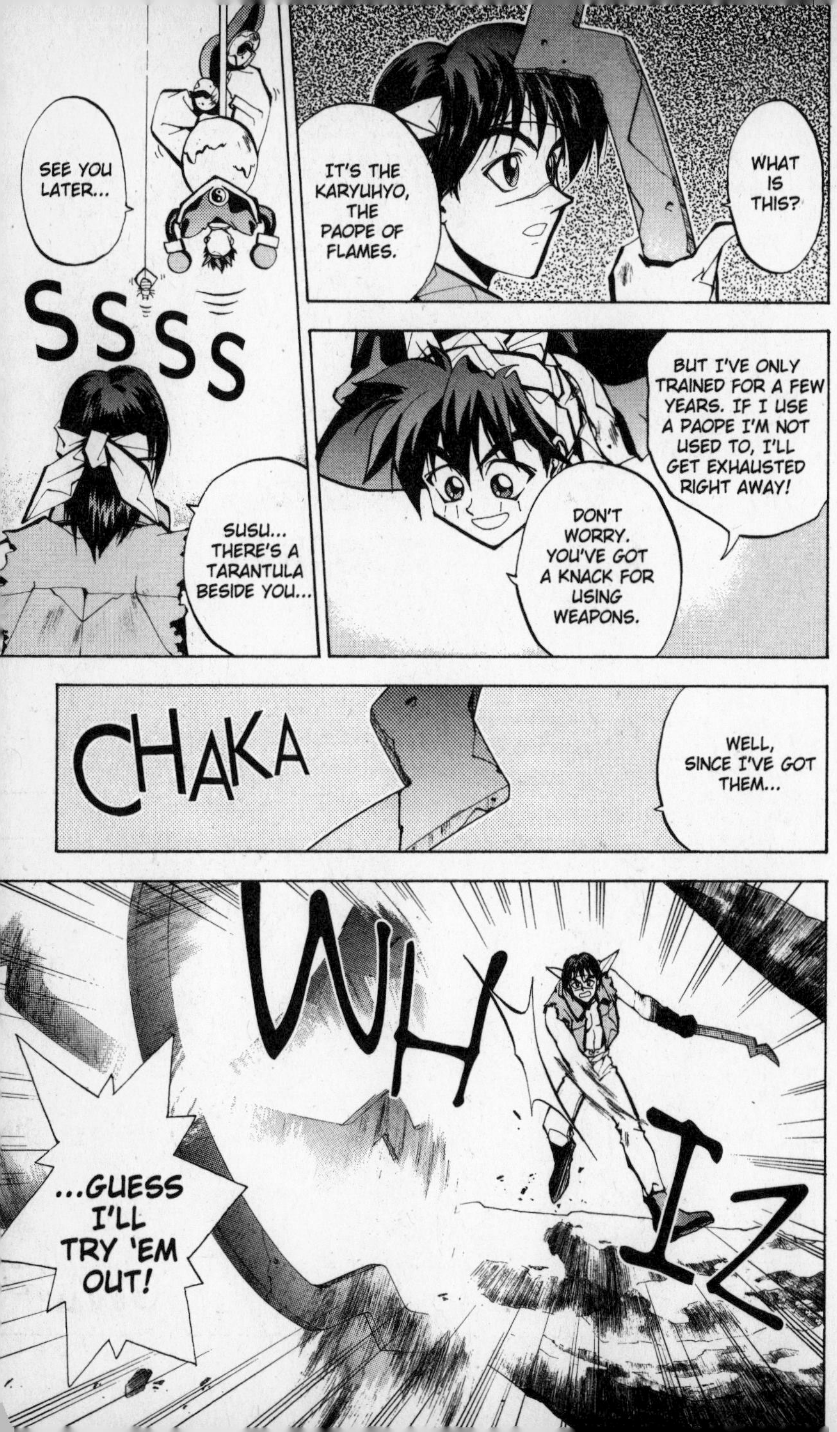
WHAT IS THIS?
IT'S THE KARYUHYO, THE PAOPE OF FLAMES.
BUT I'VE ONLY TRAINED FOR A FEW YEARS. IF I USE A PAOPE I'M NOT USED TO, I'LL GET EXHAUSTED RIGHT AWAY!
DON'T WORRY. YOU'VE GOT A KNACK FOR USING WEAPONS.
SEE YOU LATER...
SSSS
SUSU... THERE'S A TARANTULA BESIDE YOU...
WELL, SINCE I'VE GOT THEM...
CHAKA
WHIZ
...GUESS I'LL TRY 'EM OUT!

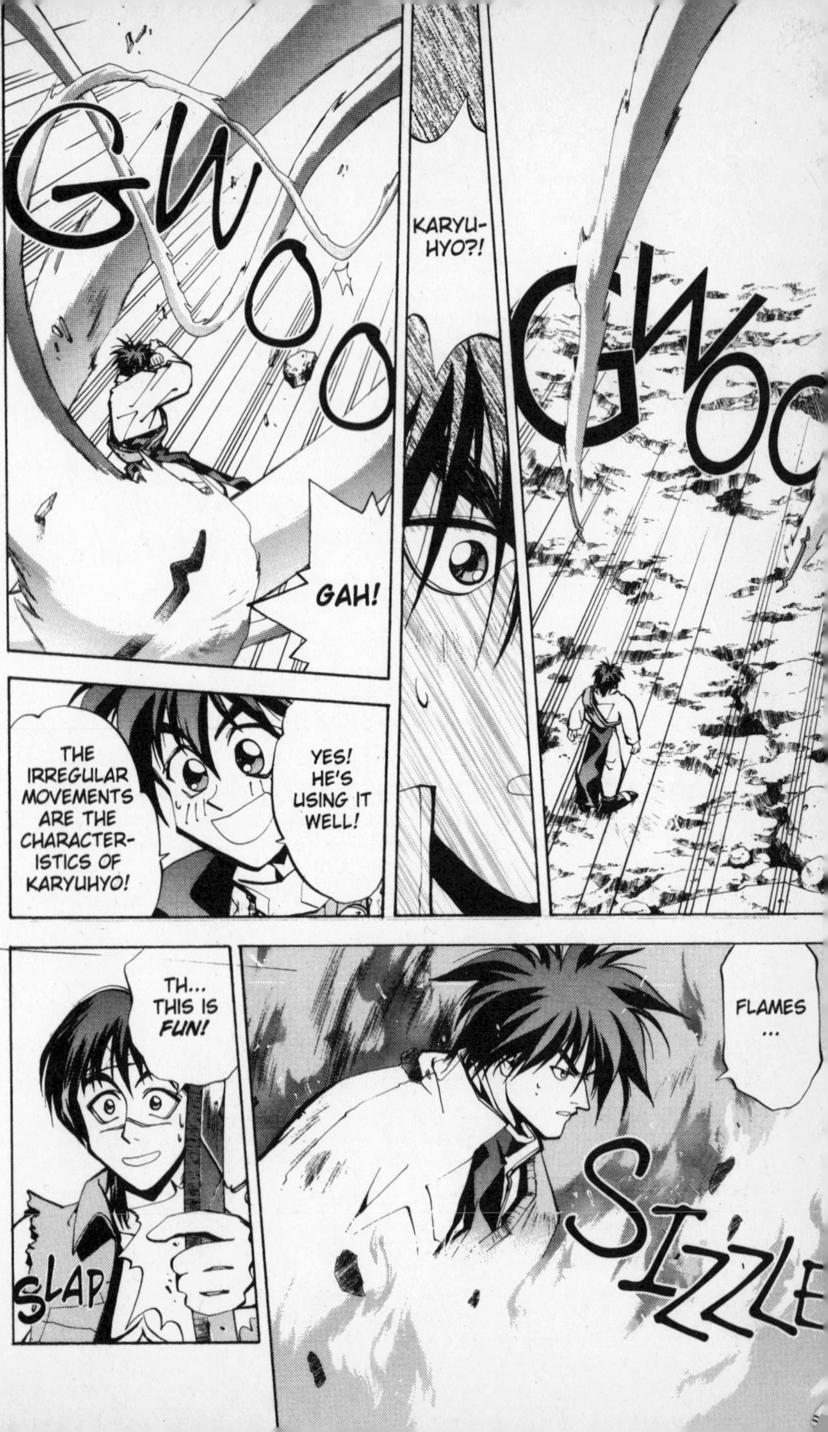
GWOO
KARYU-HYO?!
GWOOO
GAH!
YES! HE'S USING IT WELL!
THE IRREGULAR MOVEMENTS ARE THE CHARACTER-ISTICS OF KARYUHYO!
FLAMES ...
SIZZLE
TH... THIS IS *FUN!*
SLAP

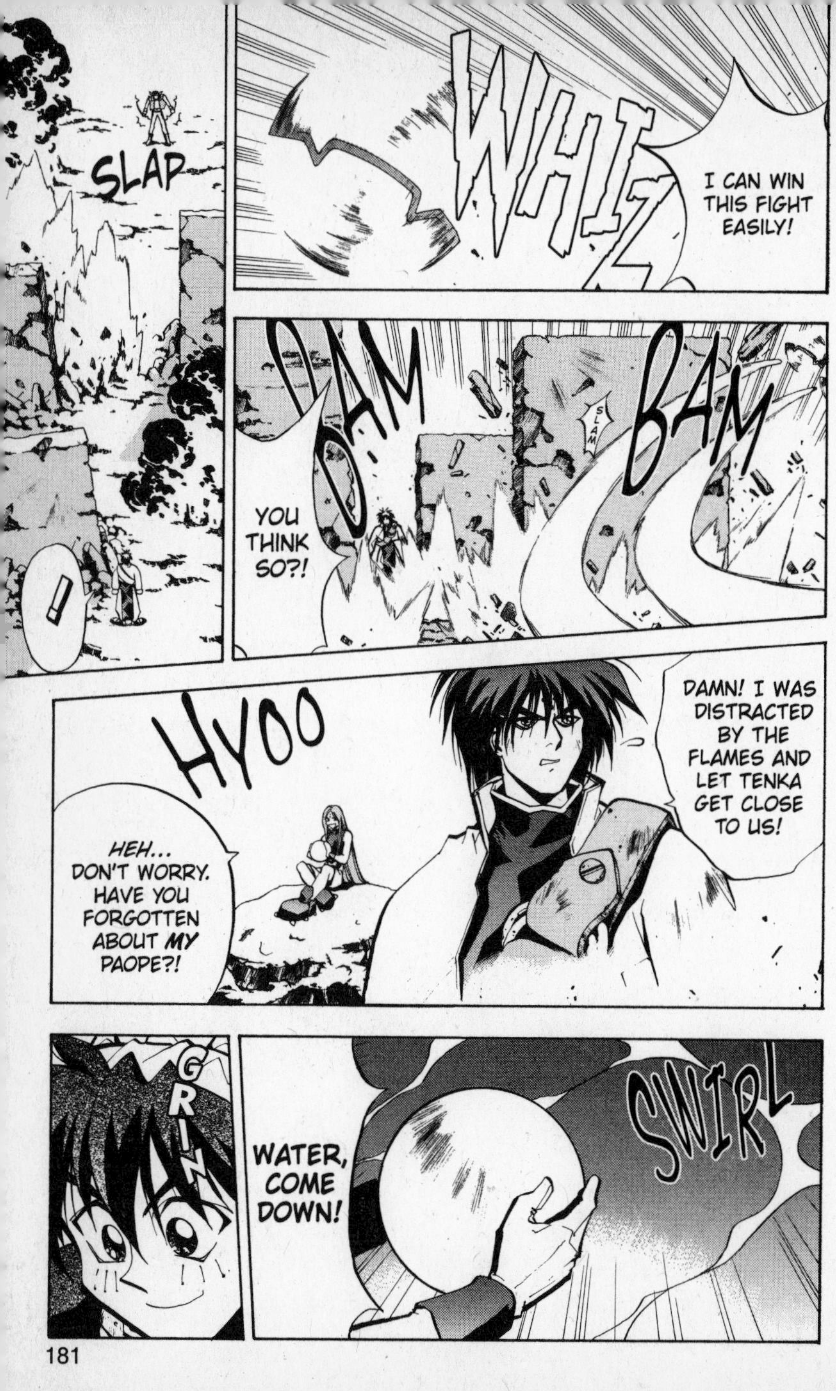
WHIZ
I CAN WIN THIS FIGHT EASILY!
BAM
SLAM
BAM
YOU THINK SO?!
SLAP
!
DAMN! I WAS DISTRACTED BY THE FLAMES AND LET TENKA GET CLOSE TO US!
HYOO
HEH... DON'T WORRY. HAVE YOU FORGOTTEN ABOUT *MY* PAOPE?!
SWIRL
WATER, COME DOWN!
GRIN

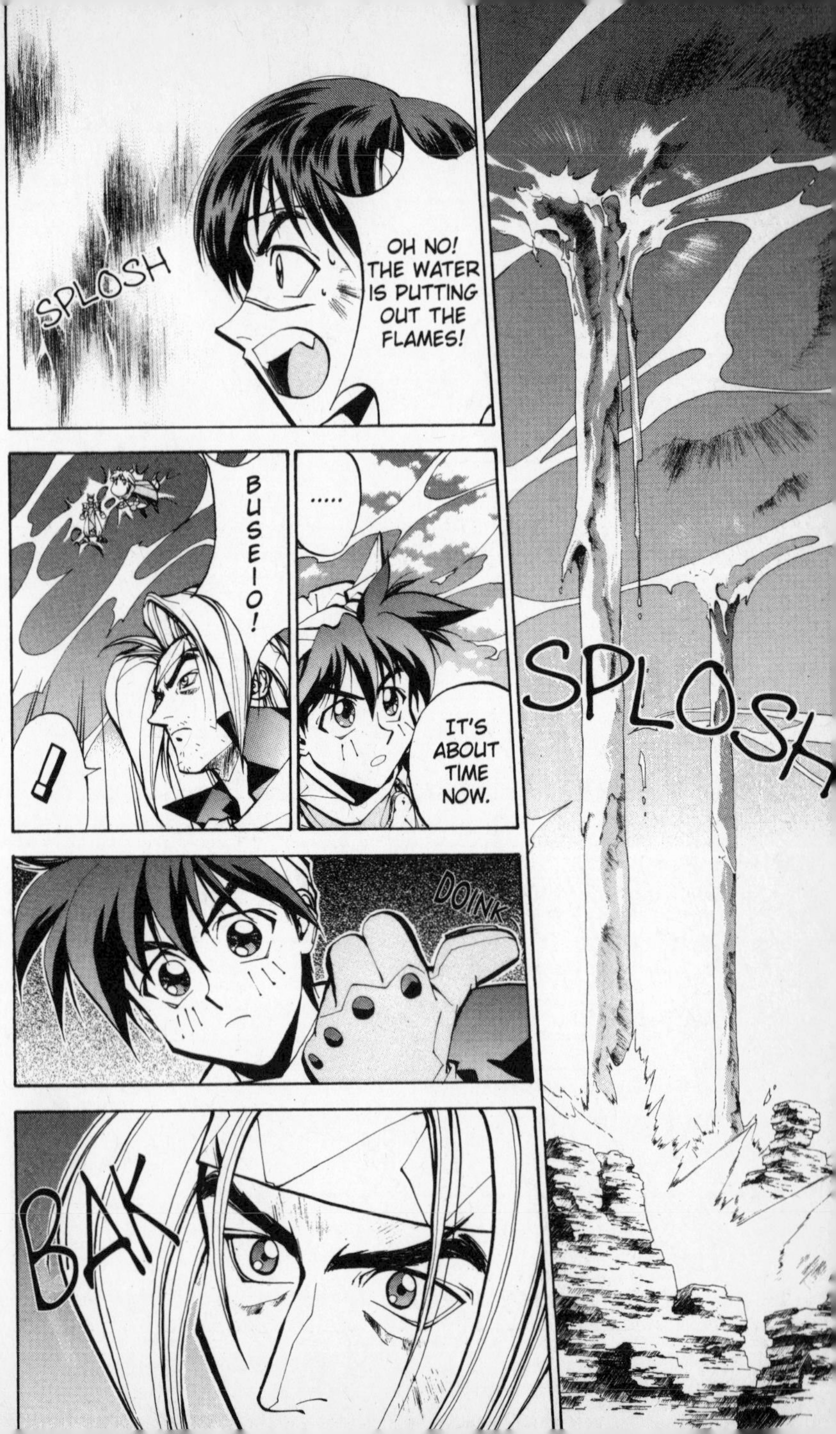
SPLOSH
OH NO! THE WATER IS PUTTING OUT THE FLAMES!
SPLOSH
.....
IT'S ABOUT TIME NOW.
BUSEIO!
!
DOINK
BAK

READ THIS WAY

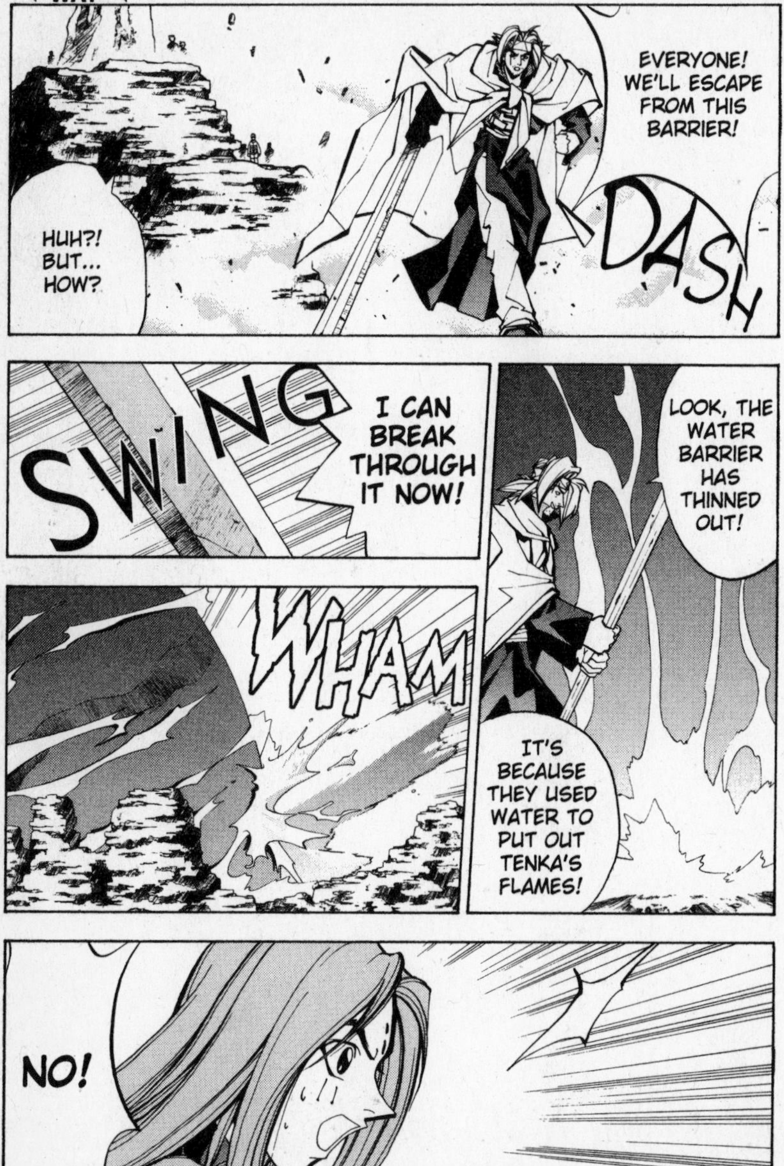
EVERYONE! WE'LL ESCAPE FROM THIS BARRIER!
DASH
HUH?! BUT... HOW?
LOOK, THE WATER BARRIER HAS THINNED OUT!
IT'S BECAUSE THEY USED WATER TO PUT OUT TENKA'S FLAMES!
SWING
I CAN BREAK THROUGH IT NOW!
WHAM
NO!

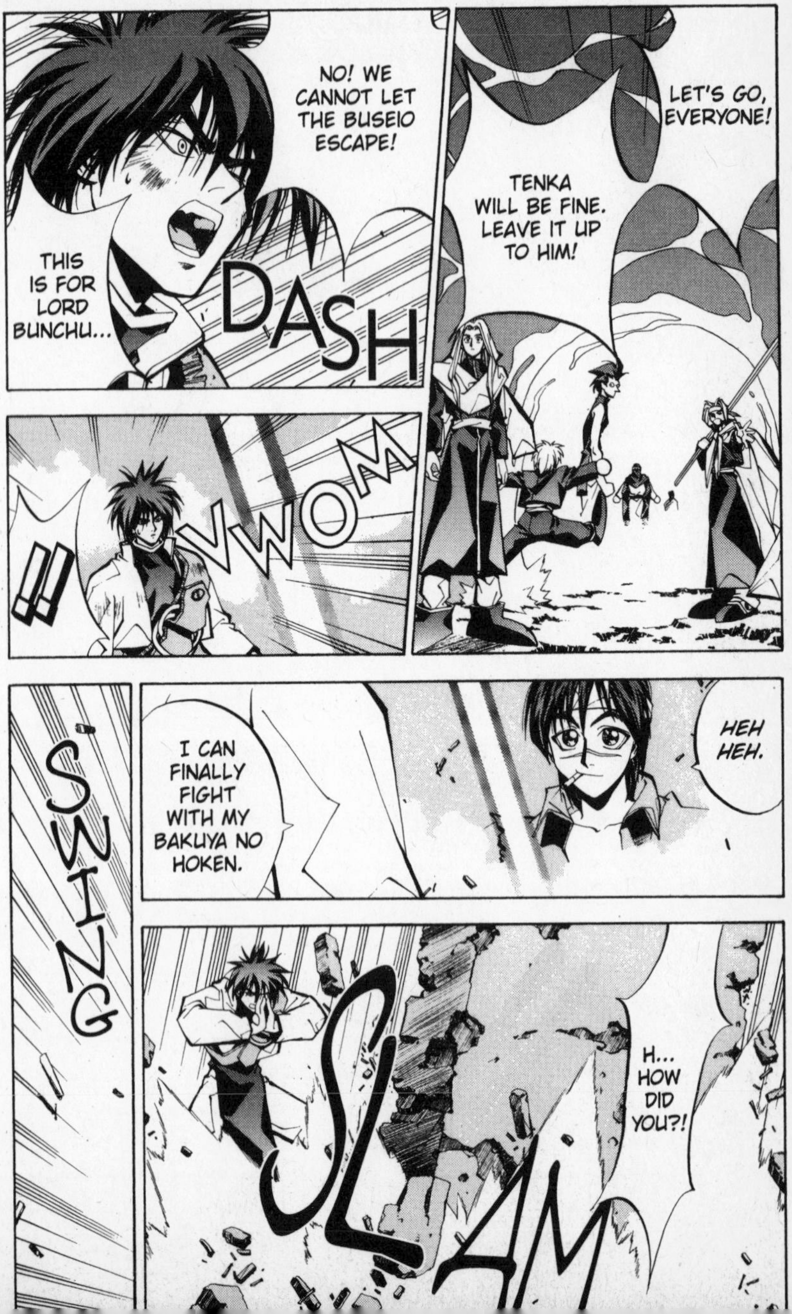
LET'S GO, EVERYONE!
TENKA WILL BE FINE. LEAVE IT UP TO HIM!
NO! WE CANNOT LET THE BUSEIO ESCAPE!
THIS IS FOR LORD BUNCHU...
DASH
VWOM
!!
HEH HEH.
I CAN FINALLY FIGHT WITH MY BAKUYA NO HOKEN.
H... HOW DID YOU?!
SLAM
SWING

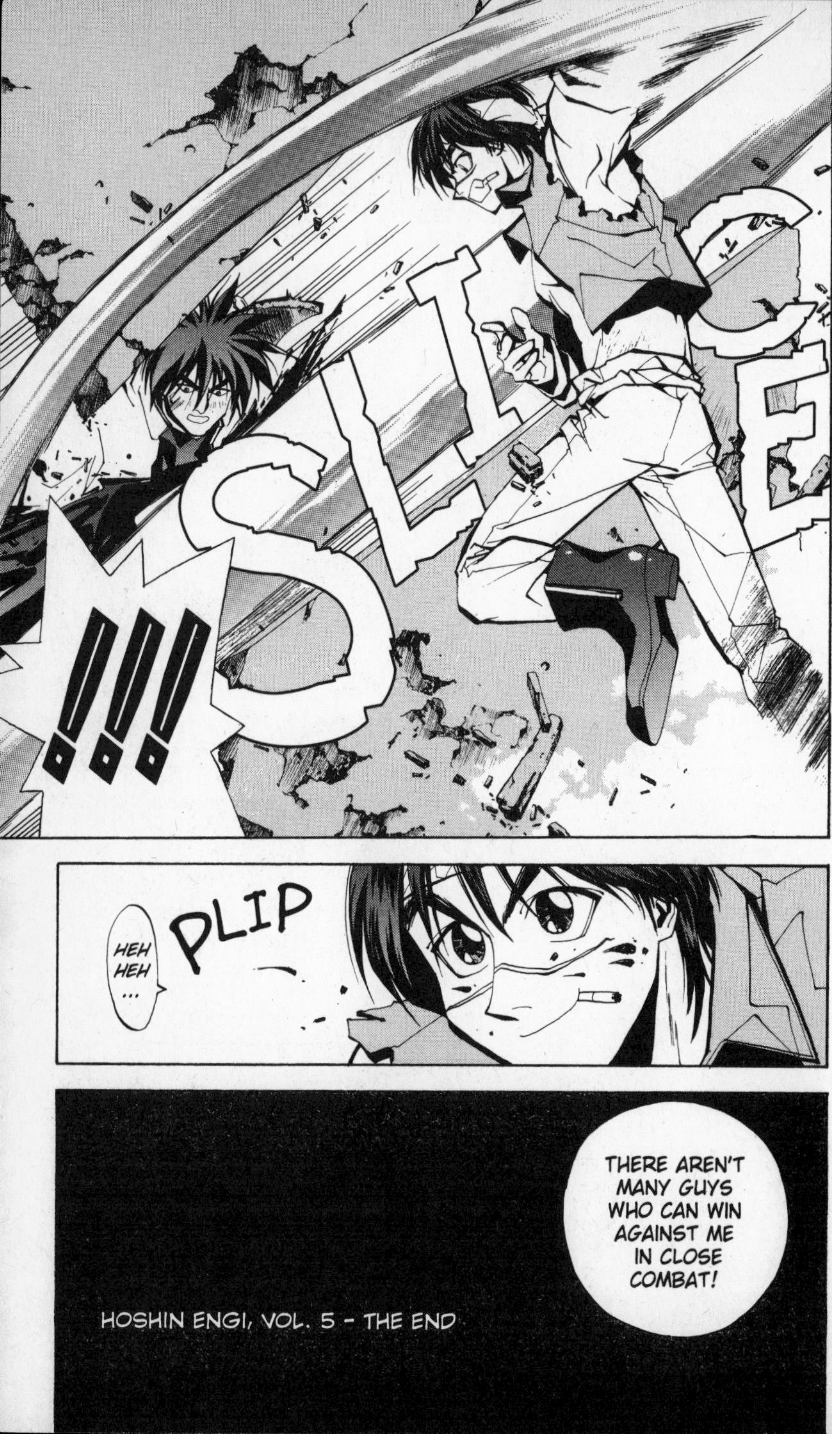
SLICE
!!!
PLIP
HEH HEH ...
THERE AREN'T MANY GUYS WHO CAN WIN AGAINST ME IN CLOSE COMBAT!
HOSHIN ENGI, VOL. 5 - THE END

RESULTS OF THE FIRST CHARACTER POPULARITY POLL!!!

A TOTAL OF 39,914 VOTES! THANK YOU SO MUCH!

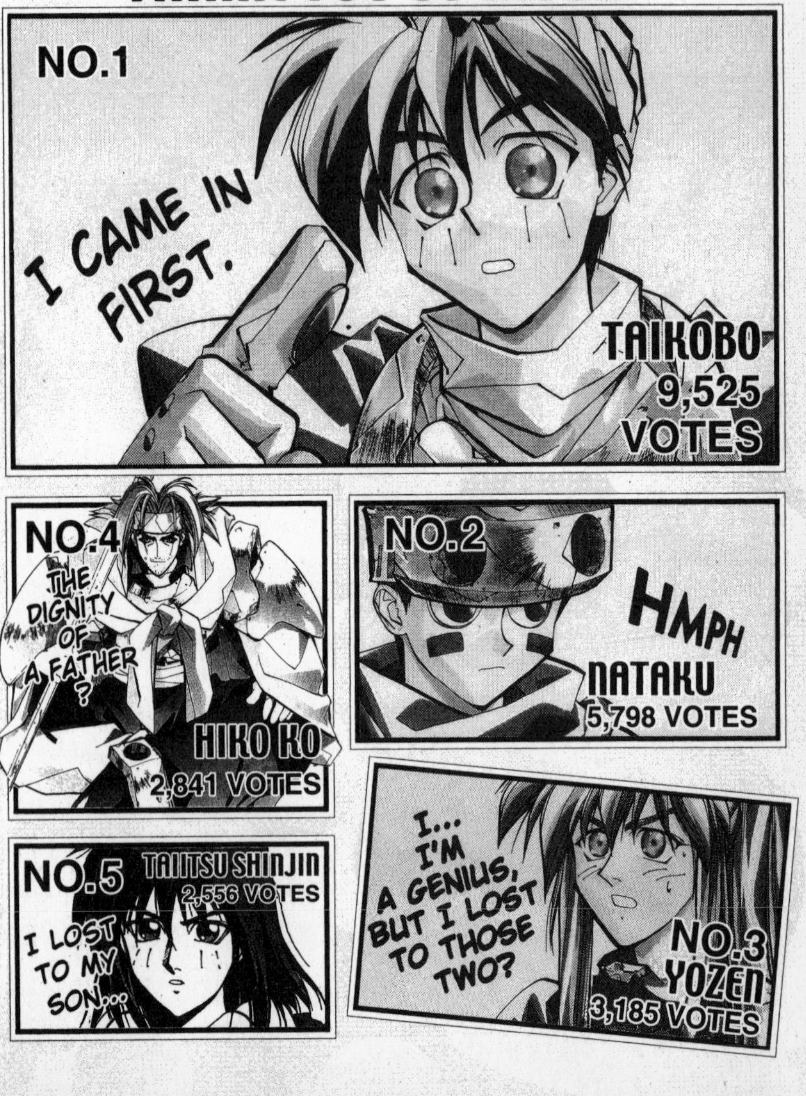
NO.1
I CAME IN FIRST.
TAIKOBO
9,525
VOTES
NO.2
HMPH
NATAKU
5,798 VOTES
NO.4
THE DIGNITY OF A FATHER?
HIKO KO
2,841 VOTES
I... I'M A GENIUS, BUT I LOST TO THOSE TWO?
NO.3
YOZEN
3,185 VOTES
NO.5
TAIITSU SHINJIN
2,556 VOTES
I LOST TO MY SON...

"HOSHIN ENGI"

went ahead and held a character popularity poll, although the series has been running for less than a year! We got many more votes than we expected. Thank you!

OBJECTIONS?

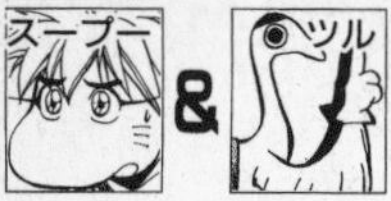
スープー
&
ツル

SUPU & THE CRANE'S FRANK TALK!!

Supu: Well, I'm glad that Master came in first place.

Crane: Hmm. And he had a clear lead. Susu must be happy about this.

Supu: But when the votes were still being counted, Nataku was No. 1, and the Master was pale about that.

Crane: Yozen hasn't appeared too much, but his popularity is amazing.

Supu: The next time, Master might lose. But the most unexpected result is Taiitsu Shinjin, who came in fifth place.

Crane: Well...I guess looking at the camera appealed to the readers subconsciously. By the way, are you satisfied with your ranking, Supushan?

Supu: Of course...actually, I'm a little disappointed.

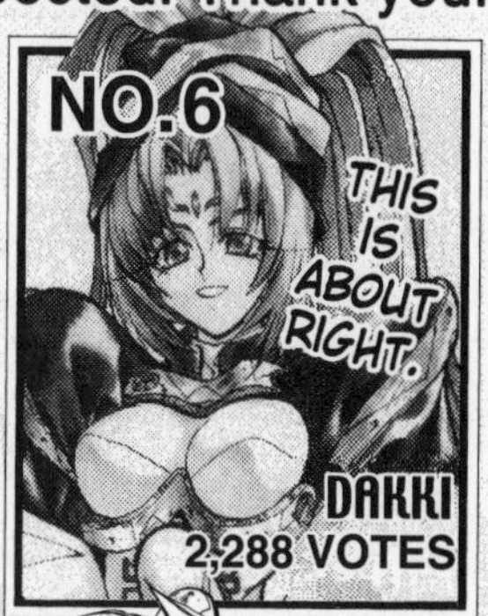
NO.6
THIS IS ABOUT RIGHT.
DAKKI
2,288 VOTES

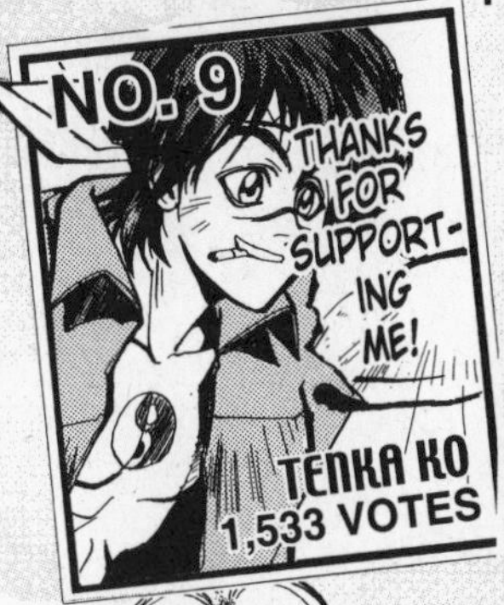
NO. 9
THANKS FOR SUPPORTING ME!
TENKA KO
1,533 VOTES

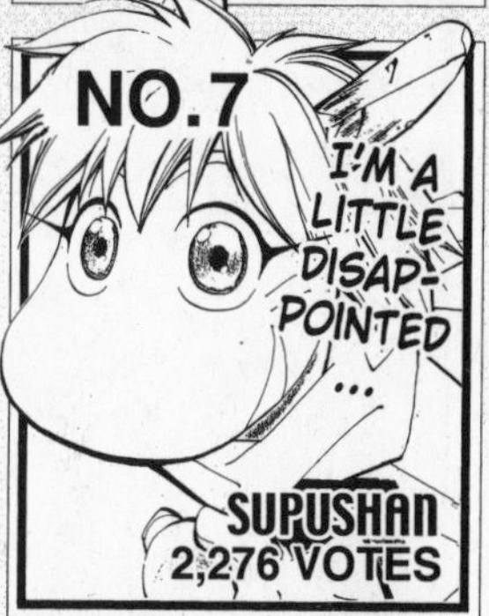
NO.7
I'M A LITTLE DISAPPOINTED...
SUPUSHAN
2,276 VOTES

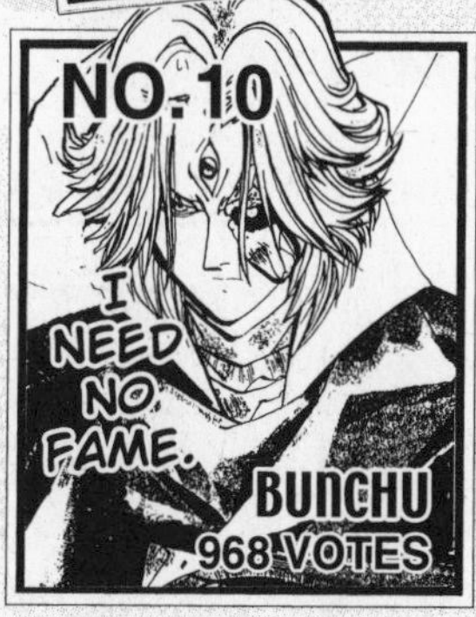
NO.10
I NEED NO FAME.
BUNCHU
968 VOTES

WORDS OF THANKS FROM FUJIRYU!!

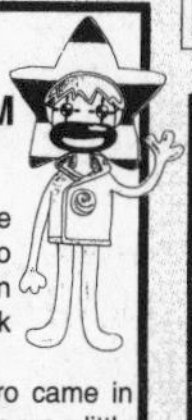

People had only one week to vote, but so many people sent in their votes. Thank you. For now, I'm relieved that the hero came in first place. The results are a little different from what I'd expected, and I find that interesting.

This article was published in Issue 24, 1997 of *Weekly Shonen Jump*.

NO. 11	KIBI, 806 VOTES
NO. 12	TENSHO KO, 688 VOTES
NO. 13	OKIJIN, 648 VOTES
NO. 14	BUKICHI, 584 VOTES
NO. 15	HAKUYUKO, 575 VOTES
NO. 16	KING CHU, 567 VOTES
NO. 17	RAISHINSHI, 499 VOTES
NO. 18	HAKUTSURU, 477 VOTES
NO. 19	KOKUTENKO, 416 VOTES
NO. 20	THE FIREWOOD SELLER, 314 VOTES
NO. 21	KASHI, 258 VOTES
NO. 22	KOTENKEN, 215 VOTES
NO. 23	UNCHUSHI, 71 VOTES
NO. 24	KOSHI, 54 VOTES
NO. 25	HATSU KI, 51 VOTES
NO. 26	SHO KI, 42 VOTES
	KOKIN RIKISHI, 42 VOTES
NO. 28	RYU FUJISAKI, 39 VOTES
NO. 29	HEKIUN, 34 VOTES
NO. 30	DOKOSON, 30 VOTES
NO. 31	GENSHI TENSON, 29 VOTES
NO. 32	DOTOKU SHINKUN, 28 VOTES
	CHINTO, 28 VOTES
NO. 34	SEI LI, 25 VOTES
NO. 35	INSHI, 24 VOTES
NO. 36	INCHON, 22 VOTES
NO. 37	KOKUKIRIN, 21 VOTES
OTHERS	HAKUMEN ENKO, 19 VOTES
	INCHI, 17 VOTES

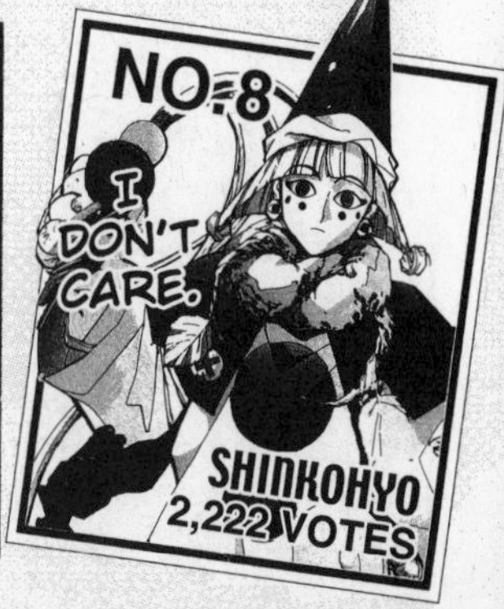
NO.8
I DON'T CARE.
SHINKOHYO
2,222 VOTES

Art by Ryu Fujisaki

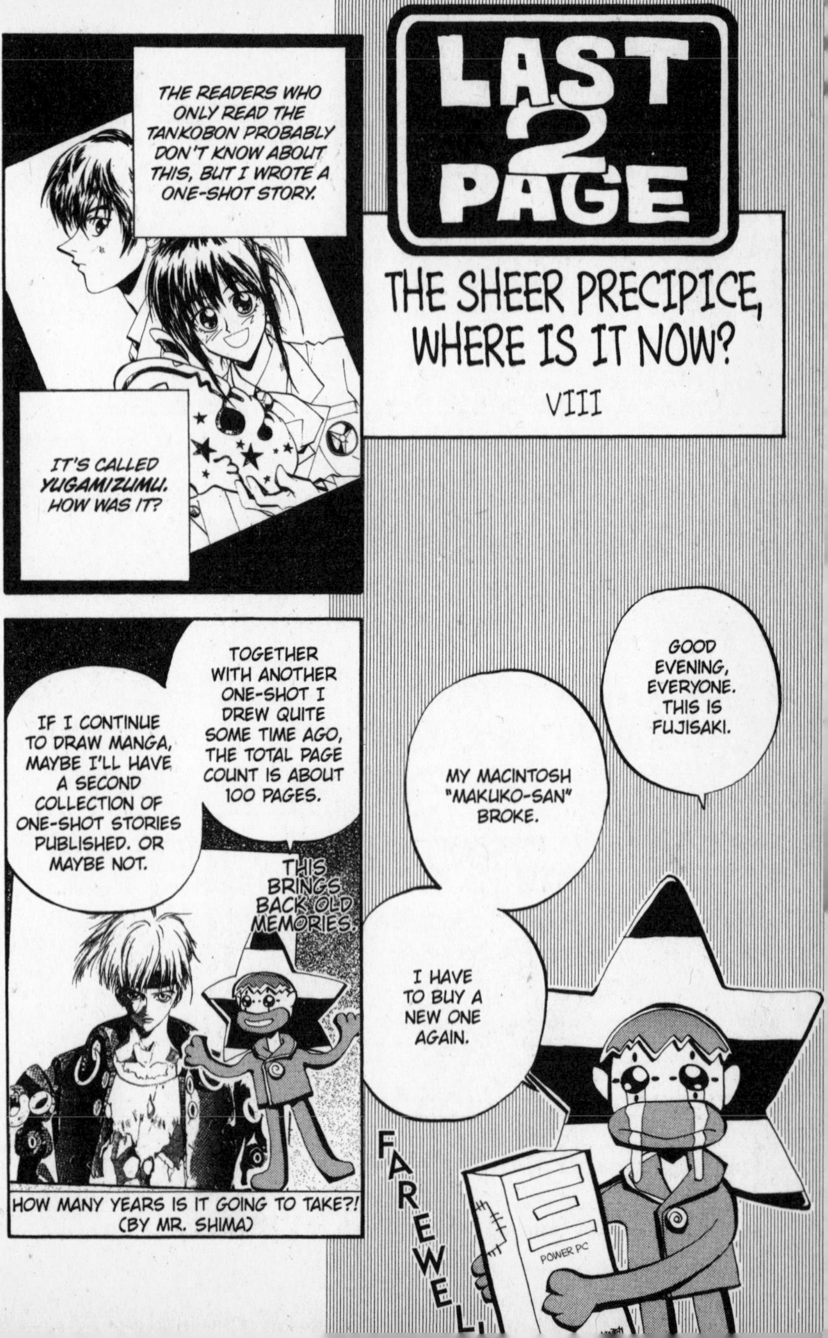
LAST 2 PAGE
THE SHEER PRECIPICE, WHERE IS IT NOW?
VIII
GOOD EVENING, EVERYONE. THIS IS FUJISAKI.
MY MACINTOSH "MAKUKO-SAN" BROKE.
I HAVE TO BUY A NEW ONE AGAIN.
POWER PC
FAREWELL.
THE READERS WHO ONLY READ THE TANKOBON PROBABLY DON'T KNOW ABOUT THIS, BUT I WROTE A ONE-SHOT STORY.
IT'S CALLED YUGAMIZUMU. HOW WAS IT?
TOGETHER WITH ANOTHER ONE-SHOT I DREW QUITE SOME TIME AGO, THE TOTAL PAGE COUNT IS ABOUT 100 PAGES.
IF I CONTINUE TO DRAW MANGA, MAYBE I'LL HAVE A SECOND COLLECTION OF ONE-SHOT STORIES PUBLISHED. OR MAYBE NOT.
THIS BRINGS BACK OLD MEMORIES.
HOW MANY YEARS IS IT GOING TO TAKE?! (BY MR. SHIMA)

READ THIS WAY

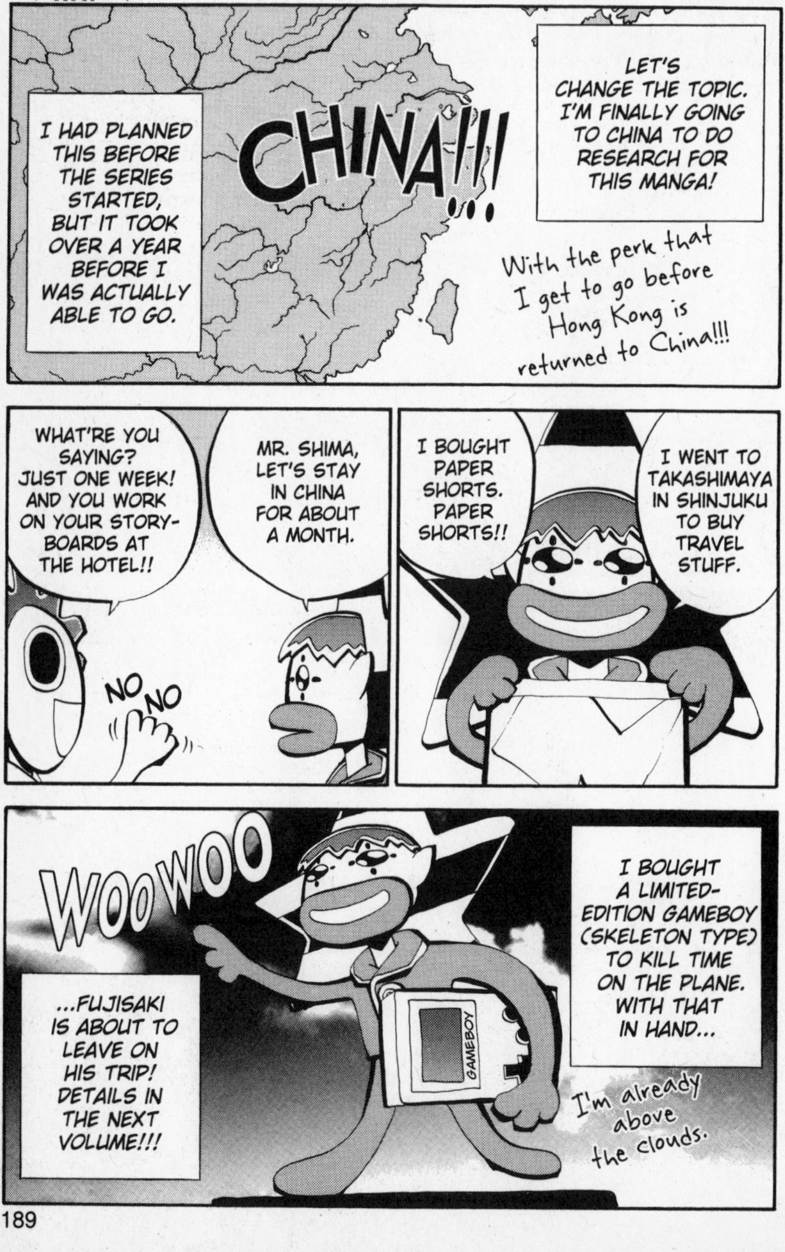

LET'S CHANGE THE TOPIC. I'M FINALLY GOING TO CHINA TO DO RESEARCH FOR THIS MANGA!
CHINA!!!
With the perk that I get to go before Hong Kong is returned to China!!!
I HAD PLANNED THIS BEFORE THE SERIES STARTED, BUT IT TOOK OVER A YEAR BEFORE I WAS ACTUALLY ABLE TO GO.
I WENT TO TAKASHIMAYA IN SHINJUKU TO BUY TRAVEL STUFF.
I BOUGHT PAPER SHORTS. PAPER SHORTS!!
MR. SHIMA, LET'S STAY IN CHINA FOR ABOUT A MONTH.
WHAT'RE YOU SAYING? JUST ONE WEEK! AND YOU WORK ON YOUR STORY-BOARDS AT THE HOTEL!!
NO NO
I BOUGHT A LIMITED-EDITION GAMEBOY (SKELETON TYPE) TO KILL TIME ON THE PLANE. WITH THAT IN HAND...
I'm already above the clouds.
WOO WOO
...FUJISAKI IS ABOUT TO LEAVE ON HIS TRIP! DETAILS IN THE NEXT VOLUME!!!
GAMEBOY

Hoshin Engi: The Rank File!

You'll find as you read *Hoshin Engi* that there are titles and ranks that you are probably unfamiliar with. While it may seem confusing, there is an order to the madness that is pulled from ancient Chinese mythology, Japanese culture, other manga, and, of course, the incredible mind of *Hoshin Engi* creator Ryu Fujisaki.

Where we think it will help, we give you a hint in the margin on the page the name appears. But in addition, here's a quick primer on the titles you'll find in *Hoshin Engi* and what they mean:

Japanese	Title	Job Description
武成王	Buseio	Chief commanding officer
宰相	Saisho	Premier
太師	Taishi	The king's advisor/tutor
大金剛	Dai Kongo	Great Vassels
軍師	Gunshi	Military tactician
大諸侯	Daishoko	Great feudal lord
東伯侯	Tohakuko	Lord of the east region
西伯侯	Seihakuko	Lord of the west region
北伯侯	Hokuhakuko	Lord of the north region
南伯侯	Nanhakuko	Lord of the south region

Hoshin Engi: The Immortal File

Also, you'll probably find the hierarchy of the Sennin, Sendo and Doshi somewhat complicated. Here, we spell it out the easiest way possible!

Japanese	Title	Description
道士	Doshi	Someone training to become Sennin
仙道	Sendo	Used to describe both Sennin and Doshi
仙人	Sennin	Those who have mastered the way. Once you "go Sennin" you are forever changed.
妖孽	Yogetsu	A Yosei who can transform into a human
妖怪仙人	Yokai Sennin	A Sennin whose original form is not human
妖精	Yosei	An animal or object exposed to moonlight and sunlight for more than 1000 years

Hoshin Engi: The Magical File

Paope (宝貝) are powerful magical items used by Sennin and Doshi. Sometimes they look like regular objects, like a veil or hat. These are just a few of the magical items, both paope and otherwise, that you'll encounter in *Hoshin Engi!*

Japanese	Magic	Description
打神鞭	Dashinben	Known as the God-Striking Whip, Taikobo's paope manipulates the air and wind.
霊獣	Reiju	A magical flying beast that Sennin and Doshi use for transportation and support. Taikobo's reiju is his pal Supu.
哮天犬	Kotenken	The Howling Dog can fly and be used as an attack Paope.
莫邪の宝剣	Bakuya no Hoken	Tenka's weapon, a light saber.
叫名棍	Kyumeikon	An object that can freeze someone's movements when their name is shouted.
紅珠	Koju	Buddhist rosary beads that can capture an enemy.
混元珠	Kongenju	A gem that can control water, it is connected to a similar gem beneath the sea.
劈地珠	Hekichiju	An object that uses the Earth's power to heal allies.
拌黄珠	Bankoju	A vehicle that shoots energy beams.
開天珠	Kaitenju	A missile that destroys anything it touches. Allows the user to fly.

Coming Next Volume:
Protector

Bunchu and the Shisei prove themselves to be more than a match for Taikobo and his allies. When his victory seems imminent, Bunchu must decide between his sense of justice and his loyalty to the throne of Choka!

AVAILABLE APRIL 2008!

Read Any Good Books Lately?

Hoshin Engi is based on *Fengshen Yanji* (*The Creation of the Gods*, written in the 1500s by Xu Zhonglin) one of China's four classic fantastical novels of adventure, magic and mystery. The other three are *Saiyuki* (*Journey to the West* by Cheng'en Wu, late 1500s), *Sangokushi Engi* (*Romance of the Three Kingdoms* by Guanzhong Luo), and *Shui Hu Zhuan* (*Outlaws of the Marsh*, by Shi Nai'an, mid-1500s).

Want to read these books? You can! They're all still in print, more than 500 years later!

These books are North American in-print editions only.

Yu-Gi-Oh! Millennium World

by Kazuki Takahashi

Yugi's soul goes back in time. Can he defeat the villains of the past and achieve his ultimate destiny?

Manga series on sale now

Only $7.95

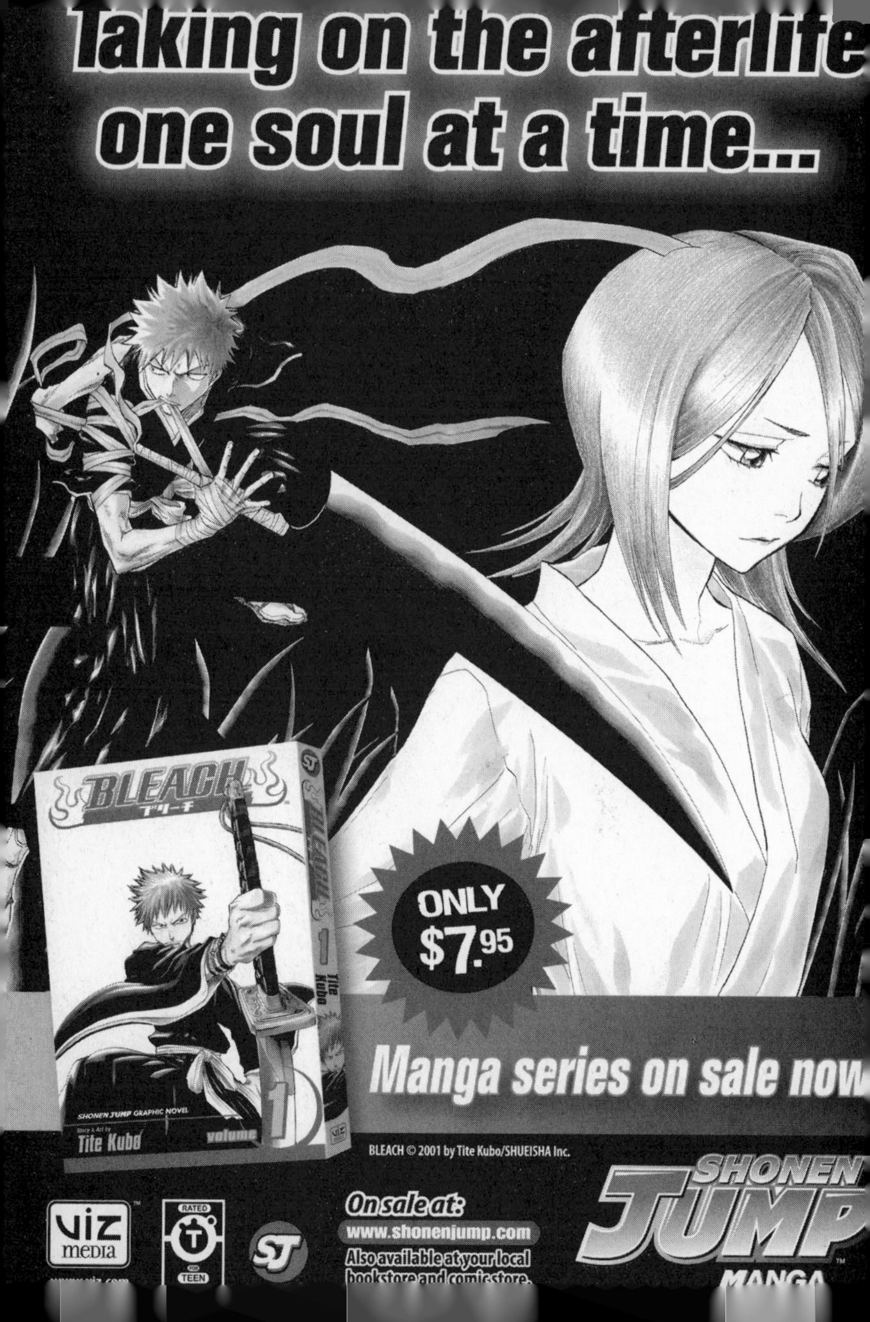
Taking on the afterlife one soul at a time...
BLEACH
ブリーチ
ONLY $7.95
Manga series on sale now
SHONEN JUMP GRAPHIC NOVEL
Story & Art by
Tite Kubo
volume 1
BLEACH © 2001 by Tite Kubo/SHUEISHA Inc.
SHONEN JUMP MANGA
viz media
RATED T FOR TEEN
On sale at:
www.shonenjump.com
Also available at your local bookstore and comic store.

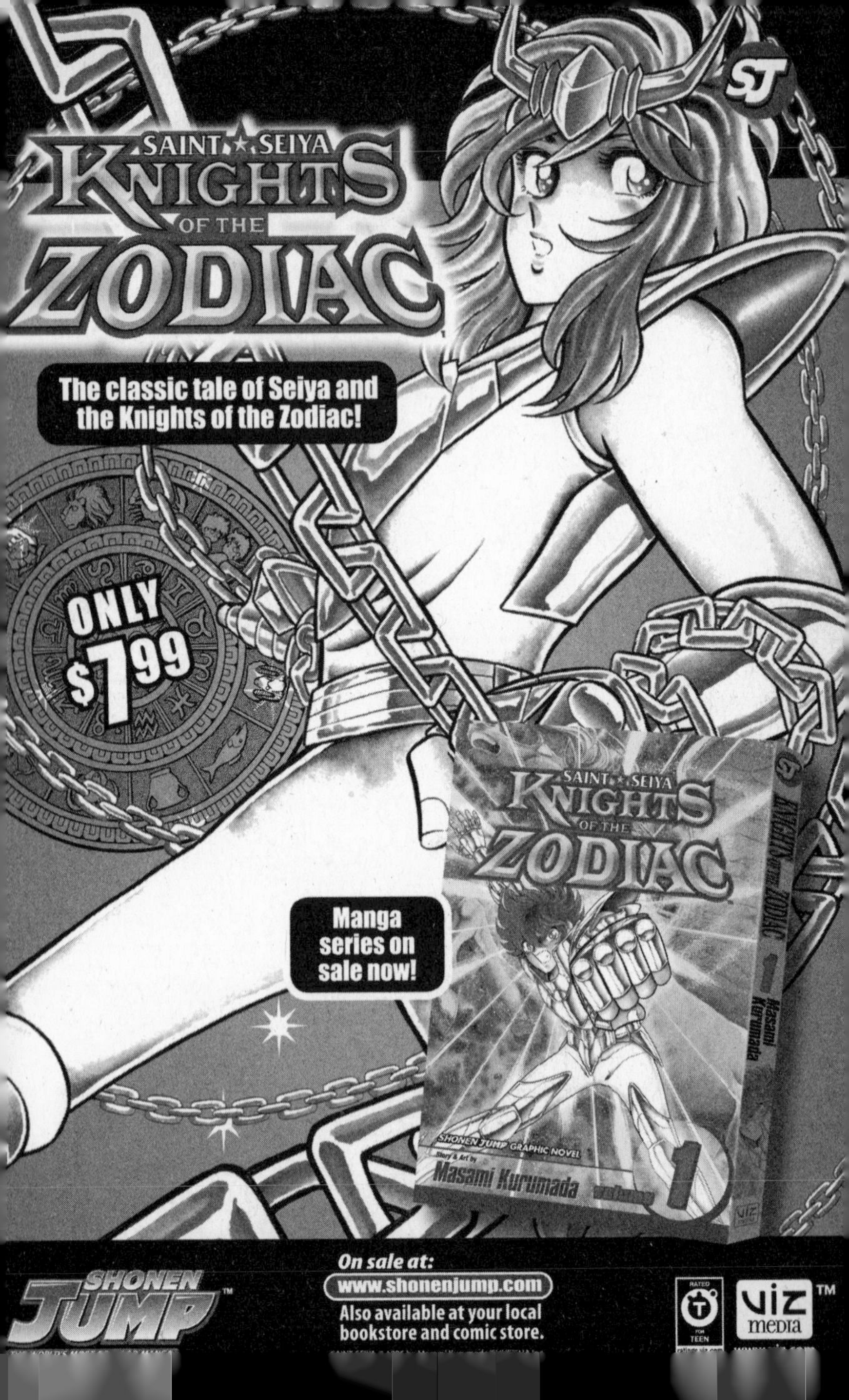
SJ
SAINT ★ SEIYA
KNIGHTS OF THE ZODIAC
The classic tale of Seiya and the Knights of the Zodiac!
ONLY $7.99
Manga series on sale now!
SAINT ★ SEIYA
KNIGHTS OF THE ZODIAC
SHONEN JUMP GRAPHIC NOVEL
Story & Art by
Masami Kurumada
1
SHONEN JUMP
On sale at:
www.shonenjump.com
Also available at your local bookstore and comic store.
RATED T TEEN
VIZ media

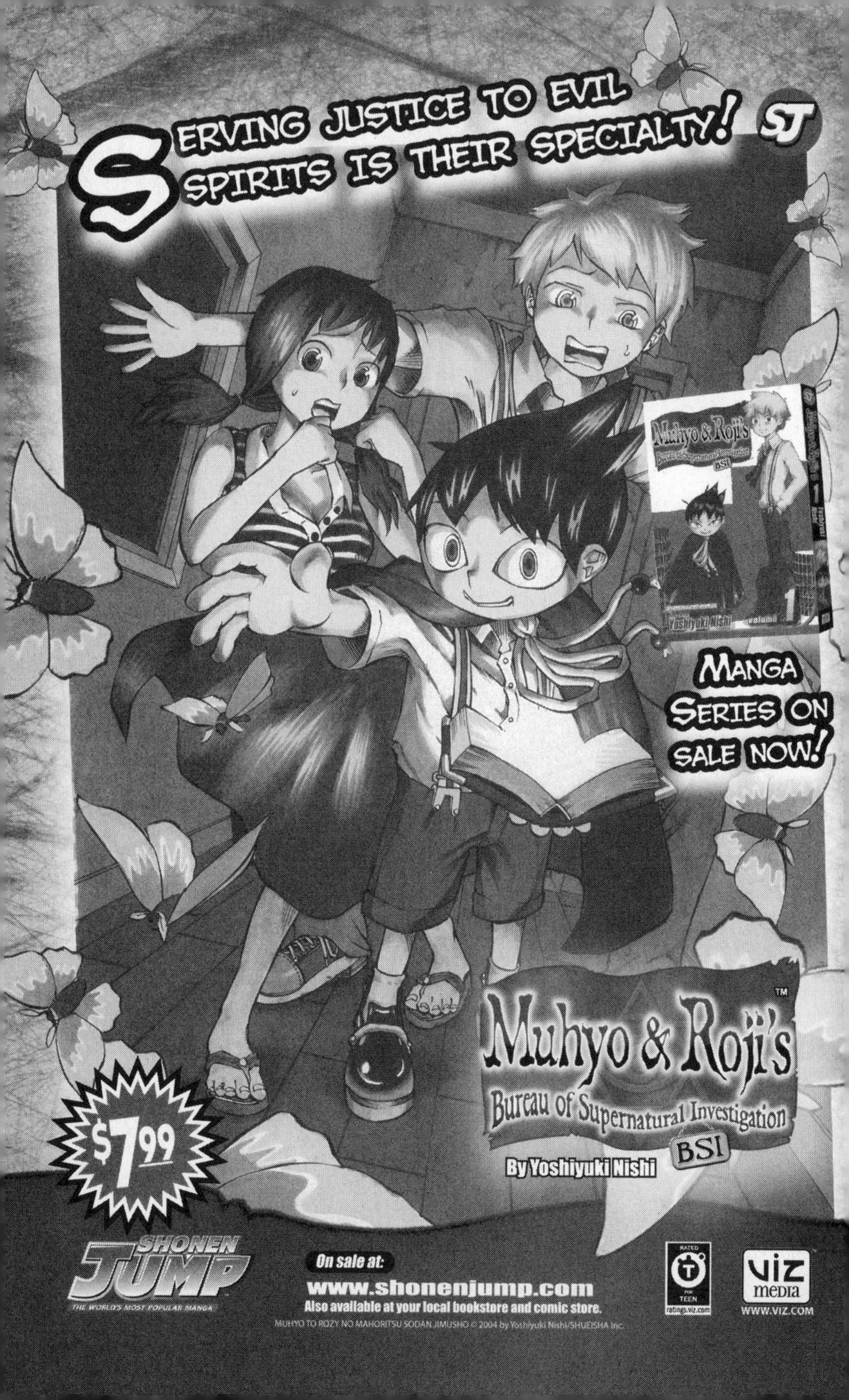
SERVING JUSTICE TO EVIL SPIRITS IS THEIR SPECIALTY!
SJ
Muhyo & Roji's Bureau of Supernatural Investigation BSI
MANGA SERIES ON SALE NOW!
Muhyo & Roji's™
Bureau of Supernatural Investigation
BSI
By Yoshiyuki Nishi
$7.99
SHONEN JUMP
THE WORLD'S MOST POPULAR MANGA
On sale at:
www.shonenjump.com
Also available at your local bookstore and comic store.
MUHYO TO ROZY NO MAHORITSU SODAN JIMUSHO © 2004 by Yoshiyuki Nishi/SHUEISHA Inc.
RATED T FOR TEEN
ratings.viz.com
viz media
WWW.VIZ.COM

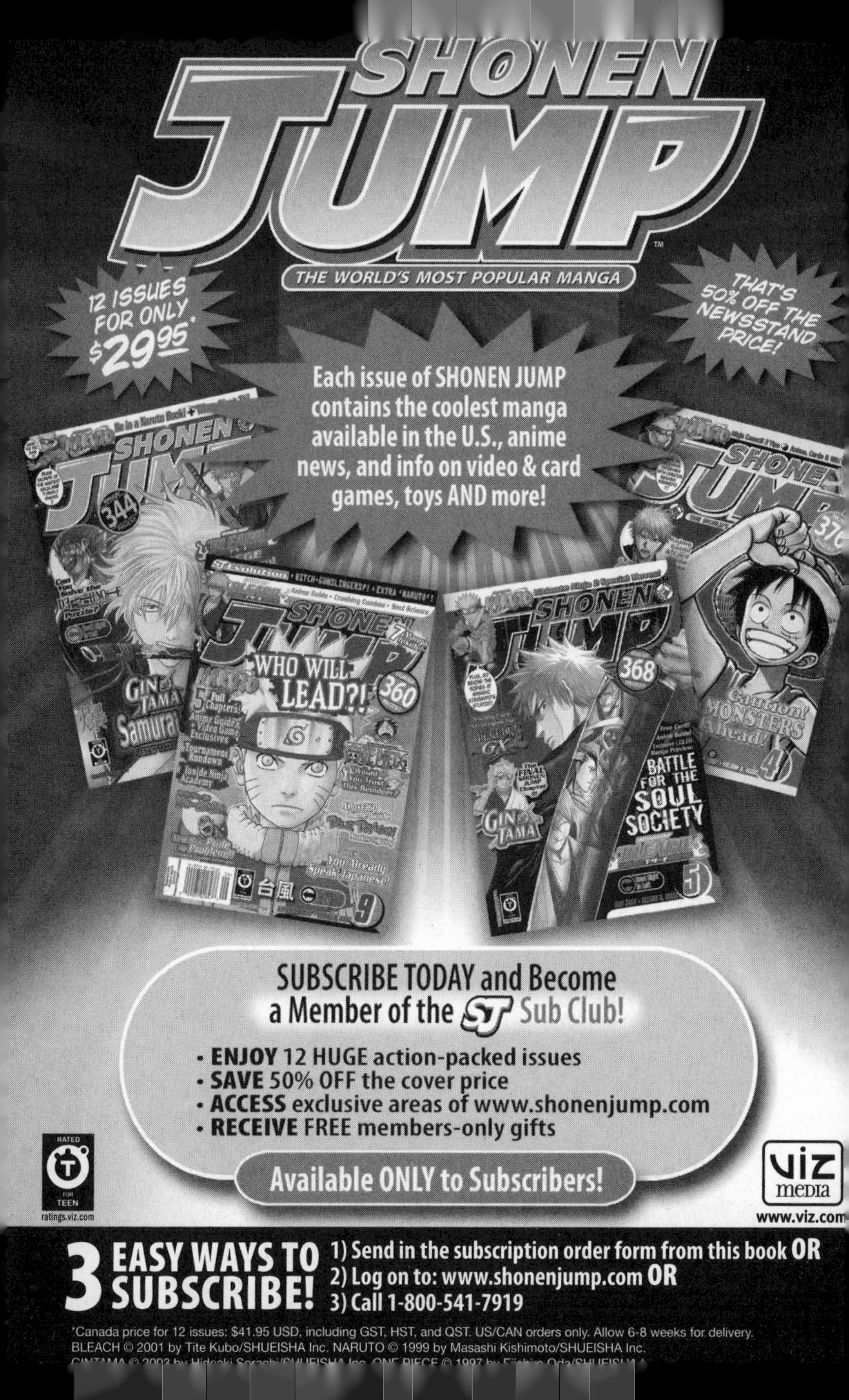
SHONEN JUMP™
THE WORLD'S MOST POPULAR MANGA
12 ISSUES FOR ONLY $29.95*
THAT'S 50% OFF THE NEWSSTAND PRICE!
Each issue of SHONEN JUMP contains the coolest manga available in the U.S., anime news, and info on video & card games, toys AND more!
SUBSCRIBE TODAY and Become a Member of the SJ Sub Club!
• ENJOY 12 HUGE action-packed issues
• SAVE 50% OFF the cover price
• ACCESS exclusive areas of www.shonenjump.com
• RECEIVE FREE members-only gifts
Available ONLY to Subscribers!
RATED T FOR TEEN
ratings.viz.com
VIZ media
www.viz.com
3 EASY WAYS TO SUBSCRIBE!
1) Send in the subscription order form from this book OR
2) Log on to: www.shonenjump.com OR
3) Call 1-800-541-7919
*Canada price for 12 issues: $41.95 USD, including GST, HST, and QST. US/CAN orders only. Allow 6-8 weeks for delivery.
BLEACH © 2001 by Tite Kubo/SHUEISHA Inc. NARUTO © 1999 by Masashi Kishimoto/SHUEISHA Inc.
GINTAMA © 2003 by Hideaki Sorachi/SHUEISHA Inc. ONE PIECE © 1997 by Eiichiro Oda/SHUEISHA

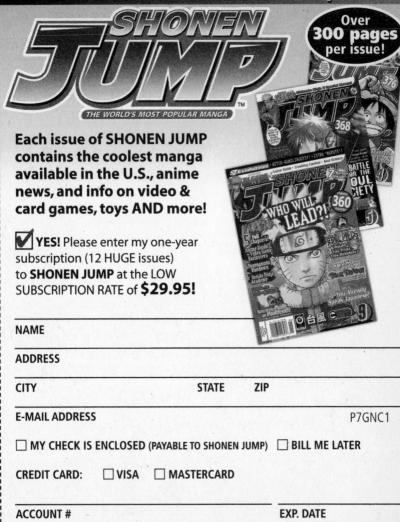